Confessions of the Critics

Confessions
of
the
Critics

EDITED BY

H. ARAM VEESER

Routledge *New York and London*

Published in 1996 by
Routledge
29 West 35th Street
New York, NY 10001

Published in Great Britain by
Routledge
11 New Fetter Lane
London EC4P 4EE

Copyright © 1996 by Routledge
Printed in the United States of America on acid-free paper

The editors gratefully acknowledge the permission of the following publishers to reprint the following essays: Blackwell Publishers, for "'Auction Block' Stories Masquerading as Objects" by Marjorie Garber, from *Critical Quarterly* 34 (1992); Cambridge University Press, for "Through the Academic Looking Glass" by Vincent P. Pecora, from *Radical History Review* 60 (Fall 1995); University of Chicago Press for "Speaking Personally" by David Simpson, from *The Academic Postmodern and the Rule of Literature*, by David Simpson; Indiana University Press, for "Pictures of a Displaced Girlhood" by Marianne Hirsch, from *Displacements: Cultural Identities in Question*, edited by Angelica Bammer.

Library of Congress Cataloging-in-Publication Data

Confessions of the critics / edited by H. Aram Veeser
        p.   cm.
        Includes bibliographical references
        ISBN 0415-91410-8. -- ISBN 0415-91411-6 (pb)
    1. Criticism. 2. Reader-response criticism. 3. Authors and readers. 4. Critics--Biography. 5. Autobiography. I. Veeser, H. Aram (Harold Aram)
PN98.R38C66   1996
801'.95'0904--dc20   95-30071
                                                      CIP

Contents

I. Is It Okay to Read Subjectively?

II. How Can a Critic Create a Self?

III. Just Do It!

Acknowledgments

❖

An MLA panel conceived this book's principal ideas and gave the volume its first resolute push into the world but for one reason and another the panelists—Jane Gallop, Marianne Barnett, and Dominick LaCapra—left the project to fend for itself. Panelist Paul Bové took the anti-patrilineal logic to its limit by not even attending the session itself, though his ideas, like the other panelists', remain imprinted here. Fortunately, the intellectually well-heeled contributors who now comprise the table of contents stepped in and gave the volume great expectations.

I too had generous benefactors. The University of Utah Humanities Center, headed by Lowell Durham and Patricia Hanna, gave me a wonderful year away from home; Gallop's thrilling visit to the Great Salt Lake first inspired the project. The National Endowment for the Humanities donated my stay at the University of California at Berkeley, where James E.B. Breslin and David Farber, themselves transposed New Yorkers, helped stamp this volume as a Bay Area book. Most recently the Center for Literary and Cultural Studies took up the role of benevolent aunt-and-uncle; Herrick Wales and especially Barbara Akiba gave their ever-generous support, and Marjorie Garber created an incomparably rich and stimulating intellectual community where ideas could divest their old clothes and do a bit of serious cross-dressing. The book comes to term back home in Wichita, where Deans Phillip Thomas, Gerald Loper, and David Glenn-Lewin, English Department Chair Lawrence Davis, and Vice-Presidents James Rhatigan, Bobby Patton, and Peter Zoller have all given unstinting succor.

My own chosen ancestors remain Stanley Fish and Edward Said, who as uncles, not fathers, need not formally disown this book however much they dislike it. My extra-Oedipal bonds extend to the widening gyre of deeply committed scholars who include Jane Marcus, Fred Pfeil, Don Hedrick, Paul Smith, Michael Sprinker, Catherine Gallagher, Dipesh Chakrabarty, and Barbara Harlow. Abdul JanMohammed offered some crucial insights into autobiographical criticism, as did Louis Menand. At Harvard's Du Bois Center, Sabine Sielke, Cornel West, Anthony Appiah, and Henry Louis Gates, Jr., gave my ear a colorful and cosmopolitan twist. Just down the road a piece, at the University of Kansas, Janet Sharistanian, G. Douglas Atkins, Cheryl Lester, Philip Barnard, and Iris Smith donated some vital conversation and occasions. My deepest debt is to Wichita State superstars Stephen D. Moore, Roger Berger, Albert Goldbarth, Deborah Gordon, Dennis Smithheisler, Rus Lopez, and Ken Pitetti. Stephen Magro, Eric Zinner, and Christine Cipriani presided at the birth of the book. William P. Germano was present at the conception and gave the book its name.

Sharon Kelley's brilliant library research got this volume off the ground. Secretary *extraordinaire* Janice Cryer lifted its chin and straightened its shoulders. Henry S. Kazan taught me all I needed to know about capital logic, and my brother Cyrus pressed forth the needed socialist corrective. To all these seen and invisible supporters: please accept my grateful hand and *un abrazo fuerte.*

Introduction

The Case for Confessional Criticism

❖

H. ARAM VEESER

Students are always shocked when they come upon their teachers out of school: incredible! The teachers actually have a life apart from the classroom! Rachel Brownstein asks you to remember the "delight and mischief and disbelief you first felt when your third-grade teacher turned up in a two-piece bathing suit at the beach. Why, that's Mrs. Fisher—out from behind the desk, in a body!" This two-sentence anecdote encapsulates that peculiarly Western duty to pass everything to do with the body through the endless mill of speech. You saw, and suddenly you are exclaiming, "Why . . . !" Teachers today have not reversed the peristalsis and ceased to speak. They have come to appreciate the attention they suddenly command as soon as they slip into a body. That most austerely impersonal biographer, Arnold Rampersad, quipped during a recent talk at Columbia, "When in doubt, wax autobiographical."

Until recently only the toughest critics dared to make the autobiographical move. Literary theory was against it. Conservative colleagues were against it. Personal critics themselves turned against it, chastising any "critic bold and clever and successful enough to shock and thrill by interposing her own body."[1]

Disapproval only eggs some people on. Stanley Fish allowed his own publisher to bill him as "the Roseanne Barr of the professoriate," and Jane Gallop dubbed herself the "bad girl" of feminist theory.[2] They knew they were outsiders.

Nowadays, autobiographical criticism has come into general use. Granted, the autobiographical segment may occupy no more than forty seconds of a forty-minute talk. But the audience will ask questions only about the forty seconds. Autobiography triggers their startle reflex. But is that good? Or is it bad?

The present volume brings together accomplished writers who consider the validity of subjective interpretation; the fashioning of critical selves; professorial isolation, embodiment, and personification; autobiographical moves in a postcolonial and global frame; historical representation; collective process writing; and the politics of performance. They enact self-writing and personal criticism in several genres: travel writing (Greenblatt), science writing (Bérubé), postcolonial deconstruction (Spivak), cultural Marxism (Robbins), African-American literary historicism (Andrews), oral history in Marxist feminism (Newton), and performative pedagogy (Tompkins).

> "Confession is but poor amends for wrong, Unlesse a rope would follow"
> —Dekker, *Roaring Girl*, 3.173

A critical practice that breaks long-standing rules is bound to encounter resistance. In this volume, anti-expressivist, radical-Left, psychoanalytic, and high-culture critiques of autobiographical criticism all get an airing:

(1.) No one will listen to anyone if one has interest only in expressing oneself.[3]

(2.) Confessional criticism builds on the hypothesis of liberal authenticity. "I felt it, therefore it is true," parodies David Simpson.[4]

(3.) The corollary—native identity politics, is invoked. Simpson paraphrases, "I felt it. I am white. Therefore, this is what white people feel."[5]

(4.) Yes, everyone has subjective reactions to literature, and our job as professional interpreters is precisely to overcome those reactions and move beyond ordinary personal responses (Elizabeth Fox-Genovese).

(5.) Autobiographical criticism has sanctioned criticism without texts. It has "interrupted reading," and reading is our day job (Brownstein).

(6.) Autobiographical critics are self-indulgent in their "naked display of ... complacent exhibitionism" (Fox-Genovese). The response from Jane Tompkins: "Self-indulgence is the charge made by people who are afraid of their own selves."[6]

To these six antiexpressivist complaints, the contributors add Leftist, psychoanalytic, and high-culture critiques:

(7.) Critics are retreating into a genre wherein (unlike the theory genre) questions of accountability and indebtedness to the public rarely arise (Altieri).

(8.) Autocritographers are playing the Romantic poet, recollecting in tranquility a moment of ungoverned excess (the moment of Theory). They promote a conservative ideology.[7]

(9.) We know that we cannot simply articulate our drives—psychoanalysis would not exist if we could—so who are we trying to kid? (Pecora)

(10.) Autobiographical criticism includes "a chummy implicit appeal to let go of pretensions to talk about anything higher" (Brownstein).

(11.) No one can *hear* anyone if everyone is talking at once.[8]

And I would add for future discussion:

(12.) Confessional criticism means drafting new rules for judging scholarship, ranking journals, and preserving decorum, etiquette, and style.

(13.) The *qu'en dira-t-on* critique. "Giving the public details about oneself is a bourgeois temptation that I have always resisted," writes Gustave Flaubert, 1879.[9] But every social class now fields its autocritographers. Anthony Appiah descends from Ghanaian kings and Linda Orr from South Carolina governors, and Candace Lang misspent her adolescence racing her father's yachts. Gloria Anzaldúa came from a migrant laboring family, and Ruth Behar's folks were Cuban exiles. Patricia Williams's grandmother was chattel and Williams can produce the bill of sale. Your move, Gustave.

(14.) The social need for hypocrisy argument. "His *Confessions* are an attempt to force the hands of God and humanity, to confess that all are equally bad," Stephen Spender said of Rousseau. "Better than this the secrecy of the confessional, in which each person reveals his shame, without challenging the appearances that make up the decent hypocrisy of society."[10]

(15.) The Rightist critique. An overpaid army of *arrivistes* and drones, who abuse their cultural guardianship by celebrating everything crude, lumpen, and *de trop*, would have the final Neroesque pleasure of teaching only books written by themselves, about themselves. Hard hearts on the Left—Fox-Genovese in this collection—would agree.

(16.) The critique from social and intellectual superiority. Sara Suleri dismisses other people's confessional criticism as a mode in which "radical subjectivity is raised to the power of inanity or functions as an excuse for intellectual shoddiness."[11] Her own prose is a frightening alternative. Consider this opaque example: "The unsequestered writing that I pose as a counterpoint takes autobiography as a strategy of dismantlement that dispenses with such dichotomies as public and private or inside and outside in order to position itself at the border of outsidedness." Sentences like that one, whatever the truths they may conceal, bring to mind Professor Irwin Corey, the double-talk artist whose act consisted in making himself incomprehensible.

(17.) The critique from ennui. Contributor Charles Altieri points out that Frank Lentricchia's life, Nancy Miller's (another founding figure of personal criticism), and Altieri's own are quite frankly boring. "The shaping events are so common, so interchangeable with events in other parallel lives" that "critics' autobiographies do not serve to highlight anything. They serve to bury something" (Altieri).

(18.) The critique of evasiveness: Altieri accuses autocritographers of burying questions of accountability. Alice Kaplan tells interviewer Scott Heller that her book is all about secrets. "The big emotional issue was secrets and hiding."[13] Gillian Brown cites another evasion: "In the present ethos of anxiety and controversy about authority, critical discourse now often entails showing some kind of identity papers: not actually an admission about oneself but a credential composed of personal matter."

Have I mentioned yet that in 1984 I went to Nicaragua for three weeks to pick coffee for the Sandinistas?

(19.) The critique of Power. Foucault's mordant *History of Sexuality* calls into question the whole confessional enterprise:

> one has to be completely taken in ... in order to believe that all these voices ... —repeating the formidable injunction to tell what one is and what one does, what one recollects and what one has forgotten, what one is thinking and what one thinks he is thinking—are speaking to us of freedom.[13] (60)

By these lights the autobiographical-literary establishment is completely taken in. Phillipe Lejeune's very influential *Pacte autobiographique* is notable for its "quasi-legalistic language of contracts, rights, obligations, promises, expectations, and pacts" (Olney, Introduction, 17–18). Phillip Lopate can simply assume, in his recent anthology *The Art of the Personal Essay* (Doubleday, 1994), that in each of the collected essays "a contract between writer and reader has been drawn up: the essayist must then make good on it by delivering, or discovering, as much honesty as possible" (xxv). Foucault would have raised his bleached eyebrows skeptically.

"I must tell the children about my body!" A Mrs. Fisher-à-la-Foucault would insist on telling all, perhaps with charts.

The contributors disagree about Foucault and the purgative power of confessing. They disagree as to whether autobiography "deprives and disfigures to the precise extent that it restores" and prolongs life.[14] They even disagree about one's simple ability to tell the truth. "Who, finally, ever writes the memoir that reveals what must remain hidden?" asks Vincent Pecora.

But why write autobiographical criticism if not to purge guilt, secure reputation, achieve community, or reveal verity? Why read it if not to overhear intimacies or absolve sinners?

What does the confessional critic want? This question, *mutatis mutandis*, stumped Freud. One may hazard this: confessional critics reject polarities. They replace a process with an erotics. They recreate the gorgeous iconoclasm of performance.

1. The autobiographical critic wants performativity.

Confessional critics no longer accept the antithesis between expressive, "process" writing and objective, logical thinking. They practice an art that falls somewhere between writing and performance, an art much akin to the erotics envisaged by Roland Barthes: "The intermittence of skin flashing between two articles of clothing: ... it is this flash itself which seduces or rather: the staging of appearance and disappearance."[15] Contributor Gillian Brown draws attention to the "hide-and-seek quality of critical personification"; Diane Freedman and Marianne Hirsch discuss the vanishing and reappearance—in photography or poetry—of the unmarked gendered subject; and Michael Bérubé develops further the concept of oscillation as described by reader-response criticism and feminist film theory. The mood was caught years ago by David Lodge when, in his 1984 novel *Small World*, he had Morris Zapp (a.k.a. Stanley Fish) deliver a paper entitled "Textuality as Striptease."[16] Then it was satire. Today it is realism.

If confessional criticism "seduces," it also "performs." "Performativity" made its spectacular and disruptive entrance as "die-ins" and theatrical "outness." It conversed with ordinary language philosophy and deconstruction; the topic was "iterativity."[17] "Mobilized by the injuries of homophobia, theatrical rage reiterates those injuries," writes Judith Butler.[18] Bérubé gives new meaning to "performativity" when he takes over and corrupts some preexisting roles:

> we look something like a cross between Johnny Rotten and Cotton Mather: just take the Sex Pistols' political tact and respect for authority, toss in the Puritans' good cheer and sense of rhythm, and presto, you've got Rotten Mather, assistant professor of English, thirty years old and not to be trusted.[19]

He reiterates damaging complaints and makes them sound ridiculous: "Amniocentesis, sonograms, Apgar ratings, laryngomalacia, polycythemia, torticollis, vertebral anomaly, scoliosis, possible sepsis; don't you despise all this barbaric jargon?" (Bérubé). He dredges up the historically destructive textbook images of Down's syndrome children "facedown in their feeding trays." Irony such as Greenblatt's in the riotously funny "Laos is Open" presupposes a certain superiority to the situation, whereas performativity implies a certain disadvantage. Each member of the Duke writing group limbers up by writing a parody of her own style. Is parody exhibitionist, inane, bourgeois, evasive, and shoddy?

These judgmental terms make no sense. Parody can be well-performed or badly performed; that is all. "The performative utterance, like the live performance event and the sexual union of two same-sex people, cannot be repeated or reproduced," according to Peggy Phelan, Department of Performance Studies, Tisch School of the Arts, New York University. "Same-sex lovers live in the present (rather than take stock of one's reproductive legacy)."[20] By contrast, Marxism, deconstruction, and New Criticism have (or had) big ambitions; they want to succeed not just on *this* text but on *any* text.

Confessional criticism takes its tempo from performance art. Split Britches' lesbian performance piece, "Upwardly Mobile Home," captures the rhythm.[21] Everything is temporary, one-shot. What you write about *King John* will not help you to write about *Richard II*. "To say 'my body,'" wrote Adrienne Rich, "reduces the temptation to grandiose assertions."[22] Performativity, too, eschews the grandiose and embraces the body. "Where is Indonesia, Professor Baker, unless in the sole of your shoe?" demands Amitava Kumar.

The humility topos allowed the socially untouchable Horace to attain every reward a Roman poet could win. Houston Baker may wear a humble Nike shoe, but he stands atop the global ladder of labor.

Is autocritography merely, then, a *faux* performativity? "Within the political economy of performance, writing is always on the side of the Law," writes Phelan, performance being on the side of the Outlaw (23). Deconstruction has nagged for twenty-five years that writing eviscerates the present: that is why it is a *dangerous* supplement. Writing hordes up, preserves, reproduces, cites and re-cites; like heterosexual fornicators, it has one eye on posterity. Even if it rarely *feels* like an operation of power, writing seeks to preserve "the beauty and folly of performance [which is] its insistence on the power and fullness of the present as such" (Phelan, 24). Writing diverts its attention to its own afterlife, whereas performance lives its present.

But the written format of these "confessions" is not fatal to their performativity. Behind autobiographical criticism stand those eminently performative writing traditions, namely the theory (not so much the practice) of *écriture feminine*, and pedagogical theories of expressive writing.

French feminists defended a style of writing that disrupted "masculine" norms of usage and logic. "Erection doesn't interest us: We're fine in the lowlands," writes Luce Irigaray, in her credo for French theories of *écriture*.[23] *Écriture feminine* had much in common with a confessional criticism that hates pouring itself into molds.[24] Confessional criticism is the writing practice, moreover, of a *gendered* subject. It puts back on the table the question of whether a particular sort of writing can be assigned to the biologically female subject. Cixous, Irigaray, and Kristeva, each in her different way, said "No." Jane Tompkins has said "Yes." "[W]hat is perceived as personal by men, or rather, what is gripping, significant, 'juicy,' is different from what is felt to be that way by women," writes Jane Tompkins.[25] And though Tompkins has since changed her mind, that earlier manifesto positions sexual difference as the irreducible premise of autobiographical criticism.[26]

Expressivist composition pedagogy—the "process" theory of writing— also defended the rights of the weak, including the open-admissions students who flocked to public universities. Expressivism embraced the idea that writing was a gendered practice. The early expressivist gurus, Peter Elbow and Ken Macrorie, considered outlining and formulaic argumentation to be oppressive, patriarchal norms. Elbow parodies a writer filled with fear that "my mind will grow soft and limp, it will atrophy; it will finally fall off. No! I'll have high standards. I'll be rigorous. I'll make every argument really stand up" (33).[27] He shows how fully male performance anxiety—"growing soft and limp," losing "rigor," wanting to "really stand up"—underwrites traditional writing instruction.

Expressivism has all sorts of problems. Susan Jarratt astutely observes that Elbow could not so readily "come out" as a woman writer were he not an established masculine author.[28] Elbow's farcical enactment of male performance anxiety would convince most of us that Elbow really has no anxiety at all. Expressivism gained prominence in the seventies, when even radical feminists were prepared to accept a sex-determined basis for behavior; when Nancy Chodorow could write that young girls have "more flexible or permeable ego boundaries," and Sheila Rowbotham could argue that women have had to identify themselves with groups "instead of viewing themselves as unique individuals."[29] Performativity assumes no essences. Rather, acts of writing "effectively constitute the identity they are said to express or reveal."[30] Autobiographical critics enact selves in the same way legislators enact laws.

Confessional critics have avoided the failings of "process." The "naked display of complacent exhibitionism," hopelessly emotional readings of literary texts, patently overconfident but really naïve self-analyses, the flushed excitement of writers bursting through blockage: Elbow, Macrorie, and Donald Murray may leave themselves open to these charges, but confessional critics avoid sophomoric ezxcesses even while they redouble the expressivists' radically democratic, risk-taking honesty.

But if confessional criticism escapes the various essentialist and identitarian fallacies as well as the risk-free, self-aggrandizing, Elbowesque "confession" of frailty, does it simply fall into another worn-out attitude, that of pervasive modernist irony? Irony crops up with unnerving frequency. Noting that "heterosexuality is regarded as an embarrassment," Judith Newton concludes that "the irony of this reversal in an obscenely homophobic culture is something to savor." Charles Altieri notes that the autobiographical critic "steps into the ironic condition." And Greenblatt's outrageous "travel" piece here piles irony upon irony. The designers of the River View Hotel in Vientiane had little experience of indoor plumbing, he observes, for "how else to explain the quaint decision to place the toilet in the bathtub?" Irony comes in many shades; one of the contributors has written a book about them.[31] Here it serves most often to deflate posturing, pomposity, and Brobdingnagian theory-speak. It is a new skill that, like e-mail, everyone will soon want to have.

2. The autobiographical critic wishes to tell anecdotes.

Confessional critics deny that a critic has to opt for chilly analysis or gritty texture, but not both. Performative criticism signals an end to the era when critics searched for what Bruce Robbins has called "allegories of vocation"—wishful thinking of the sort that identifies Charlotte Brontë's *Jane Eyre* as an antitype or prefiguration of the late-twentieth-century feminist literary critic.[32] Rejecting grandiose Hegelian unfoldings no less than the faddish fetishizing of Geertzian local knowledge, confessional criticism is fashioning a written performativity that eroticizes disclosure and concealment.[33]

One relic of the New Historicism has floated down to autobiographical critics. They cling to the anecdote. The anecdote assumes new theoretical importance when, Joel Fineman has theorized, the "large story of the exigent unfolding of beginning, middle, and end no longer carries an urgency," and the appetite for stories must be satisfied by the anecdote: "the event within and yet without the framing context of historical successivity . . . the hole and rim—using psychoanalytic language, the orifice—traced out by the anecdote within the totalizing whole of the story. . . ." The seductive opening of the anecdotal form can operate as "a breaking and a realizing interjection within the encyclopedically closed circle."[34] Tradition operates here, too: *anekdota* meant "secret," "unpublished," "risqué."

Autobiographical criticism uses the anecdote as a sluice gate for alarming emotions rather than, as in New Historicism, to provide a "representative instance." In Tompkins's "Let's Get Lost," the students take trips to Okracoke and to an old Southern plantation in order to act out what they have felt in reading *Moby Dick* and *Beloved*. She herself focuses on Ahab's "immitigable hate, so abundantly *thorough* and satisfying." "It was Ahab's hate so eloquently expressed" that determined Tompkins's own choice of career. Literature and life take on an immediate connection, and certain incantatory quotations, such as "breaking open the heart's hot shell" of hatred, move language toward a sort of dithyrambic violence that makes the post-Dachau, post–Sabra-and-Shatila world understandably nervous. In an equally uncensored moment, Judith Newton, Marxist feminist and founder of *Feminist Studies*, confesses "a certain weariness of twenty years in mainly female communities, a liking for progressive men, the heterosexual erotic"; and Timothy Brennan, who wrote the first book about Salman Rushdie, collected the "Writing of Black Britain," and defined Latin America's revolutionary "national longing for form," makes a startling homage to white, midwestern "fanaticism."[35] These authors hand us anomalies and say: "You explain it."

Certainly there is something troubling about a personal criticism that gives transcendently moving performances of execrable emotions. That is its point. Vincent Pecora writes that "the biggest villains" of Alice Kaplan's *French Lessons*, namely fascist intellectuals from the 1940s to the 1980s, possess "an excess of strong emotion, welling up from the gut, utterly transparent as to personal interest, and spewed forth directly at Jews and any other 'inferior' group."[36] Do we want, he asks,

> figures like Bardeche [the French holocaust revisionist and fascist] to be more in touch with what they feel? Or do we want them to think, calmly and rationally, about the evidence, about history, about how dominated they have been by emotional lives that are out of control?

Though Pecora plays devil's advocate, one must hear echoes, here, of the Dworkin and MacKinnon antipornography campaigns. First Amendment fundamentalists like me will cautiously hazard this: Better to "spew" in a book than to burn up a Reichstag.

Anecdote cuts a channel from mind to sensation, and is useful for intellectuals who ordinarily keep emotions to themselves. Professors learn to "love loneliness," as David Damrosch has recently argued.[37] "I didn't realize until I tried to write [*French Lessons*] what an intellectual I had become and how unused I was to expressing emotions," Kaplan remembers.[38] Confessional criticism may well provide "a solution, a ritualized resistance" of the sort that Simon Frith attributes to pop music. Intellectuals may enjoy rock music neither as a "fond look back at adolescence" nor a flaunting of proletarian roots, but rather because it expresses "the deep desire of intellectuals not to be intellectual."[39]

Readers will no doubt object that Western philosophy has no more hoary polarity than the one that positions intellect opposite emotion. Confessional criticism has the signal virtue of unsettling any certainty that the writer *knows* that s/he is evoking powerful emotions. Eve Sedgwick uses the vocabulary of gay sadomasochism to describe an autobiographical passage in Henry James. But one can hardly imagine James writing, even in his private *Notebooks* in

California, something so crude that it could be dubbed, in Sedgwick's words, "fisting-as-*écriture*":

> I sit here, after long weeks, at any rate, in front of my arrears, with an inward accumulation of material.... Everything sinks in: nothing is lost; everything abides and fertilizes and renews its golden promise, making me think with closed eyes of deep and grateful longing when, in the full summer days of L[amb] H[ouse], my long dusty adventure over, I shall be able to [plunge] my hand, my arm, *in*, deep and far, and up to the shoulder—into the heavy bag of remembrance—of suggestions—of imagination—of art—and fish out every little figure and felicity, every little fact and fancy that can be to my purpose. These things are all packed away, now, thicker than I can penetrate, deeper than I can fathom, and there let them rest for the present, in their sacred cool darkness, till I shall let in upon them the mild still light of dear old L[amb] H[ouse]—in which they will begin to gleam and glitter and take form like the old and jewels of a mine. (James, quoted in Sedgwick 208 n. 33)

And yet, having read Sedgwick, one wonders, "Could James really be saying *that?*" Confessional criticism regularly encourages just such readerly speculations, an inward tango danced between corrupt knowingness and jejune naïveté.[40]

A sublimated erotics boils in the most innocent-seeming accounts. Growing up white in segregated Virginia, contributor William Andrews used to see the family housecleaner but rarely heard her speak. Occasionally he overheard her singing, but she stopped whenever she noticed him. It was this state "of simultaneous visual connection and aural isolation" that made him eager to pick up books by Du Bois, Chesnutt, and other African-American writers. "Reading African-American autobiography that semester became a way for me to reconsider the accumulated memories, the unresolved confusion, the still unexamined lessons of a lifetime of segregation." Against the expectations and desires of white society—his mother's refrain "But why the colored, Bill?" captures the mood—Andrews made African-American literature more than a successful career. He made it a commitment.

Half-buried private emotion pokes up through remote Apollonian theorizing. Frank Lentricchia's magisterial *After the New Criticism* cannot fully inter his zany, performative *The Edge of Night*. Interviewer Jeffrey Williams elicits another such moment. "I took ten years trying to write [*36 Views of Mount*] *Fuji* and couldn't figure out how I wanted to do it," Duke professor Cathy Davidson tells him. "And then I brought in this section about sleeping in a flophouse when I was sixteen and how this reminded me of sleeping in a Zen temple the first time I was in Japan. And the group said, That's it, you've got it, that's the book."[41]

It would be nothing to convert all this to a portrait of intellectual exhaustion painted with one tired foot atop Theory and the other crushing down Politics. This tableau would cancel the most exciting interpretive opportunities that autocritography offers. Autobiography shapes itself within larger theoretical projects, but the larger projects continue in force. The excitement comes when the reader can detect bridges connecting the two. An example is Henry Louis Gates, Jr., whose memoir of Piedmont, West Virginia, reinforces his larger contention that black writers look primarily to each other for models and opponents. Replete with his youthful Uncle Earl, the *recherché* Sneakin' Deacon, who visits his female parishioners late at night; the six austere Coleman brothers, who lust after property and drink nothing stronger than iced tea; and Gates's own restless search for the perfect hair straightener, his decision to be saved, and his initiation in the mystery of Piedmont bologna —*Colored People* taps into every surface emotion and Artesian drive that courses through Gates's natal Appalachian backwater.

These refluent memories do not interrupt so much as they illustrate, enable, and empower Gates's larger academic project, which is to discover the true African-American rhetoric and to describe the whole linguistic and cultural system that he began laying out in *The Signifying Monkey*. Gates's larger theoretical project enfolds the two-hundred-page anecdote that is *Colored People* and yet is itself "inspired by the seductive opening of the anecdotal form." Gates has said that other critics amply study white influences on black authors. He wished to show that African-American writers study, acknowledge, and answer each other. Gates's autocritography about growing up in segregated Piedmont helps to locate and historicize his literary theories.[42] The Cut-Rate drugstore where only whites could sit down, Up the Hill, Colby Carroll's barbershop, Big Mom, Uncle Earkie, Miss Toot, the Fearsome Foursome, Skip Gates himself: all the staging, blocking, and character-acting leave little question that life, like criticism, asks to be played, not just "expressed."

The essays in this book offer many opportunities to discern the links that connect anecdote to career project. A gangster grandfather has some relationship to Robbins's left-wing defense of literary critical professionalism. Lang's "self" acquires its uncomfortable ambivalence about feminism and feminist criticism and its pleasure in deconstruction because she learned, early, to master big machines. The anecdotes and the careers: an arbitrary connectedness? Or a causal chain? That is for the reader to decide.

3. Critics wish to retain artistic control over their own self-staging.

The easy antithesis of celebrity and invisibility comes under equally devastating attack. Our academic "star system" has been variously savaged and celebrated; so has our academic marginality.[43] But this division of the academic landscape into an inside and an outside, center and margin, onstage and offstage, has had its day.

Instead, critics in this collection place themselves "betwixt and between." They repeatedly emphasize physical locations of scenes of initiation. Brennan locates Latin America, the source of his radical priest uncle's letters, as the site to work the "transformation of the bohemian impulse to a usable politics." Davidson recalls that the Duke writing group subjected her to "a sorority hazing"; these four nonsmokers also tend to light up and, thus, to heighten the ritual aspect of their weekly sessions. Robbins shuttles between the Belmont racetrack and Harvard Yard, inhabiting a kind of middle earth that he calls cultural Marxism; in that corridor, he can affirm loyalty to where he has been (to his lower-class origins—this is the Marxism) and loyalty to where he wished to go (to fruitful, interesting *cultural* work).[44] Amitava Kumar places himself in a succession of transitory sites—a taxicab, the University of Pennsylvania interview suite, the JFK Airport customs shed. Even the hotel room is "more like being at a foreign airport" because "I was utterly ignorant of the world that now confronted me," a world where "I wasn't yet beginning to hear words as words" and where one might confuse the sign for "bus" with the sign for "bags." Pecora imagines academic life as sort of pilgrimage, as "a search for the parent (traditionally the father) that one believes one should have had from the start." Greenblatt takes an ironic view of his "small twin-engine Chinese plane" that could not get above automatic-rifle range. It "grew tremendously hot, the cabin filled with smoke—just normal condensation, we were told—and several passengers became violently ill." Moving between margin and center requires some risk. An "origin was staged for [Gayatri Spivak]" by a psychoanalyst in France, the "foreign place" most appropriate "because [there,] a 'proper' analysis could not take place." Once outside the gravitational pull defined by "foreign" and "origin," instruments like psychoanalysis begin to function improperly.

Liminal spaces, pilgrimages, secured locales where secret knowledge changes hands—such *topoi* suggest that Victor Turner and kindred ritual theorists, important to early New Historicists such as Louis Montrose, have had a surprising resurgence. Thus, "Turner's model of social drama and 'liminality' provides a handy conceptual model for the study of exile—or border crossing 'betwixt and between,'" writes Mae G. Henderson (5). The liminal "traveler" must literally cross a threshold in order to move from preliminal to postliminal status. Between these fixed status-positions, the passenger enters a cultural "limbo," where the "blurring and merging of distinctions" permits the subject to "pass through a place or period in which [s/he] experiences freedom from the constraints of normative or oppressive social structures" (Henderson, 5). Turner finds tremendous creative potentiality in many societies' protected opportunities for "standing aside not only from one's own social position but from all social positions and of formulating a potentially unlimited series of alternative social arrangements."[45]

Henderson ascribes liminality to exiles, emigres, refugees, and expatriates, perhaps because her book must be faithful to its title, *Borders, Boundaries, and Frames*. And yet Turner was largely concerned with internal exile. His hopes for antistructures (he wrote enthusiastically about hippie communes!) evolve within a single culture. They thrust against that culture's constraints. Judith Butler stresses the creative and constructive side of Turner's oppositional anti-structures. "[V]arious acts of gender create the idea of gender, and without those acts, there would be no gender at all" (Butler, 273).[46] The liberating, antistructural moment comes, then, when a person appropriates socially established acts and repeats them subversively. Ice-T, Madonna, M. Butterfly, and Split Britches all subvert norms by repeating them with a difference.[47] In the process, these marginals make themselves culturally central.

The critique of academic celebrity and would-be centrality has come from all sides. From the Left, Laura Kipnis has trashed the "hypervisibility" of "the ideological category of the subject."[48] On the comparative Right, one finds Peter Brooks:

> A recent trend toward the personalization of criticism, indeed toward the cult of the critic's personality, seems to me regrettable, a kind of academic version of the postmodern replacement of personhood by celebrity—as if one did not really exist until celebrated in *People* magazine.[49]

But is autobiographical criticism really about hypervisibility, celebrity, and the play of signification? I think not. Critics want, rightly, to make themselves objects of desire, interest, public fascination. Why indeed should they write if their work blooms in the forest unseen?

Yet if visibility were equivalent to power, then young, nearly naked women would run the state—clearly not the case.[50] Autocritographers know the technologies of the visible; many would accept Lacan's theorum that the object of desire remains potent only when veiled. To remain desirable, the object must remain inaccessible. It must remain ungotten. That is a given. It brings me to the critic as transvestite.

Marjorie Garber's figure for the category-crisis-inducing, partly known object of desire is . . . the transvestite. The transvestite willfully creates a third space beyond the masculine/feminine dichotomy, the homo/hetero binary, the real/artificial antithesis, the onstage/offstage dualism. To take one small example, Dee Snider, male lead singer of Twisted Sister, was voted one of the worst-dressed *women* of 1984.[51]

Garber develops, in her article for this volume, a "logistics of competitive desire." Her example is the country auction, where she and her partner decline to buy, among other commodities, a large green bronze garden frog. "Part of the fascination . . . comes," she explains, "with the act of displaying whatever the item is—a rug, a table, a pair of andirons. It is held up for admiring scrutiny for as long as the bidding lasts." Could this be our allegory of vocation—the auction? Every critic held up for display? "It's a rule of thumb that everything, however bulky or improbable, gets displayed; if it's a set of eight chairs, all eight are held up, two to a person." Not just Alice Kaplan or the slender Jane Tompkins, but even the bulking Lentricchia and the slippery de Man: all are held up for view. Autobiographical criticism oscillates, then: one minute an elegant, finely crafted piece by Tompkins or Bérubé; the next minute an inelegant grotesquery—a pompous self-promotion or a weepy complaint. The present collection excludes all large green frogs.

What does this image, the critic-as-cross-dresser, suggest? Not that autobiographical criticism tells the truth, is authentic, represents an ethnos, speaks for a gender, makes criticism accountable, or repays critics' debt to society. But not that it is complacent, exhibitionist, chummy, professional, hostile to reading, *arriviste, de trop*, or a "betrayal of personhood," either. It appears to be fun, "but ultimately nothing," Garber warns, "is free" (*Vested Interests,* 161). The auctioning and hawking of critics' selves yields what Garber's country auction yields: "Another good lesson in the arbitrariness of desire."

Confessional criticism stages the anxieties that suffuse all forms of contemporary criticism. It has unsettled the firm dichotomies of expressivism and objectivity, *petite histoire* and *grand récit*, celebrity and invisibility. It has stage names galore: "plebeian autobiography" (Jill Johnston); "autocritography" (Henry Louis Gates, Jr.); "sequestered criticism" (Sara Suleri); and integrative writing (Marianna Torgovnick).[52] It divides itself into parts; Nancy K. Miller's centrally important book distinguishes autobiographical from personal criticism, the latter of which requires no autobiographical self-representation. It has incarnations that range from brief codas and cameos (D. A. Miller's *Cage aux folles* and Stephen Greenblatt's *Renaissance Self-Fashioning*) to full-scale experimental autobiographies (Carolyn Steedman's *Landscape for a Good Woman* and Alice Kaplan's *French Lessons*).[53] Contemplating this profusion, one recognizes that critics are no longer willing to settle for Nietzsche's assurances that every critical text is "a kind of involuntary and unconscious memoir," nor Wilde's assertion that "criticism is the highest form of autobiography." They abjure hypervisibility as much as silenced scopophilia. Theatrical, sexy, flashing their bodies between the folds of theory, they could hardly stand further from the neutered "third sex of Ph.D.s."[54]

They conceive kaleidoscopic variations on the theme of erotic, generative apertures. It is no accident that Gerald Graff proposes, as his preferred model for a new pedagogy, the academic conference. The conference breaks into the academic calendar much as the autobiographical anecdote breaks into teleo-logical narration: each instigates a revivifying time of raised expectations. The highly successful writer-scholars interviewed by Jeffrey Williams first formed their writing group in order "not to be alone." Initiation—an entry "inter-view"—was required, and the participants name a desire "to feel accepted," and "to be a part of something," to have "experiences that set the two of you apart for that moment from the rest of humankind." Confessional criticism offers to make a subculture out of solitude.

Autocritography offers many versions of refreshment and community. The very act of reading refreshes. Isolated by my dark coloring and my fatness, I used to cringe with embarrassment as I went to the ready-to-wear rack marked "Husky." As I prepared this introduction, I read Henry Louis Gates, Jr.'s confession. "I was fat," Gates, né Skippy, writes, "and therefore compelled to wear 'husky' clothes. . . . Whoever thought of the euphemism 'husky,'" Gates adds, "should be shot." Skippy Gates, *mon frère*!

❖

When I look at Kumar, Brennan, and Andrews *making* the bridges to Houston Baker, to a Pakistani cab driver, to Mexican-American Pinto plant employees, and to the editors of *Race and Class*, Spivak insistently returning to the tribals and the people, and all these contributors battling the fearful iner-tia, solitude, and torpor that clogs U.S. academic culture, I have hope. And I feel proud to be among them. They step beyond center and margin, beyond self-effacement and self-absorption, beyond liberal authenticity and identity politics. And they do so in myriad, enchanting ways. Better than force on these essays some spurious unity, a reader might seek to enjoy each on its own invented terms.

"I'm tired of the conventions," announces Jane Tompkins, and her exhaustion summons new, defiant energies. Few North American readers can resist her hit-the-road retort to tired, stilted scholarship. Autocritography takes us across a threshold: there was scholarship before it, and after it, and they are not the same.

Even David Simpson, who initially considered personal criticism the purest eyewash, has come around. The cult, Simpson admits, has blossomed into a culture. "For it has been nurtured and cherished awhile, and regularly fertilized; and it is, as a historical culture, inescapable, and not at all open to dismissal from some high point of disinterested inspection." Personal criti-cism—no longer compost, it is now in full flower.

These essays were for the most part written for this book. The authors had full artistic control, and the majority chose to enjoy "the power and full-ness of the present." Mesmerizing storytellers, they move at a cinematic pace.

They speak for and against autobiographical criticism, and after them, it will be harder to write a theoretical narration that lacks its own anecdotal hole, its flash of intermittence, its moment of beauty and folly. Critics of such critics might recall Matthew Arnold: "with oneself one may always, without impropriety, deal quite freely."[55] Anyone eager to see criticism step out from behind the desk should prepare for a stiff round of delight, mischief, and disbelief.

Notes

1. Brownstein, this volume. Further references to essays in the present volume will be parenthetical.

2. Advertisement for Stanley Fish, *There's No Such Thing As Free Speech, And It's A Good Thing, Too* (New York and Oxford: Oxford University Press, 1993), in *Critical Inquiry* 21 (Winter 1995).

3. D.S., "NB," *Times Literary Supplement*, April 30, 1993, 14.

4. Quoted in Scott Heller, "New Brand of Scholarship Mixes Experience, Expertise," *The Chronicle of Higher Education* May 6, 1992, A9.

5. Heller, A9.

6. Tompkins quoted in Heller, A9.

7. Mike Hill, "What's New about the 'New Belletrism'?" Paper delivered at Annual Meeting of the Modern Language Association, San Diego, California, December 28, 1994.

8. *TLS*, 14.

9. Quoted in Julian Barnes, *Flaubert's Parrot* (London: J. Cape, 1984; New York: Random House, 1990), 94. Anthony Appiah, *In My Father's House: Africa in the Philosophy of Culture* (New York: Oxford University Press, 1992). Ruth Behar, *Translated Woman: Crossing the Border with Esperanza's Story* (Boston: Beacon Press, 1993). Patricia Williams, *The Alchemy of Race and Rights* (Cambridge, MA, and London: Harvard University Press, 1991).

10. Stephen Spender, "Confessions and Autobiography," in *The Making of a Poem* (New York: W.W. Norton, 1962; rpt. in *Autobiography: Essays Theoretical and Critical*, ed. James Olney [Princeton: Princeton University Press, 1980]), 120, 121.

11. Sara Suleri, "Criticism and Its Alterity," in *Borders, Boundaries, and Frames: Essays in Cultural Criticism and Cultural Studies*, ed. Mae G. Henderson (New York and London: Routledge, 1995), 175.

12. "A Passion for French," *Chronicle of Higher Education*, 9 February 1994, A9.

13. Michel Foucault, *La volonté de savoir* (Paris: Editions Gallimard, 1976; *The History of Sexuality, Volume I: an Introduction*, trans. Robert Hurley [New York: Random House, 1978]), 60.

14. Paul de Man, "Autobiography as De-Facement," *MLN* 94 (December 1979): 919–930; rpt. in *The Rhetoric of Romanticism* (New York: Columbia University Press, 1984), 81.

15. Roland Barthes, *The Pleasure of the Text* (New York: Hill and Wang, 1975), 10.

16. David Lodge, *Small World: An Academic Romance* (New York: Warner Books, 1984).

17. J. L. Austin, *How To Do Things With Words*, eds. J.O. Urmson and Marina Sbisa (Cambridge, MA: Harvard University Press, 1955); and Jacques Derrida, "Signature/ Event/Context," *Limited, Inc.*, ed. Gerald Graff, trans. Samuel Weber and Jeffrey Mehlman (Evanston: Northwestern University Press, 1988).

18. Judith Butler, "Performative Acts and Gender Constitution: an Essay in Phenomenology and Feminist Theory," *Performing Feminisms: Feminist Critical Theory and Theatre*, ed. Sue-Ellen Case (Baltimore and London: Johns Hopkins University Press, 1990), 270–282.

19. Michael Bérubé, "Discipline and Theory," *Wild Orchids and Trotsky*, ed. Mark Edmundson (New York: Penguin, 1992), 171. See also "Public Image Limited— Political Correctness, The Media's Big Lie," *Village Voice* June 18, 1991, and *Public Access: Literary Theory and American Cultural Politics* (London and New York: Verso, 1994).

20. Peggy Phelan, "Reciting the Citation of Others; or, A Second Introduction," in *Acting Out: Feminist Performances*, eds. Lynda Hart and Peggy Phelan, (Ann Arbor: University of Michigan Press, 1993), 19.

21. Elin Diamond, "Mimesis, Mimicry, and the 'True-Real'," in Phelan, *Acting Out*, 373.

22. Adrienne Rich, "Notes Toward a Politics of Location: in *Blood, Bread, and Poetry: Selected Prose 1979–1985* (New York: Norton, 1986; qtd. in Nancy K. Miller, *Getting Personal: Feminist Occasions and Other Autobiographical Acts* [New York and London: Routledge, 1991], xiii).

23. Luce Irigaray, "When Our Lips Speak Together," trans. Carolyn Burke, *Signs* 6 (1980): 69.

24. Hélène Cixous, "Le Rire de la Méduse," *L'Arc* 61 (1975): 39–54.

25. Jane Tompkins, "Me and My Shadow," *New Literary History* 19 (1988); *Gender and Theory: Dialogues on Feminist Criticism*, ed. Linda Kauffman (New York and London: Basil Blackwell, 1989); rpt., *The Intimate Critique: Autobiographical Literary Criticism*, Diane P. Freedman, Olivia Frey, and Frances Murphy Zauhar (Durham and London: Duke University Press, 1993), 16.

26. But see also Jane Tompkins, "'Indians': Textualism, Morality, and the Problem of History," *Critical Inquiry* 13 (1986): 118; *Sensational Designs: The Cultural Work of American Fiction* (New York: Oxford University Press, 1985); "Fighting Words: Learning to Write the Critical Essay," *The Georgia Review* 42 (1988): 585–590; and *West of Everything: The Inner Life of Westerns* (New York and Oxford: Oxford University Press, 1992).

27. Peter Elbow, *Writing Without Teachers* (New York and Oxford: Oxford University Press, 1973), 33. Ken Macrori, *Telling Writing* (New York: Hayden Book Company, 1970; rpt. Boynton/Cook, 1985).

28. Susan C. Jarratt, "Feminism and Composition: The Case for Conflict," in *Contending with Words: Composition and Rhetoric in a Postmodern Age*, ed. Patricia Harkin and

John Schilb (New York: Modern Language Association, 1991), 117. See also Jarratt, "The First Sophists and Feminism: Discourses of the 'Other'," *Hypatia* 5 (Spring 1990), 27–41.

29. Barbara Kosta, *Recasting Autobiography: Women's Counterfictions in Contemporary German Literature and Film* (Ithaca and London: Cornell University Press, 1994), 20–21. Nancy Chodorow, *The Reproduction of Mothering: Psychoanalysis and the Sociology of Gender* (Berkeley: University of California Press, 1978). Sheila Rowbotham, *Dutiful Daughters: Women Talk about Their Lives* (Austin: University of Texas Press, 1977).

30. Butler, in Case, 279.

31. Candace D. Lang, *Irony/Humor: Critical Paradigms* (Baltimore and London: Johns Hopkins University Press, 1988).

32. Bruce Robbins, *Secular Vocations: Intellectuals, Professionalism, Culture* (London and New York: Verso, 1993), 190.

33. Naomi Schor, *Reading in Detail: Aesthetics and the Feminine* (New York: Methuen, 1987).

34. Joel Fineman, "The History of the Anecdote: Fiction and Fiction," in H. Aram Veeser, ed., *The New Historicism* (New York and London: Routledge, 1989), 61.

35. Timothy Brennan, *Salman Rushdie and the Third World: Myths of the Nation* (New York: St. Martin's, 1989); ed., *Writing from Black Britain*, special issue of *The Literary Review* 34 (Fall 1990); and "The National Longing for Form," in *Nation and Narration*, ed. Homi K. Bhabha (New York and London: Routledge, 1990), 44–70.

36. Alice Kaplan, *French Lessons: A Memoir* (Chicago: University of Chicago Press, 1993).

37. David Damrosch, *We Scholars: Changing the Culture of the University* (Cambridge, MA and London: Harvard University Press, 1995), 90.

38. "A Passion for French," A8.

39. Simon Frith, "The Cultural Study of Popular Music," in *Cultural Studies,* eds. Lawrence Grossberg, Cary Nelson and Paula A. Treichler (New York and London: Routledge, 179, 182; qtd. in Carrie Jaures Noland, "Rimbaud and Patti Smith: Style as Social Deviance," *Critical Inquiry* 21 [Spring 1995]: 609–610.)

40. Eve Kosofsky Sedgwick, *Epistemology of the Closet* (Berkeley and Los Angeles: University of California Press, 1990), 208.

41. Frank Lentricchia, *The Edge of Night* (New York: Random House, 1994); Cathy N. Davidson, *Thirty-Six Views of Mt. Fuji: On Finding Myself in Japan* (New York: Dutton, 1993). See also Eunice Lipton, *Alias Olympia* (New York: Meridian, 1994); Ruth Behar, *Translated Woman* (Boston: Beacon, 1993); and Marianna De Marco Torgovnick, *Crossing Ocean Parkway: Readings by an Italian American Daughter* (Chicago and London: University of Chicago Press, 1994).

42. Henry Louis Gates, Jr., *Colored People: A Memoir* (New York: Alfred A. Knopf, 1994), and *The Signifying Monkey* (New York: Oxford University Press, 1988).

43. Leo Braudy, *The Frenzy of Renown: Fame and Its History* (New York and Oxford: Oxford University Press, 1986); David Lodge, *Small World* (New York: Warner Books, 1984); Roger Kimball, *Tenured Radicals: How Politics Has Corrupted Our Higher*

Education (New York: HarperCollins, 1990); John Rodden, *The Politics of Literary Reputation: The Making and Claiming of "St. George" Orwell* (New York and Oxford: Oxford University Press, 1989).

44. Michael Sprinker, whom Robbins acknowledges, gives a rather different spin to this point about cultural Marxism in *Imaginary Relations: Aesthetics and Ideology in the Theory of Historical Materialism* (New York: Verso, 1987), passim.

45. Victor Turner, *Dramas, Fields, and Metaphors: Symbolic Action in Human Society* (Ithaca and London: Cornell University Press, 1974); see also *The Ritual Process: Structure and Anti-Structure* (London: Routledge and Kegan Paul, 1969). Louis Adrian Montrose, "The Purpose of Playing: Reflections on a Shakespearean Anthropology," *Helios* and "'Shaping Fantasies': Figurations of Gender and Power in Elizabethan Culture," *Representations* 2 (1983): 61–94. Mae G. Henderson, "Introduction," *Borders, Boundaries, and Frames: Essays in Cultural Criticism and Cultural Studies*, ed. Mae G. Henderson (New York and London: Routledge, 1995).

46. Butler, in Case, 273; see also Judith Butler, *Bodies that Matter: On the Discursive Limits of Sex* (New York and London: Routledge, 1993), especially 187–242; *Gender Trouble: Feminism and the Subversion of Identity* (Routledge, 1990); and "Imitation and Gender Insubordination," in *The Lesbian and Gay Studies Reader*, ed. Henry Abelove, et al. (New York and London: Routledge, 1993), 307–320.

47. See the anthologies edited by Case and by Hart and Phelan; Marta E. Savigliano, *Tango and the Political Economy of Passion* (Boulder and Oxford: Westview Press, 1995); Peggy Phelan, *Unmarked: The Politics of Performance* (Routledge, 1993); and Randy Martin, *Socialist Ensembles: Theater and State in Cuba and Nicaragua* (forthcoming).

48. Laura Kipnis, "Feminism: the Political Conscience of Postmodernism?" in *Universal Abandon? The Politics of Postmodernism*, ed. Andrew Ross (Minneapolis, MN: University of Minnesota Press, 1988), 149–166.

49. Peter Brooks, "Aesthetics and Ideology: What Happened to Poetics?" *Critical Inquiry* 20 (Spring 1994): 520.

50. See Peggy Phelan's article on visibility politics, "White Men and Pregnancy: Discovering the Body to Be Rescued," in *Acting Out*, 383–401.

51. Marjorie Garber, *Vested Interests: Cross-Dressing and Cultural Anxiety* (New York and London: Routledge, 1992), 354. See also Garber's *Vice Versa* (New York: Knopf, 1995), passim.

52. Jill Johnston, "Fictions of the Self in the Making," *The New York Times Book Review* 25 1993: 29. Gates is quoted in Heller, "New Brand of Scholarship," A9. Torgovnick's remark occurs here, in the interview with Jeffrey Williams.

53. Carolyn Steedman, *Landscape for a Good Woman* (New Brunswick, New Jersey: Rutgers University Press, 1987); Stephen Greenblatt, *Renaissance Self-Fashioning: From More to Shakespeare* (Chicago and London: University of Chicago Press, 1980); D.A. Miller, "*Cage aux folles*" in *The Novel and the Police* (Berkeley and Los Angeles: University of California Press, 1988), 191.

54. The phrase from Nancy K. Miller, 14.

55. Matthew Arnold, *Culture and Anarchy*, ed. J. Dover Wilson (Cambridge: Cambridge University Press, 1932), 99.

I

Is It Okay to Read Subjectively?

1

Autobiographical Literary Criticism as the New Belletrism

Personal Experience

❧

DIANE P. FREEDMAN

The primary relation most academics have to academic discourse is a sense of duty.
—Peter Elbow, "Problematics of Academic Discourse"

Personal criticism and the inscription of authorial subjectivity are a means of hijacking discourse by insisting upon a specificity that disrupts the abstractions of the canon. In self-consciously asserting one's location in the text, the personal can disrupt not only the transcendental male critic who privileges his art over his context, but also the subjectivity of the critic herself.
—Victoria Howell, reviewing Jane Gallop's *Around 1981*

Autobiographical literary criticism is a subset of "The New Belletrism" explored in a recent MLA session and in print and of what is here deemed "confessions of the critics."[1] In general, the New Belletrism refers, I think, to the increasing presence of the literary essay of personal meditation in bookstores, book reviews, and the academy—including in cross-disciplinary scholarship and in the writing asked of students as well as what they read. Especially in literature departments, autobiographical criticism may, on the one hand, also go by such names as personal criticism, narrative criticism, autocritography, public criticism, and personalist or experimental critical writing, and on the other, as the personal essay, writings "on location," or sim-ply the essay.[2] Other contributors to this collection will use additional terms as well to describe both public and academic or quasi-academic versions of the writing in this movement—or moment. "It is engaged," my co-editor Frances Zauhar wrote in her contribution to our own collection, *The Intimate Cri-tique: Autobiographical Literary Criticism*. It is accessible, as likely to be pub-lished by trade presses as university presses.

Journalist Scott Heller suggests that "the new subjectivity" is a politically and emotionally engaged, often belletristic mode that "freely mixes personal elements with research expertise" (A7). Before settling on "autobiographical criticism" I myself have also previously described it (in *An Alchemy of Genres: Cross-Genre Writing by American Feminist Poet-Critics*) as cross-genre writing (writing incorporating critical theory, textual exegesis, autobiography, poetry, manifesto), alchemical writing, border-crossing writing, hybrid writing, em-bodied writing, or a quilt, collage, or patchwork of genres—all metaphors invoked or suggested in the examples of hybrid writing on which I focused in that book: Gloria Anzaldúa's *Borderlands/La Frontera*, Cherríe Moraga's *Loving in the War Years*, Adrienne Rich's "Split at the Root: An Essay in Jewish Identity," Alice Walker's "In Search of Our Mothers' Gardens," Susan Griffin's *Made from this Earth*, Marge Piercy's *Parti-Colored Blocks for a Quilt*, Tess Gallagher's *A Concert of Tenses*, Jane Gallop's *Thinking Through the Body*, Maxine Hong Kingston's *The Woman Warrior* and *China Men*, Nancy Mairs's *Remembering the Bone House*, Jane Tompkins's "Me and My Shadow," and oth-ers. Together, these kinds of texts represent a paradigm shift in academic writ-ing, a shift that, although (as I'll explain in a moment) it has roots in a range of discursive traditions, may be said to have begun in earnest in the late 1980s.

A short list of other belletristic scholars in fields outside literature might include Anthony Appiah (philosophy/Africana Studies), Ruth Behar (anthropology), Norma Field (Asian studies), Eunice Lipton (art history), Sara Ruddick (philosophy), Patricia Williams (law), and Carolyn Steedman (sociology/psychoanalysis). Fuller bibliographies of autobiographical literary critics and autobiographical scholars across the disciplines may be found in *The Intimate Critique* and in *Nexus*, respectively, and the work of some impor-tant practitioners is well represented in this volume.

Liberty Bell-etrism

Ann Rosalind Jones has pointed out the "phonocentric emphasis" of much of the writing associated with the feminist movement (think of Gilligan's *In a Different Voice*, and Frey's "Beyond Critical Darwinism: Women's Voices and Critical Discourse"), something I find resounding in the New

Belletrism. I had considered for my "New Belletrism" talk many different terms and tropes for the personal criticism I read and write and was intrigued by the genre-naming that Jane Tompkins, Marianna Torgovnick, Alice Kaplan, and Cathy Davidson attempt in their interview reprinted in this volume.[3] I returned to some of the terms that, as I have mentioned, I had previously adopted: cross-genre writing (ungainly), autobiographical criticism (not evocative of the full range of genres used or of disciplines whose term for academic work is not "criticism"), and alchemical writing (because of its association with change, and even because of its association with the failure to transmute base metal to gold. I was interested in evoking the idea of process, not product).

Each time I began to write about the New Belletrism, I kept thinking of the Liberty Bell.

The Liberty Bell embodies its (supposedly failed) process; its makers were unable to meld several metals into a stable amalgam. Hung in 1753, "it was inscribed 'Proclaim Liberty throughout the Land unto all the inhabitants Thereof' (Lev. 25.10) [and] it was rung in July, 1776 to Proclaim the Declaration of Independence.... It was cracked in 1835 and again in 1846 and it now rests on its original timbers as an exhibit" instead of being hung and rung (*Columbia Encyclopedia*). Comprised of three different metals—silver, copper, gold?—its amalgam didn't hold. Nor should it have—the melting pot metaphor that was earlier a supposed American ideal was flawed. It is appropriate that the bell of freedom and independence at once holds together as symbol and yet symbolizes the limits of assimilation, of holding together (as our nation failed to hold itself together in the late 1800s). In fact, the bell probably "functions" better as a relic accessible for ready view than as something lifted high and away, functions better as a reminder of the several peoples and cultures that make up our United States than as a permanently harmonious blend.

In the Duke group interview, Jane Tompkins goes on to say that she wants a term for personal writing "permitting fragmentation, or permitting lots of different selves, or different aspects of the self." All of which makes me want to say that the new belletrism is somehow deeply U.S. American (though practiced elsewhere, of course—most especially in Great Britain, France, and Canada, and by U.S. Latino/as, at the moment).

Multiple Origins

The kind of writing I'm excited to hear about these days produces liberatory feelings and audible music while retaining visual evidence of its multiple and conflicted origins. In fact, Philip Lopate, in his new, nearly eight-hundred-page collection, *The Art of the Personal Essay*, speaks of multiculturalism as one reason for the turn toward the personal. Given "the growing awareness that the United States is a pluralistic, multicultural society," he writes,

> and that we need to listen carefully to the intellectual voices of minorities and immigrants.... The personal essay turns out to be one of the most useful instruments with which outsiders can reach the dominant culture quickly and forcefully and testify to the precise ambiguities of their situation as individuals and group members. It can also be, as Adrienne Rich's essay shows, a vehicle to analyze how often we are "split at the root" when it comes to our chosen and inherited identities. (li)

In *An Alchemy of Genres*, I also argued for the efficacy of the hybrid essay for creative writers split at the root or in the "shadows" personally and professionally—Rich, Anzaldúa, Moraga, Kingston, Audre Lorde. I would add Carol Taylor, a scholar of folklore, who finds herself "standing in the shadows" of institutional "plantations" ("Dividing Fences"); lawyer Patricia Williams, who writes in her book *The Alchemy of Race and Rights* that she slipped "in and out of shadow, as [she] became nonblack for purposes of inclusion and black for purposes of exclusion"; and anthropologist Ruth Behar, who was "non-Latina for purposes of inclusion and Latina for purposes of exclusion" and then the reverse (at the hands of her institution).

Autobiographical literary criticism, the most common and widely published form of autobiographical criticism, owes something, in addition, to the increasing presence of poets in the academy, the proliferation of creative-writing programs, and the historically hybrid nature of poets' prose and of English departments housing poets and novelists along with composition teachers, journalists, textual critics, and literary and cultural theorists. Autobiographical criticism shares, for example, composition theory's emphasis on writing as process, not product; reader-response theory's attention to the reactions of readers; and some French theorists' penchant for "crossing over genre lines, cross-pollinating autobiography, fiction and theory, and challenging traditional dividing lines between subject and object, self and others" (Flieger, 265). Autobiographical criticism may also be indebted to such first-person political-aesthetic (and oral) traditions as the Latin American *testimonio* and the African-American slave narrative. Perhaps China and Japan, two cultures with a strong tradition of "I" writing, as Lopate reminds us, will be the next prodigious producers of and influences upon autobiographical criticism.

> The 'I' implicated here is very precise, yet more than half unspeakable. Its descriptors are not mere political trading chips. They are vectors, inter-

locked with energy, joy, imbalance, determination, depression—themselves not free-floating emotions, but situated and socially formed.
—Rachel Blau DuPlessis, "Reader, I Married Me: A Polygynous Memoir"

My location or situation as a poet, long before I ever became a critic, and as a woman writer of mixed religious and class identity, mixed up about faith, makes me, I think, privilege belletristic writing, the self-consciously meditative and musical essay, and books and essays by persons with (and whose subject is) hybrid genealogies and social histories. In my writing, editing, and teaching, I lean towards autobiographical criticism that depicts what *An Alchemy of Genres* and the texts studied therein did—an "identity [that] oscillates among sometimes fogged-in points of reference, multiple angles of vision—and confusion" (*Alchemy*, 33).

Marianna Torgovnick, in "Experimental Critical Writing," insists that the critic must work as "a writer, not just a critic. . . . When writers want to be read they have to be more flexible and take more chances than the standard scholarly style allows: often, they have to be more direct and more personal." To her, "writerly writing is personal writing, whether or not it is autobiographical. Even if it offers no facts from the writer's life, or offers just a hint of them here or there, it make the reader know some things about the writer— a fundamental condition, it seems to me, in any real act of communication. . . ." (26–27). Surveying some early attempts at the genre while making a case for "essayistic" writing, Douglas Atkins makes clear that in personal criticism, if "the text is not . . . illuminated for another reader, the resultant writing surely doesn't deserve to be called literary criticism" (97). He continues, "if, on the other hand, the experiencing, responding critic is not interestingly and effectively represented, I don't know why anyone else would want to read him or her or should be expected to do so." So, the writer has vectors needing voice(s), and the criticism has vectors needing inclusion (literariness, illumination of literature and culture, illumination of the textual and critical personalities involved. A gyrating X marks the spot.)

Further, most autobiographical criticism, I would argue, is personal in tone (though it needn't be), self-disclosing (though it needn't be), emotional, full of concrete particulars, but it is also theoretically and historically engaged, confronting many of the reigning academic and social debates and problems today (social constructionism, essentialism, identity politics, social construction of gender, alcoholism, child abuse, pornography, sexism, classism, racial discrimination). "This balancing act—to speak from the place of personal experience and to scrutinize the assumptions of the universality of that experience—has produced a particularly persistent tension within the feminism of the past two decades," writes Bonnie Zimmerman ("In Academia and Out:

The Experience of a Lesbian Feminist Literary Critic," 116). Beyond literature departments, scholars in one discipline after another are taking a fresh approach to their subject matter and writing style as well as to their readers. As frequently unacknowledged connections between a critics's life experiences and his or her research assumptions, methodologies, and conclusions are revealed, academic prose begins to seem more intimate and honest, more inviting—and also more literary. It has become more accessible and exciting to the general public and to general-education students.

Informing Traditions

Although autobiographical criticism represents a radical shift in academic writing, its variants owe something to the essay tradition, with its writerly freedom, and much to the second-wave feminist tenet that the personal is the political; to a female psychology that allegedly favors "connected" over "separate" knowing (Gilligan; Belenky *et al.*), and to a feminist epistemology that sees social location (the nexus of one's racial, religious, gender, class, geographic, sexual, familial, and institutional histories) as necessarily implicated (and thus needing to be articulated) in one's research (Rich, "Notes Towards a Politics of Location"; Harding). As Leslie Rabine reminds us (quoting Gayle Greene and Coppélia Kahn's assumption for their coedited volume, *Changing Subjects*), "a major strength of feminist scholarship is the vital connection between lived experience and theory" (211). The New Belletrism is not a passé throwback, however: although "the 'authority of experience' was basic to feminist inquiry from the start, most academic feminists have also used a depersonalized, academic style, in order to pass" (Greene, "Looking at History"). The time has finally come to follow up on the experimentations of the few early rebels. Personal testimonies still have political-action, aesthetic, and epistemic value.

"Something is happening to the way we think about the way we think" (20) and "the instruments of reasoning are changing" (23), writes anthropologist Clifford Geertz in *Local Knowledge*. It is a happening that the writings in this volume attest to. In their present forms, writings on and from the autobiographical are inflected by social constructionist views of identity, by feminist and poststructuralist cautionary tales about "essentializing" and binary thinking. Even those like me, with materialist, "expressivist" leanings, see neither the self nor group identity as stable or unified. Even categories like gender blur and change through ongoing individual, medical, and social intervention. Race and ethnicity change through discourse and history. Biology is not seen as governing one's destiny. To the autobiographical critic, no one self, no one approach is taken as a constant.

Just for the Record

Our own profession's fascination with the belletristic personal essay (in its many variations) is evident in the many convention sessions on related topics since 1989, and in journals, book series, new books, and at least one internet discussion group. 1994 MLA sessions included: (1.) "The New Belletrism" (special session); (2.) "Autobiography and Pedagogy" (Division on Autobiography, Biography, and Life Writing); (3.) "Narrative in Non-narrative Contexts: The Critic as Narrator" (Society for the Study of Narrative Literature); (4.) "Confessional Criticism" (Division on Literary Criticism); (5.) "Using Personal Experience in Critical Writing: Theory and Practice" (Division on Nonfiction Prose Studies, excluding Biography and Auto-biography); and (6.) "The Words to Say It: Empowerment through Personal Voice" (Division on Psychological Approaches to Literature). At the 1993 convention, Madelon Sprengnether offered a panel on autobiographical criticism with Gayle Greene and others, who read from essays soon to be published in Greene and Kahn's *Changing Subjects*. In past years, beginning in 1989, Olivia Frey and I have organized sessions on "Autobiographical Literary Criticism," "Voices of Color: Autobiographical Criticism," and, at the Midwest Modern Language Association meeting in 1988, "Analytical versus Relational Discourse." I also remember a 1988 MLA session entitled "What Does It Mean to Me?"

In 1992, *The Sonora Review* announced "cash paid" for submissions published in its special issue on merged genres. In response to a query I sent Joan Marcus, the editor at the time, I was told that she had had "an astound-ing response to our announcement in *Associated Writing Programs Newsletter* (people really seem to need a market for cross-genre work) but we always want more" (personal letter October 4, 1991).

PMLA around that time featured a *Mid-American Review* call for essays for a forum on women's positions in contemporary writing for which "diverse and creative approaches [were] encouraged." It suggested discussions of a distinctive feminist poetics, experimental forms, ecofeminism, and so on. The same issue of *PMLA* featured a notice seeking "poetry, personal narratives, essays, letters [and more traditional academic forms]" for a special issue of *Women and Language* focusing on women and spirituality. In December, 1994, *Creative NonFiction* advertised itself as a new journal "for writers, teacher and readers of the rapidly emerging genre of creative nonfiction," with issues featuring writings by John McPhee, poets writing prose (Adrienne Rich, Charles Simic, Margaret Gibson), "powerful new voices ... of emerging women writers," and the New Journalism. In 1994, the University of Illinois Press inaugurated a new series in creative nonfiction.

The popular literary press has taken notice (*Times Literary Supplement, The Chronicle, Women's Review, Lingua Franca*) along with the book review editors of scholarly journals. The internet offers a discussion group or "list" on "the place of the personal in feminist work/lives." Discussed are "autobiographical theorizing, pedagogy, personal experience, life writing, literary critical theory." List subscribers are encouraged by the list administrator, Sidney Matrix, to "tell stories about their lives, work, writing, and teaching," as they challenge the idea that "'academic' work and 'personal' experience should be kept, or are, separate, opposite, or radically different things." My own working bibliography of recent book-length works in autobiographical scholarship (and not the more general-category, personal writing) stretches to seven single-spaced pages. As Lopate reports, "More and more publishers are willing to bring out essay collections."

Who is she then?

> Who is she then? It appears she locates herself only to disclose that she has no secure location. She writes herself only to falter over the necessity for a stable identity. There are too many categories available to her. The very space of location is in fact a decentered one.
>
> —Terry Caesar, *Conspiring with Forms*
>   (on Marianne Hirsch, in her book,
>   *The Mother/Daughter Plot: Narrative, Psychoanalysis, Feminism*)

Memory: my sister and I go shopping at Nordstrom's in Seattle. An English salesperson asks if we need help. Gail, a true Long Islander who drops her "r"s and dawgs her "o"s, responds in a clipped British accent, "Diane, do we need help? I don't think so." Embarrassed, I shush her. She doesn't even realize she's spoken that way, never intending, as I thought she might have, to parody the speaker.

Identity and identity markers/attributes are fluid, mutable, sometimes self-consciously so. One sociobiologist claims our genetic histories are knobs tuned by family and environment, as Michael Bérubé's essay here may well dramatize.

I suffer from depression. So do my sister, who takes an oral antidepressant, and my father, who at sixty-seven has had several ischemic episodes and suffers from long-term diabetes diagnosed when he was in his twenties. But I prefer to think of and to treat my diagnosed depression as "situational" rather than genetic, to treat it with words rather than drugs.

Exercise in comp. class: write a letter describing your car accident to your best friend from high school. Write another letter to your parents, grandparents, nephew. What do you leave out? What are you sure to include?

How and why do these letters differ in content, tone, diction, length, handwriting, format?

Are these personae, masks? Or other (authentic?) selves?

We are early occupied by many voices, many selves, I'd argue, and then, through stress, loss, change, age, reading, acquire or let go of still others.

First-person writing doesn't erase this theoretical position, doesn't mean totalization of the self or of the community of which one temporarily posits oneself to be a representative (Jewish Long Island? Middle-class depressives with advanced degrees?). It's a window in and a route to other work, other selves.

Critiques/Poetic License

I've been so distracted by critiques launched at the supposed essentialism, solipsism, and anti-intellectualism of autobiographical or personally inflected scholarly writing, that I've expended entirely too much energy explaining the ways in which this sort of writing is relational rather than subjective or objective; it is not merely a swing to a pole opposite the prevailing one, and the personal (what we mean by the personal) is as much transformed by the new practices as the professional is when we transport the "personal" into our "professional" talk. All such categories are put into constant motion. Instead, however, there is much to emphasize about the formal and aesthetic dimensions of the New Belletrism, the pleasure it brings to the ear, and the relief. Atkins seeks it as a source of a "revitalized" critical writing. I looked to poets as some of the best sources. It seems, however, that to renew or use poetic license these days in academia, one needs to have a license as large as a library or with as much storage as a pentium chip. (Of course, we all know the pentium chip is flawed when it tries to make certain, sophisticated mathematical calculations, which only argues for its efficacy as a symbol of the New Belletrism—a kind of writing no longer concerned with getting everything right or figured out to the nth decimal. . .).

In college, I liked reading poets' autobiographies and prose, with all their directness and sensory detail. I drifted from a critical and creative focus on poetry to one on the essay, in large part because, as a graduate student, I paid my way by teaching composition, courses on the essay, courses I increasingly focused on the autobiographical essay. A focus on sound and speech and verbal play seem to me more embodied than other kinds of discourse, the pleasures of mouth and ear a way to begin with the political commitment to "the body closest in" (Rich, "Notes Towards a Politics of Location"). Bass-line (as in music) discussions about actual bodies unite many of the works I'd put on the list of the New Belletrism I'd celebrate and attempt to emulate—Rich's essays; Behar's "The Body in the Woman, the Story in the Woman" (an essay about Behar's mother); Behar's "translated woman," Esperanza; Mairs's "bone house." I shift from epistemical focus on the eye to the ear and touch (Tompkins wants writing that will "touch her where she wants to be touched"). The vulnerability of the writing and writing subject—its contested status in this volume, for example—derives, probably, from the fact of the writer's body making itself so present.

What I do know is that despite its dangers for teaching and scholarship—hypersubjectivity in the assessment of literary and student writing and hypersensitivity to criticism, writing that veers towards the boring and trivial, teaching that turns psychotherapeutic or merely confessional, leaving students and teachers at loose ends and avoiding the rigors of social, academic, or publishing reality—autobiographical criticism is a moving and effective intellectual and literary practice. Joining the personal and professional, analysis and emotion, "self" and other, it powerfully connects readers to texts, to their own writing, to our own (if previously unacknowledged) critical process, and to one another.

Coda/Agency Adrift

But if belletristic, self-consciously musical, metaphorical, descriptive for description sake, at once tentative and sententious, much of the new personal criticism might additionally be called a literacy narrative, stories of how the writer came to read or write as she or he does. Inevitably metadiscursive in being a story of its own genre and technique, a literacy narrative often invites the reader to a specific book or set of books or to a place and thence to her own favorite book or place.

◈

Back against the apple tree I once cried for when my sister climbed into its then frail limbs and disfigured the tree and buds, I read, against the dinner cries of my mother and the laundry list, I read. Then, in the large closet in my new basement bedroom, in a womb within a room, I read, ignoring as best I could the clatter upstairs, the calls to chores. There, too, I played an old phonograph in private devotion to my favorite folksinger-poet, whose lyrics I learned from reading them on album covers as I listened and then sang along: "Blue—ooh-ooh-ue-ue. Songs are like tattoos. / You know I've been to sea before."

I meditated in a tall box and hid in the laundry room next to my bedroom, eyes shut tight, mind gone awandering and self-sorrowing. When my father tried to bring me out in the world and make me useful at his office—where I was supposed to pull medical charts; file floppy, oversized X-rays that resisted the rack and cut my finger ends; stick lead letters on new X-ray films; and centrifuge blood specimens—I would take any opportunity to sit on the little brown stepstool in the storage room to read out of sight of my father and his nurse-receptionist, whose affection I treasured but whose gossip I derided.

❀

I've been having the blues lately, weeping when a colleague asks me how I'm doing, unable to explain my rage at the institution that in so many ways has made me welcome. I've passed through all the stages, age ten through twenty, sung about in Joni Mitchell's "The Circle Game," I've worn out the turntable no one repairs any longer, I can't sing to myself in my closet or living room—I'm too busy with teaching, writing, child care, trying to sneak in some sleep. I'm too old to moon about the house in my nightgown and thick socks, cheery only to the dog, living on chocolate and daydreams and daytime TV. I'm supposed to be a professional, writing footnotes, finding through-line arguments, not distracted by the intrusions of the real or sentimental: Where are the sorrow songs of my youth? What of these varicose veins, the sciatica pain, these twelve visits to three dentists for the care of one old tooth? And the pain and loss and fear of loss one can't write about in less than tedious clinical detail or without seeming cruel to one's family or without banality?

I left the white kitchen of my Long Island childhood behind for college in the country and multicultural studies; for poetry workshops in Boston bars; for feminist studies in Seattle; for teaching in private preparatory schools and colleges; and, now, for teaching in a public institution in rural New England. But in my head I'm back in my red room with the poet-singer's blues, this time with the frog in my throat of age and responsibilities and too many desires beyond the good man hard to find or the good book to read in the margins of the day and office. Daily, I want first a good word (does my toddler son love me? does my partner?), then a good garden, a good dog, good words to read and write, that would be the good deed. But as with my garden, the perennials of my life are too crowded together, red aphids run rampant, moles burrowing frantically. And the perennial question: What to work on first?

Notes

1. "The New Belletrism," MLA convention special session, San Diego, 1994 (at that session I gave an earlier version of this essay woven together with a presentation by Denise Stephenson entitled "A New Belletrism: Experimental Writing." Also on the panel was Mike Hill, author of a paper entitled "What's New about the New Belletrism?" The session was chaired and arranged by Jeff Williams. I am grateful to Denise, Mike, and Jeff for a lively exchange on the subject. I am additionally grateful, as always, to Olivia Frey.) For another invocation of the New Belletrism, see Hesse, "Cultural Studies and the New Belletrism."

2. These terms are used, respectively (and this is really just a partial list), in Freedman, Frey, and Zauhar, *The Intimate Critique* ; Caws, *Women of Bloomsbury*; Miller, *Getting Personal*; about Gates, *Colored People*; in Hesse, "Cultural Studies and the New Belletrism"; the subscriber blurb for the personalist list administered by Sidney Matrix [Michelle Reynolds] and in her unpublished monograph "(Un)Authorized Discourse"; Torgovnick, "Experimental Critical Writing"; Lopate, *The Art of the Personal Essay*; Freedman and Frey, *Nexus: Writings on Location*; and Atkins, *Estranging the Familiar*.

3. Jeff Williams generously made available a transcript of the interview before it was edited for inclusion in *The Minnesota Review* n.s. 41/42 (Fall 1993/Spring 1994): 53–74 and this volume.

Works Cited

Anzaldúa, Gloria. *Borderlands/La Frontera: The New Mestiza.* San Francisco: Spinsters/ Aunt Lute, 1987.

Appiah, Anthony. *In My Father's House: Africa in the Philosophy of Culture.* New York/ Oxford: Oxford University Press, 1992.

Atkins, G. Douglas. *Estranging the Familiar: Towards a Revitalized Critical Writing.* Athens, Georgia: University of Georgia Press, 1992.

Behar, Ruth. *Translated Woman: Crossing the Border with Esperanza's Story.* Boston: Beacon, 1993.

———. "The Body in the Woman, the Story in the Woman: A Book Review and Personal Essay." *Michigan Quarterly Review* 29.4 (Fall 1987): 1–22.

Belenky, Mary Field, *et al. Women's Ways of Knowing: The Development of Self, Voice, and Mind.* New York: Basic Books, 1986.

Bernikow, Louise. *Among Women.* New York: Harper, 1980.

Caesar, Terry. *Conspiring with Forms: Life in Academic Texts.* Athens: University of Georgia Press, 1992.

Caws, Mary Ann. *Women of Bloomsbury: Virginia, Vanessa, and Carrington.* New York and London: Routledge, 1990.

Creative Nonfiction. Ed. Lee Gutkind. P.O. Box 81536, Pittsburgh, PA 15217-9966.

Davidson, Cathy. *36 Views of Mount Fuji: On Finding Myself in Japan.* New York: Dutton, 1993.

DuPlessis, Rachel Blau. "Reader, I Married Me: A Polygynous Memoir." Greene and Kahn, 97–111.

Elbow, Peter. "The Problematics of Academic Discourse." CCC Conference. Seattle, March 17, 1989. Later published as "Reflections on Academic Discourse: How it Relates to Freshmen and Colleagues." *College English* 53.2 (February 1991): 135–155.

Field, Norma. *In the Realm of the Dying Emperor.* New York: Pantheon, 1991.

Flieger, Jerry Aline. "Growing Up Theoretical: Across the Divide." Greene and Kahn, 253–266.

Freedman, Diane P. *An Alchemy of Genres: Cross-Genre Writing by American Feminist Poet-Critics.* Charlottesville: University Press of Virginia, 1992.

———. "Living on the Borderland: The Poetic Prose of Gloria Anzaldúa and Susan Griffin." *Women and Language* XII.1 (Spring 1989): 1–4. Rev. and rpt. as "Writing in the Borderlands: The Poetic Prose of Gloria Anzaldúa and Susan Griffin." *Constructing and Reconstructing Gender: The Links Among Communication, Language, and Gender,* eds. Linda Perry, Lynn Turner, and Helen Sterk. Albany: SUNY Press, 1992. 211–217.

———, Olivia Frey, and Frances Murphy Zauhar, eds., *The Intimate Critique: Autobiographical Literary Criticism.* Durham, NC: Duke UP, 1993.

Freedman, Diane P. and Olivia Frey, eds. "Nexus: Writings on Location." Unpublished ms.

Frey, Olivia. "Beyond Literary Darwinism: Women's Voices and Critical Discourse." *College English* 52.5 (September 1990). Rpt. in Freedman *et al., The Intimate Critique.* 41–65.

Gallagher, Tess. *A Concert of Tenses: Essays on Poetry.* Ann Arbor: University of Michigan Press, 1986.

Gallop, Jane. *Thinking Through the Body.* New York: Columbia University Press, 1988.

———. *Around 1981: Academic Feminist Literary Theory.* New York: Routledge, 1992.

Gates, Henry Louis (Jr.). *Colored People: A Memoir.* New York: Vintage, 1994.

Geertz, Clifford. "Blurred Genres: The Refiguration of Social Thought." *Local Knowledge: Further Essays in Interpretive Anthropology.* New York: Basic, 1983. 19–35.

Gilligan, Carol. *In a Different Voice: Psychological Theory and Women's Development.* Cambridge, MA: Harvard University Press.

Greene, Gayle and Coppélia Kahn, eds. *Changing Subjects: The Making of Feminist Literary Criticism.* New York/London: Routledge, 1993.

Greene, Gayle. "Looking at History." Greene and Kahn, 4–27.

Griffin, Susan. *Made from This Earth.* New York: Harper, 1982.

Harding, Sandra. "Who Knows? Identities and Feminist Epistemology." Joan E. Hartman and Ellen Messer-Davidow, eds. *(En)Gendering Knowledge: Feminists in Academe.* Knoxville: University of Tennessee Press, 1991. 100–115.

Heller, Scott. "Experience and Expertise Meet in New Brand of Scholarship." *The Chronicle of Higher Education.* May 6, 1992: A7+.

Hesse, Douglas. "Cultural Studies and the New Belletrism: Strange Anti-Allies for Public Discourse." *Rhetoric Society of America* (Conference Proceedings, 1992): 120–129.

Hirsch, Marianne. *The Mother-Daughter Plot: Narrative, Psychoanalysis, Feminism.* Bloomington: Indiana University Press, 1989.

Howell, Victoria. Review, *Around 1981: Academic Feminist Literary Theory* by Jane Gallop and *Getting Personal: Feminist Occasions and Other Autobiographical Acts* by Nancy K. Miller. *Journal of Gender Studies* 3.1 (1994): 103–105.

Kaplan, Alice. *French Lessons: A Memoir.* Chicago: University of Chicago Press, 1993.

Kingston, Maxine Hong. *The Woman Warrior.* New York: Vintage/Random, 1989.

————. *China Men.* New York: Vintage/Random, .

"Liberty Bell." *Columbia Encyclopedia.*

Lipton, Eunice. *Alias Olympia: A Woman's Search for Manet's Notorious Model and Her Own Desire.* New York: Scribner, 1992.

Lopate, Philip, ed. *The Art of the Personal Essay.* New York: Anchor, 1994.

Mairs, Nancy. *Remembering the Bone House: An Erotics of Place and Space.* New York: Harper, 1989.

Miller, Nancy K. *Getting Personal: Feminist Occasions and Other Autobiographical Acts.* New York: Routledge, 1993.

Moraga, Cherríe. *Loving in the War Years.* Boston: South End, 1983.

Piercy, Marge. *Parti-Colored Blocks for a Quilt.* Ann Arbor: University of Michigan Press, 1986.

Rabine, Leslie. "Stormy Weather: A Memoir of the Second Wave." Greene and Kahn, 211–225.

Reynolds, Michelle [Sidney Matrix]. "(Un)Authorized Discourse: Performing in Lesbian: Writing/Lesbian: Theory." Unpub. paper, 1994. Matrix is also the administrator of the "personalist" internet "list" or discussion group.

Rich, Adrienne. "Notes Towards a Politics of Location." *Blood, Bread, and Poetry: Selected Prose, 1979–1985.* New York: Norton, 1982. 210–231.

————. "Split at the Root: An Essay in Jewish Identity." *Blood, Bread, and Poetry.* 100–123.

Ruddick, Sara. *Maternal Thinking: Toward a Politics of Peace.* Boston: Beacon, 1989.

Steedman, Carolyn. *Landscape for a Good Woman.* New Brunswick, NJ: Rutgers, 1987.

Taylor, Carol. "Dividing Fences: Growing up Jim Crow." Freedman, *et al., The Intimate Critique.* 197–206.

Tompkins, Jane. "Me and My Shadow." *Gender and Theory,* ed. Linda Kauffman. New York: Basil Blackwell, 1989. Rpt. in Freedman, *et al., The Intimate Critique.* 23–40. Originally appeared, in a slightly different version, in *New Literary History* 19.1 (1988).

————. *West of Everything: The Inner Life of Westerns.* Oxford: Oxford University Press, 1992.

Torgovnick, Marianna. "Experimental Critical Writing." *Profession* 90 (1990): 25–27.

————. *Crossing Ocean Parkway: Readings by an Italian-American Daughter.* Oxford: Oxford University Press,1992.

————. *Gone Primitive: Savage Intellects, Modern Lives.* Chicago: University of Chicago Press, 1990.

Walker, Alice. "In Search of Our Mothers' Gardens." *In Search of Our Mothers' Gardens.* New York: Harcourt, 1983.

Williams, Patricia. *The Alchemy of Race and Rights.* Cambridge, MA: Harvard University Press, 1992.

Zimmerman, Bonnie. "In Academia and Out: The Experience of a Lesbian Feminist Literary Critic." *Changing Subjects: The Making of Feminist Criticism.* Ed. Gayle Green and Coppélia Kahn. New York: Routledge, 1993. 112–120.

2

Mourning Shakespeare

My Own Private Hamlet

❖

MADELON SPRENGNETHER

Poetic Influence is a variety of melancholy.
—Harold Bloom, *The Anxiety of Influence*

I have been thinking about *Hamlet* for a long time—much longer than I knew. I discovered this when, in the middle of an essay about my father's death by drowning when he was forty-two, I wrote the following: "When I first read *Hamlet* as a teenager, I empathized not only with Hamlet's grief as a survivor, but also with the anguish of the ghost—hoodwinked out of his life. I imagine my father, like him, bitterly feeling betrayed." In the way that writing often reveals something unexpected, this simple statement elicited a double awareness—of the extent to which I identified very specifically with Hamlet's dilemma as an adolescent, and of the general significance of mourning in the play. Beyond this, I began to think about how Freud's oedipal reading of *Hamlet* has obscured the more obvious issue of mourning, and how his own faulty understanding of this process has contributed to the state of present confusion about the importance of Shakespeare to English studies, including his influence over Anglo-American culture.[1] I want to use my own experience in this essay as a point of departure from which to explore the complex intertwining of these matters, as well as to suggest a means of coming to terms with the task of mourning Shakespeare in ways that honor the claims of the present as well as the past.

I saw *Hamlet* in performance before reading the play. I'm not sure what year it was, whether I was a sophomore or a junior in high school, but I do remember the evening of the event. The Royal Shakespeare Company was touring the states, and I was invited to go with a friend and her parents. At dinner that night, my mother announced that she and my stepfather were thinking of a divorce. Although my mother was upset, she did not raise her voice, my stepfather remained silent, and it was understood that my two brothers and I should continue to behave as before, that is to say, as if nothing had happened, though our lives were pulling apart in ways that I regarded as frightening, if not disastrous. I had no heart for going out, but when my friend arrived, I left with her as planned, not knowing what else to do.

I believe it is the context in which I saw the play that caused it to affect me so deeply. My mother's announcement had acted as a painful reminder of our recent family history, of all the raw and wounded feelings surrounding my father's death which I had been striving so hard to deny. Always hovering in the background of my consciousness, they now threatened to overwhelm me. Yet *Hamlet* engaged me on precisely these grounds. In spite of my dismal mood that evening, I found myself becoming absorbed in the play. Looking back, I would say that I was able to submerge myself in Hamlet's problems because they so resembled my own. It was more than adolescent rebellion (the usual basis for identification with Hamlet) that I felt; I knew exactly what it was like to grieve the loss of a father, to resent his replacement. Although my mother did not remarry for five years after my father's death, to me (locked in the timeless realm of childhood) it felt as "o'er hasty" as two months. Like Hamlet, I idealized my father, hated my stepfather, and cultivated my sense of helplessness and depression. Like him, too, I blamed my mother for betraying my father's memory. Forced to conceal my feelings, I was convinced that no one could understand me. Sometimes I even wished that my stepfather would die. Such thoughts, in turn, oppressed me and made me feel guilty—like a murderer. It was obvious: Hamlet was me, Gertrude, my mother, and the ghost, most terribly, my father, commanding an impossible fidelity and revenge.

My mother's threat of divorce (a threat which she never actually carried out) opened up the whole issue of my relation to my stepfather just when it was beginning to settle into some accommodation. Though I was not able to feel active liking for him, I *was* beginning to accept him, mainly because of the interest he took in my education. It was he who was responsible for my attending the private girl's school which I found so intellectually challenging and where I received the kind of approval I craved. Now that he was my benefactor, how could I want him to leave? Would we be poor again, I wondered, as we were after my dad's death? How would we survive? At the same time, my father's memory called to me, demanding its due. How could I accept a substitute for him when I still lived with his ghost? From this perspective, I believe that I understood Hamlet's procrastination. When you are torn by conflicting impulses, the easiest course is to do nothing.

What *Hamlet* elicited most deeply in me, however, were my scarcely buried feelings about my father's loss. I, too, was sunk in mourning yet prevented from giving expression to my grief. My father died in 1951, an accidental drowning victim. Although I was present at the scene, I did not actually witness his death. From my perspective, he simply disappeared, suddenly and irrevocably. Instead of pulling together around this event, my family dispersed. My paternal grandparents, aunt and uncle and their children moved away from St. Louis shortly thereafter and failed to stay in touch. My mother, evidently stunned by her own loss, withdrew from us children into her private world of pain. Because I did not attend my father's funeral, I had no graphic sense of the reality of his death. My younger brother, who was seven at the time, barely remembers him.

Somehow I understood that I was to manage my feelings by myself, that this was what it meant to be grown up. When I cried, I did so in the seclusion of my own room, half-ashamed of giving in to such a childish impulse. My mother's philosophy, as I subsequently learned, was to try to forget what you cannot change, an emotional strategy that fitted her own upbringing. Hence her silence on the subject of my father's death. To this day, we rarely talk about him.

It seemed, in my family, that my father *had* been forgotten, almost as though he had never existed. Yet this appearance of oblivion only strengthened my secret resolve; I, at least, would remember. Once, when my younger brother casually referred to my stepfather as "daddy," I took him aside to reprimand him. "He's not your father," I hissed, "don't ever call him that." Not being able to grieve fully for my father when he died, I could not let him go. I was stopped in time, arrested at the moment of my father's disappearance, as though still waiting for him to return. Like Hamlet, I would hardly have been surprised to see his ghost.

One of the points I used to make in teaching *Hamlet* is that the ghost of Hamlet sounds just like his son. Both are obsessed with the same issues: Claudius' crime, Gertrude's infidelity, the sinful nature of their pleasure, and the body's general corruption. It is as though young Hamlet carries the voice and vision of the ghost within, almost as though he were possessed. Yet the ghost tells him only what he already knows or wants to hear, exacerbating rather than relieving his condition. Communicating with the ghost contributes to Hamlet's burden of grief, focusing his thoughts even more narrowly on the pain of his situation and his physical disgust. He becomes fixated on his mourning, a tortured and tortuous process which can only come to a bad end.

I think I understood this too. While I had received no ghostly injunctions from my father, I was determined to "remember" him. Keeping him freshly in mind, I thought, was a way of staying in touch. As long as I carried my father inside me in this way, he could not finally leave me, could not be gone forever. Over time, however, something changed. The image of him that I wanted to retain kept getting mixed up with nightmarish images of his dead body—in this case images of a body that was badly decayed. Like Hamlet, I became obsessed with the fate of the body, with its gradual metamorphosis into an object of fear and revulsion. Like the gravedigger, though less humorously, I thought about the effects of water on decomposing flesh. In the early seventies, I wrote several poems incorporating references to *Hamlet* and my father's drowning. The following lines are representative.

> Water is a sore decayer. The dead pop up
> putrid, unrecognizable. They go
> without a thought, but won't stay down
> not even in the ground, weighted
> with a clean stone.

By this time, my desire to preserve my father in memory had turned into a form of haunting. I was pursued by him, inhabited by him, to the point of feeling the disintegration of his body within. In its extreme form, this seemed a kind of madness—like that of Ophelia, but projected onto other figures. In a poem about Virginia Woolf, I fused these elements into an image of suicide as a kind of lover's union. This is the last stanza.

> In my dream, I run, lightly, like a girl
> like Atalanta, not stopping
> for any golden apples.
> I am running, I think, toward some memory
> toward some dank smell
> of mud and sticks and sand and shells
> and fat flowers worse than weeds
> toward faces so eaten I cannot remember
> what they are to me,
> toward some consummation maybe
> with the water, where I can lie
> like a stone watching the flickers
> and streaks of light
> playing on the river.
> I will put one in my pocket.

What this poem now tells me is that my desperate strategy to keep my father alive in imagination was corroding my capacity to take pleasure in my own life. It was destroying me from within. I have found a word for this process in the work of Nicholas Abraham and Maria Torok—"encrypting."

Instead of coming to terms with one's grief, one creates a secret compartment in the self where it is preserved intact, like a mummified corpse.[2] Such a process represents the obverse of a successful mourning, in which the dead are remembered in a mobile, evolutionary way, instead of being figuratively embalmed. Jacques Derrida offers a gloss on this distinction:

> I pretend to keep the dead alive, intact, *safe (save) inside me*, but it is only in order to refuse, in a necessarily equivocal way, to love the dead as a living part of me, dead *save in me*, through the process of introjection, as happens in so-called "normal" mourning.... Faced with the impotence of the process of introjection (gradual, slow, laborious, mediated, effective), incorporation is the only choice: fantasmatic, unmediated, instantaneous, magical, sometimes hallucinatory. (xvi)[3]

I have come to my own understanding of what it means to refuse mourning through "incorporation" or encrypting. Once, at the end of a massage cum spiritual healing session offered to me by a friend, I said simply, "I have made my body a container for my grief."

I am reading *Hamlet* as a play not about mourning *per se* (or even revenge), but about encrypting. Even Freud, by classifying Hamlet as a melancholic, seems to understand this. Although Freud typically refers to *Hamlet* as an illustration of the Oedipus complex, he suggests a rather different dynamic in his essay, "Mourning and Melancholia." The melancholic, as Freud explains, refuses to acknowledge the reality of his loss, regardless of how it occurred, whether through death, abandonment, or betrayal. Instead, he incorporates the lost object into his own ego, thus directing any feelings of hostility or reproach against himself. In such a state, "the patient represents his ego to us as worthless, incapable of any achievement and morally despicable; he reproaches himself, vilifies himself and expects to be cast out and punished." Freud clearly understands Hamlet's state of mind in this light. "In the patient's heightened self-criticism," Freud continues, he may describe himself as "petty, egoistic, dishonest, lacking in independence, one whose sole aim has been to hide the weaknesses of his own nature," views which "Hamlet held both of himself and of everyone else" (SE 14, 246). Hamlet provides an instance of what Freud calls "pathological mourning."[4]

One does not recover from "pathological mourning." Instead, "the shadow of the object," as Freud poetically states, falls "upon the ego" (SE 14, 249). By identifying with, incorporating or encrypting the lost object, one can never escape from it. There is no possibility of letting go. Something like this, I believe, happens to Hamlet. The task of remembering is such that it overwhelms his life, compelling him to give up his own loves and ambitions in deference to his father's demand. It also acts like a contagion, destroying the innocent, or merely meddlesome, along with the guilty. Of those who are close to Hamlet, only Horatio survives to tell the story. If this is what the dead require in the way of mourning, it is too much to ask.

As a teenager, I could not have reasoned in this way, of course. I would have believed the ghost, and credited Hamlet's distress. But I don't think I would have been uplifted by the end of the play, or its implicit message—that Hamlet's acquiescence in his death is either beautiful or noble or that the general bloodshed provides release. I think I would have read the conclusion as contributing to the hopelessness I already felt. My own anguish, I might have comprehended, could only end in death.

I think that Freud understood melancholia or pathological mourning (what I am calling encrypting) better than the so-called normal grieving process, which he tends to dismiss as taking care of itself. Yet, even here, his analysis is instructive, not so much for what it reveals about the subject of mourning, as for the insight it offers into his own mental processes. For Freud, normal mourning takes place through gradual detachment from the lost object:

> Each single one of the memories and situations of expectancy which demonstrate the libido's attachment to the lost object is met by the verdict of reality that the object no longer exists; and the ego, confronted as it were with the question of whether it shall share this fate, is persuaded by the sum of the narcissistic satisfactions it derives from being alive to sever its attachment to the object that has been abolished. (SE 14, 255)

The logic here is simple, but rather cold. The dead are gone for good, and if we are to live our own lives, we must endeavor to forget them. Such is the wisdom of Claudius, and I, like most readers, feel that Hamlet is right to reject it. Severing one's ties to the deceased seems too draconian a solution to the problem of absence posed by death. Surely something more subtle occurs in the process of ordinary mourning. Yet Freud can imagine only two alternatives: either total embrace or total abandonment of the dead.[5]

I think it is likely that, in "Mourning and Melancholia," Freud offered the fruits of his own experience with grief—an experience which he theorized in the bifurcated fashion I have just described. Conspicuously missing from his account is an understanding of mourning that allows for continuing attachment in the absence of active suffering. I believe that the evolution of Freud's oedipal construct in the wake of his father's death, as reflected in his interpretation of *Hamlet,* offers some insight into this phenomenon.

Freud's father, Jacob Freud, died on October 23, 1896. The following May, Freud included some notes on mourning, melancholia, and death wishes against one's parents in a letter to his friend Wilhelm Fliess:

> Hostile impulses against parents (a wish that they should die) are also an
> integrating constituent of neuroses. . . . These impulses are repressed at peri-
> ods when compassion for the parents is aroused—at times of their illness or
> death. On such occasions it is a manifestation of mourning to reproach one-
> self for their death (so-called melancholia) or to punish oneself in a hysteri-
> cal fashion, through the medium of the idea of retribution, with the same
> states [of illness] they have had. . . . It seems as though this death wish is
> directed in sons against their fathers and in daughters against their mothers.
> (Masson, *Letters*, 250; May 31, 1897)

This passage, with its analysis of the dynamics of self-reproach in the aftermath of a parent's death, prefigures Freud's later views on melancholia, yet he
does not pursue this line of thought. Rather, he moves in another direction—
toward a formulation of the Oedipus complex.

As a necessary step in this progression, Freud abandons his earlier conception of neurosis as the outcome of childhood sexual abuse, a step which
not incidentally absolves his own father of wrongdoing. In order to sustain the
seduction theory, as Freud explains to Fliess, he would have had to indict his
own father as the instigator of his brother's and sisters' neuroses.[6] "Then the
surprise that in all cases, the *father*, not excluding my own, had to be accused
of being perverse" (Masson, *Letters*, 264; September 21, 1897). It is tempting
to view Freud's seduction theory as the expression of a "hostile wish" against
his father, one which (following his own incipient theory of melancholia) he
needed to repress or turn inward as a result of Jacob Freud's death.

As one might expect in this case, Freud expresses not disappointment but
relief at the demise of his theory. "I have more the feeling of a victory than a
defeat," he confesses, comparing himself with Hamlet in Act V of Shakespeare's
play. "I vary Hamlet's saying, 'To be in readiness': to be cheerful is everything!"
Less than a month later, Freud comes forth with a new theory: "A single idea of
general value dawned on me. I have found, in my own case too, [the phenome-
non] of being in love with my mother and jealous of my father, and I now consider it a universal event in early childhood" (Masson, *Letters*, 272; October 15,
1987). This insight, in turn, prompts a new reading of *Hamlet*:

> How does Hamlet the hysteric justify his words, "Thus does conscience
> make cowards of us all"? How does he explain his irresolution in avenging
> his father by the murder of his uncle—the same man who sends his
> courtiers to their death without a scruple and who is positively precipitate in
> murdering Laertes? How better than through the torment he suffers from
> the obscure memory that he himself had contemplated the same deed
> against his father out of passion for his mother. . . . His conscience is his
> unconscious sense of guilt. (Masson, *Letters*, 272–273; October 15, 1897)

Freud first mentions the theme of hostile wishes directed against parents, and their subsequent repression, in the context of mourning. Slowly, however, he detaches these concepts from the context of death, sloughing off the seduction theory in the process of framing his oedipal construct, which posits a son's guilty desire for his mother, his corresponding hatred of his father, and repression of that hatred under pressure of the threat of castration. While retaining the notion of hostile wishes and the self-reproach attendant on their repression, Freud reconstrues them in such a way as to eliminate the fact of death. Thus Freud's Hamlet suffers not from grief, but from an inability to cope with his incestuous impulses.

The oddity of Freud's allusion to Hamlet at the moment of renouncing his seduction theory signals perhaps his bad faith. In saying "the readiness is all," Hamlet clearly means to indicate his preparedness for death. Heavy of heart, yet fatalistic, he allows himself to be drawn into Laertes's murderous scheme. "If it be now, 'tis not to come; if it be not to come, it will be now; if it be not now, yet it will come. The readiness is all" (V.ii.195–197). Freud reads this statement, bizarrely, as its near-antithesis: "to be cheerful is everything." In his obvious distortion of these lines, Freud betrays a strategy of misreading which may also inform his oedipalization of *Hamlet*.

The period of Freud's most intense self-analysis coincides with that of his mourning his father's death. Yet few have thought to critique the Oedipus complex (the most obvious outcome of this self-analysis) in the light of Freud's grieving process.[7] Read from this perspective, the Oedipus complex seems less the unmediated product of Freud's self-understanding than an evasion of the full force of mourning. In it, Freud displaces the dynamics of loss in favor of a more "cheerful" construct, one in which sons only *wish* their fathers dead, submitting instead to their live authority. By shifting his focus to the realm of juvenile fantasy and desire, Freud in effect substitutes a resurrected and idealized father figure for the elderly Jacob Freud, who has proved so disappointingly mortal.[8]

In the face of his father's death, Freud theorizes Oedipus instead of mourning, encoding that choice in his interpretation of *Hamlet*. Yet, implicitly acknowledging this work of displacement, he elsewhere associates the play with the issue of loss, pointing out on more than one occasion that Shakespeare (or his avatar Edward de Vere) had written the play in the aftermath of his father's death.[9] Only in "Mourning and Melancholia" does Freud pursue this tantalizing clue, reading Hamlet's habit of self-denigration as a specific effect of grief.

"Mourning and Melancholia" might be regarded as Freud's repressed reading of *Hamlet*, continuing the train of thought he began in the aftermath of his father's death, yet set aside in favor of his oedipal constuct. By turning from mourning to Oedipus, moreover, Freud seems to have foreclosed certain investigative possibilities, ultimately limiting his understanding of the dynamics of loss to the extremes of forgetting (severing ties with the deceased) or encrypting (pathological mourning). Such a description, which leaves no room for poignant or even pleasurable memory, can hardly pretend to account for the full range of emotions expressive of grief.

I would even venture to suggest that Freud's two poles, rather than representing clearly opposed alternatives, tend to collapse into each other. I don't know anyone who really ever "forgets" the dead. That which is banished from conversation or consciousness merely seems to dig in deeper, inhabiting more frightened and vulnerable areas of the self. Trying not to think about someone is perhaps the surest way of becoming haunted.

I began this paper by suggesting that both *Hamlet* and Freud's confusions about *Hamlet* have contributed to our current dilemmas regarding Shakespeare's position in the canon of English studies. What I mean by this is that we have no shared understanding of how to perform the labor of cultural mourning. Instead, we tend to regard the body of Shakespeare's work as something either to enshrine or to discard. In my own department, for instance, there is a feeling among some graduate students and faculty that Shakespeare should no longer be part of our "required" curriculum. Indeed, there is evidence of declining faculty interest in teaching the multiple undergraduate Shakespeare courses necessary for our majors. Last spring, the chair made an appeal for the first time for more "volunteers" to staff these sections. Yet we do not seem able to discuss these matters with any degree of composure; our conversations tend to polarize too quickly to permit serious engagement.

There are those whose desire to "remember" Shakespeare reminds me of Hamlet, who sacrifices his own hopes and desires to a ghostly presence and command. Others seem to want to forget, dropping Shakespeare from our syllabi and requirements for the major, severing our ties, in effect, to this long-dead poet. Such conflict is not unique to our department, nor does it confine itself to terms of informal debate. Not long ago, *PMLA* published an article entitled "The Poetics and Politics of Bardicide," as if to imply that merely *reading* Shakespeare in certain way amounts to a crime against his person[10]— as if to invoke the full force of sanction, not only against homicide, but also parricide, the sin of Oedipus.

But surely there is some alternative between annihilation and repression, between Oedipus and Hamlet? Merely preserving Shakespeare, worshipping an idealized memory (what I would call encrypting), is no solution, any more than it is in grieving the loss of someone truly loved. Nor does it seem adequate to pretend that Shakespeare never existed, never touched us, never influenced us or the culture we have inherited—for good or ill.[11] Neither Hamlet nor Freud, I would say, seems to know what to do about loss.

To live life to the end is not a childish task.

—Boris Pasternak, "Hamlet"

Tradition has it that Shakespeare himself played the ghost in *Hamlet*. What did he think of while playing this part? Did he ponder the death of his only son Hamnet? Or his father John, who would have died by the time this play was first performed. Did he identify with the living or the dead? Did the ghost offer him an opportunity to see from both sides of betrayal—from that of the grieving, hoodwinked father, and that of the lost, the grieving child?

We do, of course, attribute emotions to the dead. It is as though they go on living and changing—as long as they inhabit *us*. I used to think of my father sometimes as feeling betrayed by my family. We couldn't save him, and we left him to the river (when he was already surely dead) in order to get help. It makes no difference that we had no choice. The spring that I turned forty-two, I was afraid. It didn't seem right to me to outlive my father, to have more years, more of anything. But recently, I have begun to see things differently.

Once, not too long ago, I was dancing with my husband—as we like to do on warm summer evenings, barefoot in the living room with the rug pushed back, the french doors open to breezes and smells from the garden—when I began to sense my father's presence. It was in the music that I felt him, almost as though he were summoned by it, and by us, through the exuberance of our dancing, the emanation of our pleasure. I began to sing to him, as though he were a silent partner in this scene, breathing the lyrics to Jackson Browne's "Stay," as I continued to step and twirl. "People stay, just a little bit longer." "Please, please, stay ... take a little time, don't leave us all behind, sing one more song." At first, I felt this as a kind of pleading, my voice blending with Browne's falsetto, the plaintive whine of the synthesizer, and his electric guitar. But then, it came to me differently. I began to hear my father speaking through the music to *me*; it was his wish that I keep on dancing, singing, so that he too could enjoy this moment. He was not haunting me. It was precisely my pleasure that had allowed him to appear. It was his desire that I go on dancing for as long as the music played—and then just a little bit longer.

Notes

1. Reinhard and Lupton, p. 50.
2. See Kathleen Woodward, "Between Mourning and Melancholia."
3. See Derrida.

4. See Alexander Welsh, p. 481 and p. 502; Arthur Kirsch, *passim*; Susan Letzer Cole, p. 60; Juliana Schiesari, p. 264; and, on Lacan, John P. Muller.

5. See Woodward, "Between Mourning and Melancholia," p. 116.

6. See my *The Spectral Mother.*

7. See Peter Homans, p. 104, and Mark Edmundson, p. 41 and p. 162.

8. See Woodward, "Reading Freud," p. 33.

9. See Freud, *SE* 4: 263–4; 20: 63–4; and 23: 192, n. 1.

10. See Richard Levin's two *PMLA* essays and, for arguments for and against his position, *Shakespeare Left and Right.*

11. See Peter Erickson, p. 67 and *Rewriting Shakespeare, Rewriting Ourselves.*

Works Cited

Abraham, Nicolas and Maria Torok. *The Wolf Man's Magic Word: A Cryptonomy,* trans. Nicholas Rand. Minneapolis: Minnesota University Press, 1986.

Cole, Susan Letzer. *The Absent One: Mourning Ritual, Tragedy and the Performance of Ambivalence.* University Park, PA: Pennsylvania State University Press, 1991.

Derrida, Jacques. "Fors: The Anglish Words of Nicolas Abraham and Maria Torok," trans. Barbara Johnson. In *The Wolf Man's Magic Word,* xi–xlviii. Minneapolis: Minnesota University Press. 1986.

Edmundson, Mark. *Towards Reading Freud: Self-Creation in Milton, Wordsworth, Emerson, and Sigmund Freud.* Princeton: Princeton University Press, 1990.

Erickson, Peter. *Rewriting Shakespeare, Rewriting Ourselves.* Berkeley: California University Press. 1991.

———. "The Two Renaissances and Shakespeare's Canonical Position." *The Kenyon Review* 14 (Spring 1992): 56–70.

Freud, Sigmund. *The Standard Edition of the Complete Psychological Works of Sigmund Freud.* 24 vols., trans. James Strachey *et al.,* ed. James Strachey. London: Hogarth, 1974; rpt. 1986.

———. "An Autobiographical Study." 1925 [1924]. *SE* 20: 7–74.

———. *The Interpretation of Dreams.* 1900. *SE* 4: 1–338.

———. "Mourning and Melancholia." 1917 [1915]. *SE* 14: 243–258.

———. *An Outline of Psychoanalysis.* 1940 [1938]. *SE* 23: 144–207.

Homans, Peter. *The Ability to Mourn: Disillusionment and the Social Origins of Psycho-analysis.* Chicago: Chicago University Press. 1989.

Kamps, Ivo, ed. *Shakespeare Left and Right.* New York: Routledge, 1991.

Kirsch, Arthur. "Hamlet's Grief." *English Literary History* 48 (Spring 1981): 17–36.

Krull, Marianne. *Freud and His Father,* trans. Arnold J. Pomerans. New York: Norton, 1986.

Levin, Richard. "Feminist Thematics and Shakespearean Tragedy." *PMLA* 103 (1988): 125–138.

———. "The Poetics and Politics of Bardicide." *PMLA* 105 (1990): 491–504.

Masson, Jeffrey Moussaieff. *The Assault on Truth: Freud's Suppression of the Seduction Theory.* New York: Farrar, Strauss and Giroux, 1984.

———, trans. and ed. *The Complete Letters of Sigmund Freud to Wilhelm Fliess 1887–1904.* Cambridge: Belknap/Harvard University. 1985.

Muller, John P. "Psychosis and Mourning in Lacan's *Hamlet.*" *New Literary History* 12 (Autumn 1980): 147–176.

Reinhard, Kenneth and Julia Lupton. "Shapes of Grief: Freud, *Hamlet* and Mourning." *Genders* 4 (March 1989): 50–67.

Schiesari, Juliana. *The Gendering of Melancholia: Feminism, Psychoanalysis, and the Symbolics of Loss in Renaissance Literature.* Ithaca: Cornell University Press. 1992.

Shakespeare, William. *Hamlet. Norton Critical Edition,* 2nd. Edition, ed. Cyrus Hoy. New York: Norton, 1992.

Sprengnether, Madelon. *The Spectral Mother: Freud, Feminism, and Psychoanalysis.* Ithaca: Cornell University Press. 1990.

Welsh, Alexander. "The Task of Hamlet." *Yale Review* 69 (June 1980): 481–502.

Woodward, Kathleen. "Between Mourning and Melancholia: Roland Barthes' *Camera Lucida,*" in *Aging and Its Discontents: Freud and Other Fictions.* Bloomington: Indiana University Press, 1991. 110–129.

———. "Reading Freud . . . Aging, Castration, and Inertia," in *Aging and Its Discontents.* Bloomington: Indiana University Press. 1991. 26–51.

3

Interrupted Reading

Personal Criticism in the Present Time

❖

RACHEL M. BROWNSTEIN

A year and a half ago, when Columbia University Press decided to publish a new edition of my 1982 book, *Becoming a Heroine*, the editor proposed that I write a new introduction. The idea appealed to me: teaching feminist graduate students at the City University, I was thinking about the difference between current concerns and those of seventies feminism, in the climate of which that book had been written; I was even doing a little reminiscing in class. The first chapter of *Becoming a Heroine* looked back at my passionate, girlish reading in the 1950s from the standpoint of the seventies; what could be more appropriate than placing a second lens in front of the first one?

But the project of writing the new material, which ended up as a "post-script" to the book, unexpectedly became a problem. The nub of it was an anecdote written in the style of *Becoming a Heroine*. I meant it to be a comical self-portrait, an updated version of the persona I presented in the book, now crankily vexed by the thorough decline of reading in the nineties. I had to cut it, because the editor and several other readers, and finally I myself, found that it couldn't help but be about something altogether different. Here is the outtake:

> Do people still read for themselves, these days? A young friend assures me that, in L.A., at least, they do (they're tired of talking about movies, she explains). She tells me this because I've just told her about my encounter with the fellow I think of as the antiliteracy vigilante. A thickset young man

of about twenty-five, with a neatly tucked-in white shirt and a necklace of earphones, he approached me on a subway platform where I stood, reading a book, and asked how long I'd been waiting there. Startled, I answered him, then noticed he kept on standing near me. A quick look round revealed that there were eight or ten other people in our neighborhood, none of them reading; why had he singled me out to interrupt? I wondered angrily. And why was he hanging around now? My apprehensive wariness of the hefty young man was complicated by a rush of psychoanalytically valid rage: that is, I recognized its connection with my mother, who has always seen a page before my eyes as an open invitation to chitchat. Finally the train arrived, we both boarded it, and I sat down and put up my protective volume; he stood at a little distance from me, but I felt him keep on glancing in my direction. I had already begun to scheme about what I would do if he should continue to stalk me when, as we pulled into a station, I saw him adjust his Walkman in preparation for detraining. Just before getting off, he turned to call out helpfully in my direction, "Better stop reading or you'll miss your stop!"

I wrote this story about the enormous gulf between compulsive readers like me and practical, militant nonreaders like the strange young man in the subway and my mother, who, when I was growing up, had considered my constant reading a disabling distraction from the real business of life, like getting on a train. (Belatedly, I notice that the Corot painting I chose for the cover of *Becoming a Heroine* is entitled, in English, "Interrupted Reading.") But the anecdote stubbornly refused to make that point. Was the young man black? my editor wanted to know. Yes, she had guessed as much, but was curious as to why I hadn't mentioned it. Shouldn't I do so? Could I not? She fretted: Wasn't my story really about my irrational fear of the young man? Wasn't I telling it in my relief that, after all, he didn't harm me? Was it my racism or the sexual insult I was trying to laugh—or write—off, my surprise at seeing I was being seen as an aging mom? Did I want to unpack all that in my piece—take these important issues on?

I didn't; my subject was reading. I rewrote the anecdote several times: the narrative seemed to contain a nugget of truth I needed to tell about the war between the imagined worlds of readers and the world of dailiness. Of course I was also rewriting now in self-defense, passionate to prove I was not, as my editor hinted—as tactfully as she could—untruthful, unhip, and/or unaware, not working to cover up my racism or at the very least racialism—not only, in other words, the graying, prejudiced, anxious white woman the young man had seen on the train. But no matter how I sliced it, the anecdote insisted on being about race, and class, and gender.

Perhaps the real trouble is that I failed to tell it well, to do justice to the sudden loony vision I had had on the platform of vigilantes policing the subways to make sure that people didn't read. The story as I tell it opens up too many cans of worms, the race can and the sex can and the age can, the young man as my mother and me as his, my apprehensiveness creating his reassurance, and so on. The reason I can't let it go still, of course, has something to do with this excessive, this novelistic, worminess. But the dense details that delight me cannot but be distracting, here and now. When a literary critic talks about her personal experience, these days, she is expected to make certain predictable points. Not to do so is to make a social and political and also a literary *faux pas,* to break the accepted constraints of what has become a genre. Irony has always presented problems, and so has self-writing since Montaigne, and recent developments have compounded the difficulties. In these times the categories of race and class and gender, once invoked or even implied, indelibly color all other meanings.

❖

The anecdotal first chapter of *Becoming a Heroine,* the one called "My Life in Fiction," looks, from here, like what some academic critics and publishers have called "personal criticism," a category which did not exist in 1982. One hesitates to define the term, especially if one considers everything written or even plagiarized to be in some degree a reflection or expression of the person writing. ("The highest as the lowest form of criticism is a mode of autobiography," wrote Oscar Wilde.) Defining personal criticism as a category, and considering it to be a radical, innovative, politicized practice, is part of the problem I want to consider here.

Different writers use the term to denote different things: sometimes an essay distinguished by an urgent tone of voice; sometimes one that gives a glimpse of the writer's private life (Mr. Booth reading to Mrs. Booth, who's ironing); sometimes a witty riff on what polite people don't mention; sometimes a chatty confrontation or a charged wrangle with other critics; sometimes a full-fledged confession, memoir, or even an autobiography by someone who also elsewhere teaches literature, or "does theory." For reasons that will become clear, I would like to define "personal criticism" narrowly, as a kind of writing about writing that acknowledges, points to and/or reveals—well, what one would be tempted to call the person behind it had the subject not been thoroughly problematized and fractured and rendered unstable and perhaps dead. It is a piece that reveals or pretends to reveal, shall we say under the circumstances, those attributes of the writing subject that are personlike, personal—the person, more usually than not, in the sense of the word that means the body. Personal criticism upsets the reader's expectation of staid professorial discourse. It depends heavily on a sense of generic decorum—an expectation that public academic discourse will be "high," Arnoldian or Foucauldian, but in any case philosophical—which it flirts with so as to subvert. It exploits the signature of the writer, who slips off a mask to tell about, for example, reading theory while also having to go to the bathroom—or about a young man on a subway platform who put her in mind of her mother. Personal criticism is about the reader in the process of reading, the embodied critic.

Some personal critics seem to believe they mime the radical example of postmodern poets and novelists by the mere gesture of entering and rupturing their texts, but of course it is nothing new for a writer to make a cameo personal appearance. Trollope did it, and even Jane Austen, in a few but notable pronouns. Pope, before them, put potentially damaging self-revelations into iambic pentameter: "Fools rush into my head and so I write." His readers would have recognized this as a show of bluntness, and the best personal critics today also acknowledge they're putting on a show, or performance. They also disingenuously suggest—as Pope did—that, unlike more self-concealing writers, they are honest. Their line goes more or less as follows: traditional academic critics claim—falsely—to be dispassionate, rational, apolitical, and disinterested, and I'm here, embodied, to show that this pose is a lie. Or, more radically: the academy is the apex, or the foundation, or the reflection, of an oppressive, white, heterosexist male power structure, and by talking shockingly about myself on this platform I am doing my bit to dismantle the power structure that makes people like me marginal.

❂

Not only feminists do personal criticism, but what now goes by that name has its sources in the insight of seventies feminism that the personal is the political. The genre has become problematic, I think, in a period of confusion and disorganization on the Left—and a period of excessive, obsessive concern everywhere with persons and personalities and the merely personal. In a cultural moment when almost every issue of *The New Yorker* features a celebrity profile, complete with a glamorous, warts-and-more photograph by Avedon, there are obvious reasons why professors are tempted to talk about themselves rather than about literary texts. As a culture we are committed to debunking the Enlightenment and mistrusting generalization and Olympian surveys from above; we value particulars, embodied thought, local and/or situated knowledges. And while Foucault's ideas about surveillance were surely partly inspired by his own rejection of the Catholic confessional, and Foucauldianism is an influential sect, secular varieties of confession are still valued as purgative. Everyone is doing self-writing, which makes you want to try and do it better; and if you are of a certain age, it comes easily, as you have rehearsed it already on the couch. Furthermore, you don't have to go to the library to get the material. (Personal criticism is not the only reason why this old-fashioned trip is beginning to seem unnecessary; in the January/February 1995 issue of *Lingua Franca* an article called "Why Johnny's Professor Can't Read" quotes Andrew Ross's remark to *New York Magazine* that he's given up books for glossy magazines. That *New York Magazine* is interviewing professors is, of course, another sign of the times, as is the existence of *Lingua Franca*, the *New York Magazine* of academics.)

The anecdotal, "personal" mode, for literary types, comes with the territory—certainly the territory of critics who "work," as they say, on novels. Just as the critic who thinks of poets as prophets aspires to write in the prophetic-poetic mode, the one professionally concerned with the plots of fictitious people's lives longs to write his or her own life as a work of fiction. Everyone knows that if you scratch an English professor's drawer you'll find a novel in it. But it's hard to sustain a novel; and the postmodern critic is wary of narrative. Writing bits of personal reminiscence, a.k.a. criticism, seizing on the telling detail and the nice juxtaposition of the recondite and the vernacular, the academic recounting scenes from the life is transformed into something like a novelist, a dialogist. As with a wink he or she exploits the innocence that people marvelously manage to retain since grammar school, the sense of delight and mischief and disbelief you first felt when your third-grade teacher turned up in a two-piece bathing suit at the beach. Why, that's Mrs. Fisher—out from behind the desk, in a body!

❧

Partly because literary criticism is in a bad way these days, with few people sure how to do it or why, all professorial writing about the self has come to be called personal criticism. It was not ever thus. Seventies feminist critics, fueled by politics and encouraged by reader-response and reception theory, explored the differences between men's and women's points of view; then, for the critic to "come out," as it were, as a woman and a feminist reading, rather than a disembodied, dispassionate, enlightened, critical intelligence, was an act of irreverence and perhaps defiance. I say "perhaps" because the irreverence of my own "My Life in Fiction" was meant to charm more than to defy. Girlish impudence has traditionally engaged readers: a student I knew in the 1980s dedicated her dissertation on Jane Austen "To Elizabeth Bennet, who taught me to speak up." While Elizabeth is certainly no wimp, she is not, as many have rightly observed, a revolutionary.

My aim in *Becoming a Heroine* was to seduce my readers into reading about Elizabeth Bennet and heroines like her—to see that such reading, such heroines, can really matter to one's life. In other words, I wanted them to enjoy *Pride and Prejudice* as much as I did, and to take it seriously—personally, if you will. My book came out of teaching English and Women's Studies at Brooklyn College, in the 1970s—teaching young women hooked on romances, older women returning to college and thinking about what they had made of their lives, and young men like the one who envied Mr. Darcy for having no business but the private life. I wrote as a teacher; I wanted my readers, who seemed ripe for it, to see a connection between their own lives and nineteenth-century English novels, and therefore to come to some greater understanding of the ways language and literary form made them think and dream as they did about the differences between the sexes, and the idea of a self. *Becoming a Heroine* elaborates the insight that language—the language of novels in particular—matters, that novels reflect and also affect actual lives— that they help determine what Raymond Williams called the structures of feeling. Not so much the plots and characters as what I can only call the literariness of novels—for example (but it's disingenuous to call it that, when it's the thing itself, as I see it), the sense *Pride and Prejudice* gives one of simultaneously living Elizabeth's life and watching it being lived. I juxtaposed readings of novels with anecdotes elaborating my readerly persona so as to show how a character in a novel by Jane Austen partly constructed "my" character. My object was not—or not only—the vulgar pedagogical one of bringing Elizabeth "closer" by showing she is just like you and me; I wanted to show how she—how Jane Austen—contributes to making her readers who we are. It was something my temperament equipped me to do comfortably; and feminism gave me permission to do it more or less respectably. The text, not the personal revelation, was the subject of my critical discourse—a gritty literary text, rather than an abstract, theoretical one.

This last distinguishes me from my younger and more metacritical colleagues. The men I studied with at Yale Graduate School were the text-bound New Critics, not their theorizing successors. In 1959 to 1963, in New Haven, the concerns of philosophical and psychoanalytic and linguistic circles in Paris and Frankfurt were not yet of moment in the English department; even Vienna wasn't a haunting presence there. If I departed, insofar as I wrote about my own life in a book about literature, from my teachers' austere ways, I remained loyal to their method in that my first concern was with reading. The texts that concerned me in *Becoming a Heroine* were books my teachers didn't teach, and I put myself in the picture as they had not, but I wasn't primarily concerned to attack my teachers' impersonal method. In the "personal" sections of *Becoming a Heroine*, I simply stated what all readers know, that you are what you read, and acknowledged what all women know, the tyranny of the marriage plot.[1] I wrote as a reader, and didn't try to argue against any theory of reading or knowledge. For later critics, in contrast, writing about themselves is a way of "doing" theory; finding nothing in the field of literature as interesting as their own presence there, they have moved farther and farther away from what I continue to think the critic's proper study is: the literary object as it seems to that critic to be.

Depending on the intelligence and skill of these writers, their works have been variously absorbing, intelligent, and illuminating, and some of them are of intrinsic value. The objection to them I want to register is threefold: first, that, as the genre has hardened, the different personae "revealed" in these words have come to look excessively and predictably alike; secondly, that self-writing, as it is sometimes called, is neither a development of literary criticism nor a substitute for it; and third, that when we do it, we set a questionable example for our students.

❖

"Oh yes, I know you, you wrote about how you became a heroine," the visiting academic responds when I introduce myself, meaning to flatter me by remembering my first book. To which I smile sourly and nod with resignation. I have, after all, reconciled myself some years ago to suspicion of and lack of interest in reading—as illustrated not only by my subway vigilante, but by colleagues who haven't read more of my book than the title, from which they conclude—because of the feminine form of the noun?—that it must be autobiographical. (*Becoming a Woman*, one colleague thought the book had been called.) No, I'm not distressed by this deafness to my irony. Who can be depended on to hear, in the title, my uncertainty about what a heroine might be, or the pun in "becoming"—or to consider at any length the subtitle, *Reading about Women in Novels*, which I meant to be taken to mean both Reading about the Women Who Turn Up in Novels, and Reading Novels So As To Learn About Women Generally? On second thought, I'm not resigned at all; my English teacher's hackles rise at this inattention to my carefully chosen language. I dislike being misunderstood. Doesn't she know that *I*, of all people, would only claim to be a heroine as a joke?

But how can she, if she's only just met me? How much can a writer expect from her readers? How much can one know, reveal, or conceal of one's familiar self? What assumptions must one make, and what standards of decorum obtain? Where are the boundaries and what are the rules? How can one speak personally without seeming to speak only and transparently and only well of oneself? How is it possible not to feel personally attacked and wounded when one is misunderstood? And how has literary criticism, of all things, brought us to these sticky questions?

Linda Kauffman has recently attacked an oddly constituted set of feminist theorists—Barbara Christian, Nancy Miller, and Jane Tompkins—for, in effect, setting up as heroines—that is, for reaffirming the traditional identification of women with the private and emotional life, and—worse yet—valorizing the idea of the coherent, integral subject. I think Kauffman's attack is problematic, and that it simplifies these critics' positions, but I have no interest in analyzing it so as to position myself (as they say) in the (mine)field where the politics of personal criticism are debated. I want to move to a differ-

ent field—partly because (*pace* my old professors at Yale) you can't really separate the persona or the "speaker" of a personal text from the writer behind it.
When a critic puts her feelings and her body out there, whether in all apparent
earnestness or in an elaborately playful game, it is even harder than usual to
disagree and discuss things profitably. People who write about themselves
open themselves to armchair psychoanalysis and personal attack; readers tend
not to get their favorite ironies; writers get hurt; they sulk in silence, or worse
still in print. If they don't from the start silence potential critics, who are loath
to turn on someone so obviously vulnerable, to argue against a victim of sexism or child abuse or racism, whose victimization is central to the position she
takes—or *is* the position.

At another extreme—sometimes it's the same extreme—personal writing
leads to a cult of personality: the critic bold and clever and successful enough
to shock and thrill, by interposing her body, becomes a celebrity who figures
only her own glamor and notoriety in classrooms and conferences. Which
takes me to my second point: that glamor and glitz drive out subtlety and
complexity the way bad money drives out good, and just as surely as sensational revelations and hints of oppression do. The critic's person—because it's
reminiscent of bigger celebrities?—threatens to make her merely a celebrity.
Far from disrupting or questioning the power structure, her persona—her
person—becomes its avatar and emblem.

We gobble up personal writing partly because we need the language to
live our own intimate lives with a higher consciousness: I say this, having just
read every word of a strongly written memoir about aging written by a college
classmate of mine. But it is necessary to distinguish the higher narcissism
from politics, and criticism, and literature. The critic who claims to tell all
about, or to brilliantly perform, her idiosyncratic but representative, duly
raced and classed and gendered self, cannot fairly rely on her oppression and
outrage to make her a radical, or an intellectual, or even interesting; she had
better be a good writer, too, preferably one with something new to say. Unless,
of course, the sense of what good writing might be disappears, as it threatens
to do—while the crudest gesture in the direction of self-revelation or as-you-
watch-me self-fashioning continues to bring down the house.

Juicy details by their nature claim disproportionate attention. I am told
that at a recent Modern Language Association session on writing about
motherhood, when a scholar prefaced a paper about catachresis with some
comments about the Susan Smith case, all the questions asked afterwards
were about Susan Smith. Another scholar, at the same session, showed a
photograph of herself and her daughter at the end of a paper about fictional
mothers and daughters: again, predictably, the questions were aimed at that
photo. One might argue that this anecdote illustrates a lamentable rift

between academic and ordinary discourse; perhaps the paper on catachresis was too abstract, perhaps it was too early in the morning for the audience to concentrate on it. But surely it's also true that the allusion to a still-warm scandal, like the glimpse of the professor at home, is a distraction from just about anything. Both pretend to appeal to a least common denominator of humanness, beg to let go of falsifying pretensions. Like a naked body intruded into a group of clothed ones, an allusion to the public, private life we have in common is overwhelming: the sign itself packs so much of a wallop that it obliterates what it means to illustrate or indicate. If intruding the body, the banal, the bit of familiar scandal, or the merely personal was once a useful political strategy that served to dramatize and correct the pretensions of "formal" or "male" or "traditional" academic discourse, it now threatens to foreclose thought. It also contributes to the political atmosphere of invasiveness, staged confession, and "outing," the insistence on the sexual or sociological fact of life that blots out everything else.

Personal criticism has intersected dangerously with the media, and with that monster, born of psychoanalysis and social science run amok, that is called identity politics. The contemporary reader has been persuaded to take for granted that the self of a critic—and everyone else—is not a self most deeply connected to, say, playing Beethoven on the piano, or dreaming of intellectual breakthroughs, or contemplating Nature or God. It is, rather, a drearily categorizable self: what it has is a body and a place in society. Unlike the Romantic self that rebels against its origins, the self as imagined these days tends ruefully to accept its role in the inescapable family romance, and limply to concede to biological and sociological determinism. It is a self that is impervious to the pressures of other cultural productions, being always already constructed by pre(tend)-texts of pop sociology and psychology. A writer, I think, is obliged to war against this pervasive and boring conception, this vulgar obsession with the self—or she will, in effect, become a mere effect of race, class, and gender. It's time, I think, to turn away from the distraction, the conversation-stopper, of the self as currently conceived. And for various reasons, it may be a good moment for literary critics to get back to what we were doing when we were interrupted: to reading.

I say this with trepidation, aware that it is open to interpretation, in a polarized political climate where nuance is hard to hear, as a reactionary exhortation. My point is not to bring back old-fashioned *explications du texte*—though I do admire good ones. I'm arguing that it is bracing, healthy, and necessary now to look outside the self—and also socially useful. Surely, at a time when formulaic and jargon-ridden language pollutes politics and the academy, and a radically impoverished language dulls the streets and the airwaves and the high school and college corridors, we have an obligation to focus our students' attention on good writing, let them know what it is and how to talk about it, give them vocabulary and show them syntax. More narrowly, feminist critics might usefully look again at types and techniques of literary image-making, a seventies concern that was given up when the more problematic study of the difference of women writers came in. (Not that the "images" emphasis was unproblematic, motivated as the worst of it was by an ill-advised quest for positive images or role models—"pictures of perfection," Jane Austen called them, which, she said, made her "sick and wicked." Perhaps the death of this kind of literary criticism—and the turn to celebrating the self—was linked to a disappointing dearth of positive models.)

The differences and connections between roles and models on the one hand and historical realities on the other still make an interesting subject, nevertheless. Critics can still find it profitable to look at what the heroine-centered domestic novel suggests about women and representation, and therefore about the art and the world that men and women, over the last three centuries, have made. It is useful to recognize the connections among images complex and simple, to see how they correct and intersect with one another, how they are deployed and rejected and received, how the world is changed and reflected by, say, a writer, or an actress who cleverly altered a stereotype to suit herself—and was translated by writers into a new image. The study of literary forms and tropes and traditions, and the practice and techniques of unpacking images—of literary analysis—are useful skills for citizens that people in literature departments can and should teach. It has been established, over the past twenty years or so, that different people do this from different points of view, with different political agendas, which are more and less easy to make out. The truth about the critic is, to be sure, as elusive—as complex and context-determined, and as fully constructed by language and images—as the truth about the text. But that does not make critics as inherently interesting as texts are; nor does it relieve us of the obligation and the pleasure of continuing to read.

For symmetry's sake, and honesty's, I will end on a personal note. "Anybody may blame me who likes," as Jane Eyre says when she intrudes into her text—and indeed even Virginia Woolf blamed her, or Charlotte Brontë. Her words occur to me because I expect, as she did, that the expression of my desire will alienate my readers. The truth is that I am urging a shift of emphasis away from the critic to the text, from the self to the world, for two reasons. First, I am afraid that the new brand of reductive self-reflexivity, combined with the accidental pressures of modern life and the taste for quick takes, struck attitudes, and jargon, not to mention the yen for the new and the old addiction to love or applause or belonging or blamelessness, will soon make it impossible to get any reading done—impossible, that is, to give complex literary texts the attention they demand and deserve, to enjoy them and to learn from them how to attend to the equally complex contexts in which they were written and in which they may, if we don't forget how, continue to be read. My second, related fear is that people like me will be out of business—and if that seems a very personal and unrepresentative and selfish fear, well, anybody may blame me who likes.

Notes

1. The difference between what women and men, novelists and theorists, know and say about this latter—not to mention the lack of progress in the course of the nineteenth century—is dramatically suggested by a contrast between the endings of Jane Austen's *Northanger Abbey*, published in 1818 but probably written more than a decade earlier, and Sigmund Freud's *Fragment of an Analysis of a Case of Hysteria*, published in 1905. Observing that her readers would "see in the tell-tale compression of the pages before them, that we are all hastening together to perfect felicity," Austen peremptorily marries off a sympathetic minor character to "the most charming young man in the world," who "is instantly before the imagination of us all." Professing herself "aware that the rules of composition forbid the introduction of a character not connected" with the story at the end, she invokes an earlier joke and identifies him as the man whose servant left behind the laundry-bills that Catherine Morland had humiliatingly found in the old chest she hoped would contain clues to gothic horrors. Freud, for his part, magisterially concludes his narrative of Dora's case with this tidying paragraph: "Years have again gone by since her visit. In the meantime the girl has married, and indeed—unless all the signs mislead me—she has married the young man who came into her associations at the beginning of the second dream. Just as the first dream represented her turning away from the man she loved to her father—that is to say, her flight from life into disease—so the second dream announced that she was about the tear herself free from her father and had been reclaimed once more by the realities of life." The Master Narrator's identification of the husband as the association to Dora's dream that he had drawn out of her is undercut, in the editions of 1909, 1912, and 1921, by a footnote: "This, as I afterward learnt, was a mistaken notion."

4

Autocritique

❖

CANDACE LANG

In 1985, that self-professed antihumanist and ringleader in the revolt against the Cartesian *cogito,* Alain Robbe-Grillet, not only published an autobiography, but proclaimed that even in his novels, he had been talking about himself all along, "from the inside."[1] Should we be surprised at this apparent about-face in favor of a self-expressive literature? The *nouveau romancier* himself says not, affirming that this autobiographical turn was initially an act of provocation, a deliberate contradiction of his previous theoretical affirmations intended as a revolt against the terrorism of an entrenched antihumanism that had solidified into an ideology. He soon set the project aside, though, and by the time he resumed work on it in the early eighties, a "new humanism" was becoming so prevalent that he was tempted to scrap the original opening, but instead retained it, preluded by three new introductory pages. Hence, however perplexing the theoretical maneuvering of the opening pages may be, one thing at least is immediately evident: for Robbe-Grillet, autobiographical writing is indissociable from an ongoing theoretical battle, in which it constitutes a strategic move. *Romanesques*—as the three volumes of his autobiography would be entitled—is both a personal and a theoretical work.

In an apartment of Paris's fifteenth arrondissement, during the summer of 1981, about the same time that Robbe-Grillet was presumably incubating his autobiographical project, a considerably less renowned critic was brooding over an article about "Autobiography in the aftermath of romanticism."[2] In her review of some recent publications on autobiography, she deplored the stridently antitheoretical tone adopted by the majority of the critics represented, who often depicted "theory" as the enemy of the private and the personal—in short, of the human. She argued that the critical act, as inherently self-reflexive, has much in common with the autobiographical act, and that the fates of the two were inevitably linked.

Now, over ten years later, much of what has been written continues to set the autobiographical over against the theoretical, as though the two were antithetical or fundamentally incompatible. This perplexes me as much as it did a decade ago, for, in May 1993, as I sit in a (different) apartment in Paris's fifteenth arrondissement and reread what I wrote in 1981, I find myself in fundamental agreement with my earlier contention that autobiography and critical theory are intimately associated.

More and more academics, of late, have been shifting to first-person discourse, integrating personal anecdotes and reminiscences, as well as confessions of idiosyncratic tastes and private pleasures, into their critical writings. Concomitantly, these and other critics have been hailing this emergence of a "personal criticism" as a radically new development, a move away from theory, defined as a mode of discourse that suppressed all "personal" expression, toward a new age in which the writing subject is free to come out of its theoretical closet and reveal itself as it "really" is. In *Getting Personal,* for instance, Nancy K. Miller proposes that "the efflorescence of personal criticism in the United States in the eighties—like the study of autobiography—has in part to do with the gradual, and perhaps inevitable waning of enthusiasm for a mode of Theory, whose authority—however variously—depended finally on the theoretical evacuation of the very social subjects producing it."[3] Miller is too astute, however, not to recognize that this claim glosses over a few complexities, and she recuperates theory on the following page by asserting that just as "'the personal is the political' . . . the personal is also the theoretical: the personal is part of theory's material" (21).[4]

If theory and autobiography are mutually implicated, then, the moment seems a propitious one to theorize on my own reactions to personal criticism. Spatially and temporally, this is an ideal autobiographical occasion: at the close of a year in Paris, four thousand miles from the home office, I sit perched in an eighteenth-floor apartment overlooking the Seine. Stendhal, I muse, must have felt a similarly exhilarating sense of detachment and perspective as he opened his own autobiography with an all-embracing vision of Rome from atop the Janiculum.

The autobiographical fact of the matter is that I initially got off on very bad terms with the personal subject of writing. As a college student during the heyday of psychologizing biographical criticism, I felt compelled to write papers in which I hung my interpretation of the text on distressingly flimsy biographical facts gleaned from a variety of mutually contradictory sources. The result made for tedious, impressionistic analyses leading to what I felt were almost totally arbitrary conclusions. I recall suffering from near-terminal attacks of *angst* as I tried to make, on the basis of available biographical information, some eminently forgettable (and blissfully forgotten) point about Racine's *Athalie*, when it was perfectly clear to me that I could argue either of two contradictory positions with equal conviction (or lack of it), because I hadn't the slightest idea what Racine was really thinking or feeling when he wrote certain lines, nor, frankly, did I much care. This stuff is B.S., I gloomed. Yet as a senior French major with a fellowship for graduate study in French at Johns Hopkins, I couldn't quit now. But I wondered darkly if I could really spend the rest of my life "faking it," feigning excitement and conviction as I erected specious arguments on a shaky foundation of biographical trivia, such as whether the author loved his mother, hated pea soup, had syphilis, or suffered from constipation. In short, I embraced my future career with little ardor.

Consolation came in the form of philosophy, which incredibly, I met up with for the first time that year. Almost immediately, I recognized this as my kind of thinking: the analyzing, abstracting, differentiating, categorizing—hairsplitting, if you wish—that I had always delighted in. By the middle of a year-long survey, I was so hooked that I ditched a third-quarter French course in order to take Existentialism. Not only did this new discipline turn me on, but to me, it seemed a lot more honest than literary criticism: in philosophy you were allowed to *doubt*—with conviction. You could admit the existence of opposing arguments. You could erect complex theories, rigorous in their own terms, with the awareness that they constituted ways of approaching reality, or languages for talking about it, rather than reality itself. Most of all, nobody seemed to care much about the author's heart, bowels, or genitals.

At Johns Hopkins the following fall, my first seminar was taught by a French fellow called Jacques Derrida. The course was entitled "La psychanalyse dans le texte," and the entire first session was devoted to the phrase, "le fils ne revient pas au père." I now marvel that Derrida could have dispatched such a complex sentence in a mere two hours, but at the time, it was quite a novel performance—and an intimidating one. (One student left after two weeks. This stuff was B.S.) Were we expected to do that? I doubted if I could, but I already knew this much: I would rather try to do that than snoop around in Racine's personal life.

Of course I couldn't write like Derrida; nor, after one or two pathetic attempts, did I try. But he and the parade of continental "theoreticians" who followed him through our seminar rooms during those years managed collectively to make literary criticism look like a subject worthy of the kind of passionate interest I had diverted toward philosophy. While borrowing analytic tools from a variety of disciplines, they shared a great sensitivity to language and an awareness of the stakes involved in the assumption of any given discourse. That critical self-awareness, in particular, attracted me. The emphasis on language of course entailed a de-emphasis on biography, notions of personal creativity, genius, and the like. The "theoreticians" never ceased talking about the human subject, of course, but they treated it in a nonromantic key, in a language that demonstrated the private person's inextricable implication in the social, that is, in the empirical and in the political. Through their theoretical grids, I could see for the first time what real (and not purely voyeuristic) human interest literary criticism might have. Dead was the old, abstract, Humanist subject of high culture—but not the real, concrete subject of political activity, the engaged, contestatory one that some proponents of personal criticism today seem to think needs resurrecting. The old Author was a stifling origin, an oppressive voice, a critical Big Brother who knew me but whom I could never know, looking over my shoulder as I erroneously pondered his inscrutable utterances. His deposition opened a space for live subjects to act and speak.

The dark side of this liberating scenario was that this rethinking of subjectivity was rapidly becoming a dominant ideology, with all the excesses that entails. For fear of public ignominy or worse, French grad. students dared not mention the person of the author anywhere in the vicinity of Gilman Hall. Even upon a Saturday evening, as we shared a joint in the privacy of a friend's apartment, we spoke of such things only in hushed tones, and avoided windows, unnerved by the Baltimore Police helicopters that hovered menacingly above graduate housing. Had somebody turned us in to the poststructuralists?

Already, by the time I wrote my dissertation, certain forms of theoretical discourse had acquired the authoritative ring of a party line; both the old, biographical, critical model and the new, textualist one were easily caricatured and abused, and I sensed I had to negotiate for myself a position I could maintain with some conviction, for it was also evident to me at some level that the biggest stake (for me) in all this was *moi*. There could be no going back to the old "humanist" subject: I didn't believe in it, any more than I believed in God or any other ultimate authority or ground. The old expressive model was just too simple, too obvious. I have always been suspicious of the simple and the obvious; I associate them with religious fundamentalism, racism, historical revisionism, Reaganism, all ideologies that I literally cannot stomach. The only remedy for the nausea induced by such conceptual junk food is a good dose of "theory"—of questioning, dissecting, and analyzing, to bring out the complexity of the issues. That is why theory has never been for me a purely abstract, cerebral activity, but one in which I got physically involved: everything I have ever written in a theoretical voice has literally constituted a "gut" reaction.

The foregoing is meant to imply that the most essential component of what I consider to be theoretical activity is the reflexive (self-reflective) moment in which the critic attempts to define her own presuppositions, methodological tools, and the consequences of those choices. Thus it seems to me that the recent trend toward autobiographical or personal criticism is a necessary development in the evolution of critical theory, a further elaboration of the self-reflexive moment of theory through a move beyond the ostensibly "rational" determinants of reading, in order to identify some of the highly specific, localized (both spatially and temporally), empirical factors affecting the critical agent.

In this respect, the theoretical moment is overdetermined by the cultural moment, as American society moves away from an ideal of assimilation toward one of differentiation, that is, multiculturalism. It is no accident that the majority of the practitioners of personal criticism thus far have been speaking from within and for minority and/or marginalized groups, such as gays, blacks, and women. As witnesses for the group for which they strive to achieve recognition by endowing it with a voice, they evoke their personal experiences as members of it—but of course the private or personal experience mobilized by representatives of such groups is already theoretically determined, that is, informed by theoretical concepts and definitions of race and gender categories.

At the risk of irreverence toward academia, I would further suggest that the autobiographical move afoot in scholarly writing today is part of a larger trend that I call the Phil Donahue syndrome: the multiplication of talk shows, audience participation shows, call-in shows, and so on, featuring guests who bare it all, figuratively and sometimes literally, before a fascinated audience. Are academics suddenly admitting they have emotions and entrails and genitals, that they have hit their wives, or have to go to the bathroom, or prefer anal sex for the same reasons as the folks on TV, whatever those reasons? I suspect so, and I suspect that our confessional urges may stem from a growing malaise about the insulation of the intellectual from the "real" physical world of bodies and politics, but I leave it to the sociologists to produce documented hypotheses.

I can, however, argue for the literary-theoretical claim that, as more and more academics seize the occasion to let it all hang out even while adding a line to their vitas, they fall right into line with a certain Christian autobiographical tradition. Like the religious who violated the injunction against excessive preoccupation with self in the name of a higher religious duty to profess her faith by relating her conversion, the academic who violates a law of genre by incorporating personal anecdotes into her scholarship can justify it by appealing to theoretical rigor—and political correctness.

In the case of the religious, the ultimate goal of the conversion narrative was the renunciation of the past self through a symbolic death and rebirth. The traditional autobiographical narrative, undertaken as a retrospective totalization of one's life, had an equally deadening effect, as Sartre so wittily demonstrated in *Les mots*. However, a subtle but essential twist in the conversion narrative scenario is effected when, in the wake of a personal crisis, the subject chooses to interpret that crisis as a turning point, and narrates the events leading up to it as the necessary prelude to the new course her life is to take. While such a turning point is in many ways analogous to the symbolic death of a religious conversion, it differs from it in that the act of writing is, in this case, perceived not as a gesture of devotion and surrender, but as a reappropriation, a *prise en main* of one's own life at a time when it seems to have been lost or taken away. One could argue that the distinguishing characteristic of secular (and the "modern") autobiography is the underlying conviction that writing can and should be a productive, Promethean act, rather than a mimetic, subservient one.

This rebellious, Promethean potential of autobiographical writing to destabilize traditional authority and to transform the self over and against that authority has much to do with why it is becoming a tool of choice for contemporary literary critics. Traditionally confined to the relatively passive or defensive role of spokespersons for and guardians of authority, many academics are eager to move onto the offense. Doubtless the multiplication of sexual revelations in critics' texts is symptomatic of this desire to belie, metaphorically, as it were (but where the concrete functions as vehicle for the abstract), the myth of the impotent scholar. The obedient child hides its sexuality; to flaunt it is one of the most blatant acts of disrespect toward the censoring instance.

Perhaps, then, for academics the autobiographical conjuncture is a moment of revolt against the constraints of tradition, but it is a mistake to cast poststructuralist theory in the role of the now-dead authority, and to proclaim that we have resuscitated the subject it had so brutally repressed. If anything, we have finally assimilated the lessons of the seventies, and are beginning to turn them to constructive use by building upon the ground that they cleared; we had to finish bemoaning the death of the father/subject/author before we could rejoice in the freedom his disappearance gave us. The recent trend in autobiographical criticism is not a return to some kind of healthy referentiality after a long bout with textualitis, but a *mise en oeuvre* of the Promethean powers of language, of its potential for restructuring our world by readjusting our relation to the referent.[5]

Autobiographical writing, then, can be a powerful theoretical instrument, and I would contend that it is most productively exploited as such. That I have a personal stake in this argument should be evident enough, given the elements of intellectual autobiography I have introduced into the preceding pages. The capacity for and the need to engage in theoretical reflection constitute an essential element of my personal identity, so that to oppose the theoretical and the personal is for me simply unthinkable. Furthermore—and this brings me to another and perhaps even more intimately personal interest I have in the personal criticism debate—I am even more dismayed when theory is gendered by feminist scholarship, that is, when rational discourse or abstract analytical thought are stigmatized as instances of phallogocentrism, that is, male intellectual oppression. As a preamble to this second, gendered (?) phase of my confession, then, I will lay my critical cards on the table by declaring that I have never felt repressed, disfigured, disembodied, unsexed, or otherwise alienated by the constraints of logical or theoretical discourse; *au contraire*, I have always found it to be liberating and empowering.

"Empowering," one could say, belongs to the aggressive vocabulary of maleness. I have sold out. Yet what are we in this arena for, if not to fight? You can't always choose your own weapon or fight on your own territory. I am confused by what often appears to me to be the passive-aggressive attitude of feminist critics, by the mixed messages they emit when aggressively denouncing men for being aggressive. An example I ran across recently: in response to Denis Donoghue's query, in "A Criticism of One's Own," as to whether he is "really guilty" of all those things feminists accuse phallogocentric male critics of, Nancy K. Miller writes, "Yes, Denis, since you ask, you are 'really guilty'; in every line of this article of yours, beginning with the cheap shot of its title; you're doing it now in the flamboyant bad faith of your rhetoric."[6] Indeed, while Donoghue makes some good points, his tone is unbearably supercilious, and it irritates this female reader, too. But then Miller goes on to comment that "Donoghue's language is inhabited by a metaphorics of the Law: crime and punishment, guilt and innocence, enforcement and entitlement, rights and wrongs. In fact it is the constant recourse to this language, the preferred codes of phallocentrism itself ... that make Donoghue guilty as charged" (137–138). I fail to see in what respect Miller's own counterattack is not also a recourse to the vocabulary of guilt and innocence; surely she is charging him with something in respect to some code of rights and wrongs. And why shouldn't she?—and recognize it openly? Much feminist writing is in fact heavily laced with such accusatory vocabulary and often seems to be proclaiming a new law without acknowledging it. Surely we don't want to replace Big Brother with Big Sister.

Throughout my academic career I have resisted such segregationist or separatist tactics. Nonetheless, I have often felt guilty about it, as I sensed the accusatory gaze of Big Sister upon me. This, then, may be taken as an apology in the Socratic sense of the term: as an "explanation or justification of one's motives, convictions, or acts." I confess that, while female colleagues on all sides have been vocally joining the ranks of feminist criticism, teaching seminars, sponsoring colloquia, and publishing innumerable pages on female writers and feminist issues of all sorts, I have continued to produce syllabi and articles in which male figures dominate. Oh, I have consciously added some female writers to my syllabi (sometimes out of real interest, sometimes for fear of the disapproval of my feminist students and colleagues), and I have certainly learned to read and to teach with a sharper eye for gender bias, but I have also consciously avoided jumping on the feminist bandwagon. Why? For one thing (beyond the simple fact that I liked what I was already doing), because I felt as though a new imperative had been issued to do so, from some now-female-based authority. More importantly, however, I simply did not recognize myself in much of the feminist discourse I encountered.

To return to the specific domain of personal criticism, I will take as a case in point an article that has often been seen as a feminist (anti)theory manifesto of sorts: Jane Tompkins's "Me and My Shadow."[7] When Tompkins suggests that theory-writing is somehow an inherently masculine activity, and protests that "the female subject *par excellence,* which is her self and her experiences, has once more been elided by literary criticism," I feel as though I have been cast as a sexual deviant. When she writes that "what is perceived as personal by men, or rather, what is gripping, significant, 'juicy,' is different from what is felt to be that way by women. . . . we are really talking about . . . what is important, answers one's needs, strikes one as immediately *interesting.* For women, the personal is such a category" (134) I want to say, please speak for yourself, not for women. While I admire immensely Tompkins's (and any woman's) courage to stand up and speak *for herself* (something I have too often failed to do), I do not care to have her speak for me (I am doing that myself now).

In the course of writing her way to these conclusions about women and the personal, Tompkins supposedly rises from her chair to peruse some books on her shelves. She first picks up Guattari's *Molecular Revolution,* Bloom's *Poetry and Repression,* and Foucault's *History of Sexuality,* and finds their impersonal and abstract style off-putting, particularly in the cases of Guattari and Foucault who, it seems, are not interested in the personal or in concrete situations. This is a curious critique, given the interest both writers accorded the personal and the concrete insofar as they were ignored, precisely, by traditional Freudian and Marxist theory. It is true that they discuss the personal and the concrete in an abstract, that is, theoretical, way, but *some* abstraction, at least, is a condition of communicability; the absolutely personal is incommunicable. Verbalization itself is a mode of abstraction, hence inherently theoretical.

Jessica Benjamin's essay, "Master and Slave: The Fantasy of Erotic Domination," however, gets a thumbs-up—despite its impersonal style and use of generalities—because it deals with experiences Tompkins can relate to. So it turns out that what is at issue is not so much style as content. Now, there is nothing unusual or reprehensible about being particularly attracted by works that appeal to one's personal experience; however, it seems to me that an important part of scholarship is studying subjects outside the realm of our personal experience, and that the additional intellectual effort that is required to understand these more "distant" texts is justified.[8] And it is precisely abstraction and formalization that render accessible to a wider audience of other subjects problems that might, if left in a rawly "personal" form, appear to be purely idiosyncratic and therefore inaccessible and uninteresting to all but a few.

The real stakes of Tompkins's article appear at the conclusion, however: she is angry, very angry, at authority, which in our society has mostly been incarnated in male figures, and at the way in which females have generally been the victims and the tools of that authority. For many reasons, some already evoked, I can identify to a great extent with Tompkins' anger: I understand the authority problem; I grew up in the same stereotyped world she did. For my father, a retired Navy captain and engineer, women were created to cook, clean, and rear children, and the current crisis in the U.S. economy, along with the increasing violence in our society, is the fault of all those women who have abandoned their children to go out and take jobs away from men. A womanizer who thought himself the center of the universe, he was incredibly stingy, and had a violent temper which manifested itself mostly over monetary matters. My mother had been to art school, but naturally gave it up to get married, have children, and be active in the Junior League. She was a good cook and hostess, who put her art training to use making Halloween costumes and Christmas cards, invitations and decorations. The perfect lady, she hardly drew a breath without consulting Emily Post, and taught my sister and me to curtsey (CURTSEY!!!) to adults, not to scratch ourselves at the table (Queen Elizabeth would never do that), and to write charming thank-you notes. She had a pathological case of math anxiety, was a terrible driver, and so terrified of capsizing that she eventually gave up sailing. At forty-five, she divorced my father, was awarded a pathetic amount of alimony, and has been an angry, bitter, lonely person ever since.

So I could be very angry at my father, and I could generalize my anger and direct it at the entire male sex; to some extent, I am and I do. But I am also angry at my mother for her total abdication of self in favor of the law of the other, for her perpetual obsession with what the neighbors would say, the *qu'en dira-t-on*, and for her constant dissatisfaction, her incessant criticism of everything and everyone (evoking, of course, some transcendent criteria)—all the revenge of her thwarted ego against the oppressive other. I am angry at her math anxiety, her lousy driving, and her fear of sailing. I am angry because she bought into the male authority system with all her psychic capital. And I am angry at her incapacitating anger: the fact that she continues to blame all her problems on her father, her ex-husband, on outside agencies. This is unfair of me perhaps, because she *has* been a victim; but she has turned victimization into a vocation. Finally, what angers me most is that she has spent her entire life trying consciously and unconsciously to transmit her submission and her anger to me, and has to a great extent succeeded. For having allowed that to happen, as I said earlier, I am angry at myself. *Mea culpa.*

If I "caught" some of my mother's servitude and anger, however, I did not catch all her phobias and insecurities. It may well be that my father himself unwittingly inoculated me against them, for since he had no sons, he had to make do with daughters, and taught me (a "tomboy," or "*garçon manqué*," as the French say, suggestively) to drive and to saw, sand, drill, hammer, caulk, and rewire; he took me deep-sea fishing at dawn and on ocean sailing races with the fellas, lectured me at length on the functioning of engines, four-cycle versus two-cycle, and gasoline versus diesel, and when (after getting my Ph.D.) I got my first car (a decrepit Renault 12), made me a special tool to remove the odd-sized oil drain plug, and even devised an extension for my lug wrench to give me enough leverage to undo what had been done by men twice my size. He believed you could do anything you set your mind to, a principle that occasionally caused him to foul up royally, thus giving me a glimpse into the dark secret that he—and doubtless men in general—weren't a wit smarter or more competent than women, they just acted as though (and perhaps believed) they were.

I remember a Dagwood comic strip that made a vivid impression on me when I was a child: Blondie is trying to vacuum under Dagwood's armchair, and has him get out of it and lift it off the floor. She next asks him to pick up one foot, and finally the other (without putting the first foot down). Exasperated, Dagwood protests, but that's impossible, hasn't she heard of Newton's law of gravity? To which Blondie responds, oh, poor Mrs. Newton, how does she ever get the housework done? Although I couldn't have articulated it then, I think I sensed that this situation epitomized the distribution of male and female roles in my fifties world as well as within my own family: the male as the thinker, the theorist, versus the unintellectual, pragmatic female, for whom such abstractions as Newton's law of gravity seemed foreign and irrelevant to her sphere of activity. As I recall, I was immensely irritated at the Blondie character for her inanity; by now, of course, my irritation has shifted to the cartoonist whose work served to perpetuate such an image of female unintelligence. Thank heavens, I think, times are changing.

But when I read that theory inhibits the expression of the female subject, I blink in disbelief as a vision passes before my eyes of Blondie denying the relevance of Newton's theory to her housework. My object is not to disparage housework—or any other activity that has traditionally been attributed to women and devalorized as such—but to point out that the act of revalorizing "women's concerns" need not, indeed should not, entail the rejection of all that has traditionally been associated with male authority. I heartily applaud the introduction of courses devoted to women writers and gender issues into university curricula, welcome the revision of the canon and the rethinking of the notion of canonicity it entails, approve the institution of women's studies programs to actively promote the study of writers and works that have heretofore been given short shrift. But, when I attend a faculty gathering where nearly all the women I talk to are writing a work with "women's" or "feminist" in the title, when virtually every prospective female graduate student I interview announces her intent to write a similarly entitled thesis, when I hear that a student has declined to take a course of mine despite her interest in the topic covered, simply because "there aren't enough women writers on the syllabus," my stomach grows queasy and my palms sweaty, as I wonder if I am about to be guillotined by a revolution which I have always believed I supported by trying very hard (and successfully, I think) not to be Blondie.

Like it or not, Newton's law has a lot to do with vacuuming, and "men's" Theory of the seventies has everything to do with Experience, women's or otherwise. It shot the notion of objectivity full of holes, and along with it, that of pure subjectivity: it taught us that everything is indeed "experience," but that experience is always mediated, in a circle that passes through the personal, but always on the way from and to the "unpersonal," or other. In the terms of the current discussion, it taught, in a Nietzschean tradition, that values, laws, or theories are always founded in personal experience (or desire), but that, at the same time, experience also takes form as such in terms of existing narratives that impose a structure on it; "raw" experience is inaccessible as such. The consequence for the genre of autobiography is not, as some would seem to believe, that there can be no such thing, because there are no more subjects out there to write them, but that autobiographical writing is not and cannot be an innocent, naive form of expression: it is a strategic one that mobilizes particular "experiences" and "events," into narratives—or antinarratives—with a view to particular effects.

The point I wish to make here, in respect to the exploitation of personal criticism by feminist and minority groups, is that it seems not only theoretically but also pragmatically untenable to hail the recent emergence of personal or narrative criticism as a return to concrete reality, to the revelation of the "real" people behind the text, to the liberation of an authentic form of subjectivity that has been cowering in the closet during a theoretical reign of terror. The friendly "I" that beams out at the reader from the "personal" critical essay can be every bit as oppressive and subtly seductive as the detached, authoritative voice of the "impersonal" "third-person" text. Rather than eliciting your consent by speaking as though it were the oracle of eternal truth, it entraps you by inviting you in for tea and appealing to your sense of humanity and *politesse* and perhaps, of femaleness, gayness, and so on. (Therein lies also the danger of such a mode of writing: by so narrowing your nets, you risk losing some people as you close in on others).[9] The "I" of personal criticism disarms you by appearing to drop all pretense and speak frankly, honestly, and candidly, *sans arrière-pensée*. But, as they say, get real: there is always a hidden agenda, and even the "truest," most "sincere" autobiographical narrative in some way conforms to a motivated program of self-representation.

Anyone who has studied a number of autobiographies can report that they are peppered with "factual" errors and deformations: Stendhal was not

on the Janiculum the day his autobiography claims he began it with a panoramic description of the city; George Sand retouched some of her father's
letters to present him in a more favorable light; Gide *did* leave his Bible behind
when he left Paris for North Africa, but he wrote back to ask for it from
Montpellier. Lies, perhaps, but also devices exploited to make points more
important than mere "facts": Stendhal's panoramic view of the eternal city
becomes emblematic of the act of autobiographical writing, Sand's editing
responded to a need for dramatization and to follow her self-imposed rule of
"charité envers les autres"; Gide's omission serves his emphasis on the religious
crisis he was undergoing at the moment of his departure.

I point this out in order to draw attention to one of the greatest strengths
of personal criticism: its potential strategic effectiveness. Autobiographical
elements incorporated into a critical argument become, by virtue of their
inclusion in such a context, staged events, corralled to produce, among other
things, a sincerity effect, regardless of their conformity to "objective" reality.
To return to the example of Tompkins' article, let us reread the passage on
pages 130–134, in which she compares the three dry, male texts to the juicy,
female one. (At this point, I reach across my desk for her article, to make sure
I have got this right.) It begins in the past tense, as though she were simply
reporting an incident that had occurred a little earlier: "Looking for something to read this morning, I took three books down from my literary theory
shelf. . . ." But the sentence concludes with: "in order to prove a point." The
question immediately arises: what point was she trying to prove when she
chose those books? the point she knew she was going to make later in this
article? or did this conveniently relevant incident occur by chance, to be subsequently mobilized in the argument she was about to write? The narrative
situation is about to be complicated by the fact that between sentences two
and three, Tompkins slips almost unnoticed into the present tense: "The first
book was Félix Guattari's *Molecular Revolution*. I find it difficult to read, and
therefore have read very little of it . . . according to a student . . . it has to do
with getting away from ideology. . . . It is specific," and so on. (130).

Initially, this shift appears fairly insignificant, as the deployment of a
timeless descriptive present, but soon we become aware that the action itself
has apparently become contemporaneous to the writing—which accounts for
my first impression, referred to above (and which I shall leave in its inaccurate
form, for the record) that Tompkins claims to have gotten up in the middle of
writing this page to look at the books—for the passage continues: "So I open
at a section entitled. . . ." From this point on, the text continues in the present
tense, presumably, given its inaugural preterit, in order to dramatize the scene,
render it more "alive," in the manner of the French *"présent historique,"* which
introduces us into the heat of the battle and the heart of the heroine. Clearly,
the scene is staged for the purposes of the article, which does not, to my mind,

make it one iota less "authentic"; I believe that Tompkins did, at some point, look at these books, and react more or less in the manner described here. But ultimately, I don't really care if the action actually occurred, any more than I care if she really, as she claims in her now-famous statement on page 126, needs to go to the bathroom. Both events are entirely *vraisemblable,* plausible, and equally unverifiable; they serve to make a point, and make it well, and if it took a little *mise en forme* to achieve their effect, what of it? All writing entails such a tailoring and trimming of materials in view of an end.

So Tompkins's sincerity is every bit as calculated an effect as the authority of the old impersonal writing. She has tried to rope me in by appealing, initially, to my supposed personal interest in her as subject behind the text, and secondarily, via at least two generalities (women are interested in the personal, and men/men's theory oppress female subjectivity) designed to drag me, as a female reader, into her camp to share her anger. In my case, however, it backfires: this reader feels excluded by her implied categories.[10] I notice with interest, though, how the repressed returns, as theory creeps back into her discourse in the form of abstraction-through-generalization. Q.E.D.

To return to my own little autobiographemes, I am quite aware that the portraits I have painted of my parents are caricatures. I said nothing false, but I did not "tell the whole truth." I used reductive, clichéd expressions, like "perfect lady," and "womanizer." My mother came out looking like a dingbat who taught me nothing; my father fared a little better in that he got more airtime, but there was so much more to tell (I had pages of notes on both of them). Nonetheless, the caricatures were absolutely accurate, in the context of the discussion. Furthermore, since I am in the confessional mode, I am not in Paris on the eighteenth story of a tower overlooking the Seine, not more than Stendhal was in Rome on October 16, 1832, but in Decatur, Georgia, on the second floor of a yuppie apartment complex, looking out at a cozy, grassy, bushy spot. My father, here for a visit, is in the living room on the couch, watching the Phil Donahue show, a factoid the irony of which does not escape me. Despite myself (my father is not well, and I *am* fond of him), I feel irritated because the TV is so loud (he is hard of hearing) and because I have to get up in a few minutes and fix him lunch. *Peu importe,* I am nearly done. Tomorrow I can get back to work on my Robbe-Grillet chapter, writing in my usual "impersonal" style. Still talking about myself, but from the inside.

Nearly everything I have said here is very personal; some of it is autobiographical; all of it is true, whatever that means.

September 12, 1993[11]

Notes

1. Alain Robbe-Grillet, *Le miroir qui revient* (Paris: Minuit, 1984), 10 (hereafter referred to as MR).

2. *Diacritics,* 12 (Winter 1982), 2–16.

3. Nancy K. Miller, *Getting Personal: Feminist Occasions and Other Autobiographical Acts* (New York and London: Routledge, 1991), 20.

4. "The personal is the political" early became a slogan of feminist criticism, as Jane Gallop remarks in her essay entitled "The Body Politic," in Jane Gallop, *Thinking Through the Body* (New York, Columbia University Press, 1988).

5. For the record, throughout my years at a grad. school which some perceived as a hotbed of poststructuralism, nobody ever tried to tell me there was no referent, only that our access to that referent was always mediated by language. I distinctly recall one of our most outspokenly self-proclaimed poststructuralist professors lecturing in 1971 on the persistence of the referent. Yet just last year, I ran across a new book in which the author devotes two hundred pages to a misguided and repetitive defense of the referent. Isn't it time we moved on?

6. "Man on Feminism: A Criticism of His Own," in *Men in Feminism,* eds. Alice Jardine and Paul Smith (New York: Methuen, 1987), 137. The Donoghue article to which Miller is responding is reprinted, in an interestingly subordinated fashion, at the end of Miller's article and in smaller type.

7. Jane Tompkins, "Me and My Shadow," in *Gender and Theory: Dialogues on Feminist Criticism,* ed. Linda Kauffman (New York: Basil Blackwell, 1989), 121–139.

8. Tompkins effects a subtle confusion of *difficulty* and *impersonality* that enables her to condemn the former under the guise of the latter. A not-very-close reading of her argument reveals that the real reason she dislikes Guattari's writing is that it is so hard to understand, not that it ultimately lacks interest: "I will return to this essay some day and read it. I sense that it will have something interesting to say. But the effort is too great now. What strikes me now is the incredibly distancing effect of this language. It is totally abstract and impersonal" (131). Furthermore, as I have said above, "impersonal" turns out to have nothing to do with style, but rather to refer to works that do not evoke women's personal experience (more precisely, experience Tompkins has shared). While I too, may be daunted by extremely difficult texts (I put off reading Deleuze and Guattari's *Anti-Oedipe* for years), and am frankly exasperated by those I deem to be excessively involuted, abstruse, or recondite (and *intended* to mystify), it doesn't seem argumentatively cricket to denounce difficult texts in the name of feminism. Moreover, French feminist writers, in particular, have certainly proven that obscurity and abstruseness are not monopolized by male scholars.

9. I notice, while working on revisions, that Miller makes a similar observation about the dangers of personal criticism: "At its worst, it runs the risk of producing a new effect of exclusion, the very 'chumminess' of the unidentified 'we' of Foucauldian self-effacing authority that Tompkins set out to displace" (25). It has recently occurred to me, however, that there is a worse possible effect: that what is presented as merely *descriptive* (how I feel as a woman or a black or a gay) become *prescriptive* (here is how women, blacks, gays should feel, talk, and act) by the authority invested in it through publication, which turns the private into the public.

10. To recall a point I made earlier, a problem raised by personal criticism is that if you criticize the ideas expressed therein, you almost inevitably appear to be launching a personal attack on their author. This is frustrating. I don't know Ms. Tompkins, but I respect her as a scholar and would probably like her if I did meet her. But I do not like a number of the claims made in this article, nor do I find the argument coherent.

11. Editor's note: According to the reports of her friends William Ray and Kate Nicholson, Lang did in fact write a significant portion of this article in the Parisian high-rise she describes; her plane ticket stubs and passport attest to the fact that she returned to the United States on June 5, 1993. According to her father's testimony, he could not have been in Decatur on September 12, as his last trip there was in mid-July; he does, however, remember watching the morning talk shows on her TV. She seems to have been more faithful to the facts than to the dates. In our opinion, this does not affect the overall veracity of her narrative.

5

What Is at Stake
in Confessional Criticism

❧

CHARLES ALTIERI

I must begin with a confession, but one that has very little to do with anything distinctively autobiographical because it is so bound to the logic of my situation. I do not know who to be, or to present myself as, in this essay. Can one speak about confessional criticism without being confessional oneself? Or is that impulse to confession to be resisted in the name of more impersonal analytic stances capable of partially resisting both the charms of the personal and the curiosity of strangers? And how are we to adjudicate these questions without having always already chosen the perspective establishing the relevant criteria? Even if one takes Nancy Miller's suggestion that this interchange between the personal and the positional is exactly what personal criticism cultivates,[1] there still remain the same questions about how to negotiate that interchange.

There is no theoretical way to resolve these issues. They are too abstract—not "too theoretical," since theory may be able to specify why they are too abstract in their rendering of what personal or analytical can mean or how they might join. But such theory can only help us clarify our terms. The larger questions here require a more pragmatic discourse about the practical gains and losses involved in focusing academic, critical intelligence through the lenses provided by the kinds of personal concerns that invite autobiographical contexts. So I will turn to that discourse in order to argue that, for most academic critics, the autobiographical is not the fullest means of rendering or fostering personal investments in the work literary critics typically do.

❖

Initially I thought I had a clever way to challenge the current cult of the autobiographical. I would offer my own autobiographical account explaining my resistance to the autobiographical. At the end I would confess that the story was false in its details, then ask what difference it made that my account did not actually refer to my specific life history. For it might still be the case that the narrative defined a typological situation that actually did clarify the motives shaping my views on autobiography, since one can be empirically false and still capture causal structures: perhaps any analysis sensitive to embarrassment about the ethnicity of one's parents, the effects of philosophical education, and gendering into mainstream American maleness might provide a plausible genetic explanation of my views. And, for me more important, such accounts might help indicate how what establishes identities is less the specific facts of our lives than the particular ways we have of investing in them, so that my truth would be in my falsehood.

Several reasons led me to reject this strategy. First, it is not easy to be entirely false. Clearly I could not invent the details without betraying my fantasies. So I thought of having my friends invent a version of me. But they were not willing, perhaps because of what that would reveal about them. And even if they had been willing, their fantasies might have told more about the "me" I was trying not to denote than my own version would have. It would be much easier, and almost as effective, for me simply to describe the desire for the experiment, since that would make the analytical or philosophical point, and it would do so without the seductively scenic cast even of false autobiography. Moreover, by avoiding such scenes, I might the better be able to show how in much of our academic discourse being personal is a matter of qualities and concerns at stake in some practice, while being autobiographical or confessional is only one way of thematizing and contextualizing those qualities.

❖

One can be suspicious of current trends without (quite) sharing Peter Brooks's view that autobiographical criticism is little more than the academic version of replacing personhood by celebrity.[2] At its best, the confessional dimension of recent academic work has opened significant new directions and provided us with moving and thought-provoking ways of elaborating an intricate interplay between the individual and the representative. (1.) As a mode of witnessing (like Henry Louis Gates's *Colored People: A Memoir*), autobiographical criticism can register ambivalent feeling, moral outrage, and an awareness of complex competing social patterns that more abstract, impersonal discourse is likely to displace. In fact, telling stories about one's own past is probably our culture's richest way of characterizing the effects of social injustice and developing what it takes to become sufficiently empowered to resist various kinds of victimage. More abstract discourses tend to deprive suffering of its immediacy, and most academic efforts to clarify the causes of that suffering or to sanction change tend to reduce the persons seeking expression to the analtyic methods defining the underlying structures or shaping the political values that might facilitate the change. Only attention to individual lives keeps the actual situations in focus, and perhaps only an emphasis on personal situations keeps the situations elemental enough that we can at least envision the sublime possibility of producing agreement across cultural divides.

(2.) As a mode of expression, autobiographical criticism provides the kind of texture, detail, immediacy, sense of idiosyncratic difference necessary to extend contemporary culture's struggles against the hegemony of universals, or the hegemony of its apparently more modest brother, the quest for the representative. Autobiography dramatizes the ways in which individual lives are woven out of the crossing of diverse discourses, and it shows how, in individual cases, truthfulness can replace the kinds of epistemic concerns required if we are to speak more generally about truths and rational obligations.

(3.) As an ethical mode, autobiography paradoxically provides a counter to fantasies of powerful, autonomous selves, because it forces us to confront how determined we are by contingent forces that we cannot control. As Charles Bernheimer put it in conversation, we are now realizing that the first obligation of an intellectual may be to clarify the conditions of the person's own subject-constitution, since all the person's values may be extensions of that particular orientation. Then ethics cannot be a matter of universalizing and communication not a matter of simply of sharing practices. Central to both is the capacity to attune ourselves to one another's contingencies. And theory done in this spirit can claim a tight connection to practice, if only because the person's own life becomes the measure of what the theory makes possible.

(4.) Finally, as a political mode, autobiographical criticism redefines relations between authors and communities. Authors offer at least the appearance of intimacy (although it is astonishing how often academic autobiographical details evade anything deeply embarrassing, and hence symptomatic, and hence, according to Lacan, fundamental to singularity[3]). And by bringing in the extradisclipinary, such writing opens the possibility of bonds to its audience's lives which also "supplement" the disciplinary. On a more philosophical level, Steven Shaviro makes a powerful Deleuzean case for the personal as the basic norm for criticism because what matters is not some descriptive truth but the possibility of enticing an audience to further discourse or application.[4]

Even if we grant that personal criticism performs important tasks, we also have to recognize its limitations, as well as the problematic influences that are inseparable from its astonishing currency. Speaking practically, I would say that this mode works well for discussions of practical policies and for many aspects of the politics of reading, but it remains quite thin as a stance for appreciating what authors accomplish or for making substantial cultural claims—unless the critic goes on to develop a theoretical case in which the personal works primarily as a representative example, offered as a means of extending knowledge rather than a means of fostering intimate relations with some community. Contingency, in other words, requires to be addressed in a variety of ways—some directly attuned to specific voices, some devoted to describing what is most significant in the ways that other contingent agents perform, and some enabling us to develop provisional generalizations about the causes and structures shaping our investments, one of which is our current obsession with individual voices.

If one shifts to arguing in more theoretical terms, it becomes possible to elaborate two basic lines of criticism—that autobiographical criticism is not sufficiently attuned to how persons are engaged within literary experience, and that as currently practiced, it does not satisfactorily serve the social and critical purposes often motivating it. The second of these claims seems the easier one to support, since it follows directly from the practical observation I have just offered. Autobiographical criticism is not likely to provide full accounts of texts or of cultural issues (although it may stimulate or illustrate such accounts) simply because it has only the representative anecdote to work with, so it must deprive itself of all the other analytic frameworks that contemporary intellectual life offers, or it must measure those frameworks only in relation to a very limited position, when in fact the mind can take more capacious stances by binding itself to disciplinary procedures.

The claim that autobiography may not provide an adequate model of the personal engages more intricate and resonant issues. Autobiography relegates the personal to those investments we can evoke or perform by providing narrative accounts focalized in terms of a single, self-historicizing perspective. But if we take Deleuze, on the one hand, and traditional humanism, on the other, we find versions of subjective agency which cannot easily be foregrounded in narrative accounts—primarily because they require careful attention to the object in order to appreciate what the subject is capable of. For example, much of the intensity that I feel in relation to works of art can enter self-reflection only if I can imagine subjectivity breaking down into radically contingent and fluid emotions, where strange and surprising links with other persons become possible. Consider how bodies are disposed by films or by something like a Pollock painting. Correspondingly, the opportunities for imaginative identification afforded by art enable us to explore alternative ways to organize our deepest mental and affective energies—we for moments literally become Lear, or find ourselves desiring to experience as Cézanne or Picasso did. An autobiographical focus, however, limits us to attempting to interpret such appeals only in terms of how we bring a life history to bear on them, so it tends to minimize the degree to which such experiences allow our exploring possible selves we might pursue. For teachers that is an especially severe loss.

Perhaps more important, autobiographical criticism finds difficulty acknowledging or elaborating those aspects of personal experience which do not take narrative forms, especially the senses of power and self-delight afforded by committing ourselves to the most demanding disciplinary practices—whether these be modeled on the sciences or on what Nietzsche called the infinitely more difficult labors of artistic expression. Precisely because subject positions are culturally constituted, they afford permissions or fields of play wherein agents learn what they are capable of. As we take on different positions, we develop new appreciations of audiences we can address, communities we might participate in, and interests and values we might pursue. And as we shift positions, we find new ways of experiencing objects, as well as new ways of participating in communal enterprises for dealing with those objects. Personal agency becomes manifest in a variety of forms that extend beyond autobiographical contexts into modes of self-reflection defined by the social practices they are embedded within. There are states of subjective agency distinctive to playing chess or working out physics problems, and even something as private as reading lyric poetry can also be seen as participating in an activity we share with the most fundamental concerns of others who share the relevant disciplinary orientations.

❖

One could insist here that it takes autobiographical accounts to appreciate such permissions, and even to make concrete what they might offer to others. In response I would have to grant the general argument, but also point out how rarely the autobiographical stretches itself to accommodate such personal intensities. And then I would finally have to concentrate on the actual limitations of a specific representative example, so I will turn to Frank Lentricchia's essay "My Kinsman, T.S. Eliot," in large part because of the intricate relationship to theory that the essay elaborates. On the one hand Lentricchia casts the theoretical impulse as the devil of paranoiac self-doubt, from which one seeks relief in the concreteness of autobiography. There he hopes to render and to capture the force of "art as stubborn specificity, as untheorizable peculiarity. Art for life's sake." And yet Lentricchia is also after significant theoretical game, since he enages Eliot in order to give a contemporary cast to Eliot's own experiments in self-reflection as a means of freeing himself from having "a self to reflect upon."[5] However, I think Lentricchia's autobiographical framework makes problematic both his claim about the limitations of theory and his efforts to escape the confines of personal identity: autobiography narrows the concreteness Lentricchia idealizes to the infinite ironies of irresolvable self-analysis, while also imposing pressures on the self that generate a melodramatic model of escape which I consider inadequate to the positive imaginary identifications offered by the arts.

It would take too long to summarize Lentricchia's subtle and inventive narrative. So it must suffice to say that he develops an elaborate set of analogies to Eliot's *Waste Land* as his means of contrasting his own cultural traditions for mixing art and life to Eliot's mandarin ideals, and ultimately as a way of reaffirming his choice to become a teacher of literature, despite the threats to his formative values that he now sees in the dominance of "theory." Autobiography takes the form of a quest romance, in which the hero comes fully to appreciate the central place in his life played by the the aesthete's concern for art's particularity as "the only place to find deliverance of the specific from the habits of abstraction":

> That's why I look for the beautiful everywhere, why I coax and stroke it when I find it stirring in front of me. And I do mean "in front of me" in a restaurant in little Italy. 146 Mulberry Street (honor to the site) at Angelo's (everything is in a name). Art as stubborn specificity, as untheorizable peculiarity. Art for life's sake. (56)

Lentricchia had been to mass, seeking "something good I thought I had met in a monastery six months before," then met again at a church in North Carolina, four Sundays in a row (56). But on this day, the Protestant part of his soul gets the best of his Italian, Catholic half (57), so ritual will not do. Like Eliot's quester, he must sojourn in the demotic aspects of urban city life that Eliot cannot bear because of his class biases. Lentricchia's Italian-American heritage, on the other hand, helps him focus his attention on the complex multicultural scene that unfolds in the aptly named Angelo's. For Lentricchia, rendering the scene immediately triggers defensive self-consciousness: "Is someone waiting for me to give the sexist and homophobic dimensions of my Angelo's text?" (61). (No wonder he wants liberation from theory.) And that defensiveness, in turn, leads him back to autobiographical narrative, situated in relation to Eliot, as if this parallel might help clarify the question, "What does it mean, exactly to say 'myself'?" Where Eliot grew up with little else than bookish escape, Lentricchia could experience the bookish only as the part of his life simultaneously alienating him from friends and family and affording an escape from that alienation. But these dilemmas allow him to appreciate how much a particular teacher meant to him, and hence to understand both the grounds for his own choice of careers and the difficulty of keeping those grounds alive in the present. Reflecting on that teacher even helps Lentricchia deepen his resistance to abstract theory, since the teacher opened for him the secret of how Shakespeare could come to live within a particular "flesh and voice," and hence how the ego could become somehow more itself by undergoing the very process of losing the self that Lentricchia wants to accomplish. Eliot, on the other hand, could not enter the pub, could not accept a secular alternative to the chapel of Magnus Martyr, because of the self-consciousness fostered by his physical condition and his patrician upbringing.

Ultimately, an imaginary dialogue with Eliot's snobbishness leads "Frank" to spin out all the morals of his tales:

> I could weave Angelo into the seminar, easily, but it might be a mistake. They might say, You went in, ethnic Frank, Eliot didn't.... They might say, You are a privileged reader of Angelo's text. And then we would all sing the multicultural rag. Better to tell them you were a transparency at Angelo's. Tell them that you didn't want to be noticed, that you wanted to disappear into all that you beheld.... No I am not Marie Lloyd, nor was meant to be.
>
> I could, but I don't live on the second floor of a two-family house in East Utica. I left Utica for good in 1966.
>
> Having sacrificed yourself to something more valuable, in the text of Angelo's, or in the formal text of a poem, you are tempted to move above, in an effort to tell the stories you do about men with important bodies [like the husband he observed at Angelo's].... Having yielded, having taken a vacation from who you are, having in a way forgotten yourself in order to find a more satisfying self, you begin to reflect on your "position" and "allegiances." You want to announce principles of literary criticism. You would propound a theory. You've been having a good time, but now, should you yield to the devil, you are going to have a very bad time. So bad, should you yield, that you'll tell yourself you made a serious mistake when almost thirty years ago you wanted to teach literature and write about it. (72)

And on this basis our hero manages to resist the temptation to theory by remembering three written texts that have given him pleasure, and that, as touchstones (not his word), can silence the devil for good because their concrete, evocative power avoids the abstraction that is the stuff of his kingdom.

❖

However, before we let the devil of theory be silenced, I would like to play his advocate for a few minutes. For when writers work so hard (and in this case so well) at seduction, it seems naïve to grant them only the sympathetic reader they call for. Those that would banish the devil rather than make peace with it have a good deal of the devil still working in their prose. Let me then develop three lines of criticism pointing out problematic consequences in Lentricchia's reliance on autobiography.

First I think it important that Lentricchia's very intricate grasp of Eliot nonetheless fails to respond fully to crucial aspects of Eliot's work, along lines that prevent Lentricchia from seeing how Eliot's work calls his own values into question. Consider first what Eliot would have thought of Lentricchia's efforts to recuperate "something good" that had happened in previous churchgoings, and to equate that something good with bringing the aesthetic into ordinary experience. Eliot's religion is far more severe and resistant to humanist ideals. For him, religion begins not in a sense of having felt something good, but in an intellectual conviction about one's own fundamental worthlessness without some nonhuman ground, so that one then submits to the discipline enabling a person to maintain a life of duty and self-renunciation which may, only may, blossom into a positive faith. The enabling condition for such faith is not epiphany, not the sudden conversion autobiography longs for, since faith cannot come simply from the kind of scrutiny that self-consciousness affords. Instead, self-consciousness opens a path to religion only when it recognizes its own inadequacy and uses that inadequacy as the basis for committing the self to an overall intellectual structure addressing that very sense of need. Angelo's, in other words, cannot take the place of the necessary angel without turning the transcendental into something close to what Nietzsche called "spilt religion."

This failure to engage Eliot's theology is paralleled by a severe blindness to much of what is most powerful in the concrete, spiritual experience offered by *The Waste Land*. For Lentricchia's concern for specific modes of attention rendered in particular scenes within *The Waste Land* leads him to ignore the compositional, structural forces organizing the poem's various moments of attention. These relational patterns created by the poem's juxtapositions and internal patterning invite us to see that the poem puts at stake not simply how we engage particulars but also how we grasp the needs and projections of the psychic states shaping how investments are made in those particulars. Eliot is less concerned with how life becomes art than with how the demands we make on life force us beyond art to confront those lacks within us that simply will not be satisfied by the hope of momentary epiphanies. Such hope, in fact, may be what condemns the voices in *The Waste Land* to their wandering. The only antidote to that hope, I hasten to add, is bringing poetry very close to the condition of theory by having the structure invite levels of abstraction and qualities of transpersonal voicing not reducible to personal memories and private histories. We can share the experiences of these various voices, and even turn back to their implications for our lives, but we trivialize them if we find their relation to life only within our memories rather than within our own capacities for thinking beyond what memory affords.

Ironically, Lentricchia is nowhere closer to such modernist theorizing than in his own attack on theory. But Lentricchia's attack relies only on modernist rhetoric about concreteness, without attending to the ways that the art then uses constructivist principles in order to foster an abstraction that makes concreteness itself a complex space for ontological speculation. Concreteness for modernist art is not a matter of autobiographical denotation but of constructing sites that dramatize a play of ideas working against the constraints of autobiographical narrative—that is why it is so difficult, and so exhilarating, to determine who is the speaker of *The Waste Land* or to track the working of memories within it.

If Lentricchia's theorizing against theory is not adequate to the art it idealizes, it is even more problematic when seen in connection to the discourse about the self that he relies on to thicken his autobiographical approach. So addressing these problems will constitute my second line of criticism.

Lentricchia's is no naïve attack on theory in the name of lived experience. In the long passage quoted above, he presents theory as dangerous because it stands in for the dynamic process by which we move from sacrificing a self to those moments when we feel we have achieved more "satisfied" modes of being. In the effort to stabilize those satisfactions, we in fact impose rigid categories on experience. And in doing that, we evade the concreteness distinctive to autobiography—an irreducibly ironic subsumption of ideas within the vagaries of their telling. Within the autobiographical situation, within this "unabstract representation of a desire for abstraction that subverts itself in the act of announcing its desire" (75), ideas must be seen as aspects of the gestures by which we elaborate figures for the self. There is no standing outside the intricate tonal and contextual modalities by which they are presented, and hence no way to develop criteria that do not destroy the writerliness in which they are embedded. Instead, abstract ideas appear only as temptations or indulgences to be sympathized with, or, more generally, as manifestations of who and where the person is at any given time.

If I am right about this ironic dimension to Lentricchia's thinking, I have to admit that he is not wrong. His is a rich sense of what in our lives resists conceptual formulation.[6] But it is not a rich sense of how we nonetheless have to find provisional, public terms for assessing ideas in terms of their effects on society—which means it is also not a rich sense of the multiple registers necessary to give an adequate accounting of the investments on which we base our senses of personal identity. Even if the personal imposes tonal intricacy on the conceptual, the conceptual still plays a substantial part in the bid that the autobiographical makes on our attention, so that we have to judge the way ideas are handled, and, more important, the way ideas create the values developed in the narrating.

Lentricchia on the self is a good example of these limitations, since I suspect that both his notion of sacrifice and his notion of what comes to satisfy the self are somewhat melodramatic and inaccurate versions of what is at stake in the ways art and life manage to nourish one another. On the level of the writing, Lentricchia never loses himself—he only finds Utica merging with Eliot's pub. All his talk of loss of self takes place within a genre fundamentally self-satisfied because of its capacity to talk of losing the self. Moreover, when he explicity thematizes satisfaction, he has what seems to me a strange notion of it residing in managing to escape an uneasy self-consciousness without submitting to some abstract faith. This view requires autobiographical writing, because such satisfaction depends on identifying oneself with the activity of writing, where one can achieve concreteness by the constant qualifying of anything that might reach for the conceptual. But then satisfaction can consist of little more than being able to invite one's audience to accept the ironic as the precondition of reaching attunement with the life offered to us, or aggressively confronting us with its satisfactions. For the more insistent the text is on the complex forces set to work in the concrete writing, the less this autobiographical mode can develop any more substantial ways that a positioned memory can frame its responsibilities in any publicly assessable terms.

We see most clearly what this view of satisfaction costs Lentricchia when he explicity casts his writerly ideal as managing "an act of homage to the real state of my affairs" (53). Statements like "the real state of my affairs" invite theory because it is extremely difficult to align them with any observable situation. If such a reality is to be something that the text can picture or denote, and hence some truth that the author discovers, then all his irony can be adequately contained within some actual state of affairs that we can test various ways of describing and deriving values from. And if "real" means what the writing discloses as it absorbs the world into conditions of autobiographical self-reference, then Lentricchia can be charged with letting the autobiographical model of self-reference blind him to what might be much deeper and potentially more satisfying ways of imagining how the personal might be intensified, enriched, and even socialized. By idealizing the "real" and insisting on it as ultimately depending on "my affairs," Lentricchia severely underplays those satisfactions that come from exploring possible interdependences between subject and the postulating of objects. Those explorations do not involve a quest for some underlying reality but allow us to track the various aspects of selves that are articulated and called upon by changing situations or modes of discourse.

Lentricchia's efforts to formulate his stakes for autobiographical writing, then, provide a strong contrastive background within which to see why I propose alternative views borrowing from Deleuze and from traditional humanism. Rather than speaking of a real state of one's affairs, we have to realize how much we displace by seeking to bring the multiplicity of experience under any single rubric such as "this self with this history." What happens in Angelo's can be mapped onto Eliot without having to lead back to Lentricchia's own position. In fact, imposing ideas of self on the fluid intensities that such texts afford will only deepen the temptation to turn to abstract theory because one has to secure for notions of the self what are in fact only tangential relations to the actual emotional processes involved. Conversely, as we come to appreciate why Eliot's work invites such analogues, we enter an Hegelian or Bradleyan theater: Eliot's art leads beyond moments of attention to elaborate subject positions that are irreducibly public and shareable and historically specifiable (and therefore amenable to further theorizing without the rhetoric of alienation that follows upon isolating the autobiographical subject, then lamenting what it takes for resocializing it). So even an autobiographical stance as complex as Lentricchia's proves neither sufficiently intimate nor sufficiently sociohistorical to understand the stakes involved in feeling satisfied by central aspects of Eliot's poem.

❖

My final, and most pressing, difficulty with Lentricchia's essay requires our turning to the most practical aspects of the relation between art and life. I do not see much point to autobiography for lives like Lentricchia's or mine, where in fact the shaping events are so common, so interchangeable with events in other parallel lives, that one begins to suspect that the very claim to concrete individuality is evading some underlying social pressures. What white literary academic from working-class, ethnic backgrounds, or even from middle-class, third-generation backgrounds, does not have essentially the same story to tell, albeit with somewhat different details? Given America's anti-intellectual traditions, the love of books and ambitiousness in grammar and high school will, in most communities, alienate a person from the social world in which he or she most desires to be accepted. One might even add that very few professors of literature from such backgrounds do not also share the general desire to link art to life or even to postulate concreteness as an alternative to the devil's abstract theorizing. Similarly, what young Jewish woman from a slightly higher-class background, now between forty and sixty, teaching at a prestigious literary institution did not share Nancy Miller's fantasies about Paris, or experiences with groping instructors? And what suburban WASP teaching in the same institutions does not have a history of community and school service ranging from the football team to class vice-president? (The class president probably went on to medical school.)

It may be precisely because there is so much overlap in our lives that we can readily use another's autobiography to provide representative examples for our own "theoretical" concerns. In fact, now that our specific teacherly and scholarly interests have become so diverse, we may be turning to autobiographical ways of talking about differences because they provide the only common structure for organizing information that we can (almost) trust. These are clearly laudable interests. But problems begin when it seems as if all of us simply accept autobiography as an adequate means of serving our deepest concerns about value, without including the healthy suspiciousness we have cultivated about other textual performances. What might this turn to autobiography be evading that is deeply problematic within our current sociocultural situation?

I put my question in a form familiar in Marxist and deconstructive readings. But the hypothesis I propose as a partial answer derives from my Jesuit education: autobiographical criticism gravitates towards alienation stories, and even towards conversion stories like Lentricchia's, because critics want to displace into the realm of the personal the disturbing fact that they are among the most intelligent members of a democratic society that grants them privileges but does not have any set of values which might justify those privileges (in contrast to its values about medicine, say). We are stuck in a situation where we cannot produce a language that might convince society we can repay its investment in us—hence Lentricchia's obsession with the failures of theory. So rather than face our failures to produce a public language adequate for our social position, and perhaps also to our failures to live up to the vague, ideal expectations that certain segments of the society do have of us, we hide within personal histories, where questions of justification and debt rarely arise.

Consider what it is that upsets us most in the current right-wing bashing of political correctness in the academy. We react less to specific arguments than to the reminders of how pervasive anti-intellectualism remains in America, and of how difficult it would be to find the terms for convincing the populace, and perhaps ourselves, that we lead significant lives. Because we enjoy considerable freedom and pleasure within our work, and because society makes substantial investments in training us, we find ourselves owing substantial debts to a social order we tend to despise, and often feel superior to, even as we congratulate ourselves for engaging popular culture (in ways that the populace would find very strange).

Autobiographical criticism does respond deeply to this situation. As I have suggested, much of it is intensely concerned with fostering community, often with the pedagogical goal of producing a society in which each individual has the resources and sense of self-importance allowing them to offer autobiographical writings to others. But these public concerns need to be made more explicit, and they need to be better connected to other versions of empowerment through education that might also help justify society's investments in us. Otherwise it will seem that we turn to the intricate self-consciousness produced by our training as if it were only an individual possession whose major troubles with connecting to the quotidian world consisted in whether to theorize or not to theorize. And then we will deserve the autobiographies we now read and write.

Notes

1. Nancy Miller, *Getting Personal: Feminist Occasions and Other Autobiographical Acts* (New York: Routledge, 1991), 16. Miller suggests that feminist theory is in large part "the effort to analyze that relation." This leaves us with the question I must avoid here, about the ways in which the personal does and does not bring to fruition the analytic force of feminist theorizing.

2. Peter Brooks, "Aesthetics and Ideology: What Happened to Poetics," *Critical Inquiry* (Summer, 1994), 520.

3. There is an interesting test case for my claim in Nancy Miller's remarks on Jane Tompkins famous passage in "Me and My Shadow" about her postponing an urge to go the bathroom. For Miller, this passage is an exemplary rendering of the kind of embarrassment distinguishing the author-reader relation in personal prose, and also distinguishing, to some degree, a female community from what males expect and do (5–7, then 23ff as examples of an "anxiety about feminine exposure"). But in my view, there is nothing humanly embarrassing about the detail—we all do that. The risk of embarrassment is in the writing, and that is because it is a break in decorum, not a revelation. Moreover, that writerly gesture is not intimate; it is entirely melodramatic, driven by theoretical considerations about how to write personally, and motivated not by communication but by desires to stage the self for certain effects. In other words, Tompkins here uses the personal as a very clever theoretical gesture.

4. Steven Shaviro, *The Cinematic Body* (Minneapolis: University of Minnesota Press, 1993), 8–9, 265–266.

5. Frank Lentricchia, "My Kinsman, T.S. Eliot," in Mark Edmundsen, ed., *Wild Orchids and Trotsky* (New York: Penguin, 1993), 56, 53.

6. I share enough of Lentricchia's wariness of what the theorists will say to need here to address the question of gender. There may be some who think what I say about irony represents male self-defensiveness about personal talk, while female cultural constitution allows very different attitudes about self-expression. However, I think it is at least arguable that, insofar as any autobiography steps outside personal conversation into self-conscious writing, it also steps into this version of the ironic condition. For it must personalize by deflecting away from the public order or domain of third-person assessments. And the more one realizes how autobiography creates its own distinctive site for self-representation, the more one has to worry about the price of such hard-won concreteness in the processes of self-presentation.

6

Confession versus Criticism, or What's the Critic Got to Do With It?

❖

ELIZABETH FOX-GENOVESE

Let us go on, O Lord my God, to explain the meaning which the next verse of your Scripture holds for me. I shall speak without fear, for if you inspire me to give the meaning which you have willed me to see in these words, what I say will be the truth. If any other than you were to inspire me, I do not believe that my words would be true, for you are the Truth, whereas every man is a liar, and for this reason he *who utters falsehood is only uttering what is natural to him*, what is his alone. If, then I am to speak the truth, let me utter not what is mine, but what is yours.
—St. Augustine, *Confessions*, Box XIII, Section 25[1]

At the close of *West of Everything*, Jane Tompkins reflects upon the similarity between the actions of critics toward one another and the actions of the heroes of Westerns toward their enemies.[2] Like the action of the Western, she notes, the action of academic exchange combines "elements of admiration, bloodlust, and moral self-congratulation" (230). Above all, she suggests, academic violence is directed at "characterological defects" of a colleague's style or point of view. "Following traditional lines of thought was translated into cowardice, dependence on another scholar's work into toadyism, failing to mention another critic's work into lack of generosity" (230). Thus do academics "accuse one another of stupidity, ignorance, envy, pride, malice, and hypocrisy," translating intellectual disagreements into failures of "social conscience and moral virtue"—what might once have been called sins. As Tompkins notes, such denunciations embody feelings of righteousness and moral superiority, which are felt to justify them. Yet the notion of sin as that which is displeasing in the sight of God has been transformed into a lapse from a prevailing professional fashion. "We feel justified in exposing these errors to view, that they may be scourged not in the sight of God, since no god presides over modern warfare, but in the sight of our professional peers and superiors" (231).

These reflections remind Tompkins of an occasion on which she had engaged in similar behavior. And she finds "myself focusing inward," recalling the exhilarating feeling of the attack. "It is an experience of tremendous empowerment. You feel invincible" (232). Tompkins fails to note that, at the center of her moment of confession, she retreats to the impersonality of "It is" and the projection of displacement of "you feel." Suddenly, the confession of personal experience becomes diluted in its elevation to a general condition. Sin thus moves from the personal failing to the human—or at least the academic—condition. But if she fails to note her reluctance to claim the sin as specifically her own, she does notice that her reflections have "a moralizing tendency" that might be expected to lead to an exhortation to treat other critics as you would yourself be treated. She refrains. "I believe in peace and I believe in the Golden Rule, but I don't believe I've earned the right to such pronouncements. At least not yet" (232). The most she can bring herself to say, borrowing from *High Noon*, is that there has to be a better way to live.

Throughout *West of Everything*, Tompkins explicitly draws upon her own feelings, beginning with the opening sentence, "I make no secret of the fact: I love Westerns" (3). Her love for the genre does not, however, deter her from using—or, more accurately, exploiting—it to explore herself through her response to a distinct strand in American culture. A leading exponent of reader-response criticism, Tompkins constantly returns to her own conflicted feelings about Westerns, notably her ability to identify with their heroes as well as with those, mainly women, whom they objectify. Her refreshing capacity to appreciate Westerns and, by extension, a male perspective distinguishes her from those feminist critics who reject most manifestations of masculinity as inherently oppressive; her willingness to acknowledge the savage sanctimoniousness of much academic exchange bespeaks a rare clear-sightedness about her own club. Yet, in the end, by pushing reader-response criticism to its logical conclusion, she writes a book that is much, if not more, about herself than about the Western.

Tompkins' confessional criticism grows directly from the premises of reader-response criticism, which also account for her reluctance to assume the authority to transform personal beliefs into pronouncements. St. Augustine, in contrast, willingly assumes that authority, for he rests on God's promises. *"Everyone that asks, will receive; that seeks, will find; that knocks, will have the door opened to him.* These are the promises, and who need fear to be deceived when Truth promises?" (281). The certainty that truth exists does not fore-close Augustine's anxious questioning of texts, nor even lead him to deny the possible validity of multiple and even apparently contradictory interpreta-tions. Listening to people who claim that Moses meant this or that, he won-ders if it not be more "truly religious to say 'Why should he not have had both meanings in mind, if both are true? And if others see in the same words a third, or a fourth, or any number of true meanings, why should we not believe that Moses saw them all'?" (308). Indeed, he insists that, were he to be called upon to write a book vested with the highest authority, "I should prefer to write it in such a way that a reader could find re-echoed in my words whatever truths he was able to apprehend" (308). And if this is true for Augustine, how could it not have been more true of Moses?

Augustine's reflections upon the many possible interpretations of Scrip-ture seem to foreshadow some of the assumptions of reader-response criti-cism, notably his appreciation of the validity of various interpretations. Yet this appreciation never leads him to confine the ultimate meaning of the text to the ways in which different fallible humans read it. For him, the ultimate truth resides in the words of the text itself, and Moses—the author—"was conscious of every truth that we can deduce from them and of others besides that we cannot, or cannot yet, find in them but are nevertheless there to be found" (309). Thus the possibility that Augustine himself may speak the truth requires that he transcend his personal experience. If he is to speak the truth, he must put himself aside.

Today, the confidence in sacred texts that embody the Truth, which critics may at best hope partially to discover, has broken up on the shoals of secular-ism, doubt, and individualism on which, more recently, the very notion of legitimate authority of any kind has foundered. Confidence's journey from Augustine to Tompkins nonetheless passed through a long transitional stage best exemplified in the notion of the Romantic artist, whose ghost so relent-lessly haunts anxious modern critics. As Raymond Williams has argued, the first great, postrevolutionary generation of Romantics effectively transferred the notion of the sacred from the divinity to the work of art and transferred the notion of authority from hierarchical social structures to the artist—preferably themselves.[3] For the Romantics and many of their heirs, the work of art—today familiarly known as the "text"—inherited the sacred quality of Scripture: it embodied an authority of creation that defied the reductionist temptations of readers and critics. Its glittering surface invited appreciation and awe even as it refracted presumptuous attempts to demote it to the ebb and flow of the experience of ordinary mortals. Williams's argument, like many brilliant interpretations of complex cultural developments, simplifies the play of contradictory currents, but contains an important kernel of truth. And the temptation for denizens of an increasingly secular world to deify the work of art persisted long after the Romantic era proper had passed. Traces of the sensibility informed the claims of the New Critics of the 1920s and 1930s, who claimed to be rescuing art from the demeaning hurly-burly of various forms of materialist criticism.

Tellingly, the very folks who invented the Romantic artist and deified the work of art also bequeathed us both the modern autobiographer and modern critic. It requires no great insight to suggest that a deep kinship might bind the three roles of artist, critic, and autobiographer, but it is worth noting that, even as the roles intertwined, they also remained distinct. And although any given individual might, during the course of a lifetime, successively occupy all three roles, the roles themselves remained bound not by the accident of common actors but by their common commitment to the lingering—and secularized—ghost of creation as sacred and to the individual soul as some-thing more than the playground of impersonal forces. In these twin commit-ments lies the core of what poststructural and, especially, postmodern critics contemptuously dismiss as essentialism.

Both critics and autobiographers were wont to confuse their efforts with those of the artist. It would have been astonishing if they had not. Once the vision in the mind's eye effectively replace the deity as the locus of an irre-ducible truth, it would be a rare soul who could entirely elude the seduction of viewing his—or, more rarely, her—vision as less interesting or truthful than that of the artist. In this climate, the self itself emerged as the appropriate object of reverence, and, should the soul in question be flawed, those very flaws could be assimilated to the essential truth of the self. In this respect, as in so many others, Jean-Jacques Rousseau blazed the trail. In the various guises of artist, critic, autobiographer, and even political theorist, Rousseau increas-ingly assuaged his ghosts of doubt and guilt by proclaiming that that was what he was and, in some way, what he was must be good.

If contemporary confessional criticism needs a forebear or, indeed, would acknowledge one, Rousseau would serve as well as any. For, writing at the dawn of modern individualism, Rousseau took his own soul, complete with self-pro-claimed warts, as the subject *par excellence.* His differences from Augustine are, in this regard, instructive. Augustine, too, began the work of criticism or, as he preferred, interpretation, with his own flawed self. But, in his case, the self acquired excellence only in the measure that its inescapably sinful, human attributes were conquered or transcended. For Augustine could not see the self as an end in itself. For him, in contrast to Rousseau, the minutia of self-examination acquire interest only in relation to the higher truth, which, if properly contained, they may serve.

Seeing self-knowledge as an end in itself, Rousseau was inclined to treat it as a work of art. Augustine, in contrast, saw self-knowledge as a necessary stage of atonement for the sins that self-knowledge too glaringly revealed. In this sense, his self-examination did not directly inform his work of interpretation: it merely prepared him for it. The significance of the preparation should not be minimized. Augustine did conjoin confession and interpretation of Scripture. But the conjoining was sequential rather than intermingled. Nor did he assume that, even when properly undertaken, his interpretation enjoyed an authority superior to that of other (presumably Christian) critics, much less an authority equal to that of the author of the text, whom he imagined as having foreseen and allowed for all possible interpretations of his words.

As against contemporary critics and even their Romantic predecessors, Augustine enjoyed the inestimable advantage of certainty. Like his successors, he was intimately acquainted with the anxiety of doubt; like them he lived with the temptations of pride. Unlike them, however, he viewed doubt and pride as demons to be cast aside in the service of Truth. Moderns, and especially postmoderns, readily dismiss certainty and what they view as the illusion of Truth as themselves symptoms of pride, if not philistinism or bigotry. Who are we to claim either certainty or Truth, knowing as we do, that others disagree. But then, living on the other side of the Romantic divide, we tend to see both certainty and Truth as extensions of the self—mere matters of personal opinion. Our jaded spirits have long since rejected the idea that any work of art enjoys sacred or even quasi-sacred status. The text has drowned in the rising tide of a pseudo-democratic intertextuality. Pretenses to the contrary display an alleged elitism that values the words and expressions of some over those of others. One may imagine that the revolt against the sacralization of art might have taken another form. Augustine would assuredly have protested it, as did Terence, who impatiently queried, "What has Athens to do with Jerusalem?" But rather than repudiating the Romantic infatuation with self, the postmoderns have taken it to its ultimate conclusion. And, in good global capitalist form, they have waged a revolt against art that elevates the consumer over the producer.

One need not preach a return to the long-gone worldview of Augustine in order to suspect that something has gone awry. If the sacralization of art embodied what Mario Praz viewed as a Luciferian revolt against authority, the recovery of humanity is not to be found in extending that revolt to a repudiation of the discrete claims—the integrity—of artistic texts themselves.[4] However hostage to the vicissitudes of location, privilege, and even revision, the text remains a (permeable) entity more indebted to the craft and talent of its author than the self-reflections of its reader, if only because it triggers or provides the occasion for those self-reflections.

As the example of Augustine suggests, self-reflection has an important place in criticism or interpretation, which it may wonderfully serve. But the emphasis should fall on the serve. As readers, each of us sees a text through a glass darkly—through the prism of our own experience and demons. The better we understand the demons, the better critics we become. Once again, Tompkins illustrates the point. To read or review a Western unself-reflexively as a woman is likely to evoke a host of unconscious feelings. At one extreme, those feelings may include rage and resentment at being figuratively represented as marginal or, worse, as the custodian of constricting ties the hero is attempting to escape. At another, they may include a narcissistic pleasure in imagining oneself as the object of the hero's desire. And between the two extremes lies the tangle of feelings that play upon any woman who imaginatively experiences herself as the other in the imagination of a male writer. Some women, as Tompkins suggests, resolve the conflicts by identification with the male protagonist, although that identification normally entails significant doses of repression or sublimation. Whatever the specific response, both female and male readers engage texts driven by emotions they do not always recognize or understand.

A critic who espouses the responsibility of making the text more accessible to other readers suffers from the same problems. Contemporary confessional critics have attempted to respond by explicitly introducing their personal responses as readers into their work. In the spirit of reader-response criticism, this tactic has a nice, democratic aura. It is as if the critic were admitting that he or she is just one reader among many, thereby shedding the privilege that might be thought to accrue to the literary scholars. If indeed this were the case, it might be possible to defend it, although we might retain doubts about the virtues of shedding the responsibilities of scholarship— unless we were genuinely prepared to shed graduate stipends and professorial salaries as well. In theory, critics differ from other readers not because of their freedom from sin or even necessarily their innate intelligence, which may occasionally be questioned, but because they are professional custodians and practitioners of a craft. Where critics resemble other readers is in their susceptibility to the subjective resonances a text evokes in them. Once we have acknowledged this similarity, the responsibility of the critic is to overcome it. But how? Confessional critics apparently believe that the solution lies in public exposure of those personal responses, as if they were what would preeminently interest readers of the text.

Another solution, albeit one that receives little attention these days, might lie in a private examination of conscience and motives as the necessary precursor to the work of the critic. Knowing that we respond personally to texts, we might well explore the whys and wherefores on the assumption that under- standing the forces that drive us gives us some freedom from subservient obedience to them. Popular misperception notwithstanding, the goal of psy- choanalysis was never to free one to act out one's murderous impulses but rather to recognize them so that one would not be condemned randomly to enact them on the wrong people—or even those against whom they are directed. Similarly, an understanding of the motives that bedevil us as readers need not condemn us, in self-congratulatory fashion, to continue to misread texts in their light. Ideally, such an understanding might even free us to read better—more impersonally—and thus better meet our responsibility to open the text's pleasures to others.

In the end, the goal of the critic should ever be to share the pleasures of the text with as wide an audience as possible. And that sharing above all requires admiration for and delight in the ways in which the authors of texts accomplish their purposes—a self-effacing pleasure in the craft, artistry, and, sometimes, genius of another. The attitude does not require sacralization of text or author, but it does require a measure of humility on the part of the critic. And naked display of one's personal failings, as Rousseau's *Confessions* long since should have taught us, more often than not falls into a complacent exhibitionism. But if self-exposure does not reliably guarantee humility, may it not at least embody a commitment to the democracy of readers, each of whom is invited to take the text as a mirror of his or her personal concerns? Some would have us believe as much, but I remain doubtful. For it is hard not to believe that the critic who glosses the text with personal responses is not effectively substituting the self of the critic for the work of the author. As I tell my students when I advise them never to use highlighters on the pages of a book, once you have marked the text, you will never again be able to read it afresh. In so marking texts, confessional critics proudly claim them as their own, thus reenacting the hubris of the Romantics, no longer as rebellion against God but as rebellion against art—no longer as tragedy, but as farce.

Notes

1. Saint Augustine, *Confessions*, trans. R.S. Pine-Coffin (Baltimore, MD: 1961), 337. Augustine's assertion that every man is a liar is taken from Romans 3:4; and the assertion that he who utters falsehood is uttering what is natural to him is taken from John 8:44.

2. Jane Tompkins, *West of Everything: The Inner Life of Westerns* (New York: Oxford University Press, 1992).

3. Raymond Williams, *The Long Revolution* (New York: Columbia University Press, 1961).

4. Mario Praz, *The Romantic Agony* (London: Oxford University Press, 1933).

7

Through the Academic Looking Glass

❖

Vincent P. Pecora

"I can't explain *myself*, I'm afraid, sir," said Alice, "because I'm not myself, you see."

"I don't see," said the Caterpillar.

Most academicians secretly love to read about academia, even when the popular portrait is not flattering. This may be due to hunger for public recognition. But it may also stem from the faint *frisson* of having the arcana of academic life revealed, like sacerdotal mysteries, to the uninitiated. Yet the university is more than a secret society. It is also the site of the grandest family romance around, and the family romance—the search for the parent (traditionally the father) that one believes deeply one should have had from the start—generally makes for good reading. Novels would be impossible without it. And so would a large part of the literary academy's (largely unwritten) institutional history, at the center of which one finds the young scholar being refashioned by parental substitutes. As in most families, and all family romances, there are also family secrets, secrets that may simultaneously embarrass and attract, but always serve to guarantee (and enforce) membership in the clan.

Alice Kaplan has written a memoir[1] and managed to do it before she hit forty. It is her version of the family romance, inside and outside the academy. The book is organized around two imbricated motifs: the young scholar's search for a replacement father (hers dies as she turns eight), and the discovery of a kind of solace, but also a kind of escape, in French language and culture. Kaplan's account is driven by her desire to be the good daughter, even toward men (such as literate Nazi collaborators, the eventual subjects of her scholarship) she might be expected to despise. But it is even more focused on the ways French provided an ambiguous substitute paternity of its own: in vaguely Lacanian tones, Kaplan notes that "learning French," "learning to think," and "learning to desire" (140) are all mixed up for her—she cannot tell the difference. It is a curious conceit, implying that desire itself became an academic pursuit. Indeed, while strenuously insisting on the need for including the "personal" in academic work, Kaplan's memoir yields an oddly inhuman truth—that her strongest desires are for a language, one that will never be intimately her own. (Kaplan's reach for sympathy in this regard produces a howler near the end, where she professes envy "of her friends in the English department who teach their own national literature" [209]. Does she really believe everyone in "English" teaches American literature?) Kaplan recovers "personal" feeling within the arid wastes of academia, but only by turning a language into the object of her sincerest affection. I'm not sure this is exactly the lesson she intended to teach.

Kaplan's desire for French takes her into a Ph.D. program at Yale, where she studies briefly with Paul de Man. One can assume that it is primarily *l'affaire de Man* that has made Kaplan's book of interest to reviewers; it is unlikely to have been noted otherwise, unlikely perhaps to have been published. The revelations in 1987 that de Man (whose uncle was a collaborator) had written a literary column for the Belgian collaborationist newspaper *Le Soir* in 1941 and 1942, a column at times pro-Nazi and, on one occasion, anti-Semitic, supplies the big academic family secret in this memoir. Kaplan makes almost no personal reflections on de Man—she seems not to have known him very well—and he remains an enigmatic figure here. But as a symbol he serves mightily. Her grand act of rejecting de Man's impersonal, rhetorically bound, "deconstructive theory" allows her to join her private family romance—her father had been a prosecutor at Nuremburg—with the academic and political romances around her. What she discovers abroad, ironically, is that even French children know what Americans "are rarely called upon to explain: the connection between family history, family prejudices, and big history, with a capital H" (97). Her dissertation (not guided by de Man) turns to French literati who collaborated with the Nazis, figures de Man had discussed in *Le Soir*, though Kaplan had no way of knowing de Man's journalism. Suddenly, this allows her to share things with her father that they were unable to share when he was alive: their Jewish heritage, the trauma of the Holocaust, the persistence of historical memory.

Learning French thus provides a victory over lost time: Kaplan can be proud to identify herself with a heroic father she barely got to know, to bask in the reflected glory of family history in a way common Americans (and Paul de Man) cannot. But this triumph does not come without a struggle, for from Céline to Sartre, Kaplan's French lessons have taught her to disregard "personal motivation" (173) in favor of disinterested intellection and aestheticism. Deconstruction too "was about keeping person-ness away" (148). The climax of Kaplan's story is, quite literally, a lack of climax, a failure of intimacy. "As we got closer to writing our term papers, Guy [her de Man-worshipping boyfriend] lost interest in sex. . . . He couldn't spend the night. He had a paper to write on metaphor" (156). As Guy scrutinizes his dictionaries, Alice is "hungry for plot . . . and a little human contact" as well. She feels mentally inferior, daunted by his energy, his books, the glowing comments from his professors, his knowledge of German philosophy. She wants more human contact than Guy is willing to give. "I demanded he stay the night. I clung to his sleeve; he yelled; I yelled louder; he stiffened up; I grabbed harder. He slapped me across the face. Hard" (157). Kaplan is liberated on the spot, from Guy and from his de Manian rigor. "Suddenly I wasn't lazy anymore. . . . I wondered— in that secret part of my brain where I admitted my responsibility—if I hadn't provoked Guy into hitting me." This is the turning point of the memoir, however silly it may appear. By the next page, Kaplan has decided to concentrate on French fascist writers, and she is "dying to show how screwed-up intellectuals could get about the truth" (160). She has rediscovered history, real feelings, passionate writing; "desire passed through" (163) her work now, so much so that her adviser wants to sleep with her. To top it all off, an "anti-deconstruction backlash was in gear; I was going to benefit from it" (163). She does.

Soulless Guy winds up with a five-hundred-page manuscript no one can read, and soon leaves the profession. Kaplan winds up, after minor detours, with a "dream job" (166) at Duke. Along the way, Paul de Man is unmasked. "Every deconstructionist in the country wanted to know what fascism was, and I was in a position to tell them. . . . My happiness was complete" (168–169). Yet, as in a later interview with Maurice Bardèche, a fascist intellectual and Holocaust revisionist, she pulls her punches on de Man's wartime writings. She refused to turn prosecutor, as her father had, acknowledging—*à la* de Man himself—"impossibility and the confusion of theory and life." Kaplan is still trying to be the good daughter, she says, and her book ends in a strange reconciliation with the merchant prince, "Mr. D," who had first unveiled to her the secrets of Paris when she was but fifteen. The genre of family romance has its demands, too, after all.

It is an engaging and yet frustrating book, with a prose style stubbornly determined to be innocent, generous, and unaffected, and a plotline that swerves coyly away to something else at just the right moments. Kaplan likes the savor of revelation that only a memoir promises, but she has little stomach for working through what she appears to feel. Her father, we learn the toward the end, seems to have been an alcoholic. But we never know what this means to her. She questions her mother's excuse—"Everyone drank" in those days; it was "the times" (202)—but then stops. Just before this, Kaplan writes: "Why do I keep circling in my work around intellectual men and their political crimes, their innocent or noble or charming surfaces and their shameful undersides?" (201). Does Kaplan also see her father as shameful? She does not say; his heroism wins out, in any case. Are we supposed to see a comparison with de Man, excused by some acolytes with words similar to those of Kaplan's mother? What would that mean? We are not told.

I raise such issues because acknowledging the importance of one's emotions is what Kaplan's book is all about; the denial of a personal life is for her the great error of deconstruction, de Man, and much of academic life. The primary opposition in Kaplan's thinking is a dependable one, if nothing else: feeling versus reason, interests versus knowledge. Yet we learn remarkably little about what Kaplan feels about anything—it is a weirdly childlike and stylized account. Despite her best efforts to leave de Man behind, things remain shrouded in "impossibility" and "confusion." When Bardèche hurls his invective at her by letter, long after the polite interview, and revels in their complicity (196), Kaplan reports that it took her five years to react. A native speaker of French reading Bardèche's words aloud—it is the native voice that counts most, apparently—finally frees her repressed emotions, but even then we are told only of her "disgust" (198). Nothing more.

The point I'm trying to make here is that *French Lessons* unintentionally demonstrates how difficult it is to show "feelings" in writing, how oddly recalcitrant our sincere efforts at self-display may be. It is simply impossible not to see *French Lessons*, despite (or perhaps because of) Kaplan's claims about her increased self-awareness, as terribly self-serving. Much of the memoir reads like a transcript of the censored narrative one occasionally gives to one's therapist—lots of smoothly hinged surfaces, with all the nasty work of finding out what one actually feels still to come. Kaplan asks interesting questions—"Why am I still fighting the battles of another time and place?" (199), for example—but seems to have little interest in trying out answers on her readers. And how could she? Who, finally, ever writes the memoir that reveals what must remain hidden? In June, the month her father died, she cannot bear to be away from France, or near home; she suddenly starts speaking and dreaming in French. She thinks, "maybe this book will put a stop to it" (208). I can't imagine any of her readers believing it will be so.

Moreover, there is something troubling at the heart of this project. It is perfectly clear that the biggest villains of the piece, fascist intellectuals from the 1940s to the 1980s, suffer (unlike de Man) from the same thing—an excess of strong emotion, welling up from the gut, utterly transparent as to personal interests, and spewed forth directly at Jews and any other "inferior" group which happens to be available. Do we want figures like Bardèche to be more in touch with what they feel? Or do we want them to think, calmly and rationally, about the evidence, about history, about how dominated they have been by emotional lives that are out of control? Do we really need a clearer sense of their personal motivation, as Kaplan's story would lead us to believe? Or should we instead hope that just a little bit of disinterested reason enters their stunted minds, even if it means smothering their all-too-expressive souls?

This brings me back, finally, to the case of de Man. I hate to say so, but I have the strong "feeling" that de Man's role in this memoir is rather exaggerated. Graduate students at Columbia, where I trained, also responded poorly to stress, even as they tried vainly to hide merely personal responses. From what Kaplan reveals, it was much worse than at Yale, though de Man never showed his face; "politics" and "commitment" were the tools that people used most often to repress their emotions, or those of others, when the need arose. We hated fascism more than any other graduate group in the country, I think, but our sexual relations were still fraught with bitter competition, emotional violence, deep anxieties over what we didn't know or understand—all of which we kept hidden under a burning desire to be *engagé*. I too refused to spend the night with a girlfriend, who refused angrily to understand, because I was too anxious about my work, and I can testify that de Man had nothing to do with it. The personal was supposed to be the political, a slogan that Alice Kaplan's colleagues in her writing group at Chapel Hill surely remember and endorse even today. But it didn't make being emotionally honest with oneself or with others any easier, and in lots of ways, it made things much worse. I can't begin to recall all the times people repressed what they felt, for fear of seeming right-wing, or aestheticist, or, worst of all—disinterested and impersonal. All of us knew—it was the reigning doctrine—just how political literature was. But it didn't help us deal with our personal dilemmas any better than deconstruction helped Alice Kaplan.

I say this reluctantly, for Kaplan's approach to the de Man affair elicits my sympathy. De Man obviously knew a great deal about the subtle links between the personal, the political, and the literary, but he chose not to address them with his students or his readers. It's our loss, and Kaplan has the right to wonder, as many others have before her, whether de Man's emphasis on the rhetorical conundrums of language provided some hideout from a personal history he could not confront openly. But about other of her claims, I have grave doubts. Was the ultimate failure of Guy "and many like him" due to the fact that they "got too far into deconstruction" (172) and couldn't get out? I doubt it. Kaplan writes: "we were a tense, ambitious, and fearful lot" (173). So were we. And why not? When only one out of every three Ph.D.s got a tenure-track job, even with sexy writing, and then only if they came from the best schools, who could feel secure? Kaplan hints at this in passing. She also tries to indicate, in an unfortunate cliché, that deconstruction did some good: "we were sharpening our minds like razors" (171). But she still leaves the reader, especially the reader outside the scholarly family, with the impression that people like Paul de Man single-handedly ruined good minds, created the tension, the ambition, and the fear, and caused people like Guy to avoid the first-person singular pronoun in private conversation. I don't buy it. I have no great desire to defend de Man or deconstruction; I too believe that his work ignored all the important and most of the interesting problems. But I think Kaplan is doing a real disservice to her nonacademic readers by indicting this scapegoat. Paul de Man had a number of very successful students too, remember. And worse teachers are easy to find.

In the end, Kaplan reveals personal feeling of any depth only when it comes to the French language. This is where her juices begin to flow, in long passages devoted to the mysteries of French grammar, the rhythms of native speech, the indescribable joys of learning to pronounce the French "*r*." For Kaplan, French is the Wonderland on the other side of the mirror of self-recognition, a thoroughly enchanted world filled with stereotypes right out of Disney. When she teaches, she reinforces them by asking her students to divide their bodies in half: "Our English side slouches, while our French side is crisp and pointed" (134–135). The French are rigorous, Americans are slovenly—it was what she struggled with at Yale, before Guy's slap taught her that she could be French without necessarily enslaving herself to de Man. French is father, mentor, and lover all in one; it is, more than she admits, the fetish around which her real emotional life has revolved since her father died. When Kaplan feels most deeply, what she feels most deeply about is French. And this is what is supposed to lend pathos to the final page of her memoir. For she has come to realize that "French did me some harm by giving me a place to hide," that there's no simple "American" self to recover. But she also believes that only by writing about French has she been able to "air my suspicions, my anger, my longings, to people for whom it's [sic] come as a total surprise." I must confess that I am hard pressed to say just what those suspicions and longings involve, and I am not at all sure who, or what, is at the root of her anger. All I do know by the end of the book is that Alice Kaplan loves French, even though she believes it may not be unambiguously good for her. I thought I would know a lot more.

Note

1. Alice Kaplan, *French Lessons: A Memoir* (Chicago: University of Chicago Press, 1993).

8

Speaking Personally

The Culture of Autobiographical Criticism

❖

DAVID SIMPSON

My first effort at presenting the argument of this essay went under a different subtitle: "The *Cult* of Autobiographical Criticism." I was clearly thinking of myself as a courageous, nineteenth-century anthropologist going out into the world's dark corners with a rationalist or, worse still, Christian faith in the primitive status of alien forms of worship. This is the self-image I take to be implicit in the word "cult." And I do still plan to take a tilt at today's "mock lyrists, large self-worshipers,/ And careless hectorers in proud bad verse."[1] But the word I really have to use is not *cult* but *culture*: the *culture* of autobiographical criticism. For it has been nurtured and cherished awhile, and regularly fertilized; and it is, as a historical culture, inescapable, and not at all open to dismissal from some high point of disinterested inspection—as if it were a problem for them, or you, but not for me.

One is tempted to refer to a "cult" of autobiographical criticism because such criticism has recently taken on a visibly new lease of life, as signaled in books, conferences, English Institute sessions, and articles in *The Chronicle of Higher Education.* Many of us are now uncritically at ease with speaking for ourselves, saying where we are coming from and inviting others to tell us where they are coming from, in gestures that are at once the most necessary and the laziest rhetoric called for within our variously multicultural society. For indeed, we are all deeply implicated in the culture of autobiographical criticism, in personal particularity, and the only choice is how to cope with it and use it (for we will always also be used by it). In the casual English mode in which I grew up (that is, the part of me that grew up before Althusser, *et al.*), the personal is at once omnipresent and deemed irrelevant. It is omnipresent as a stylistic marker—the anecdote, the fireside voice, the eschewal of the pontifical—at the same time as it is no obstacle to the proper elucidation of a text. I.A. Richards was quite comfortable with the personal, as long as it remained "genuine and relevant," and he thought that, as such, it could successfully "respect the liberty and autonomy of the poem."[2] His pupil, William Empson, described personal investments as minor markers along the road to good judgment and tolerance of other judgments: "A critic had better say what his own opinions are, which can be done quite briefly, while recognizing that the person in view held different ones."[3] Even the Welshman, Raymond Williams, seems quintessentially English in his use of personal experience as a rhetoric of validation, of making real, while refusing to theorize subjectivity or use the self as a place to begin theory.[4] For Richards and Empson, the personal can be sidestepped, while for Williams, it is an authorizing principle. But in no case does it interfere with the credibility of what is spoken about as somehow objective.

Now, and here in America, we live with more exigent formulations of the personal, which has become much more nerve-wracking, existentially and epistemologically, and occasionally revolutionary (though often spuriously so) in its rhetoric. We demand enough of ourselves that we have to figure out and then figure in what is personal and what is not, and whether anything at all can be more than contingently consensual within some or other subculture of class and/or race and/or gender and/or whatever else that is shared by persons like ourselves. In so doing we are putting a contemporary spin on what may well be a defining condition of modernity itself. Wherever one cuts the historical cake, whether with Descartes, with Hume, or with Hegel (and it is of course all of these, and more), one of the most compelling definitions of the modern is that which specifies the emergence of subjectivity as a methodological and philosophical question. Without being rigidly deterministic—for we cannot deserve to be that—it seems fair to say that when state and society adapted themselves to or enabled a middle-class, entrepreneurial culture, and when the legal, philosophical, and theological disciplines began to reflect and explore that transition, then subjectivity came onto the agenda in a very big way as the primary explanatory principle in accounting for failure and success, virtue and vice, being and nonbeing. And this brought the *problem* of subjectivity into compulsive coexistence. For it has never not been a problem, if we read between the lines, however apparently assertive and confident the rhetoric may be. It is there in the dalliance with solipsism and performativism in Descartes's *Discourse on Method,* and it explains why models of universal psychology are always being most vigorously proposed just when they are on the point of visible collapse (witness the short cycle from Kant to Hegel to Marx and Nietzsche).[5]

Foucault illuminates the paradox most elegantly and economically in his account of the "analytic of finitude" as the defining condition of modernity. He explains that all knowledge is thus positioned as both knowledge (in itself) and knowledge *production* from within bodies and minds in places and times.[6] (This is the deep compatibility of Foucault's project with the Marxist methods he so often disavowed or qualified). As soon as knowledge is thus connected to a knowing subject—and over three hundred years of philosophical speculation reflects this connection—then we are compelled to an endless concern about whether what we know is also known to others, whether what is known is real or phenomenal, and whether we know anything at all in claiming to know ourselves (for the unconscious also appears at this moment of modernity, and it has not yet left us). One could go as far as to say that the idea of the self relies for its very existence upon these problems, which are only problems because we believe that their resolution will provide that self with some plausible substance, a thing to correspond with the word.

Literary criticism has adopted a peculiar and particular relation to this general condition of modernity in its culture of autobiography. I will present two models, one of which is simple but pseudoiconoclastic, and the other of which is so difficult to formulate that it has not been much attempted, but is I think worth working at. Both correspond with a general *overemphasis* by literary criticism of its general implication in modernity's predicament of subjectivity: for literary criticism has celebrated more often than it has resisted this syndrome, by virtue of its own original appearance as a mechanism for social bonding by common sense for a population without university education and subsisting within a nationalist ideology. Hence literary criticism's appeal, over the years, to such validating categories as lived experience, the concrete embodiment, empathy, sympathy, sincerity, and so forth. And hence, inevitably, the bitterness of its internal debates between those who would propose the self as real enough to provide a foundation for knowledge and communication and those who would disperse its definitions among other and nonbiological agencies.

My first example is perhaps predictable and even, by now, done to death, but it remains exemplary nonetheless: Jane Tompkins's essay "Me and My Shadow." Tompkins writes as follows about her long-standing discomfort with what she feels to be the norms of academic propriety:

> The problem is that you can't talk about your private life in the course of doing your professional work. You have to pretend that epistemology, or

whatever you're writing about, has nothing to do with your life, that it's more exalted, more important, because it (supposedly) *transcends* the merely personal. Well I'm tired of the conventions. . . .[7]

This is a memorable passage, and I won't comment on it at length. But notice that Tompkins can claim that this situation is unreasonable, in a way that would be much harder if she were not a literary critic but another kind of "professional." She can do this because of the subjectivizing predisposition of literary criticism, which makes her outrage as implicitly conventional as it is rhetorically bombastic. Indeed when I first read this, I couldn't imagine where she located the model of dry objectivism and masculinized impersonality with which to repress herself. My own students, I thought, are far readier to talk constantly about themselves than to master any technological vocabularies. They are very happy to affirm that a reading of a text is valid because that's what it means to them, because they have been there, or because life is like that. And yet, I went on to realize, Tompkins certainly does have a point when one thinks of graduate school, much of the time in many places. New Critics, structuralists, and deconstructors have all, successively, taught us to analyze and transcribe how an "it" works, largely without reference to an "us" performing the analysis. Professionalized criticism *has* made heavy use of an objectivist rhetoric. And it has arguably done so exactly because preprofessional pedagogy has made equally heavy use of the opposite rhetoric of subjectivity—of "feeling" with and "being" like. And that's the point. Literary criticism as a social-educational complex is neither wholly objectivist nor personalized, but subsists by a seemingly immanent struggle between the two, between a masculinized professionalism and a traditionally feminized subjectivism. Adherents of one camp or the other have proven, by their very adherence, unable to see the setup. By defining objectivism as the besetting norm, Tompkins can offer the private voice as a would-be revolutionary alternative, with all the rhetoric of existential decision-making. Thus she writes that "people are scared to talk about themselves . . . they haven't got the guts to do it."[8]

To talk about oneself may, in someone's language, signify having guts, but bears not at all upon whether there is a significant "self" to contain those guts. Tompkins's assumptions are foundationalist, depending on exactly the "metaphysics of presence" that Gerald MacClean has found in her essay, and asserting, as he says, the place of a "self that is capable of self-knowledge."[9] To talk a self is to have a self whose prior and repressed existence is the very license for speech itself. Tompkins takes no philosophical risks, and she might reasonably contend that she intends no truck with assertions of foundational selfhood. And indeed no one will find it useful to dispute the veracity of whether or not she went to the bathroom, to take the now-best-known item of personal situatedness in her narrative. Some questions are beyond the point of skepticism. Nothing important is proven or disproven either way. But the existential bravado of her essay relies upon our agreement that it *is* important to talk about these things, that they are in fact implicated in the business of interpretation. The urinary motif might appeal, I suppose, to those who are searching for a whiff of the carnivalesque within the desiccated routines of scholarly argument. But there's nothing here of the Rabelaisian abandon that might fulfill such a desire: the author, after all, is "not going yet" (126). Instead, the mention of going to the bathroom functions as a conventional instance of the *vraisemblable*. Because there is no point to this, it is only mentioned to inscribe the reality of the story: it is mentioned because it really happened. And so, by contagion, we are talking about a real person, with a real self. Or, to say it better, *this* is the kind of reality Tompkins values for herself, precisely as an avoidance of the problem of theorizing selfhood, about which going to the bathroom has absolutely nothing to say, for or against— as if one could say, for instance, "I pee, therefore I am." This mention is used to make professionalism seem unreal, but it has nothing to do with professionalism, at all.

Tompkins's self is the liberal-expressive self. It has been around a while, and will surely live on. It flowed in the poetry of Walt Whitman, and it is now articulated within a certain subculture within academic feminism: the "guts" to which she lays claim are in fact already collective. Tompkins is right to say that there was a gendered exclusion of that self from the graduate schools of twenty years ago, and this in turn explains the vigor of the current attack on objectivism in the very same graduate schools now occupied by women and feminized men. But to find a conflict of languages is not to prove an essence. After Foucault and many other critics and philosophers, we might propose that the private voice of Jane Tompkins or anyone else bears no more obvious relation to a self than the front page of the newspaper she might have been reading. Indeed, some might say, less so. Even Whitman's pleasure in a poetically announced self can be read as nothing more than a string of attributes and contingent connections masquerading as an entity.

By the time of the British Romantics, the problem of self (which is, as I've said, nothing less than the question of whether there is such a thing) was more or less dominant in methodological discourse. Utilitarianism was ingeniously devised as an attempt to get around the question, but it has never left us for long. It appears in the transcript of what they called experience—the unfortunate Keats, the overmuddled Coleridge, the hallucinated De Quincey—and in their theorizing about it. Wordsworth's formulation is typical of many others:

> Hard task, vain hope, to analyse the mind,
> If each most obvious and particular thought,

Not in a mystical and idle sense,
But in the words of Reason deeply weighed,
Hath no beginning.[10]

The mode of Romantic writing is the mode of transference and of repetition. To wonder thus about and with Wordsworth is to wonder about ourselves as we wonder. It is also to wonder, infinitely and inconclusively, about how to tell the difference between what is mystical and idle, and what is deeply weighed by reason.

This kind of wondering, this skepticism, must be central to any critical or dialectical historicism, but it is mostly either ignored or trivialized. Paradoxically (as with Tompkins) it has often been the rhetoric of repression that has served to reestablish a foundational self: what has been repressed finally comes out, therefore it seems to be real and authentic. Marginalized voices can sometimes seem to claim an identity precisely by virtue of marginality. Polemically, this can be a necessary and even an inevitable move. But cultural theory is now well aware of the reciprocal reification that enables such formulations.

The kind of confidence in the present self of which Tompkins-in-print might stand as prototype is clearly the symptom of an exhaustion with or resistance to theory, with its painstaking attempts at excluding or contextualizing the self. And its currency within today's theoretophobic culture will not diminish as a result of pure/mere critique. Tompkins never makes the argument that all understandings of the past are always and entirely about the present: that meanings cannot exist except as wholly remade. But because she is uninterested in any resistances to pure personalism and presentism, or in theorizing their limits and exact potential, the position she represents can easily be taken to lead to just that conclusion. Stanley Fish made headway some time ago with a weakly socialized formalization of personalism in his model of interpretive communities. He recognized that "solipsism and relativism" are "modes of being" that "could never be realized."[11] No reader stands alone. The reasonable truth that we do indeed inhabit interpretive communities was then deployed to justify turning our attention away from supposedly immanent textual meanings and toward the meanings governed by the remaking and rereading of those same texts. Fish's interest was entirely in the presentist side of this relation, and in the legitimation of "institutional" determination, which his argument rendered (though he never says this, and there are potential alternative implications) as precisely a socialized form of identity: identity in community. Here he shares an emphasis with old-style cultural Marxism, though he differs, of course, in restricting his attention to the institution and not to any social totality within which it is articulated and mediated. The self is made by outside forces, but it is a whole, because the institution that contains it is a whole, and gives us our entire language.

Presentism is a very convenient attitude and perhaps even a pragmatic one, in a number of ways. First, it tells us that our knowledge-production, however apparently arcane, is always relevant to the here and now. If all looking at the past tells us about the present, then we can never be accused of pedantry or mere antiquarianism. We might well need this argument again, as the research agenda of the American university comes under attack— though it was devised, I think, to address a student constituency primed to appreciate an explicitly political urgency, which Fish sought at once to acknowledge and to limit (like de Man) by embedding "social" reference within an isolated professional subculture. The implication of presentism in Fish's model (and the more-than-implication in Tompkins's essay) may still prove to have good consequences for the practical legitimation of English departments in troubled times.

Nonetheless it has inhibiting effects on the development of any critical historicism, one that includes but is not restricted to the presentist component. Pure presentism gets us out of some very hard and perhaps insoluble questions. As such it is a refusal of skepticism. This is its second function. If the past is actually and wholly present, then there is no need to fuss about historical difference or a method of describing it. The problem of reference can then be limited to the here and now. This too has strategic advantages. As long as we are seeking to credit our preferred discipline of literary criticism with producing a useful knowledge (as we almost inevitably will be in the age of instrumentalism), we had better avoid the vertiginous attempt at critical historicism, which so far has produced an indefinitely splittable atom. It is not simply that the past is deemed irrelevant, but that there are now such strains on any objectivist attempt to do "history" that we risk having nothing intelligible to say for ourselves when people ask us what we do.

Third, the presentist argument once again works to inscribe, foundationally, the self doing the perceiving of the past. If all meaning resides in *me*, then I must be somebody (and the same goes for "us"). Fourth, and most banal, and thus perhaps most important, it is pedagogically convenient, as it returns us, as professionals, to the preprofessional level of talking about ourselves, which has always been a mightily easy way to run through the clock in the classroom. Immense resources of time and patience are required to read the past *as* the past. The reproduction of methodological skepticism and documentary density are well beyond what can be done in the average lecture or seminar. It is much easier to talk about what someone thinks of *King Lear* than about what *King Lear* might mean, and how we could ever claim to know what it means. Teaching has traditionally tried to use the one approach—what I feel about it—as a means to the other—what it means; but this is becoming much harder to do as the face of "history" itself becomes so complex. (Much new historicism has elegantly but visibly avoided the problem by eschewing totalities and excavating a new "piece" of history, which is then worked into a refigured, text-based exposition.)

Now for my second example, which does not yet have a name because it has yet to come about, so that it is hardly an example at all so much as the prospectus for a future method. It will have to construe, without reification of any of its interrelated terms, the self in time and place reading the past in time and place. Sartre's massive efforts, in *The Search for a Method*, in the *Critique of Dialectical Reason*, and in *The Family Idiot*, are required reading. But Sartre ignores precisely what the liberal-expressive tradition can never let us forget—his own position as another self in another history, as an interpreter in a fully historical rather than an existential-ontological sense. He shows us that past selves were neither unique nor passively generic, but always something of each. There is always particularity-in-generality. But he too was a simultaneously idiosyncratic and general subject. He used psychoanalysis to break the spell of naïve Marxism, but that is no longer as common now and here as it was then and in France. So his use of psychoanalysis was partial and unskeptical (by virtue of his disavowing the unconscious as a problematic construction, one that might obscure and not simply clarify interpretation). After Sartre we know better than to try to explain every pulsation of the artery as a symptom of crude economic determination, and we are prepared for circles within circles of mediations. But the model remains immanent, frozen in time: the past is the past, and can be scientifically described as such (in, for instance, the career of Flaubert). How can we read the present in the past, without reducing each to the other? Or, in the existential mode of individual totalization, how if at all can we extract *knowledge* from the practical orientation to *action* that typifies the recuperation of the past for an individual present?

At this point the problems threaten to seem insurmountable. Invoking Foucault, we might suggest that we can only wait out history, wait until the next epistmemic break has refigured our way of seeing so that we are outside the analytic of finitude. Then we will have solved the problem by no longer having a problem to solve. But I'm not sure I'll live long enough for that. In the meantime, what tools are there for thinking about the problem of the self in relation to the problem of history; for describing the interaction of a present self-in-history with the written records of other selves-in-history, and all this in language? The resulting *critical historicism*, if I may so call it, would seek to be at once objective and unfinal. It cannot be an immanent method, because it has to anticipate continual reformation in unforeseen circumstances. It will always produce more and new "facts." But facts they may be, in the most pertinent sense of the word. What is produced when an "I" reads an "it" is a combination of continuities and discontinuities, understandings and nonunderstandings, whose objective component resides in the general determination provided by local syndromes (for instance, class or gender) as well as in the arguably idiosyncratic formulations of those syndromes. This evidence does lead to hypotheses about various kinds of totalities—those describing the relation of the elements of the past to each other, in some tentative synchronic (if always incomplete) whole, and those describing the continuity of the past with the present, both as a similarly incipient diachronic whole conditioning the specific subject position of the individual observer. (Wholeness, let me emphasize, might be aggregational rather than organic— or something of each. It must allow for both reaction and redundancy.)

This dialectical skepticism—I mean skepticism as applied to both present and past, as each relates to selves and to social wholes—is our best hope of saying something insightful about a being-in-time-and-place that is at once inherited and prefigured and also new and unpredictable. To say that all history is mere reproduction is a fallacy appealing largely to those of us bored with our jobs in the more stable sectors of the First-World economy, and even here it is mere ideology—it could be argued that things are changing very fast indeed. Conversely, to imagine that history is always changing in all its parts at a steady pace such that there are no continuities between any past and the present is a fallacy of presentism. To say with Heraclitus that we do not step twice into the same river is only trivially true if the river contains the same volume of water and works upon us in the same way.

Any forthcoming critical historicism may tend in its methods to resemble the paradigms of evolutionary biology in their predilection for models of punctuated equilibrium. The attempt to describe uneven development across the entire historical-individual and past-present spectrum is going to have to seem very complicated. We must be prepared to investigate what *is* residual and long-term and even indefinite in particular human events, as well as what is changing in gradual or revolutionary ways. All too often criticism has redescribed the long-durational as the "human," but what we are after are the components of *particular* human lives. I may share certain features of a class position with William Wordsworth even as I have not lived through the French Revolution.[12] What has been called the "human" is more often the mark of exceptionally long duration. (If we are going to use the term "human" it is most effective for prohibiting pain, as in torture and genocide, and not in publicizing preferred forms of living). When we understand a Provençal love poem, we understand love and longing, but that is not the "human," it is a long-durational formulation of heterosexual bonding.[13] And it is embedded in much that we will not understand unless we work at it—a religious, allegorical dimension, a social dynamic, a topical allusion, and so on.

Could we call such a method "objective," or propose objectivity as one of its goals, without reverting to a discredited fantasy of Enlightenment reason? Yes and no. No in the sense that what might be produced can never be immanent. All knowledge is discovered in time, even if about past times. But to limit our notion of the objective to this sort of impossibly atemporal paradigm is self-defeating and unnecessary. We may feel comfortable with the absolute objectivity of some or other fact about the past, but the place of that item within any totality will likely change as other facts come to light, and as the pressures upon this segment of the past alter through present times. But it is possible that the conjunction between my or our knowing, and something posited as known, *has* indeed an objective function, by being *within* temporality. That is to say, our recognition of something in the past might take place from *within* an objective, "really there" component of our ongoing history—a class position, a gender position, and so forth. At the same time the synchronic totalities within which the items of the then and the now need (for historical analysis) to be configured will surely not be the same. There will be elements of Wordsworth's class position which I do not share.

This is the point at which liberal relativism or perspectivism and what remains of a Marxist critique part company. The first supposes that there can be no knowledge that is more than perspectival, that there can be no conjunction between a perspective and a social-historical totality, not in the present and therefore certainly not about the past. The ethic emerging from this is pluralist and contingent: let a hundred voices speak, but let no one dare to speak for others. The Marxist critique conversely suggests that what is perspectival *can* conjoin with a totality, and can thus induce knowledge. Lukács notoriously "solved" the puzzle by proposing the proletariat as the emergent truth of history—a solution now almost universally found implausible. But suppose that a perspective might at least articulate a microcultural condition (let us not say "class," but let us not forget class), the account of which might involve other such conditions, and so on toward a general social-historical constellation? Why could we not call this objective, in the only sense of the word now useful or credible: a conjunction of the subjective and the analytical in and for time and place?

If I read her correctly, this is close to what Ellen Messer-Davidow, in the important essay from which Jane Tompkins actually takes (and perhaps mistakes) her inspiration, in fact proposes, although she chooses to call it "perspectivism," and restricts it implicitly to a presentist analysis. She writes of this perspectivism as something between objectivism and subjectivism, something that:

would bring together, in processes of knowing, the personal and cultural, subjective and objective—replacing dichotomies with a systemic under-standing of how and what we see. It would explain how we affiliate cul-turally, acquire a self-centered perspective, experience the perspectives of others, and deploy multiple perspectives in inquiry.[14]

If this "systemic analysis" were to become also *systematic*, then we would be on the way to a critical historicism. Messer-Davidow does not take the next step in acknowledging the usefulness of a Marxist vocabulary for this task, perhaps because she is not here interested in the hermeneutic problems of recovering and relating to the past as a primary component of historicization. She thus refrains from suggesting that a feminized Marxist method is in fact the way forward. But she articulates, here, much of what I would want to hang onto within a terminology of the objective.

It is at least clearly the case that there *is* within the subcultures of femi-nism a model that does not simply replicate the inherited conventions or reproduce the assumptions that Jane Tompkins, I think, reproduces. Trying to be objective, then, does not preclude being oneself and being in time, indeed being in time is the only condition of and motive for objectivity (why else would one bother to read and research?).[15] And objectivity is itself, and recip-rocally, not atemporal. We don't need, except heuristically, to specify a history that is itself outside time. We can stop the clock imaginatively, as the movie director stops the film, to look at the makeup of a single shot. But models of cause and effect applied to complex shots will always fail as long as they assume the absolute sufficiency of what is seen there for explaining what is happening and why things compose themselves as they do: as if the airplane roaring overhead but out of the picture could not be the cause of the child's putting its hands to its ear, while the butterfly flying across the foreground in the picture explains everything.

There is, then, much to do that has not been done in the effort toward a critical historicism. Speaking personally, I get very nervous talking about objectivity. It has been for a while a dirty word, and whenever I use it in public, I want to cover my head as I wait for the beer cans to hit the chicken wire. Objectivity has lately been imaged as one of those things the tech-nocrats believe in. And indeed we cannot rely upon the sort of experimental evidence that does still obtain in some scientific disciplines to decide how and when we are right or wrong about reading the relation between past and present. No compound ghost comes back to warn us. Everything is moving, developing, and disappearing at different rates of change and with different resistances. Scientific knowledges, social formations, individual experiences, all happen within and because of each other. Any objectivity about these events will be wisdom after the whole event, even as we may still inhabit part of the event. But there has been no proof that the mirror of the present is always and entirely a distorting one: there often was no "there" there anyway, except in the empirical sense, a sense that was thus either obvious or immediately indecipherable and requiring theorization from the start. Attempting a critical historicism, I will at least no longer speak of a self, but as a subject seeking its own historical coordinates in time, place, class, gender, and whatever else it takes to make sense of my interest in a particular moment in the past. To move beyond "speaking personally" is to leave behind the comforts of self-assurance; perhaps one could mischievously say to Jane Tompkins that those who do not do this have not got the guts to do it—they are afraid of the not-self in the subject. And to make this move is to accept, in the more-than-notional but strictly methodological sense, the prospect of incompletion—or, more positively, of constant inclusion. When this happens, we will be beyond the cult, and will perhaps begin to understand the culture, of autobiography. In particular, in literature, in history, and perhaps, occasionally, in general.

Notes

1. *John Keats: Complete Poems*, ed. Jack Stillinger (Cambridge, MA and London: Belknap Press of Harvard University, 1982), 366. An extended version of the argument of this essay appears in my *The Academic Postmodern and the Rule of Literature: A Report on Half-Knowledge* (Chicago: University of Chicago Press, 1995), pp. 71–92.)

2. I.A. Richards, *Practical Criticism: A Study of Literary Judgment* (1929: rpt. London: Routledge and Kegan Paul, 1966), 240.

3. William Empson, *Using Biography* (Cambridge, MA: Harvard University Press, 1984), 142.

4. I have discussed Williams's reliance on a "voice" in "Raymond Williams: Feeling for Structures, Voicing 'History'," *Social Text*, 30 (1992), 9–26.

5. For a statement (and an overstatement) of the solipsistic element in Cartesian method, see my "Putting One's House in Order: The Foundations of Descartes's Method," *New Literary History*, 9 (1977), 83–101.

6. Michel Foucault, *The Order of Things: An Archaeology of the Human Science* (1966; rpt. New York: Random House, 1973), 303–343.

7. Jane Tompkins, "Me and My Shadow," in *Gender and Theory: Dialogues on Feminist Criticism*, ed. Linda Kaufmann (New York and Oxford: Basil Blackwell, 1989), 123. For a critique of this essay, close in spirit to my own, see Gerald M. MacClean, "Citing the Subject," *Ibid.*, 140–157.

8. "Me and My Shadow," 123. Tompkins repeated this conviction in a recent interview: "Self-indulgence is the charge made by people who are afraid of their own selves." See

The Chronicle of Higher Education, May 6, 1992, A9. Personally I think it important to remain afraid of myself.

9. Gerald MacClean, "Citing the Subject," 141–142.

10. William Wordsworth, *The Prelude: 1799, 1805, 1850*, eds. Jonathan Wordsworth, M.H. Abrams and Stephen Gill (London and New York: Norton, 1979), 77. (1850, 2: 228–232).

11. Stanley Fish, *Is There a Text in this Class? The Authority of Interpretive Communities* (Cambridge, MA and London: Harvard University Press, 1980), 321.

12. For some brief examples of this conjunction, see David Simpson, ed., *Subject to History: Ideology, Class, Gender* (Ithaca and London: Cornell University Press, 1991), 15–18.

13. See Sebastiano Timpanaro, *On Materialism* (London: Verso, 1980), 50–52.

14. Ellen Messer-Davidow, "The Philosophical Bases of Feminist Literary Criticism," in Linda Kaufmann, ed., *Gender and Theory*, 88.

15. On this subject, see Donna Haraway, "Situated Knowledges: The Science Question in Feminism and the Privilege of Partial Perspective," in her *Simians, Cyborgs and Women: The Reinvention of Nature* (New York: Routledge, 1991), 183–201. Haraway is reluctant to abandon all aspirations to objectivity and very concerned about the politically disabling consequences of admitting a universal perspectivism as the last word in the debate about knowledge.

II

How Can a Critic Create a Self?

9

Self-Interview

❧

GERALD GRAFF

Q. You became known as a polemicist in your early work, and now you're associated with the idea of "teaching the conflicts." So would you say that combativeness is a deep *personal* motivation of your work?

A. Partly but not entirely. People think I must *like* conflict because I promote it as a pedagogical and curricular strategy. In fact I dislike conflict as much as anybody. In an odd way, my interest in conflict and polemics has always been tied to a longing for community. I just don't think a democratic community can be sustained by papering over its divisions. "Teaching the conflicts" for me is a way to get beyond the conflicts. My assumption is that the more we avoid confronting conflicts the uglier they can only get.

Q. What do you mean by your "longing for community"?

A. When I was first contemplating graduate school back in 1959, I sought advice from one of my professors about "the profession," which seemed pretty nebulous to me. "The great thing about this job," he said, "is nobody bothers you." His remark has stayed with me all these years so I guess even then it must have struck me as odd. What an ambition for a profession—not to be bothered! And what a commentary on an institution that calls itself an academic "community"!

It's the isolationism of the academic ethos that I've always disliked and struggled against, both in my work and personal life. That's why, after years of being a solitary professor, I jumped at the chance to become a department chair and later a university press director, mostly just to have somebody to talk to.

Q. But aren't you exceptional in seeing this as a problem?

A. Well, another writer who does is David Damrosch, in his new book *We Scholars: Changing the Culture of the University,* an excerpt from which has just appeared in *Lingua Franca* (January/February, 1995). Damrosch argues that the university is dominated by an "ethic of alienation and aggression" that "has bred isolated and peripatetic professors, estranged from their colleagues on campus and from the communities in which they live." Well said!

Q. Yet surely there is plenty of "community" on campus—black studies, women's studies, neoconservatives, all sorts of groupism.

A. Yes, but these communities tend themselves to be isolationist. Damrosch writes that "all too often the groupings that form within departments and within fields actually function as anti-communities: small coteries who band together as much to ward off outside influences as to foster collaborative work." He adds that such scholarly "anti-communities" are "essentially defensive in nature, a bonding by which an insecure subgroup tries to gain a sense of self-worth at the price of learning from divergent views."

Q. But if academics cherish their isolation as much as you say, how could you hope ever to change things?

A. As Damrosch points out, academics are often tremendously ambivalent about "the pleasures of isolation" that they cultivate. Why else have academic conferences and symposia become so pervasive if it isn't that they answer to a longing for community that isn't being satisfied by their home campuses? You can sense this longing in the hyperexcited atmosphere at such events— suddenly, for a few days, here are people you can talk to about your work —metonymy in the Elizabethan lyric, or cross-dressing in the eighteenth century, or what you will. These are conversations you aren't likely to have at home because anybody who shares your interests is probably by definition disqualified from being your colleague—they've already got *you* who does that!

Equally pathetic is the abyss of local silence and indifference into which we academics send our publications. When we publish an article or book, you'd think our departments or colleges would look for an occasion to discuss it publicly or in a course or two (our colleagues' research is vastly underutilized in our courses, for example). Instead, the "publishing scholar" is made to feel almost embarrassed about committing a public act, even as he or she is rewarded at salary time. Again, when you go to a conference, your publication becomes a reference point, but to make it a reference point on your home campus would be like making one out of your sex life, or your religion.

Q. Why do you think this academic "ethic of alienation and aggression" has taken root, if in fact it has?

A. Damrosch hints at a reason when he speaks of the "insecure" status of the academic subgroups that bond together against the threat of outsiders. Academic culture is grounded in insecurity and fear—as any environment would be where the rules are revised so frequently that nobody can be sure where one stands, where in fact revising "the paradigm" before your competitors do it is the name of the game. Students fear professors, those distant and unfathomable beings whose arbitrary laws change from course to course without notice; professors fear students, who can humiliate them by their mere silence and passivity; professors fear their colleagues as rivals and competitors. Because the university provides no institutional arena for discussing these fears out in the open, they get channeled into the self-protective, isolationist behavior Damrosch describes. Of course, all this could be as readily said about American culture as about academic culture.

Q. What about administrators?

A. It's their job to manage the economy of fear while also being objects and subjects of it. When American universities became large bureaucratic and professionalized institutions at the turn of the century and the relatively common culture of Christian gentlemen was replaced by specialized disciplines that were largely opaque to each other and to the public, academic administration emerged as the art of neutralizing fear and contention by keeping potentially clashing groups separate. This usually means appeasing clashing individuals and groups by giving each their separate space—a new course, a new department, a new program, eventually a new building. The administrative premise is that professors are brilliant children who obviously can't be expected to cooperate with one another and have to be kept apart. Consequently, professors tend to behave like children, if not always brilliant ones.

Q. This begins to sound like the accounts in your books of the origins of the "cafeteria counter" curriculum.

A. Yes. The American curriculum has evolved in very much the same way as the American city: when a threatening innovation appears, it is neutralized by the device of adding a new "suburb"—the new course, department, building, or whatnot. This conflict-free method of assimilating change goes hand in hand with a tacit philosophy of armed truce: I won't interfere with what you want to teach or study if you don't interfere with me. Since frank public discussion across the differences is assumed by definition to be impossible, this state of uneasy peaceful coexistence has to be held together by bureaucratic administration, which becomes a substitute for intellectual community. The bureaucratic art of crisis management aims not to create a vital community out of the academy's controversies, but to keep clashing factions isolated so they won't wash their dirty linen in public.

Q. For example?

A. A recent case in point is the celebrated battle over the "Cultures, Ideas, and Values" requirement at Stanford, which was "resolved" by creating separate course-tracks for traditionalists and revisionists so that no communication need take place between the two. When Stanford revised the requirement it was widely reviled by conservatives like William J. Bennett for caving in to pressure from multiculturalists and other insurgent groups. But if Stanford "caved in" to pressure, it caved in to pressure from *all* the factions involved, including the conservatives. In a familiar academic "Let's Make a Deal" game, a more or less multicultural track was established to satisfy multiculturalists while several more or less traditional tracks remained to appease traditionalists. I oversimplify, but I think I fairly describe what took place.

The dispute was resolved, in short, by creating separate but equal curricula, or separate but not so equal, depending on which faction you talk to. By evading the issues that divided the community Stanford managed to neutralize them for a while, but now, five years later, the whole battle has predictably erupted again.

The excuse for this kind of refusal of community is that it at least preserves peace and quiet, but it really does so only in the short run. In the atmosphere of repressed conflict, poisonous fear, hatred, and paranoia build and erupt periodically, as we see in recent flare-ups over hate speech, demands for ethnic studies programs, and political correctness. And of course now a shrinking economy is depriving universities of the luxury of avoiding fear and conflict by adding new "suburbs."

Q. How is all this related to your critique of what you've call "the course fetish"?

A. For me the academic *course*, which so frequently idealized in the rhetoric of community, is in some ways the ultimate expression of Damrosch's anti-community. The academic course does create a kind of community, but it does so at the expense of another, given the structural requirement that no course be aware of what goes on in any other course, that the left hand not know what the right is doing. That is, instructors must not know that the signals they send to students conflict in all kinds of ways, for again, dealing with such a recognition would require confronting repressed fears and accepting the responsibility of community. So it's important that we stay safely inside the protection of our courses. Of course, students have no such protection, being exposed every day to their teachers' conflicts in a way that their teachers are not.

Q. Your call for community makes you sound at times like Jane Tompkins, who has been writing (in essays like "Me and My Shadow" and "Pedagogy of the Distressed") about the competitive individualism and lack of community in academic institutions.

A. Yes, and I share Tompkins' complaint up to a point. But I'm not attracted to the kind of community Tompkins seems to want, which is emotional or physical rather than intellectual. For Tompkins intellectuality—argumentation, debate, analysis, reasoning—seems to be inherently selfish, competitive, and antithetical to the emotions and the body, part of the problem rather than part of the solution. For me the antidote to Damrosch's academic anticommunities lies in reconstructing rather than abandoning *intellectual* community, which need not and should not exclude emotion and the body.

A. What about the view of some feminists that that model of aggressive argumentation is essentially male?

Q. It's interesting that those feminists don't hesitate to use aggressively "male" argumentation in asserting that view when it suits them. Like Tompkins, such feminists (who do not speak for all feminists by any means) assume that community and intellectual argumentation are inherently incompatible. As if to make the critiques of demagogues like Christina Hoff Sommers look respectable, this thinking produces touchy-feely classrooms in which students get in touch with their own "voices" instead of learning to analyze, criticize, or make an argument. Teachers who practice this species of feminist pedagogy (which again must not be confused with feminist pedagogy as such) are in effect withholding from their students the cultural capital of argumentative discourse that they themselves command.

A. But haven't womens' studies programs established alternative models of community to the isolationism you attack?

Q. They've made a start, to be sure. But unless womens' studies programs themselves are put into regular dialogue with other sectors of the university, they become another of Damrosch's anticommunities, closing themselves off from threatening outsiders. It's unfair, however, to single out womens' studies and other new "revisionist" fields for "separatism," since these new fields are merely copying the time-honored, respectable separatism of established academic departments, whose maxim has always been: consolidate your own turf and wall yourself off from anybody who might disagree with you. In other words, my problem with the new politically oriented fields is not that they're acting like subversives but that they're acting like traditional academics.

Q. Are you suggesting a change in the culture war strategy of the academic Left?

A. Yes. The Left has achieved an impressive degree of academic power and solidarity (though nowhere near as much of either as its critics attribute to it). But the power and solidarity on the Left have been achieved by circling the wagons and talking primarily to itself rather than to outsiders. "Cultural studies," for example, has become a euphemism for Left Studies, meaning in effect that no admirers of Matthew Arnold need apply. Quite apart from the dubious ethics of such behavior, this strategy of preaching to the already converted may be successful awhile longer within the university, but it seems disastrous outside, where the Left is losing the struggle for the middle to the Right.

I think it's time therefore that the academic Left reopened negotiations with the rest of the university instead of occupying positions of "oppositional" purity. It's in the interests of the Left, in other words, to help create a real academic community (not just a subcommunity of opposition), in which it would be able to speak to others besides itself. Now that the main opponent is the Christian Coalition and the Contract with America, even academic "traditionalists" and "radicals" may have interests in common.

A. It's all well and good to talk about "community," but wouldn't such community seem intolerably coercive to those academics who unequivocally *like* their privacy or isolation?

Q. I wouldn't deny privacy to anyone. I just don't see why the whole university has to be organized to suit the people who want to avoid having a discussion!

10

Critical Personifications

❖

GILLIAN BROWN

As the title of this essay collection suggests, the rhetorical mode of late twentieth-century academic criticism appears to be confessional. Selected facts of critics' lives—such as body size, hair type, car preferences, travel encounters, sexual proclivities, familial, marital, and pedagogical relations, religious beliefs, fantasies, dreams, phobias, diseases—now regularly punctuate literary and cultural criticism. Any aspect of individual experience, however particular, can be included in what composes the critical ethos.

The rhetorical stature of personal details, their value as currency in critical discourse, consists not in their intimate nature and hence their proximity to and evidence for the truth a critic is telling. Rather, what is most telling about personal details is that they get told: that they get moved from the private to the public sphere. Personal details can be compelling only because they are public representatives of persons. Going public with information about one's person means charging that data with representational agency. Envoys and proxies of persons, personal data and details stand in for the persons they convey into print and public. They thus surmount as they emblemize the physical limits of the individual bodies that they represent. While a body can be in only one place at one time, its designated agents or stand-ins can extend and even magnify personal presence. Beyond individual bodies, personal matters can become types; in being typical, the personal attains a wider compass than bodies can enjoy.

In thus sublating the personal, confessional critics not only represent but surpass themselves. When critics include materials about themselves in their work, they transfer parts of themselves from their bodies to linguistic or other representational forms of their bodies. Whatever seems most essential to and about persons, most intrinsic to their existence, gains both magnitude and longevity when abstracted from a specific and finite corporeality. Transubstantiating critics' bodies, critical confessions can attain a wider and longer presence than bodies alone afford. Critics are therefore characteristically metaphysical, and perhaps most impatient with the metaphysical character and direction of their activities, when they are getting personal.

The profession of personal matters might, at first, seem a concretizing enterprise, especially since irreducibly corporeal matters now figure so prominently in criticism. The inventory of disclosure includes the body's pains and pleasures, what bodies experience by virtue of color, composition, constitution, condition, location, affiliation, capacity, time, desires, suffering—with all of these understood as cultural configurations. Obviously there are many differences in the critical uses, effects, and effectiveness of these various rhetorical instances of the personal as well as different valences to particular forms of the personal. Though directed toward sundry purposes, and conducted from diverse perspectives, critical acts of invoking personal essence invariably entail movement beyond the physical and experiential. The representational instrumentality of personal matters depends on the convertibility of the personal into the representative or typical. By this logic of transubstantiation, in which the value of the personal consists in its availability as a metamorphic object—indeed, upon not being personal—the confessional becomes authoritative. The personal gains force only by not remaining a discrete and individual entity.

As the qualities of persons become their emissaries, they become figures of speech. The rhetorical form in which persons most often appear, or in which the features of personhood are most vividly displayed and employed, is personification. Personification involves a transfer between persons and nonpersons that proceeds in two different directions. On one course, objects take on life or personality; things or animals come to appear as persons. On the other course, persons or human figures typify or embody some quality, thing, or idea. Persons become symbols, figurative materials. Both courses reveal an order of resemblance governing the definition of a person. In the first case, things or animals act or appear like persons: that is, they speak or think or have a gender. Personified entities are endowed with characteristics that only humans possess. The discrepancy between, for instance, a cat and the human speech with which the Cat in the Hat is so rhythmically adept, or between a train and the virtuous effortfulness of the Little Engine That Could, highlights particular human skills and traits. These linguistic and moral human attributes appear more vivid when ascribed to nonhumans, and thus suggest the special distinction available to all those who really can possess the same attributes. Resembling persons more than animals or machines, the facility of the Cat in the Hat or the Little Engine That Could furnishes persons with flattering models of themselves to imitate, or, depending upon the example and point of view, with negative models of themselves to repudiate.

On the second path of personification, an idea, thing, or quality attains its clearest expression, its best representation, in an imaginary or idealized human form. Personified embodiment traditionally confers perfection upon the corporeal representative, presenting in the form of a person the perfect example of something incorporeal. For a body to epitomize some quality or idea, as Cupid personifies love or Santa Claus, good cheer and beneficence, the body must (be conceived to) match what it symbolizes. Resembling what he or she typifies, the representative person suggests a proximity between persons and propensities. Again, just as the first path of personification shows a way for persons to choose to resemble models of themselves, the second path of personification likewise supplies paradigms of personhood. Persons embody magnified versions of human qualities with which they may associate, or from which dissociate, themselves. In the operations of personification, persons personify themselves in order to appraise and reconfigure the materials of personhood. Put another way, personifications provide persons with portrayals of themselves, patterns to be imitated or avoided or altered.

Personification is thus a technique for surveying the posssibilities and limits of human agency. Abstracted from historical (that is, real) persons, human traits appear in dramatic relief, as representative constituents of persons. A personification may amplify the excellence or evil or absurdity of particular human attributes, thereby developing a celebratory or critical account of humanity. Specific attributes become positive or negative standards of human activity. If persons readily furnish the matter of personification, personification provides a mode by which persons view and revise themselves.

When critics introduce something of themselves into their expositions of cultural forms (literary, cinematic, visual, or otherwise), they contribute new or different signs of personhood to the catalog of personifications. Such human qualities as faith, hope, and charity familiarly operate as freestanding agents. It makes sense to think of these attributes not just as motivations for our actions but as themselves agencies in action that we might then emulate or abjure. I am suggesting that more recent modern descriptive categories or designations of personhood have also attained the status of exemplary agents. Race, gender, and sexuality, for example, function not merely as human characteristics but as forms of agency. In concepts and terms like race memory, gender consciousness, sexual orientation, the very nomenclature for categories of individual experience remembers, perceives, or directs. Denominations of self such as race, gender, and sexuality do not simply operate adjectivally, specifying and qualifying persons, but also operate *as* persons—persons with whom individuals can identify themselves.

In light of the personifying function of personal data, the confessional style is a fitting and powerful technique for promulgating views about cultural formations of identity. Significantly, the present autobiographical vogue in criticism accompanies a vigorous critical engagement with what has come to be called identity politics: the interests of specific persons who identify themselves with, or are identified by others with, a set of persons possesssing some similar particular feature. In the common particularity of one's class or race or ethnicity or nationality or sex or gender or sexuality (to mention only the most prevalent categories of identification), a person finds her prototype. From the commonality of experience that a group of individuals share emerges a unit of identity, a representative figure, a persona.

Like other forms of personification, contemporary critical personifications of identity appeal to resemblance. What is crucial about resemblance for contemporary critical discourse, however, is not only the possible likeness between persons and human properties, but the proliferation of persons that a standard of similitude can generate. By resemblance to a standard or prototype of personhood, individuals once excluded from recognition and rights qualify for personhood and its entitlements. Submitting different materials to the personifying procedures of resemblance widens the scope of personhood, allowing previously unentitled individuals to secure (more of) the title and rights of persons in modern society. This is precisely what late twentieth-century feminists have attempted to accomplish by implementing the dictum that the personal is the political. In stressing personal experience as an epiphenomenon of politics, this dictum generalizes and substantiates the particular experiences of women. Collectivizing and publicizing female individual experience—hitherto private matters such as rape, sexual harrassment, domestic violence, childbirth, menstruation, menopause, and employment and income discrimination—circulate types with which women can identify. In the respectability of numbers, a woman's experience and testimony gain density, probability, and valence.

Like other platforms in the public sphere—radio and television talk shows, advice columns, personal newspaper ads, interviews, memoirs, tabloids, gossip magazines, e-mail bulletin boards—contemporary literary and cultural criticism is a stage on which individuals emphasize what they take to be the crucial matters of individualities, the definitive materials of persons. Making these matters public, making them count as markers for persons, critical confessions solicit authority for the individuals that they personify. The confessional style thus highlights the individual not only by the use of personal voice and anecdote but by the invocation of types of personal experience written large. Individual experience gains credit and force in numbers. As the specificity of individuality emerges as a representative experience of many individuals, the personal does not disappear. Rather, the personal attains a greater authority by virtue of being typical.

Yet anxiety rather than confidence about critical authority pervades contemporary criticism. What critics most recently have been telling, with varying degrees of charm and candor and clarity, and for very different purposes, are stories about the limitations of critical authority. Acknowledging the presence of bias and conditionality in criticism as well as in culture, late twentieth-century critics debate what authority, if any, can be accorded perspectives that are necessarily partial. Identity politics and its rhetorical medium of confession have emerged in the wake of the poststructuralist critique of the authority of the individual subject. Since Lacan's explication of subjectivity as fragmentary and provisional (an insight also developed in Saussure's linguistics, Lévi-Strauss's anthropology, Foucault's history, Kristeva's semiotics, and de Man's deconstruction, to mention only a few of the primary poststructuralist influences), identity appears a matter beyond the self's mastery. Poststructuralists stress the subject's constitution in culture, its interpenetration with cultural symbolic orders. Rather than developing and directing themselves, individual subjects register the interests that control or circulate through the symbolic orders they inhabit.

One way to understand the contemporary prominence of personal details in criticism, then, is to see it as an acknowledgment of poststructuralist insights about the positionality of any and all subjects in language, culture, and history. Drawing attention to individual experience, the critic underscores the particularity as well as partiality of any critical view. From this perspective, the invocation of personal experience is a confession of critical limits, of one's bias or ignorance or historical horizon. At the same time, however, such confession can amount to a claim of critical authority based upon one's very limitations. Proclaiming or apologizing for personal limitations, critics present themselves as figures of critical inadequacy—they personify their critical fallibilities. The very conditionality and interestedness of criticism thus become critical objects, the figures of speech that critics now use, study, and teach. The recitation of *mea culpa* enables the critic to continue professing because the recitation is now the content, indeed the *raison d'être,* of her profession. A penitential stance accordingly allows a critic to do what she initially disavows: to claim authority. Professed awareness of one's necessarily limited perspective—often called critical self-consciousness—

furnishes the critic with features mirroring the fractured nature of existence. In other words, the critic adopts the personality accorded to the culture she studies. Matching the poststructuralist description of identity, the critic claims the prerogative granted by resemblance: the choice of personhood.

For unrepresented and underrepresented individuals, the poststructuralist focus on the provisionalities of subjectivity threatens to eliminate the status of personal matter that they want to attain. Another way to read the prevalence of the rhetoric of the personal, then, is to see it as an explicit rejection of, rather than an accommodation to, the poststructuralist conception of the subject as a fantasy of wholeness and independence. Against a perceived disappearance of subjects, identity politics promotes personal realities and perspectives, reasserting the authority of individual experience. Returning to the individual as a locus of authority, identity politics seeks to increase the number of subjects recognized by cultural canons and entitled to civil rights. To achieve this goal, identity politics tethers the personal to the typical, conceiving fully recognized individuals from representative excluded figures. Thus, in criticism and syllabi, a new paradigm of authority has emerged, embodied in the most disenfranchised. Critical authority discovers an ideal model of itself in figures of the disenfranchised whose individual bodies come to count (or to matter more) when they become typical—standard forms of being. In the imagined bodies of the disenfranchised, just as in the rhetorical figures of critical fallibility, critics find more substance and warrant for their undertakings. This is not in any way to trivialize the importance of rhetorical tactics in securing recognition for the disenfranchised, but to highlight how the disenfranchised have become a conventional personification of critical authority.

Whether critics style their confessions after or against poststructuralist formulae, their confessions follow the paths of personification in order to claim, or more precisely, reassert critical authority, to reestablish it as they reorient it. In the present ethos of anxiety and controversy about authority, critical discourse now often entails showing some kind of identity papers: not actually an admission of something about oneself but a professional credential composed of personal matter. By this formality of disclosure, critics acquire exemplary forms, bodies in which the singularity of bodies can be both recognized and sublated. The rehabilitation of persons that personification epitomizes provides a progressive model for critical activities: a vista of new, improved models, of ever-better bodies. It is not just a flattering portrait that critics get from their personifications, but a protean facility to take other shapes. Personification makes available a stock of essences for critics to sample.

Yet, if critical personifications seem to offer an endless supply of corporeality and authority to criticism, the most significant feature of personified bodies is their intangibility. They are, as the saying goes, beyond criticism.

The best advantage of a significant body—of a personified figure—is its imperviousness to judgment. In personification, critics gain both the authority accorded exemplary bodies and the immunity of forms, a simultaneous critical identity and anonymity. The hide-and-seek movements of critical personifications exhibit the truly *ad hominem* and *ad feminam* project of criticism: to merge persons only to disengage and then have the last and most authoritative word.

11

Overcoming "Auction Block"

Stories Masquerading as Objects

❖

MARJORIE GARBER

> The immediacy of the auction, the split-second to make up the mind before the hammer falls, when added to man's naturally acquisitive nature provides a formula which few are able to resist.
> —Brian Learmount, *A History of the Auction*

The first things we bought were an old pine table and a concrete chicken.

"Is there anybody here who has never been to an auction before? Raise your hands." The auctioneer reassured neophytes. "That's it. That's all you have to do to be an auction-goer—raise your hand."

It was a dank mid-spring weekend on Nantucket, the island of whaling captains, lightships, canny Quaker merchants (R.H. Macy, the department-store magnate, was an early inhabitant), and, most recently, vacationers and tourists. We had just taken title on a part-eighteenth-century cottage full of wide board pine floors and rental furniture. And we wandered into the auction in part because there was nowhere else to go in April on Nantucket, and in part because we'd never been to one.

Like all losses of innocence, this one was at once exciting, nervous-making, and risible. Unfamiliar apparatus—in this case paper plates with numbers written on them in Magic Marker, to be waved by the bidder and displayed once the booty was won—and a ritualized language, full of evocative cadences: "one-hundred-ten dollars, one-twenty, one-thirty is where? one-thirty, one-forty, one-fifty anywhere? one-forty once, one-forty twice . . .

one-fifty, thank you, one-fifty, one-sixty. . . ." The suspense, and the deferred gratification—would once and twice ever culminate in three times, in the climax of going, going, gone (just like in the movies?)—kept up our interest, as did the logistics of competitive desire. The erotics of the auction are complete and satisfying. Here, if anywhere, is mimetic desire in play. Why do those people want *that* chest of drawers, *that* armoire, *that* folk art pig, rather than the other one? Is it the dovetailing of the drawers, the bun feet on the armoire (how quickly we picked up the infralanguage of auctionese)? Who could possibly want a large green bronze garden frog? Or an antique potty-chair (a surefire seller at country auctions)? That little side table, the one we said we had no use for—it's going really cheap. Up with the hand or the paper plate. We can always find a place for it. "Gone! Your number please, the lady in the second row? You—you got it—it's yours."

So it was with the concrete chicken. It was part of a whole menagerie of masonry—a birdbath, some crouching lions, a frog. It looked pert—and it was going cheap. Twenty-five dollars (I remember—it's quite symptomatic—the auction price I've paid for just about everything in the house, by now dozens of items) and it was ours. With the pine table—the real object of desire—still to come.

The pine table, still the centerpiece of the kitchen, represented an object lesson of its own. We've bought a lot of pine pieces since—an old grain bin, three (or maybe four) trunks, a dry sink, a meat safe (do these archaisms mean anything to you? needless to say, both are just furniture to us, we neither wash in the sink nor store food in the safe), several farm tables, two armoires: but this first pine table, its surface scratched and stained—as the auctioneer says, "it has some age to it" (a euphemism that could mean ten years or a hundred)—taught us the best, and most dangerous, auction lore of all. *You can get it if you want it.* If you really want it. If you want it enough to keep bidding. At least at country auctions.

I don't know why I always thought auction bidding was an arcane technique. Sometimes it is. Sometimes you can hit the bounces just right (one hundred, one-fifty, two hundred to you, two-twenty-five?) which means, among other things, catching the auctioneer's eye (if he skips over you twice, the bidding will have escalated before you get in the rhythm, like entering the dance floor or the roller rink from the side benches) and, above all, playing the rule of the hundred-dollar barrier adroitly. (Many bidders will hesitate to go over, or up to, a new hundred level. That is, they will bid two hundred seventy-five dollars but quail at three hundred, or, more frequently, quit at three hundred. If you're willing to bid three-twenty-five you can almost always win, since your competitors fear that you will keep on rolling. We've bought a lot of things for one bid over the hundred mark.

But with the pine table, that first pine table, the bidding was perfectly straightforward, and we kept bidding and the others dropped out, and it was ours. Amazing. Our first auction and we'd got what we'd come for. Now we were hooked.

I should pause here to say a word about the "we" of all this. My most adroit move in all of this auction-going—and we've now been to lots of auctions—was to delegate the actual bidding to my partner. It's I who have the desire for *things,* and she who has the interest in the game (there's a confession). Where Barbara is not only indifferent but actively resistant to retail shopping (that is, in a store) she finds auctions a combination of strategic challenge and erotic satisfaction, with a periodic dose of anthropomorphizing empathy thrown in (nobody wants that writing desk? But it's a *nice* little writing desk. If nobody else wants it, we should ... "Fifty!"). She's about to teach a new course on "Persons and Things," and our auction-going has, I contend, provided a template and a rhetoric for such speculations. So I get the object, and fall energetically to work Bri-waxing and buffing it, while Barbara gets the thrill of conquest, and a new vocabulary to go along with it. Left bids. Rose medallion china. Firkins and dough tables. An old-er chair with new-er paint. This last is the auctioneer covering his vulnerabilities—last summer some people apparently protested against being sold reproduction furniture (albeit at bargain prices) when they thought they were getting a "real" bargain, that is, a nineteenth-century immigrant's trunk for two hundred dollars. Summer tourist auction-goers want a story—with themselves as Bargainman, the feckless antique detector—more than they want the item they're bidding on. I'm reminded of my favorite sentence from the work of psychiatrist Robert J. Stoller, "A fetish is a story masquerading as an object."[1]

Auctioneers—perhaps especially auctioneers with captive populations, like summer tourists or island-dwellers—make it their business to excel at storytelling. This "primitive chair" came from a house belonging to "one of the oldest families on the island"; that pencil sketch is from the hand of an artist "familiar to everyone on Nantucket"; the Pembroke table is walnut— "well, it looks to me like walnut"; the platter "appears to be old," or, again, "to have some age to it"; the Oriental rugs are selling for less than half what it would cost you *wholesale.* "A quick story," says our local auctioneer, just about every week (he runs two auctions each weekend), and then launches into the same account of a man who bought a rug from him and then checked with two rug dealers "in Pennsylvania": the rug he had bought for $700 was available at one dealer's showroom for $7,000 and at the other for $9,000. Then the punchline: "but at the second dealer's it was on half price sale." The story is not quick, but its point is effective. And even when we ourselves figure in the story ("this little white table [a charitable description of one of our pieces of inherited rental furniture, remanded to the auctioneer for resale] comes from a beautiful home right here on the island") we are in general persuaded by the rhetoric: on an island, a barter economy makes sense, as does recycling. Whether or not we find compelling an abstract literary-theo-retical concept like "the circulation of social energy," we approve in practice of pragmatic materialism, the circulation of social goods. For the same reason, the island garbage dump has a section labeled "take it or leave it," where one person's discard becomes another person's proud new possession. "I found that ginger jar lamp on the dump," I heard one householder explain with pride, in the course of one of the house tours that are periodic Saturday entertainments on island.

Nantucket has at present two auctioneers, not one, vying for the business of natives and tourists. One is long-established, smooth, and apparently knowledgeable about furniture, jewelry, and objets d'art; the other—the one I've been describing—an up-and-coming entrepreneur, bumptious, comic (both intentionally and inadvertently), and a quick study, though given to moodiness. Sometimes he will lecture his audience about their supposed indifference to his wares; at other times he's manic, performing little vaude-ville routines that I find tiresome (remember, I'm really only interested in the merchandise) but that others, on balance, appear to regard as entertaining. The most amusing episodes, though, are those that are clearly improvised, like the evening three men held up a set of abstract painted screens ("by Bobby Bushong, the well-known island artist, the brother of Polly Bushong," the even better-known island artist). Part of the fascination of auctions always comes with the act of displaying whatever the item is—a rug, a table, a pair of andirons—it is held up for admiring scrutiny for as long as the bidding lasts. Three or four assistants are on hand to do the exhibiting, which can be arduous, when the item is heavy or awkward, and sometimes comes to nothing, if the initial bidding is not high enough, and the auctioneer decides to "pass" on it. It's a rule of thumb that everything, however bulky or improbable, gets displayed; if it's a set of eight chairs, all eight are held up, two to a person.

With the Bobby Bushong screens, an un-Colonial yellow-and-orange pattern and a hard sell (they'd been around for several auctions without a nibble from the audience) the three men holding them up had, it was evident, little faith in the desirability of their wares. They stood side by side, each holding up a huge panel which completely hid them except for their feet. "They're out of order," someone in the audience shouted; the pattern, however abstract, had a discernible sequence. Dutifully, the men changed places. "Still out of order." They changed places again. "No, no." At this point the three men began a kind of morris dance, changing and exchanging positions, three rectangular panels moving solemnly on little sneakered feet. We broke down with laughter, at the combination of the formal moves, the ridiculous screens, and the amused assistants, happy to be toting canvas rather than mahogany at that late hour. I can't recall whether the screens sold, but they must have, because they never appeared again. (They're probably now installed in "one of the finest houses on the island," from which they will emerge again in a few years if the auctioneer stays in business.) A similar round-robin occurred with a kind of bench cum low table, clearly marked with indentations for the human bottom, a five-seater, as the auctioneer and four henchmen gleefully demonstrated. And with the box of ladies' hats modeled by one stalwart displayman. And with the rowing machine demonstrated by a blond male assistant with the impervious good looks usually described as belonging to "a Greek god." "Does he come with it?" a lady in the audience asked. As it happened, he did not.

The brash, entrepreneurial auctioneer on Nantucket violates one apparently cardinal practice of auctioneering, which is the list of items inventoried. If you attend the auction preview, get a list, and find that you are interested, say, in items 278 and 304, you can usually show up some three or four hours into the auction (seventy to ninety items an hour is the going rate for the more experienced auctioneer here) and be in plenty of time to bid on your chosen objects. But if there's no list, you have to be there for the whole time, lest your fancy be gone by the time you show up. This happened to one young couple who had their hearts set on an antique pine sideboard, the kind of item that usually doesn't come up until fairly late in the auction, after the audience has been limbered up. On this occasion, however, someone requested that it be put up early, it fetched a good price, and was sold before the young people arrived. All evening they kept mourning it, in disbelief.

The established auctioneer, by contrast, does have a list, filled with enticing and mystified descriptions: "Green Tole Chinoiserie Tray on Custom Bamboo Turned Stand; Mahogany Canterbury with Tiger Maple Drawer; Custom Burl Demilune Hall Table; Sailboats Patchwork Quilt Made by Mrs. Balton of York, Nebraska, 1933; Large Carved and Polychromed Duck". He, too, has his familiar routines—novel the first time you hear them. An antique hairbrush, comb, or jewel case is inlaid with "mother of pearl, father of John." Tablecloths come with large, "pasta-sized" napkins. He is determinedly if unreflectively heterosexist; jewelry is always thought to be purchased by men, for their wives, and when he tries on an opera-length rope of cultured pearls it's always good for a laugh. One of his tricks—especially effective before you realize that it is a staple—is to pick out, and then pick on, some unappealing object that isn't selling: a quilt in strident shades of yellow and green, for instance, or pair of portraits of someone's rather dour-looking ancestors. If no one bids on it, he'll dump on it ("get that ugly thing out of here"), even though he has sold, or lauded, arguably less prepossessing objects in the course of the auction. He'll do this with one and only one piece (or pair of pieces) per sale; the result is to suggest that he has taste and standards, and that the items he doesn't stigmatize are authentically attractive. To me this smacks of wallflower-bashing, especially in the case of the homely ancestors, whom I quite liked. Also, its not unheard-of that the wallflower of one auction becomes the swan (to mix my metaphors) of the next—this happened with the formerly-despised green and yellow quilt. But there's no gainsaying the fact that such techniques tend to humanize the process, and that that in turn speeds up sales.

The elegant auctioneer—and he is elegant, suave and cool-looking even in mid-July—handles some quite expensive items. When the bidding gets high—that is, over a thousand dollars— he frequently gives bidders time to consider before upping the ante, a courtly gesture that earns him points with me, and doubtless helps to produce satisfied rather than dismayed customers (the frenzy of bidding can sometimes lead to desire just for desire's sake, and result in a postauction depression when the object is finally in hand). When the bidding is high and spirited he also thanks the bidders who *don't* win, but who have bid up the price, another graciousness that is, I have since learned, a common practice, but that seems to impart a certain tone.

The most unexpected bidding war we've witnessed was for a collection of miniature carved wooden boats, a representation of the famous Nantucket "Rainbow fleet". This item—of no interest to me whatever, I was glad to note—started at about two hundred dollars and wound up, surprisingly, at over two thousand. Peanuts, of course, compared to Sotheby's and Christie's, but a hush came over the room as the bidding closed, and there was a spontaneous round of applause. At other times we'll be exhorted by this auctioner to "change your style of bidding!" which means that the next item he's putting up is worth a lot more than the ones that have preceded it. This tends to have the appropriate aphrodisiac effect—I still lament a magnificent black and red quilt sold under that intoxicating rubric—but, once again, it's not always clear that the praised item *is* of a different order of magnitude from its fellows. Instead of the wallflower the teen model here is the "popular girl" (and, indeed, the "popular boy") of high-school legend, never the most beautiful, but the one that everyone wanted to date, because everyone else wanted to. Another good lesson in the arbitrariness of desire.

The most fascinating thing about the elegant auctioneer, however, is not his ability to impart and direct desire, but rather his astonishing continence. He starts his auctions at ten in the morning and ends at five or five thirty in the afternoon, and never excuses himself to go to the bathroom. We are completely in awe of this performance, and dying to ask him how he does it (does he fast the day before, and abstain from liquids? do all auctioneers? does he wear a catheter?) but have never gotten up the courage. There is no question, though, but that this adds to his mystique; the up-and-coming auctioneer, by contrast, drinks water and Diet Pepsi by the glassful, sometimes breaks the furniture he's exhibiting by standing on it or abruptly pulling out a drawer, and has been known to absent himself for a few minutes, handing the auction tasks over to a confederate, while he leaves the room. Human, all too human, we think. But we spend most of our money with him.

Our experience is almost exclusively with the American country auction, a kind of upscale, competitive flea market. I've been to a couple of auctions that were more solemn, even hushed occasions, where the auctioneer is more obviously a "professional person," like a surgeon or a mortician, brought in for a special purpose, announcing his expectations in an authoritative monotone ("two hundred, I have two hundred, thank you now three hundred, three hundred I have four hundred. . . ."); less fun, higher prices. I have never been to Sotheby's or Christie's, though I know many people who have, and came away with what they declared to be bargains. I've seen, with some pleasure, the John Malkovitch movie *The Object of Value,* which concludes with an auction scene so upscale and hushed that the bidding is barely perceptible, and the prices astronomical—decidedly not a raucous occasion.

Anglo-American assumptions to the contrary notwithstanding, the so-called "English auction," in which bids are taken in ascending order, is only one of several possible auction modes. The "Dutch auction" or "upside down auction" (again, the perspective is Anglo-American) works in the reverse fashion, the auctioneer calling out quotations in descending order until someone accepts the price; this is often used for the sale of commodity lots, like fresh fish. The "Japanese auction" involves simultaneous bidding by many prospective buyers, all raising their hands or shouting at once.

There are also time-interval methods, one of the most picturesque of which, popular in Great Britain in the seventeenth century, utilizes a burning candle; bids are only accepted while the candle stays lit, and the last bid "before the final flicker" takes the lot, or, as in the case of a 1932 auction, the tenancy of an estate.[2] A sand glass could also be used to the same effect. Then there is the "handshake auction," said to have originated in ancient China, in which buyers standing in a semicircle each squeeze the auctioneer's fingers, which are covered discreetly by a piece of cloth. The number of squeezes, multiplied by the figure orally given ("tens"; "hundreds") indicates the amount offered. The bidder can disguise his intentions from others by grasping fewer fingers and squeezing more frequently, and may secretly cancel the bid by scratching the auctioneer's palm as he is bidding. Obviously, this is a technique which gives some latitude to the auctioneer in selecting the high bidder. The same is true of the "whispered bid" auction, reportedly in practice in Singapore, Manila, and Venice, in which the buyers each whisper bids in the auctioneer's ear, without knowing what their competitors are offering, a method which is less painful than the handshake but equally open to favoritism or corruption, and more suited to commodities—fish, agricultural crops—than to art and antiques, or what are these days referred to as "collectibles," a self-referential term describing anything anyone cares to collect.[3]

In fact, as this quick tour of alternative auction modes suggests, the auction as social and anthropological event is an ideal topic for today's cultural studies critics. Consider this random sampling of items recently auctioned off for high prices: rock-and-roll related memorabilia auctioned by Sotheby's in New York, including Buddy Holly's homework (biology, math, and Latin; the auction catalogue specifies that some lots are signed and others unsigned); Jimi Hendrix's Pam Am Flight bag (Pan Am, like Hendrix, now only a memory trace), and a "Reserved" table card, marked "For guests of the Bruce Springsteen band." The London Sotheby's, for its part, has sold English straw boaters once owned (and worn?) by Elton John, and several pairs of John Lennon's sunglasses.[4]

All sports items are currently very hot, from old golf clubs to baseball cards, the kind that used to be given out free in packets of chewing gum (a baseball card from 1910 depicting shortstop Honus Wagner was sold to ice hockey star Wayne Gretsky and a partner for $451,000, about four times the previous record).[5] A baseball jersey belonging to former New York Yankees star Mickey Mantle, signed, twenty-five years later, by Mantle, went for big bucks, as did two 1930s seats from Fenway Park, the home of the Boston Red Sox baseball team, described in the auction catalogue as "in fine oak with original monster green paint [the high left field wall of Fenway is colloquially known as the "Green Monster"] and elaborate iron railings."[6]

Comic books, that other reliable index of popular culture, are likewise skyrocketing, with Batman, predictably—in view of his movie celebrity—fetching the highest prices among superheroes,[7] and celluloid images of cartoon characters doing still better: early Mickey Mouse, for example, and that darling of the cartoon counterculture, Bart Simpson, immortalized in a nicely meta-auction moment, "Bart Auctions His Sister Maggie."[8]

At the opposite end of the scale from the inflated celebrity or pop culture auction are other signs of the times: items auctioned by the New York City Post Office because the addresses on their packages were illegible, incomplete, or wrong (a suit of armor, a camel saddle, a pair of panties with a built-in cassette player),[9] and, in every local newspaper, pages and pages of home foreclosure auctions, or what is known in some circles as "distressed real estate";

as the *Boston Globe* recently noted, "The economy goes bust, and auctioneer-ing goes boom."[10]

Historically the auction has often been the site of (non)differentiation between persons and things. The earliest known Western reference to auction technique, perhaps predictably, is the description in Herodotus' *Histories* of a Babylonian marriage market in which the auctioneer in each village began each year with the best-looking girl of marriageable age and went down the line to the least attractive. For the latter he sought to find the lowest price the *bidder* would accept—in effect a kind of dowry.[11] (Discovering this not only made me feel feminist outrage but also gave a further ironic twist to my anthropomorphizing of objects as "wallflowers" and "popular kids." Clearly I identified with the uncharismatic ancestors and the leftover Babylonian maidens rather than with the "Very Fine 19th Century Golden Oak Roll-Top [Tambour] Desk.")

The ancient Romans held auctions to sell house contents and liquidate property, as well as to dispose of war booty.[12] The word "auction" itself comes from the Latin word for "increase," and what was auctioned as a result of conquest was not only goods but also captive peoples sold as slaves.

The most notorious modern accounts of slave auctions, of course, come from records of the American Old South, where human beings were prodded and examined like dray horses. Frederic Bancroft provides a poignant account of the cosmetic dressing-up of slaves for the auction block in coats, pants and waistcoats, strong shoes, and hats or turbans; of the "indifference" of purchasers and spectators to the nudity of slaves, male and female, stripped for inspection; of the artificial lifting of the slaves' spirits by "gifts" of liquor, tobacco, or candy, to make a better show; of the irony of some slaves' competition between themselves to see who could fetch a better price, "as money was the measure of a slave's value," and of the auctioneer's practised patter, curiously rendered in three pages of fictionalized dialect as if in direct observation and quotation:

> come heah, boy. None o' yo' gentlemen don't want no likelier boy'n him. Now, do I heah *six?* Thank yo', Jedge. Six hundud dollahs is bid fo' this prime lot, but he's wo'th three hundrud *mo'.* Six; make it six fifty; six say *fifty,* give me *fifty,* go *fifty; fif-ty*—do I—heah? . . . "Six-*thirty*" someone called out. And the auctioneer again rattled out the figures and sputtered the short phrases, sweeping every face with his rapid glance, sure to detect the slight-est nod or expression of assent, and all the while speaking, moving, gesticu-lating and occasionally clapping his hands with a rhythm that had a fascination. . . . And once more he juggled the phrases, then slackened and drawled his speech: "*Seven—hun-dud*—an'—five—*is*—bid; let me have *ten; do I heah ten?* Yo'll *lose* 'im! Ah you-all *done?* Seven-hundud—an' five—dol-

lahs! Once-twice—third—an'—*last*—call; goin', *goin'*" and as his right hand struck the palm of his left making a loud crack—"*sold fo' seven hundud an five dollahs* to Mr. Jenks."[13]

Having sat through several dozen Nantucket auctions—and Nantucket, incidentally, prides itself as being a hotbed of nineteenth-century Quaker abolitionism, the home of an early African-American meeting house, and the site of a major address by Frederick Douglass—I found the ritualized patter of Bancroft's composite slave trader disquietingly familiar. Rhetorically speaking "this prime lot" is always what is on offer, touted by what Florida's Jim Graham School for auctioneers describes as "The Professional Auction Chant." The Graham School, a quintessentially American how-to institution, also teaches aspiring professionals "How to Determine Values," "Bidders Body Language," and "True Self Confidence."[14] From the Old South to the New? The seduction of the personalized, "interactive" sales pitch, in an age of slick media packaging and impersonal merchandizing, has its own basilisk fascination—and its own power of narrative.

It is not that the auction is intrinsically a space where persons become things, but rather that its escalating mechanism of mimetic competition exposes the fragility, impermanence, and insistence of desire. It can be—though it is by no means always—a space for the contrary transmigration, the reminder that things, because they have belonged to people, take on some of their characteristics, their pride, their pathos.

What then does a cultural critic—a *psychoanalytic* cultural critic—seek, and find, in the rhythm and interchange of auction-going? Theater. Stand-up comedy. Fantasy. History. Above all, perhaps, a story. A story of discovery (a copy of the U.S. Declaration of Independence found in the backing of a flea market picture frame, later sold at auction for $2.4 million[15]). A story of provenance ("taken from one of the finest homes on the island"). A story of savvy personal enterprise and superior knowledge ("no one there knew what Pueblo pottery was worth. I got it for only. . . ."). Stories. Stories masquerading as objects. In today's technocommodity culture the country auctioneer's podium, like the lecture stand it so closely resembles, is one of the last vestiges of the narrative of community, a Home Shopping Channel where the other buyers are visible and audible. At least for the time being. Going, going . . . gone.

120 ❧ *Marjorie Garber*

Notes

1. Robert J. Stoller, M.D., *Observing the Erotic Imagination* (New Haven: Yale University Press, 1985), 155.

2. "A Curious Survival: Sale by Candle," *The Conveyancer,* XVII (May 1932), 138.

3. Ralph Cassady, Jr., *Auctions and Auctioneering* (Berkeley: University of California Press, 1967), 55–75.

4. Peter Watson, "With Due (and Undue) Pomp, Rock Upon the Block." *The New York Times,* July 14, 1991, section 2, H27.

5. Rita Reif, "Yesterday's Whatnots Set Auction Records," *The New York Times,* February 13, 1992, C1.

6. Rita Reif, "Auctions," *The New York Times,* July 19, 1991, C5.

7. Rita Reif, "Holy Record Breaker! $55,000 for First Batman Comic," *The New York Times,* December 19, 1991, C15.

8. Rita Reif, "Are Cartoons Still a Hot Ticket?" *The New York Times,* April 12, 1992, section 2, H33; Rita Reif, "Auctions," *The New York Times,* June 28, 1991, C25.

9. Eleanor Blau, "What's Lost in the Mail Is Found at Auction," *The New York Times,* November 7, 1991, B3.

10. Nathan Cobb, "Going Once, Going Twice. . .," *Boston Globe,* May 18, 1992, 41.

11. Herodotus, *The Histories of Herodotus,* trans. Henry Cary (New York: D. Appleton and Company, 1899), 77.

12. Frank Tenney, ed. "Rome and Italy of the Empire," *An Economic Survey of Ancient Rome,* V (Baltimore: Johns Hopkins University Press, 1940), 39–40 n. 12, 26 n. 47.

13. Frederic Bancroft, *Slave-Trading in the Old South* (Baltimore: J.H. Furst Co., 1931), 111.

14. Brian Learmount, *A History of the Auction* (London: Barnard & Learmount, 1985), 198.

15. Eleanor Blau, "Declaration of Independence Sells for $2.4 Million." *The New York Times,* June 14, 1991, C3.

12

Pictures of a Displaced Girlhood

❀

MARIANNE HIRSCH

for Angelika, Marta, and Mona

Displacement is an exile from older certitudes of meaning, a possibly permanent sojourn in the wilderness.

—Mark Krupnick

Borderlands are physically present wherever two or more cultures edge each other. . . . Living on borders and in margins, keeping intact one's shifting multiple identity and integrity, is like trying to swim in a new element, an "alien" element . . . not comfortable but home.

—Gloria Anzaldúa

I am sitting on an airplane crossing the Atlantic. It is September 1991, a few days before my birthday, and I am returning to the U.S. from a study trip through Kenya and Tanzania. This is the second leg of a long journey, and I am tired though happy to be going home after visiting so many unfamiliar places and feeling so much like an outsider, a tourist. I spend my time reading: it's what I most enjoy about airplane travel—reading in a state of suspension, a no-place between home and abroad which gives me the possibility of immersing myself entirely in the space of the book I have selected for the occasion. Only this time, I am not prepared for what happens. I am reading Eva Hoffman's *Lost in Translation*, a book I have owned since it was first published in 1989, but which I have put off even though friends have urged me to read it right away. Actually, I was going to get to it on a previous vacation but lost it on the way and had to wait to purchase it again when I came home. Now this trip is almost over, and I have finally settled into Hoffman. I am reaching the end of the first part of Hoffman's narrative, the end of her sea journey from Poland to Canada at the age of thirteen. *I discern the outlines of massive gray shapes against the cloudy sky,* I read. *Closer still, the shapes resolve into buildings, tall and monolithic to my eyes. Montreal. It actually exists, more powerful than any figment of the imagination. We look at the approaching city wordlessly. The brief* Batory *interlude is over and so is the narrative of my childhood.* (95) But now I can no longer see the page. Tears are flowing down my face, I realize I am sobbing. These sentences have released a loss whose depths I had never, until that moment, allowed myself to feel or remember.

❖

It is July, 1962. I am almost thirteen and I am crossing the Atlantic, from Brussels to New York, on only the second airplane journey I have ever taken. But I am not sitting by the window. I do not want to see the expanse of ocean that will separate me from the familiar world I am leaving behind forever and, indeed, from my childhood. I do not want to see the shapes of the cities, rivers, and mountains that are to be my new home, the spaces of my adolescence and adulthood. Am I reading a book on this trip? I don't remember—all I remember is crying through what feels like the entire flight (fourteen hours), crying with abandon in public, so that everyone can see that I do not want to go. I take some small pleasure in the tears and the attention they are getting me, especially from the handsome young Lufthansa steward, who keeps bringing me snacks and drinks so that I might stop. My parents have given up trying to make this move seem acceptable; they are just letting me cry as they deal with their own excitements and anxieties. But I know I am miserably unhappy, and I am determined to remain so. I con-tinue to cry as we land in New York, and as we go through the endless bureaucracies of immigration. I cry on the plane to Providence, Rhode Island, where, from a window seat, I see an empty expanse that seems totally unpopulated to the European eye. I cry as we are picked up at the airport by Mrs. Hoffmann (no relative of Eva's I'm sure) from the Jewish Family Service, and I cry as I enter the South Providence flat—the upper floor of a brown, wooden house on what looks like a desolate street—she has rented for our adjustment period. My mother waits for Mrs. Hoffman to leave. And then she too starts to cry.

❖

Eva Hoffman's story is my story, and the only lens through which I can read it is a totally unreconstructed form of identification—a response quite unfamiliar to someone who has been studying and teaching literature for twenty-five years, and one which makes me uneasy. Yet I recognize so many of the scenes she evokes. Like Hoffman, I too *come from the war,* from that generation of the immediate postwar in Eastern Europe which grew up hearing stories of hiding, persecution, extermination, and miraculous survival every day, and dreamt of them every night. *This—the pain of this—is where I come from, and . . . it's useless to try to get away.* I recognize myself in her portrait of *children too overshadowed by our parents' stories, and without enough sympathy for ourselves, for the serious dilemmas of our own lives* (230). Her Cracow is so much like my Bucharest, her parents' urban middle-class respectability and relative material comfort, and their simultaneous marginality and discomfort as Jews, so much like my parents'. Equally similar are our parents' far-reaching ambitions for their children's happiness and success, ambitions which do not offset the attitudes of *modernist nihilism* and deep skepticism with which they raised us. So many details are similar, down to the remedy for colds made from milk, egg yolk, and sugar (only my mother, unlike Eva's, never added chocolate, perhaps because cocoa was only rarely available). I too remember vividly the day of Stalin's death and the somber funerary marches through the city under the enormous images of Lenin and Stalin and "the two grandfathers" (as I called Marx and Engels). I still feel the *cognitive disjunction* in which my friends and I grew up, hearing at home that we are to disregard most of what we might hear at school. Around the same time, in the late fifties, her parents and mine made the enormous decision to get out—to leave the place that was both *home* and *hostile territory*—and at roughly the same age, Hoffman and I left behind the only world we knew.

It is with smiling recognition that I read Hoffman's first impressions of Vancouver; I nod through her bafflement at the shaggy bathroom rugs, at the toilet paper that comes in different colors, at her paralysis when it comes to choosing among brands of toothpaste. I recognize her inability to understand American humor, her incompetence at telling a joke. I empathize with the loss she experiences when her name is changed from Ewa to Eva—more slightly than mine, who had to switch from Marianne to a Mary Ann whose "r" I could not pronounce, making it "Mady Ann." *These new appellations which we ourselves can't yet pronounce, are not us. They are identification tags, disembodied signs pointing to objects that happen to be my sister and myself. We walk to our seats, into a roomful of unknown faces, with names that make us strangers to ourselves.* (105)

❧

The relentless rhythm of the wheels is like scissors cutting a three-thousand-mile rip through my life. From now on, my life will be divided into two parts with the line drawn by that train (100). The flight across the Atlantic is for me what the train ride through Canada is for Hoffman. That is why it is so hard for me to write about the period of transition—my adolescence. My childhood remained in Rumania. It is in Vienna that I have my first period, my first crush, wear my first stockings, try on lipstick. My first date, my first kiss, my first dances and parties, are all in Providence. That's where I lose my pudginess, grow another two inches (or is it two centimeters?), have my teeth straightened, become a teenager. But which of those changes are due to chronology, which to geography? I have never been able to sort them out. I remember during my year in Vienna being unable to find a single comfortable item of clothing—everything itches and scratches, everything feels wrong against my skin, everything makes me miserable. Is that because I have just turned twelve, gotten my period and am going through puberty, or is it because everything I wear is too childish and totally "square" by Viennese standards, and I go through each day feeling wrong, ashamed, out of place? I try to make the transition from ankle socks to nylon stockings, from soap and water to face creams, makeup and cologne, from sandals to heels, from childish freedom to flirting and an obsessive interest in boys in the space of a few weeks, but what is the cost? What gets silenced and censored in the process? And how do I manage, in the space of another few adjustment weeks, to make a second transition to small-town American teenagehood—another set of rules and standards, for me only another set of *faux pas* and embarrassments? Like Hoffman, I feel *less agile and self-confident with every transformation. I hold my head rigidly, so that my precarious bouffant doesn't fall down, and I smile often, the way I see other girls do, though I'm careful not to open my lips too wide or bite them, so my lipstick won't get smudged.... In its elaborate packaging, my body is stiff, sulky, wary. When I'm with my peers, who come by crinolines, lipstick, cars, and self-confidence naturally, my gestures show that I'm here provisionally, by their grace, that I don't rightfully belong* (109, 110). Like Hoffman, *I'm a pretend teenager among the real stuff* (118).

But does any girl *come by crinolines, lipstick, cars and self-confidence naturally*? Were my discomfort and Hoffman's the result of our cultural displacement, or were they due to a chronological transition that teenage culture and the demands of adult femininity have made inherently and deeply unnatural for even the most comfortably indigenous American girl? In their recent research into female adolescence, Carol Gilligan and her colleagues find that girls use images of violent rupture, death, and drowning when they describe the transition between childhood and adolescence, a transition they locate between the ages of twelve and thirteen. Gilligan's reading of Margaret Atwood's poem, "This is a Photograph of Me," allows her to characterize this transition topographically as a form of displacement. When she moves out of childhood and into adolescence, Atwood's persona simply disappears by drowning. As she describes the lake, the poet locates herself at the center, beneath its surface.

> It is difficult to say where
> precisely, or to say
> how large or small I am
> . . . but if you look long enough,
> eventually
> you will be able to see me.

Around the age of thirteen, Gilligan suggests, girls lose their place: without their voice and their certainty, they become "divided from their own knowledge, regularly prefacing their observations by saying 'I don't know'" (*Making Connections*, 14). Whatever knowledge they preserve from their earlier selves must go underground; if they want to preserve or to perpetuate it they must "join the resistance." Gilligan describes this underground world as a "remote island," implying that every transition into female adulthood is a process of acculturation to an alien realm or, could one say, an experience of emigration? The lessons of femininity acquired during adolescence, therefore, require a move into a different culture with a different language. Girls must unlearn what they knew as they gain, sometimes through gestures of mimicry and impersonation, new skills and new selves.

But if, for American girls, to move into adolescence feels like emigrating to a foreign culture and learning the new language of femininity under patriarchy, what additional pressures confront girls like Hoffman and myself who, in addition to learning the language of patriarchy, literally had to learn the English language and American culture? Reading Carol Gilligan's work on adolescent girls has been an astounding discovery for me, who had, like Hoffman, attributed my awkwardness and alienation to my status as a "newcomer," and was therefore unable to perceive the similar discomfort and alienation of my female peers. At my recent twenty-fifth high school reunion, classmates confessed their own insecurities, but remembered me as completely "together" even as early as tenth grade—only a year after I came. I can only marvel at my own powers of impersonation, but I realize now what I could not see then: that they also had to exercise a form of mimicry in their performances of feminine behavior. Yet unlike theirs, my own and Hoffman's process of unlearning and learning, of resisting and assimilating was a double one which must have been doubly difficult to negotiate. It must have left us doubly displaced and dispossessed, doubly at risk, perhaps doubly resistant to assimilation. If most girls leave their "home" as they move into adolescence, Hoffman and I left two homes—our girlhood and our Europe. But, despite the common structure, the effects of this double displacement were different for me and for Hoffman, as were the strategies of relocation we were able to develop.

❖

On the cover of my paperback edition of *Lost in Translation* there is a picture of a photo album, set at an angle, facing a beautiful pink flower. A small, black-and-white photograph, mounted with old-fashioned, black triangles, shows two little girls in a bleak-looking forest or park. It's clearly autumn, the leaves are on the ground, and the two little girls in the photo are wearing winter coats and hats. Presumably the older girl (she seems to be six or seven) is Eva, and the younger, who must be about four, is her sister Alina. Eva is smiling self-confidently as she protectively puts her arm around her sister in her plaid coat, white tights, and high-top boots. Alina looks more tentative, less comfortable. This is Eva (or Ewa) in the Polish surroundings she inhabits with such effortless comfort, the home which in her book is cast as *paradise* and *the safe enclosures of Eden.* Later Hoffman describes another photo, one she obviously rejected as an image for the cover of her book: *About a year after our arrival in Vancouver, someone takes a photograph of my family in their backyard, and looking at it, I reject the image it gives of myself categorically. This clumsy looking creature, with legs oddly turned in their high-heeled pumps, shoulders bent with the strain of resentment and ingratiation, is not myself* (110). A third photograph described towards the end of *Lost in Translation* mediates Hoffman's astonished reunion, in New York, with a childhood friend from Cracow: *In this picture three little girls are standing on a riverbank holding hands and showing off the daisy wreaths on their heads. I remember the day when this picture was taken quite distinctly—the excursion on the Vistula during which we disembarked on a picnic, and how the three of us looked for flowers to wave those wreaths, something little girls in Poland did during those days. But as Zofia and I look back and forth from the photograph to each other, we feel the madeleine's sweet cheat: "Oh my God," Zofia keeps saying in mixed delight and befuddlement. We can't jump over such a large time canyon. The image won't quite come together with this moment* (222). The two women are unable to *recapture their past.* At this point I wonder about Hoffman's obsession with the canyon, with a disjunction that defines her life and her book: I begin to notice the pervasive nostalgia that clings to everything Polish. Suddenly alienated by the way she has constructed her story, I resist identification, start shaking my head in disagreement, resent her for breaking the ease with which I had been making my way through her book.

The three photographs trace Hoffman's journey from *paradise* into *exile* and to *the new world*. In *paradise*, she is at home with herself, smiling self-confidently; in *exile*, she has become not herself, someone she is forced to reject, denigrate. *The new world* is defined by the unbridgeable canyon at the center of her life. Eva and Zofia can look at the photo, but they cannot recapture their childhoods. They cannot find themselves—for Eva locates herself more in that childhood image than in her adulthood. An adult in New York, a Harvard Ph.D., an American writer, Eva still describes herself as a newcomer, an immigrant, unable to read her husband's emotions, unable to feel comfortable in English. Her friends are always either *Polish* or *American*; to them she remains, throughout her over thirty years on this side of the Atlantic, a foreigner, a *silly little Polish person*. When she describes relationships with friends and lovers, it is to point out how differently she sees the world from them; it is to analyze their consensus and her own exclusion. Even when she feels that she is in her world (*I fit, and my surroundings fit me*), her consciousness splits off, and there is *an awareness that there is another place—another point at the base of the triangle, which renders this place relative, which locates me within that relativity itself* (170). This doubleness and relativity I understand, but I cannot identify with Hoffman's nostalgic attempt to overcome it by returning to her Polish childhood. Her discomfort with her present double vision is clearly motivated by her construction of Poland (or is it childhood?) unequivocally as paradise, home of *the first things, the incomparable things, the only things. It's by adhering to the contours of a few childhood objects that the substance of our selves—the molten force we're made of—molds and shapes itself. We are not yet divided* (74). Thinking about my own experience, I want her to see that in Poland, as a child, she was already divided.

As I continue to read, I am more and more bothered by the contradictions between the Edenic construction of Cracow—her smile in the cover photo—and the prehistory of her parents' hiding in a *branch-covered forest bunker during the war*—perhaps the same forest where the two little girls' picture is taken? What repressions are behind the feeling that Cracow is *both home and the universe* when only a few years before all of her parents' relatives had died there, including her aunt who *was among those who had to dig their own graves, and . . . her hair turned gray the day before her death* (7). What does it take for Hoffman to consider this place *paradise*? Why would she want to recapture a childhood that rests on such a legacy? Hoffman's denial is painful to read, yet it is basic to her construction of her narrative and her world, of her self: *this is real*, she says about the eyewitness account of her aunt's death. *But is it? It doesn't have the same palpable reality as the Cracow tramway. Maybe it didn't happen after all, maybe it's only a story, and a story can be told differently, it can be changed.* With her evocation of childhood plenitude, Hoffman has displaced the reality of the war, of the anti-Semitism she admittedly still experiences, but which she simply dismisses by calling it *primitive*. Canada, to her own Polish self, was *an enormous cold blankness*, but to her parents, in their wartime forest confinement, it spoke *of majestic wilderness, of animals roaming without being pursued, of freedom*. Born of this prison-house imagination, Canada is freedom, but, in spite of so many assurances to the contrary, Hoffman, in what may well be an understandable childish strategy of survival, has displaced her parents' suffering with her own happiness, and Canada is only *exile* for her.

❖

I identify neither with Hoffman's nostalgically Edenic representation of Poland, nor with her utter sense of dispossession later, nor do I share her desperate desire to displace the relativity, the fracturing, the double-consciousness of immigrant experience. For me, displacement and bilingualism preceded emigration; they are the conditions into which I was born. Even as a child, in the midst of those first affections so eloquently celebrated in *Lost in Translation*, I was indeed already *divided*. If displacement is indeed an "exile from older certitudes of meaning" as Mark Krupnick suggests in the epigram to this essay, then I was already born into "the wilderness." As I recognize these differences between us, I see that I can read Hoffman only as a pretext for my own narrative of cultural displacement.

❖

The legendary place of origin I will never see is Czernowitz, capital of the Bukowina, a province of the Austro-Hungarian Empire which, in 1918, was annexed by Rumania and in 1945, by the U.S.S.R. This is where my parents, their relatives and friends, everyone I know and respect, came from—the city where they continued to speak German through years of Rumanian and Russian rule, where they studied French and poetry, went to concerts, swam in the Prut river and climbed the Tsetsina mountain, strolled down the Herrengasse on Sundays, ate delicious "torten" at each other's houses and cheese dumplings at Friedmann's restaurant. Here my maternal grandfather was a lawyer, and my mother grew up in a comfortable apartment with Persian carpets and a set of brown leather furniture in their "Herrenzimmer," a room whose uses I have trouble imagining. My father's family was poor, his mother a widow with four children, but he told other glamorous stories of socialist and Zionist youth movements, of hard work and its rewards, and of youthful camaraderie with friends who continued to be important throughout his life. Here also is where my father was beaten up for being a Jew, and where my mother could not study medicine because Jews were allowed only into some university faculties. These scenes and objects are more real to me than the scenes of my own childhood, especially when it comes to the narrative of my parents' survival during The War: these moments from my parents' history easily displace my own narrative. When I later learn that "our" Czernowitz is the home of Paul Celan, Aharon Apelfeld, Josef Schmidt, Rose Auslander, and other well-known "German" artists, I merely nod—this is, in fact, the image I always had of it. I know many of the details of the two years of Russian occupation and the two years of the Antonescu collaborationist regime. For years I have located myself in the courage of their survival, of my parents' unique marriage in the ghetto the day before they thought they might be deported, the two times they evaded deportation, the night my father got out of bed to answer a knock by the Gestapo. Their subsequent escape from what had become a Soviet republic to Rumania after the war and the three years preceding my birth—the pain of leaving everything they knew behind, the hardships of dislocation, my mother's two miscarriages—in my mind displace my own loss and dislocation.

Throughout her thirteen Polish years, Hoffman lives in the same house, sleeps in the same bed, speaks one language. I am born in Timisoara, a city with a sizeable German and Hungarian population, and move to Bucharest before I can remember. Timisoara remains a second home. This is where my grandparents stay, but they move, and I see the building where I spent the first two years of my life only from the outside. In Bucharest we move again when I am eight. In Timisoara I grow to the age of two speaking only German—my grandmother knows only enough Rumanian to buy eggs and vegetables at the market. In Bucharest I learn Rumanian, but I speak it with an accent. I go to a German school, and I am more fluent than my classmates, many of whom are Rumanian and speak a strongly accented and grammatically incorrect German. But in third grade my best friend is Marianne Döhring from East Berlin, and I quickly realize that my German, of which I had been quite proud, is literally a Balkanization of the real thing. I learn to mimic Berlinerisch, and I learn to be embarrassed about the way I speak my native language. This gets worse when I move to Vienna, and my German is no longer recognized as native—at this point, though I express myself with ease and am proud of my writing, I don't have a language any more. I thus cannot share Hoffman's shock at her linguistic dislocation: *But mostly, the problem is that the signifier has become severed from the signified. The words I learn now don't stand for things in the same unquestioned way as they did in my native tongue. "River" in Polish was a vital sound, energize by the essence of riverhood, of my rivers, of being immersed in rivers. "River" in English is cold—a word without an aura. . . . I am becoming a living avatar of structuralist wisdom; I cannot help knowing that words are just themselves. But it's a terrible knowledge, without any of the consolations that wisdom usually brings.... It is the loss of a living connection* (106, 107). For me, this is a connection I must never have known, since I was never located in one language as firmly as was Hoffman.

Like Hoffman, I am conscious of my Jewish identity throughout my childhood in Rumania. We never go to synagogue—after a rabbi refused to marry my parents in the ghetto on a Friday afternoon, my father stays away from rabbis—so being Jewish is the history and the reality of anti-Semitism and persecution, it is the cultural legacy of Czernowitz, it is, as for Hoffman, a sense of cultural superiority. It is also my difference from my Rumanian friends. ("How do you cross yourself, with two fingers or three?" they ask to determine whether I am Catholic or Orthodox. My shameful reply, "I don't cross myself," reveals that I am nothing.) And being Jewish is the fear of repetition, the nightly dreams of The War. It is what makes us leave and what allows us to leave. When we get to Vienna, my parents decide it might be easier not to be Jewish any longer, and they truthfully put "atheist" on our forms. But it is a lie I have to defend in front of Sabine, the only other Jewish girl in my class. She eventually guesses, of course, and I confess. But when I join the Hashomer Hatzair to which she belongs, I only feel more left out because I don't know any of the songs and stories about Israel, even though my father belonged to the same group thirty years earlier. Jewishness is an ambiguous and complicated location: one in which I both am and am not at home.

For us, Vienna is just a way station on the way to what will be our future home. We consider Israel, Canada, Australia, the United States, and we spend eight months waiting for our American visa. I desperately want to stay in Vienna: in spite of the lie about our Jewishness, in spite of the fact that my German sounds wrong and that I am much more childish than my classmates, in spite of the damp and dark two rooms without kitchen privileges we rent, I begin to feel at home here.

I have a cousin who is three years older and who introduces me to the mysteries of Western consumerism ("there's this drink called Coca Cola, and it is so amazing that once you taste it you will never be able to stop drinking it"). I spend the summer at an international camp, where I use the little bit of French I learned in Rumania to interpret between the Austrian and the French girls. By the end of the summer, I can actually speak French. In the neighborhood Gymnasium I attend for the year, I have a best friend, Angelika, who also feels like an outsider—her mother is an actress, her parents don't live together, she has less money than the other children. Through Angelika I want to become Austrian, but when there is a chance to act in a television commercial with her, I am rejected because of my "foreign" accent.

Looking at pictures from that year, I see the sadness and discomfort I displaced by fighting not to emigrate further. In most of the photos I anxiously

Marianne and Clementine
Vienna, 1962

Angelika and Vladimir
Vienna, 1962

hold on to Clementine, the brown-and-white guinea pig I acquire to consolidate my friendship with Angelika, who has a black guinea pig named Vladimir —we want them to play together and marry. In the pictures, Clementine and I look rather forlorn—she is the repository of my loneliness and desire for love and acceptance. But I smile in the picture Angelika takes—the guinea pigs bring us closer together. I have often come back to this girlhood fantasy of relocation through a friendship which, by way of the guinea pigs, becomes a fantasy of relocation through a friendship which, by way of the guinea pigs, becomes a fantasy of marriage, home, and lasting togetherness. It works, because by the end of the year I look happier. My hair is wavy, I a wearing a petticoat, I pose in front of various Viennese monuments, I look a little more like the other girls in the photos: I have to prove that this has become home. I don't want to leave. When I do leave, Angelika keeps "Tinerl," now indeed wedded to Vladimir, but not quite as we had imagined.

My history of multiple displacements—linguistic, religious, relational— makes displacement (and relocation) my strategy of survival. When I get to Providence, I don't know English—I have resisted learning it so as to have some control over my fate. I eventually have to learn, but I continue to raid the public library for all the French and German books they have. A girl named Jennifer is the only one who expresses an interest in my story, but even she finds me hard to take on. I know so little, I am younger, I do everything wrong.

In the pictures from our first summer, I wear a sailor dress that is much too small for me and I look grotesque: a chubby child infantilized by my linguistic paralysis, I look much younger than I do in the Vienna photos taken only a month earlier. I try to repeat the comfort Clementine gave me,

Marianne in Providence, 1962

but this time I have a hamster who dies two months later. Other hamsters follow, but it never works; they are single hamsters, not the instruments of relationship like Clementine. The cages they live in show my distance from them and emblematize my own confinement in this lonely new American teenage identity I reject.

I stop crying when Mona arrives with her family from Egypt. She's a year older but she's in my class, we can speak French, we can try to read the cultural signs together. The French we speak is our own private language; we both roll our "r"s, and there are many words I don't know, so we mix it with the English we are both acquiring. To her I am not "Mady Ann," but "Marianne" pronounced in French. I become comfortable with the Arabic sounds I hear at her house, and I learn some Arabic words. Her family is also Jewish, but it means something totally different to them. I prefer the Middle Eastern dishes they serve to the tuna fish sandwiches on spongelike white bread I get at American homes. I become involved in her brothers' and parents' adjustment problems. We try to teach her mother enough English to do the shopping, and we explain to her that American girls should be allowed to go out. I'm better in school, but Mona is much better at learning the styles, the songs, the gestures that will make us American—something we both want and do not want to be. She's better at flirting and more attractive to boys, but I

Marianne and Mona
Providence, 1963

join in the talk, I have crushes on the best friends of the boys she has crushes on, we go to dances at the Jewish community center where I have to lie about my age to join, and we have our first boyfriends. Mona is in every picture taken during that time. I am blond, she is brunette; my hair is thin and straight, hers is thick and wavy; yet we have the same outfit, the same posture, the same hairstyle, in every photo. Mona is the mediating figure who allows me both to acculturate and not to. Together we create a space at the border, a space that is not Rumanian nor Egyptian nor American, with an idiolect that is not German nor Arabic nor English, but some mixture of all of these, translated into the French that is "our" language.

When I go to France for a summer and learn a more authentic accent, I cannot use it when speaking with Mona. My pride in my good accent is mixed with regret at losing French as the borderland home I shared with Mona. And when I meet Mona later, and we both have children nearly of the age we were then, we speak English, and I know we cannot be close in this "foreign" tongue in which we have after all come to lead our lives.

At the end of ninth grade, I know enough English to write a composition about what it is like to lose one's country—to be located nowhere, and have no cultural identity. I so eloquently express the pain and nostalgia of homelessness and so feelingly describe patriotic feelings that have no "patria" to attach themselves to that I am asked to read it at a school assembly. Some people weep, and I get much praise, but I am a bit embarrassed by the nostalgia I have been able to evoke and which I cultivate so I can remain on the border. I also want Mona to participate in the glory and help her write her own version of this story; our origins could not be more different, but the feelings of displacement are the same. They are me, communicated to the whole school in English, but they are also an acting job, an impersonation of what I think it all should sound and feel like. But in our graduation picture from Nathan Bishop Junior High School, Mona and I sit in the front row, our hair is teased just the right amount, we smile just like the other girls and we fold our hands on our laps with just the right modesty; we pass. Only some of the inscriptions on the back give me away. Most are generic: "To Marianne, a great kid whom I'll never forget, Love ya, Nancy Weisman"; "To Marianne, A real sweet kid, AFA, Mary Beth." But some note the difference: "To 'Maddy Ann,' a wonderful kid with the cute accente (sic), Karen Powell"; "*À* Marianne (Mady Ann), The Silent One, It's been great knowing you and since we live so close, I'll see you *dans l'avenir*, Good luck, *ne jamais*, Mike Dickens." And Mona, of course, grew up with a different style of dedication:

À ma soeur Marianne
Tombe du 1er étage

Nathan Bishop Junior High School, 1963

tombe du 2ème étage
Tombe d'où tu veux
Mais ne tombe pas amoureuse
Mona Chamuel,

she writes and places an elegant squiggle under her signature. This formulaic verse actually says a great deal about our struggles with adjustments to American teenage girlhood: our sense of falling and the ways in which we caught ourselves and literally held on to each other in our friendship.

After Mona goes to a different high school and we begin to spend less time together, I do not replace her with an American friend but choose Marta, who came to live in Providence from Brazil for several years. This time I can initiate her into the ways of American teenagehood. Her experience is different from mine, for she has already spent one year in the U.S. and is determined to go back home as soon as she can. Still, we share both a basic alienation and a pervasive cultural relativism through which we observe the practices of our peers. I hear a lot of Portuguese, learn how things are done in Brazil, and my borderland existence continues. I don't have the right "r" but I know how to pronounce the "t" in her name, avoiding the more common "Marda" or even "Martha" she has become. We even speak some French together, and for years people comment on the

Marianne and Marta
Providence, 1965

Eastern European accent Marta acquires in English. In all our pictures, we
wear the same outfits and hairstyles, our postures and gestures are identical,
and through high school and, later, college we are inseparable. We need
each other to mediate our acculturation, and I identify with Marta's desire
to go back home, though I don't have a place to return to. I am homeless
and, in a different way, so is she since she has recently lost her mother. We
understand each other's pain.

We join the group of outcasts in our high school. They all smoke and
wear black and act out their rebellion, but for us it is more reasonable to
watch and join in the conversations about Dostoevsky as we safely continue
our good-girl existence. We cannot afford to alienate our parents quite as
much as they can; we have to be more cautious, more measured in our rebel-
lions. Our families, after all, are on the border with us: my mother is especially unhappy about everything "American" and needs, demands, protection
and support, not adolescent rage and rejection. I get annoyed by her unhap-
piness, but in retrospect I realize that my own strategies of displacement act
out *her* ambivalence about assimilating, that feeling perfectly acculturate
would be a betrayal of my connection to her. Again relationship becomes the
place of relocation, the substitute for assimilation. Thus cultural displacement requires different negotiations in the process of separation and individ-

Marianne and Marta
Brown University, 1967

uation from those theorized by psychoanalytic models. Marta and I negotiate together the contradictions between sixties adolescent rebellion and the strong familial bonds forged by the experience of emigration.

As it turns out, Marta stays in the States, and we both go to Brown, take the same courses, and major in Comparative Literature, the academic counterpart of the borderland. We share emotional and intellectual passion. Our English gets good enough to love T.S. Eliot and Yeats and our French to read Baudelaire. We study for exams together, read each other's papers, share each others' anxieties, and reassure each other. We live with our parents and study together in the snack bar and the reserve room of the library. We provide for each other the peer experience others find in dorms and clubs and sororities. She still sees her high school boyfriend, and I quickly find a steady boyfriend in college. We always go out together—both boys are American—and we marry within a week of each other. Eventually we are both divorced.

The late sixties offer many opportunities for group identity, but even as I protest the Vietnam War and become involved in curriculum restructuring, I do so from the margins. The Women's Movement changes all that. I join a consciousness-raising group in 1970 and experience a feeling of group allegiance for the very first time in my life. The perception of commonality, the feelings of connection and mutual recognition are exhilarating, and I become addicted to them. Not only do I see my own experiences validated and mirrored in those of others, but there is a mission in common, a politics based on those experiences—the life-sustaining, relocating friendships with Mona and with Marta, but now practiced on what feels like a global scale. Things really come together when I am able to incorporate female/feminist bonding into my work as well as my life. I have recently described

my personal and professional "coming-to-feminism" as a "story of affilia-
tions and collaborations":

> It was through several collaborative writing projects and through repeated
> dialogic encounters with other feminist critics that I was able to develop a
> feminist reading practice and a feminist critical voice of my own. To see my
> ideas mirrored in those of others, to develop together a politics and a prac-
> tice of mutual support, was not only to acquire professional confidence, but
> also to experience thinking as powerful and radical. I see now (and I appre-
> ciate the irony) that I learned in those years to fear conflict and disagree-
> ment. Was it my personal history that made consensus so precious? Or was
> it that our commonalities were made precarious by institutional pressures?
> (*Conflicts in Feminism*, 381).

Feminism is an enlarged borderland space for me, one which over the
years has changed, reshaped, and transformed itself. At first, ironically, cultural differences seemed to fade into the background, suddenly unimportant
in the face of female bonding that had replaced culture, had become a location. Later, I could begin to look at differences again. From a polar geography
dividing the feminine from the masculine world, from studying the specificity of each, I have moved to a multiple topography that sees difference
within masculine and feminine locations. Again, my history of multiple displacements has prepared me to conceive of identity as fractured and self-con-
tradictory, as inflected by nationality, ethnicity, class, race, and history. But it
has also made me appreciate those moments of commonality which allow for
the adoption of a voice on behalf of women and for the commitment to social
change. I now understand how my feminist work is inflected by my girlhood
adjustments. During adolescence, friendship provided a form of displacement and resistance: to cultural assimilation as well as to femininity. It was a
place on the border between cultures, between girlhood and womanhood.
Like those early friendships, feminism itself became a space of relation and
relocation, a place from which I could think and speak and write, a home on
the border.

❖

*Everything comes together, everything I love, as in the fantasies of my child-
hood; I am the sum of my parts* (Hoffman, 226). Yes there are such moments,
but I am suspicious of them. Displacement, or "Verschiebung," Freud says, is
the transfer of psychic energy from one idea to another, one which originally
had little intensity but which, in the process, gains centrality and importance.
A strategy of defense and survival, it offers a way to appease the censor. As an
aesthetic, it favors metonymy over metaphor.

As I finish reading Hoffman through the lens of my own experiences, I see the differences between us in terms of displacement. Both of us were culturally displaced. Yet displacement for Hoffman was the removal from one mythic place of origin and plenitude to another space of exile. Except for her passionate involvement with music, which mysteriously disappears in the third part of the book, there was no visible reinvestment of energy, no relief in the Freudian sense of displacement as "Verschiebung." This direct, unmediated confrontation of cultures accounts for what Hoffman calls her *immigrant rage* and the *trained serenity* with which she has learned to disguise it.

I chose a different strategy, that of the border, which can be seen as a kind of "Verschiebung" in the Freudian sense. In fundamental ways, I remain in this shifting space. Often longing for a more singular and straightforward sense of identity and identification, I nevertheless embrace multiple displacement as a strategy both of assimilation and of resistance. The issue of my name, for example, is never resolved—it's Marianne [Märiäne] in German and Marianne [Märiän] in French, Mariana [Märiänä] in Rumanian, but in English I accept many versions, from Mary Anne to Maryanna [Maryanä] to Mary Anna [Märyänä] to Marian [Marien]. I sometimes find it hard to remember which I am to which friends, and I do wonder what this multiplicity means, but it simply doesn't bother me as much as it does some of my friends, who have to get used to using different signifiers when referring to the same person.

Instead of engaging directly the America I was placed in, I came to it through a chain of displacements and attempts at relocation—through Vienna, through my involvement with French, through my friendships with Mona and with Marta. I do not shuttle between the surface control and the internal rage that define the sides of Hoffman's Archimedean triangle. Instead, I invest my psychic energies in a series of (dis-) and (re-)locations that allow me to live in this "permanent sojourn in the wilderness," this "alien element," which is, and always has been, "not comfortable but home."

Works Cited

Anzaldúa, Gloria. *Borderlands/La Frontera: The New Mestiza.* San Francisco: Spinsters, Aunt Lute. 1987.

Freud, Sigmund. *The Interpretation of Dreams.* 1900.

Gilligan, Carol, Nona P. Lyons, and Rudy Hanmer, eds., *Making Connections: The Relational View of Adolescent Girls at Emma Willard School.* Troy, NY: Emma Willard, 1989.

Gilligan, Carol, Janie Victoria Ward, and Jill McLean Taylor. *Mapping the Moral Domain: A Contribution of Women's Thinking to Psychological Theory and Education.* Cambridge: Harvard University Press, 1988.

Gilligan, Carol, Annie G. Rogers, and Deborah Tolman. *Women, Girls and Psychotherapy: Reframing Resistance.* Binghamton, NY: Harrington Park Press, 1991.

Hirsch, Marianne and Evelyn Fox Keller, eds. *Conflicts in Feminism.* New York: Routledge, 1991.

Hoffman, Eva. *Lost in Translation: A Life in a New Language.* New York: Penguin, 1987.

Krupnick, Mark. *Displacement: Derrida and After.* Bloomington: Indiana University Press, 1983.

13

The MLA President's Column

❖

AMITAVA KUMAR

I was headed for the Omni Park Central Hotel in New York City at nine in the morning. The Pakistani cabbie suddenly became solemn when I confided to him in Urdu that he was transporting a candidate for a job interview at the Modern Language Association Annual Meeting. "Do you have a green card?" the driver asked me. "No, but I'll apply for one if I get a job." "In this motherfucking country," he opined, "you only get jobs when you know something about cars."

It was my first interview. I was given the empty seat by the window and from that vantage point took in the sight of the ten University of Pennsylvania professors impressively arrayed around me. Houston Baker was preparing himself a cup of tea and, when I admitted that this indeed was my first interview of the day, he smiled broadly and said, "Well, we'll put you in good shape for the others." Or, words to that effect. I wasn't yet beginning to hear words as words: it was more like being at a foreign airport and following the signs that meant Bags but could also mean Bus.

That year—I'm speaking of 1992 —Baker, who now sat sipping tea, was the President of the MLA. I had read his rap on race only months after my arrival in this country, a fresh immigrant in the land of theory-speak, utterly ignorant of the world that now confronted me with its divisions between the signifier and the signified. But six years later, in this hotel suite, I entertained a different feeling of closeness with Baker. I felt it'd be worth talking to Baker not because I had become acculturated and had truly internalized the social mores of our profession, but more because I had been reading the "President's Column" that he wrote in the MLA *Newsletter*. In each of his columns, drawing upon an autobiographical voice that joined itself to the interests of minorities, women, and even graduate students, Baker had come across to me as someone who was very seriously taking his position at the top to announce that decisive changes *below* had put him there.

In the Fall *Newsletter*, Baker wrote that, like the ethnographic accounts that anthropologists brought back from their travels to other lands, "a common fund of apprenticeship experiences and memories constitutes what I would call fieldwork in our disciplines." In each of his columns, and as I was to witness later on the day I had my interview with him, in the course of his Presidential address, Baker would skillfully use his personal experiences as an African-American student as well as teacher of literature to present telling details of the changes that have become a part of our profession. Everywhere, he conveyed a sense of participating in an energetic defense of what June Jordan has called "the multifoliate, overwhelming, and ultimately inescapable actual life that our myriad and disparate histories imply."[1]

Thus, speaking that night as the President of the MLA, Baker would remark on the different look the annual convention bore back in 1968 (Baker's first MLA meeting) when he saw only one other person of color at his hotel. "The most unsettling moment came when I stepped off the hotel elevator on the second morning. I felt a hand on my shoulder and turned to encounter a ruddy-faced giant who drawled, 'Excuse me. Do you know where I can find any good Negro boys to teach at my school?' I balked, sputtered, and felt goose bumps rising but managed to respond that he might have more luck if he tried looking for black *men*. His companion guffawed, and I hastened to escape."

I am less willing than Baker to grant the MLA the multicultural virtues he so easily bestowed on it (in his final column he wrote that "the Modern Language Association is not just a room but truly a building we feel is *our* own"). I choose to put more emphasis on Daphne Patai's assertion that: "As for African-Americans, their scant presence on university faculties is a national disgrace."[2] However, I am accepting of the pride that Baker claimed unabashedly for himself and others who are "proud and civil directors of buildings such as the Center for the Study of Black Literature and Culture at the University of Pennsylvania" and similar centers at Harvard, UCLA, Cornell, and Ann Arbor. More than mere pride, I had also come to expect a struttin' defiance, recalling that exchange cited by Frantz Fanon: "'Look how handsome that Negro is! . . .' 'Kiss the handsome Negro's ass, madame!'"

I myself had understood, with Baker, that my "skin is, in fact, what the West Indian novelist George Lamming metaphorically claims it is—a castle of one's own."[3] Not too long before my interview, in a diary that I had published in a scholarly journal, I had quoted my poem which addressed the reality of my foreign body in the classroom of the U.S. academy.[4] That poem ended with the words:

> I turn from the board: black
> wall with weak ribs of chalk.
> My voice rises, fills the room
> and moves out of the door.
> It dances in the corridor, tripping
> with its foreign accent
> those calmly walking past.

And, again with Baker, I realized that the field of pedagogy is a place where the personal and the public meet to give rise to a provocative kind of politics. Baker rightly claimed a certain pride in announcing the establishment of multicultural programs; I had displayed my share of defiance in spelling out an activist, anti-imperialist agenda. In the diary that I had published, I found a militant pleasure in describing the role of one of my students, Melinda, in a rally to protest the assassination of six Jesuit priests under the death-squad Arena government in El Salvador. A law firm that did the public relations work for that government and secured U.S. aid for the

military was holding a banquet in Minneapolis. Allow me to quote a part of my entry for that night:

> We're outside in the cold chanting: "One, Two, Three, Four. . . . U.S. Out of Salvador" and "Hannan-O'Connor you can't hide. . . . We charge you with genocide." Policemen are protecting the city's elite, whom we can see through the glass walls. We keep up the chanting while Hannan and O'Connor's guests drink wine and converse amidst lighted candles. Then, someone says we should move and stand outside a door in another part of the building. We knock, no response. A minute later, the door opened. It's Melinda who, I learned later, had hid in the bathroom earlier in the day to let us in. . . . The banquet is disrupted and the local television stations present our protest on the nightly news. The law firm has been clearly embarrassed and the reality of civilian killings brought out in a manner that will be impossible to hide for any public relations firm.

My job interview, at least the one that I began this narrative with, was a lengthy one and involved engaging discussions with several people in the room. (I didn't get the job at Penn, however, and I'm reasonably certain that my ignorance about cars wasn't a factor in that decision.) As far as my professional chat with Houston Baker is concerned, what we argued over has pertinence for this column. During the interview, I had begun explaining my work as an attempt to speak in divided tongues, hoping to produce a global, hybrid discourse that would correct and critique the mystifying divisions and disjunctures under late capitalism. At each point, I was politely contested by Baker. The idea of following a mode of global pedagogy that linked the shoes one was wearing with the labor of post-colonial workers did not seem to impress Baker beyond a point. To paraphrase his vigorous queries: But how would you understand a local pedagogy? It is all very well to attend to workers in Indonesia but what about the here and now? How do you respond to the needs and anxieties of students which need to be addressed in their own specific contexts?

Unknown to me then, Baker was to deliver that evening his Presidential address entitled "Local Pedagogy; or, How I Redeemed My Spring Semester." At the end of that talk, which brought the staid MLA audience to its feet, Baker had moved from mere autobiography to a more particular performance: he had tapped into the idea of a confession to provide a narrative of redemption for himself and, miraculously, for the profession he was representing as a leader that night. Baker's main story, in a large nutshell, was the following one. A black, female undergraduate in his class on Black Women's Writing asked Baker why they weren't discussing Phillis Wheatley's poetry in relation to the black community *per se*. Baker's response had been that the class was going to concentrate on conventions and reading skills. The semester was generally a failure and, during the evening's lecture, Baker was redeeming that past by acknowledging that, instead of falling prey to some abstract, generalizing rhetoric about shared, democratic interests, he should have respected the concrete, local geography of concerns through which the student's question had made its way. The suppression of blackness and of female agency was a foolishly censoring act. A more responsible pedagogy would be one that did not flinch from being what conservatives might call "narrow" or even "partisan."

In my estimation, the turns of this argument represented a consummate, political skill. The mode of the confession ushered into the ranks of the professionals, who still might hold dear something called "the literary," a sense of local concerns that gave meaning and weight to politics; at the same time, for those who might grandly and even routinely invoke the categories of race, class, or gender, Baker was serving a reminder that all that talk meant nothing if you couldn't deal with immediate realities like the kind of hostile, social spaces that women and minorities traversed on their way to their class. And yet, I found this performance, even with its strategic strengths, curiously lacking. The experience was doubly dissatisfying for me because I felt that in my discussion with Baker that morning I had failed to advance a more compelling account of pedagogy as well as of performance that transcended the barren binary of "local/global."

So, let me mimic Baker and attempt a revision of my own. I cannot expect redemption because this is not intended as a confession. The self-reflexivity of a confession is a rather limited one: you failed once, and after you have confessed, you and even your listeners who pardon you can now be absolved. I want to enact a less triumphalist gesture, and the contradictions I want to keep alive are not unrelated to the tension between the local and the global that Baker in his lecture rather quickly foreclosed.

Where is Indonesia, Professor Baker, other than in the sole of your shoe? As a local line of query, this question allows us to begin with what your students have on their person, both as object and as ideology. As a global mode of questioning, it refers to the task of making visible those relations that are effaced by the workings of late capitalism, in this case, the invisible labor of the Indonesian who produced your Nike shoe. Nothing prompts, in other words, my question to be inherently local or global. Moreover, a moment of reflection suggests that, as a pedagogical strategy, it'd require a great deal of hard work and imagination to actually remain in any one mode of intellectual operation. In that case,

the more productive move is that of recognizing that the real labor of critical pedagogy lies in doing the dialectical dance between the two terms. We have to produce the effective kinetic motion on the floor of history that opens the space of one to the other. It is in that that genuine dialogic interaction—of modes of knowledge, of forms, and of people—lies. To return to Baker's classroom, then, the choice shouldn't be between questions of conventions and issues of communities. Rather, the histories that make unstable the divisions between those two different modes of inquiry should become an active part of the course.

As we know, Fanon wrote with lyrical power against Sartre's assertion that the idea of race is concrete and particular and that the idea of class is universal and abstract. Fanon's foe was a deracinated socialism. An overly localized understanding of blackness in Baker poses the same problem from the other end—even when it is invested in strategy or the demands of rhetoric. And this of course is not an argument that needs to be advanced only against Professor Baker. When Charles Barkley defends his aggressiveness against Angolan players at an Olympic game by saying that "It's a ghetto thing, you won't understand," he needs to be heard; at the same time, Barkley needs to understand too that there are ways of broaching historical links with the Angolans that would help explain what put him in the ghetto in the first place. Or, dammit, just help explain why the folks King Charles grew up with remain in the ghetto while he is a star selling his powerful body and a brand of cologne on TV.

The personal voice, in Baker's columns as well as his other reflections, has achieved the greatest critical purchase when it expresses a complexity that would have remained beyond the reach of the traditionally academic commentary. It has encompassed rage and longing, given voice to memories as well as to the experience of reason making sense of those memories, putting the brutality and the beauty of the past in perspective. Sometimes, it has also touched on the sensibility of silence, when there has been no possibility of redemption and only the chance of finding a brief reprieve. In solidarity with the more enabling use of the personal voice in Baker's writing, I offer the concluding section of my "Poems for the I.N.S." This section is set in the U.S. embassy in New Delhi, a site of the local that is always already also a marker of the global:

> "You can't trust them," one
>   officer says.
> I'm prepared to bet he is from
>   Brooklyn.
> There is no response from the other
>   one. He is not angry,
> just sad that I now work in his
>   country.
> This quiet American has pasted a
>   sheet with Hindi alphabets
> on his left, on his right there is a
>   proverb from Punjab.
> "You just can't trust them," the first
>   one repeats,

> shaking his wrist to loosen his heavy
>   watch.
> The one sitting down now raises his
>   weary eyes.
> "Did you, the first time you went
>   there,
> intend to come back?"
> "Wait a minute," I say, "did you get
>   a visa
> when you first went to the moon?
>   Fuck the moon,
> tell me about Vietnam. Just how
>   precise
> were your plans there, you asshole?
> And did you when you went to
>   Panama the first time
> know that you'd come back, guns
>   blazing, a century later?
> And this," I fist my cock when I say
>   this, "and this
> is what I think of your trust. Do you
>   understand
> that every time a doctor,
>   teacher, engineer, or scholar
> comes to the United States
>   from India
> you save more on bills
> that what you and Charlie here
> would be able to pay
> till the year two thousand and
>   four?
> So that your saying that we
>   can't be trusted
> is like the owner shouting his
>   worker's lazy
> after he has stripped his skin and
>   taken his soul.
> He's sold . . . do you hear me?
> Hear me
> because I want this fact to be
>   stored
> like a bullet in your heart."
> Maybe I did say all of this, and it was
>   fear
> that I saw in the officer's eyes
> when in response to my shrug
> he slowly turned the pages of my
>   passport and stamped it.

Notes

1. June Jordan, "Toward a Manifest New Destiny," *The Progressive*, February 1992, 18–23.

2. Daphne Patai, "Minority Status and the Stigma of 'Surplus Visibility,'" *The Chronicle of Higher Education* 30 October 1991.

3. George Lamming. *In the Castle of My Skin.* New York: McGraw-Hill, 1954.

4. Amitava Kumar, "Brecht and His Friends: Writing as Critique," *Journal of Advanced Composition* 11 (Fall 1991): 301–14.

14

Me and Not Me

The Narrator of Critical and Historical Fiction[1]

❖

LINDA ORR

The ideal of scholarly writing is a rhetoric that arose with nineteenth-century realism and empiricism. Besides footnotes and references, scholarly writing was defined by the absence of the I and any mention of the present or writing process.[2] Before the codes of empiricism held sway, Romantic historians, like Michelet and Carlyle, didn't worry about mixing subjectivity and objectivity in their narratives.

Impersonal writing of this scholarly tradition conveys an ideological message. You cannot appear to think for yourself except within the limits of authorized theoretical frames. We teachers of literature read a richness of first-person writing in our classes (autobiography, essays, fiction, testimonio, journals) which we and our students should be able to adapt for our own uses. Think of the different first-person perspectives available to us: camera, engaged witness, minor or major protagonist.[3] When we self-consciously explore the techniques associated with these other forms, we are doing literary criticism. We are performing our readings.[4] Performing the necessary personal and cultural connections between ourselves as readers and a literary text or historical problem adds focus and power to the argument. The presence of an observing and thinking subject adds to the truth value.

I chose first-person narration for the book I'm writing on a French family now and during World War II (from which I include two short selections at the end of this essay), because it allows me to show my own critical process. Although the book is based upon much of my own experience, I'm writing fiction, and the narrator is me and not me. But I consider this fiction as pro-longing my work as a literary critic interested in historical discourse.

Half of the book reconstructs the story of Jean Zay, a former Popular Front Minister of Education, convicted on trumped-up charges of military desertion and imprisoned in Riom by the Vichy government from 1940 to 1944. Zay was also considered Jewish by Vichy, because his father came from an Alsatian Jewish family, although Zay was brought up in his mother's Protestant church. While Zay was imprisoned in Riom during the war, his wife and two young daughters could visit him every day in his cell. Two weeks after the Allied invasion in 1944, Zay was taken from his cell and assassinated by the *Milice,* or French Gestapo.

Alternating with this reconstructed past is the other half of the book, the account of how the American narrator comes to know the Zay family and their history. This present-day story concentrates on the women, the widow and two daughters, neither of whom remembers her father. The older daugh-ter, Catherine, was seven when her father was shot; Hélène was three. At the center of this present-day story is the push-pull relationship between Hélène, a short French woman with closely-cropped brown curls, and the first-person narrator, a tall American with dark-blond hair named Charlotte. During summers in Orléans, on a walk or bike ride, Charlotte asks Hélène what her father's death has meant to her, and Hélène does and does not want to talk about it.

The reader also sees Charlotte doing research, reading Zay family corre-spondence, going to local and Parisian libraries. Certain documents become the reason for a scene, like Charlotte's discovery of Hélène's birth in the film, *The Sorrow and the Pity.* Charlotte's access to Jean Zay's three prison diaries, only one of which has been published, finally makes it possible and inevitable for her to write the book that the reader is reading. Early in the book, the reader realizes that Charlotte has written the historical scenes, told mostly from Jean Zay's third-person point of view. Charlotte filters everything through her subjectivity.

My book is about writing history—the way I would like history to be written, with much of what has been taken out, ignored, or repressed put back in. The narrator returns, anything but omniscient. Stories ordinarily consid-ered insignificant about the research process counterbalance the report of research results, for instance: why someone chooses a certain problem; what personal and cultural experiences inform the questions asked; what colors the relationship between researcher and researchee in the present or historical past; how a constant negotiation evolves between them, what the emotional costs are, the surprises and failures.[5] The low clouds on the way to interview Madame Zay, the light in the room, the furniture, all impinge upon Charlotte's interpretation of events. In this thirst for detail, I'm perilously close to Romantic history. What often kept me going was Hélène's or Madame Zay's historical understanding, always out of Charlotte's and my range. Michelet's "silences of history."

I'm not writing my book on the Zay family solely as an intellectual challenge. When Hélène told me, standing there in the hall of her house, about her mother wheeling her in the baby carriage every morning into her father's cell, leaving her there with him while she did errands, that image gave me chills. I said: "Someone has to write about this." The story fascinated me, but so did Hélène, especially the connection between her silence and learning language with her father in prison. Charlotte thinks she'll get closer to Hélène by approaching that cell. Hélène is moved and attracted by Charlotte's ardor, but Charlotte's invasiveness also repels her. As Charlotte gets more involved in her research, she becomes consumed by her own desire to know Hélène's father to the point of wanting his memory for herself.

So why do I call her Charlotte, instead of Linda? Although I change the last names of Hélène and Catherine, I keep their first names. Jean and Madeleine Zay are historical figures. I couldn't bear to change their names. Do I use Charlotte because I can't say those things about myself (stealing the memory of a friend)? I don't think so. Very early on in the writing, I used my own name, but quickly found Charlotte. I was already writing fictional scenes based on documents for the 1940s and transposing and altering dialogues with Hélène to get the interpretation I wanted. Finally I invented a few scenes that had to be there. I had gone past the boundary of history or memoir. Using "Linda" would have set up expectations that Hélène, Madame Zay, Catherine were all real people. No matter how trained we have become, because of literary theory, to read history and autobiography as fiction, I worried about the presuppositions of the genres.

The hardest task lay ahead: making Charlotte work as a narrator. At first she was too close to me, and too far. I was tough on her (as I can be on myself). I shed my disdain and hostility onto her. She was too naïve, awkward, self-analyzing, and pushy. I had to give her the sensitivity and knowledge she showed working on the project (also me). We had to undergo a painful fission. She had to take off on her own, more American than I am, less intellectual, with a cultural innocence that can also be smart and perceptive. As Charlotte went about her affairs, I also saw how much of myself was poured into the other characters. Jean Zay is a lot me, in his solitude, anxieties, and insomnia. His young wife Madeleine has a tenderness I'm convinced is hers but may well be a projection of a part of myself I only recognized in writing the book. I lovingly portray children—I who have no children and casually refer to them as little crumbsnatchers.

I've chosen to include here a scene from my book in which Charlotte does less of the talking, but her presence makes the dialogue happen between Hélène and her mother, Madame Zay. The old Madame Zay also provides a bridge, or divide, between the present and the past. The short piece I include from the historical past is written from Jean Zay's third-person point of view and narrates the moment when his family enters his prison cell in Riom for the first time.

In the first selection, Hélène takes Charlotte to her mother's house, which is right around the corner. This is the house in which Hélène grew up, now also occupied by Catherine and her family. Charlotte has been there before, but never to talk specifically to Madame Zay about visiting her husband in prison. Charlotte is the observer here, the camera, because she has to go through Hélène to speak to Madame Zay about such private, delicate memories. Madame Zay is not only old, but showing signs of Alzheimer's disease. For the first time, Hélène, who is not always so helpful to Charlotte, gets emotionally involved in Charlotte's project. A reference is made to Jean Zay's prison diaries, *Souvenirs et solitude* (Memory and Solitude), which had just been republished that year, 1987.[6]

In the second extract from my book, Jean Zay sees his family after eight months of separation. Zay had been arrested in August, 1940, after he, his family, and other political colleagues and opposition figures (Daladier, Mandel, Mendès France) had taken a boat to Morocco to set up a French government in exile. While this boat was at sea, Pétain signed the armistice with Hitler, and accused those who had left the country of "desertion." At the time, Madame Zay was eight months pregnant with the baby that would be Hélène, born in Morocco after her father's arrest. Madame Zay did not see her husband again until May, 1941, when she, Catherine, who was four, and Hélène, nine months old, entered his cell.

The scene of their arrival is told from a "close" third-person point of view, that is, from as intimate a view of Jean Zay's emotions as I could get. Here I'm departing most radically from analytical or historical writing. I give myself the chance to be emotional. These scenes, which are close to Jean Zay, show how involved Charlotte is in his and Hélène's stories. That intimacy is the truth she wants. Maybe everything is so filtered by her that she has filled Jean Zay with her own yearnings. Or maybe she has conveyed Hélène's feelings about her father that Hélène has and has not expressed. It is even possible that Jean Zay might recognize himself here, that this is what actually happened.

Orléans, June, 1987

The noon traffic was building up on the bridge that led onto the Avenue Dauphine. Exhaust fumes hung in the air despite a river breeze. Sultry clouds were low in the sky.

Madame Zay, in her eternal black skirt and sweater, answered the door. She and Hélène kissed cheeks. Madame Zay shook my hand, and we followed her down into her living room. Her white-blond hair was flat at the back where she leaned against her recliner. Some rose blossoms without stems were floating in water. The room was stuffy.

"Please sit down," she said. I turned the dining chair around at the end of the long table to face the side of her recliner. Hélène moved another dining chair out in front of her mother and turned the television's silent picture off. Then she walked around me to the low cabinet against the wall, and took out a bottle.

"There's not much left, *ma mie*."

Madame Zay shrugged and smiled. Her red morning lipstick was barely wearing off.

"I don't want that much," I said.

"There's enough for three. I'll buy another bottle later," Hélène said.

It was a heavy, syrupy, brown port. I touched my lips to it, licked my lips, before taking a swallow. It wasn't so good on top of my late morning bowl of granola and milk.

"Is Catherine at the bookstore?"

"Yes," her mother said.

"Do you go to the coiffeuse tomorrow?"

She nodded.

"Is what's-her-name still doing you?"

"Melanie," her mother said.

"Well, to your health, Mother. To our health." Hélène lifted the glass. Madame Zay smiled and lifted hers too, glanced around at me with my little glass raised.

"Are you reading his book?" Hélène leaned over with a gesture toward the low bookshelf under the two high windows that faced the the street. There on top was the new, glossy edition of *Souvenirs et solitude*—the circle close-up of his face in his tortoiseshell glasses, his dark hair thinning on top. The book had a red leather marker in the middle.

"Sometimes," she answered.

A brilliant lead-in, I thought. So quick and to the point. I had expected more of a warm-up. The silhouette profiles of a man and a woman passed on the other side of the white, crocheted curtains.

"Do you like it?"

"Yes," Madame Zay said.

"Any particular parts?"

She hesitated. "All."

"Nothing in particular?"

Her mother just smiled.

"Do you remember the trips he talks about?" I asked. She slowly turned her head, lifted her glass for a sip.

"Yes," she said.

"England," I went on, "the United States, Egypt."

"The Duke of Kent." Hélène added, draining her glass.

"Oh, the Duke of Kent." Her mother barely lifted her left hand with the diamond ring and put it back on the arm of the chair.

"Do you remember Riom?" Hélène asked.

Madame Zay looked at her glass; a frown passed over her face.

"It was an awful time," she said.

"What was the prison like, Mother?" Thank you, Hélène.

We waited. Her mother didn't answer.

"Was the cell as large as this room?" Hélène asked.

"Yes."

"Was it bigger?" Madame Zay stared at her daughter. She was concentrating hard.

"Maybe."

"Can you describe the cell? Where was the bed?"

"On the far wall," Madame Zay offered, tentative, as if waiting for Hélène to tell her if her answer was right or wrong. "No, by the door," she added.

"Are you sure?" Hélène asked, hunching slightly forward, still holding her empty glass. "Think about it for a second."

"I don't know," she said. "It was a terrible time."

Hélène leaned back in her chair. I let out my breath. I was glad we had tried, but it wasn't worth pushing.

"Are you skipping around in the book?" Hélène asked.

"Yes," her mother said. Her smile started to return.

She drank the last of her port. Hélène got up, took her mother's glass, and put it with her own on the table. "Is this the brand you like best?"

She nodded.

"It's very good," I said, taking another swallow.

Hélène stayed standing. "If this was the cell, Mother. . . ." She went over and stood behind her vacant, straight-backed chair at the door. "If this was the door. . . ." I was surprised, I thought we were giving up. Madame Zay looked at her daughter, her dark, almost navy blue eyes wide, imploring. I gave a grimace, hoping Hélène would see and know it meant I had had enough. Stop.

"If this was the door, here where you came in from the hall, and there was a window here," she pointed to the table, "and the table where you ate and later my father sat and wrote. . . ."

"We didn't eat there," her mother said.

Hélène was thrown off for a second. "You mean you ate over here?"

"We didn't eat there," her mother repeated matter-of-factly. It sounded as if she meant they never ate in the cell at all, but I knew that was impossible because I had read in the diary where he tells about the meals.

"Of course we did," Hélène said. Hélène had told me how she had this image, maybe a memory, of watching—from a crib, a bed?— she was always watching from outside the circle as the family ate at the table.

Madame Zay didn't change expression, but I thought I saw a flicker of sadness in her eyes. Hélène gripped the back of her chair and looked down at her feet. Her mother stared at her daughter's bent head. Then Hélène went over and gave her mother a kiss. "Are you hungry for lunch?"

Her mother nodded, the big smile back, her eyes bright.

"Catherine should be home soon."

I put my glass on the table. Her mother leaned forward in her chair as Hélène took her elbow. "You don't have to come to the door," she said. But her mother kept rising. We walked to the door.

"Come again," Madame Zay said to me, with her outstretched hand.

We closed the big door behind us. Madame Zay stood at the door and smiled, then disappeared back into the shadows.

Riom, 1941

The key turned. The key had trouble, no, the key turned. The bolt. Taking an hour! The bolt gave way. The door swung open. He saw them. Out in the darkness of the hall he saw an elegant woman, a baby carriage, a little girl. His wife and daughter, daughters. Madeleine, he said, but no voice came out. She pushed the carriage into the dim light of his cell. He saw her small, familiar ears under the rain hat, her blond hair tucked neatly in its twist. The brim of the hat darkened her blue eyes that were fixed on him.

She smiled and continued to push the low, wide carriage inside. "Cathou," he whispered. She gripped her mother's hand and stared. "It's Papa," Madeleine said, "go give him a hug." Catherine, in a navy blue coat, lifted her thin arms, staring at him. What should he do? She came toward him. Madeleine waited. He squatted and lifted Catherine up, high into the air. Her coattails and skirt flew out. She clutched his neck and pulled him toward her, hugged him a long time. He held the fragile body up against him, felt the damp of her coat and the small, hard places of ribs underneath, not moving for a long time, then rocking in place from side to side. She made no sound. Is she breathing? He pressed her lightly.

The cell door slammed; he heard the lock. Madeleine maneuvered the carriage closer until he saw the blanket shapes of two tiny feet. He kissed his wife on the mouth. "I'm so happy," she said, tears pooling in her eyes. "I am too," he said. The skin of his face was on fire. She smelled of air and sea. Catherine leaned back, took a quick look at him, then grabbed tight and stared behind him again. Madeleine bent down and lifted up a blanket-spun body with a white knit hat on top and curls sticking out, hands and feet punching the blanket away.

Madeleine turned the baby around.

"Your father," she said.

A round, fat-cheeked face opened big brown eyes on him. He knew he had a silly grin on his face, a giant clown face with glasses, but she didn't look afraid. Her eyes grew larger. Skin soft and clear, just under each eye a tiny wrinkle, and the mouth drawn so precisely, tearose lips, a line so smooth, and the pug nose, nostrils barely moving, polished like sacred stone. He wanted to reach out and touch, put his finger out for the tiny hand to take, but he held firmly to Catherine who was still silently clamped onto him. "Hello," he said as much to himself as to Hélène. "Hello, little one."

Notes

1. The following essay is a revised talk from the 1994 MLA session on "Confessional Criticism." My thanks to Catherine Gallagher and Nancy K. Miller for this occasion.

2. Roland Barthes, "Historical Discourse," *Structuralism: A Reader,* ed. Michael Lane (London, 1970), 145–155. On the rhetoric of history, see also the work of Frank Ankersmit, Stephen Bann, Philippe Carrard, Lionel Gossman, Hans Kellner, Dominick LaCapra, Ann Rigney, and Hayden White, especially *A New Philosophy of History,* ed. Frank Ankersmit and Hans Kellner (London: Reaktion Books, 1995).

3. See Gerald Prince, *A Dictionary of Narratology* (Lincoln: University of Nebraska Press, 1987) for a more precise array of first-person points of view and terminology.

4. After teaching and reading all kinds of memoirs, Alice Kaplan found her form by combining the American sensitivity of Mary McCarthy and Vivian Gornick with the French notion of a language memoir, Hélène Cixous's "coming into language" and Nathalie Sarraute's memory tags of words in *Enfance.* See Alice Kaplan, *French Lessons: A Memoir* (Chicago: University of Chicago Press, 1993).

5. Historians have written memoirs and *ego-histoire,* but have rarely mixed the genres with their "serious" material. But this is changing. My colleague William M. Reddy, encouraged by a North Carolina French history reading group, wrote a chapter in his forthcoming book which ties together his memories as the child of an alcoholic father and his study of shame opposing honor in nineteenth-century France. Robert Rosenstone's *Mirror in the Shrine: American Encounters with Meiji Japan* (Cambridge: Harvard University Press, 1988) was also a reference for me. It describes parallel voyages to Japan, his own and the one he was researching. Using the first person in his forward only, Jacques Rancière in *The Nights of Labor: The Workers' Dream in Nineteenth-Century France,* trans. John Drury (Temple University Press, 1989) completely integrates historical analysis with an intense meditation on the relationships of "intellectuals" to their subjects. Because of this preface, the reader senses throughout the book the troubled, ambiguous identifications of the historian with workers who aspired to be intellectuals and writers, reformers or utopian socialists who played out complicated scenarios with their "subjects."

6. (LeRoeulx, Belgium: Talus d'Approche, 1987; orig. 1946), with a preface by Pierre Mendès France and introduction by Antoine Prost.

15

Writing in Concert

An Interview with Cathy Davidson, Alice Kaplan, Jane Tompkins, and Marianna Torgovnick

❖

JEFFREY WILLIAMS

WILLIAMS: First off, what was the impetus for your writing group? What made you get together in the first place?

TOMPKINS: Well, I was in my second year at Duke, and I was on an NEH fellowship and I didn't know that many people. I was writing alone and going more and more inward and feeling sort of isolated and forlorn. Many years ago I was in a similar situation when I was living in Baltimore, and trying to finish a book. I had been reading Peter Elbow's *Writing without Teachers* at the time, so I called up a couple of people, both graduate students, and asked them if they were interested in doing a writing group. And that had really been a good experience for me. I finished *Sensational Designs*, and they both finished their dissertations, which didn't exist when the writing group began. And then we all left and went to various points of the compass. So I found myself in the same position here, and I called the two people that just came to mind. I mean, I don't remember any rationale about this. I just called Marianna and I called Alice. I'd read something of Marianna's, the Roger Fry chapter of what was then the very beginning of *Gone Primitive*. I don't know if it even existed in your mind as a book yet.

TORGOVNICK: Oh, yes. In fact, I had already written a description of the chapters. When Jane called me, I was writing a chapter on the Tarzan novels, and had been thinking of asking Jane to read it. I had been going over and over the chapter—doing microlevel revisions. I had also met Alice at a party, and we had had a wonderful conversation. But in the way that things often happen in universities, we might never have gotten to know one another without the writing group. So I said yes to the idea of a group, although I felt a little nervous at the prospect. My only prior experience had been trying to get readings from friends who would avoid me for two years after I'd sent them a book manuscript. All in all, I felt game.

KAPLAN: I came in from a different angle. I teach primarily in a Romance Studies department and come totally from a French training. Anyway, I had this idea that I wanted to write about Americans' relationship to France, and at first it was a very sociological project, not an autobiographical project. I got an announcement in the mail from Jane about an American Studies discussion group at the Humanities Center. I wrote and I said I was trying to write about Americans interested in French culture, and I didn't know how to do it. I thought that learning something about American Studies would be a good idea. And then Jane called me with the idea of a writing group.

TORGOVNICK: I remember very vividly the founding meeting which was on the deck at my house. We all stated what our ambitions were....

TOMPKINS: What we were wanting to do....

TORGOVNICK: And the common element in one way or another was that we all wanted to experiment with different kinds of writing.

TOMPKINS: That's what pulled us together, gave us some sort of common ground.

KAPLAN: And I think that's what attracted us to Cathy's work, her versatility and skill as a writer and editor.

DAVIDSON: I came to Duke because this is the one university that seemed to value the full range of writing, without making a clear boundary between scholarly and creative writing. I used to write under various pseudonyms, and do fiction under one name, journalism under one name, criticism under another name. It felt schizophrenic. And then Jane and Marianna mentioned this writing group, and my heart started beating very hard because I thought this would be just perfect, a great way of helping me put all my different people together in one person. But I had never met Alice, so we had this funny meeting at a restaurant where she was interviewing me. I walked into the restaurant and suddenly felt hostile because it felt like a sorority hazing.

WILLIAMS: You had to be initiated?

TOMPKINS: Interviewed.

DAVIDSON: And I was probably very . . .

KAPLAN: We were both very stiff. . . .

DAVIDSON: Nothing was working. I kept thinking, I'm not going to be in this group. And then suddenly we both confessed that we didn't like a writer whom we were supposed to admire very much . . .

KAPLAN: Who shall remain nameless. . . .

DAVIDSON: Who shall remain nameless. . . .

KAPLAN: We bonded over a writer that everyone admired. . . .

DAVIDSON: And who should have been the model for our kind of writing. And we both thought she was fake and superficial. And we bonded. And I went to the bathroom and I had to take a deep breath and I thought, Oh my God, now I *really* want to be in this group.

KAPLAN: That broke the ice: we finally got to where we were saying what we really thought.

TORGOVNICK: We felt that we needed another person because we were traveling too much and it was hard for us to meet.

KAPLAN: Three is a hard number.

TORGOVNICK: We started in the spring of '87. Cathy joined in the fall of 1989.

WILLIAMS: I was curious to see the author's blurb on Cathy's new book, which is different from the blurbs on a typical academic book, since it mentions that you've published in *Vogue, Ms.,* and places like that.

DAVIDSON: Actually, I think the first time I ever talked to Jane was when I managed to do a review of *Sensational Designs* in *Vogue* magazine, which I thought was a coup. That was the first academic piece I did in *Vogue.*

WILLIAMS: I want to ask more about the question of audience, but first, what are the logistics of the group? How do you go about it? When do you meet? How often?

TORGOVNICK: That's changed over time. At first we met episodically, maybe once a month. . . .

WILLIAMS: You mean if you were working on a project....

TORGOVNICK: No. The founding rule of the group was that everybody had to bring something, a piece of writing.

WILLIAMS: Every meeting?

DAVIDSON: Every meeting everybody had to bring writing.

WILLIAMS: So it would be hard to meet every week or two....

TOMPKINS: Maybe about every three weeks, or something like that....

TORGOVNICK: We'd meet for a long time, as long as it took, and we frequently read things ahead of time. Sometimes we'd distribute them.

KAPLAN: I forget when, but then we decided we would read at the group and not everyone would work every time. Then we started meeting more frequently, so that we've been meeting every week with the idea that if somebody's traveling, they don't come. Now, nothing works perfectly, because sometimes somebody'll have a longer piece, and they'll feel frustrated that there's not enough time during the group to read it all.

WILLIAMS: You meet every week?

TORGOVNICK: Now we do.

WILLIAMS: That's quite often.

TOMPKINS: One thing that happened: I remember this meeting we had at Alice's house in the summer. I think it was the first meeting of the school year. We were just back—maybe it was in August—and it was one of those where we all kind of went out of control. We were all trying to have stuff read, and we hadn't seen each other in a long time, and we all had all kinds of agendas and hopes and desires and needs and expectations, and we talked a blue streak, and we all felt ravaged at the end, after that meeting. For me, that was a crucial experience that led to a fairly regimented format, where only two people are ever on on a given day, and we can't bring more than ten pages, or just a few more than that. When we come, we check in and say what's on our minds, so we know where people are, and then we divide the rest of the time in two. The person who's stuff is being read says, "Well, let's read for so long, and then we'll have time for discussion." When the reading time is up, then the respondents, the people who have been reading, have a time period in which to give their feedback.

DAVIDSON: Without interruption.

TOMPKINS: Without interruption from anybody, from the writer, or from other people in the group. Then, when that's over, the floor's open, and the person who wrote the thing can say, "But I didn't mean that," or, "I took that part out," and make all the defensive moves and explanatory gestures. And then everybody jumps in, and sometimes we have a really good discussion where we move the whole thing up to another level. But the reason that we went to that was that we were interrupting each other and butting in, and some people didn't get to give their feedback fully, and other people talked too much.

KAPLAN: We got some help on that. In the fall of 1992, we brought in a consultant. I had gotten some great help on the penultimate draft of *French Lessons* from the novelist Laurel Goldman. She runs fiction groups, and I had heard about these fiction groups from my colleagues, Terry Vance and Linda Orr. So she came to our group, and we worked in front of her. She sat down and watched us work. She said, "You guys go too fast." And she gave us a lot of tips and ideas. One of her ideas was that if you're getting feedback, you should sit and think about it. Don't get defensive right away, don't argue, just try to soak it in. When everyone's had their piece, then you can speak. And boy, I felt that took the pressure off all of us.

DAVIDSON: We have talked from time to time about having Laurel come back to see how we've implemented everything. There are certain things that have worked and other things don't work as well.

WILLIAMS: How long do you usually meet altogether?

UNISON: Two hours.

TORGOVNICK: We restrict that now. Some of my fondest memories were doing *Gone Primitive* when everybody was chiming in. On the way it became very confused, but that actually moved things forward in a way that probably would not have happened if there had not been a pooling of responses. So I feel some nostalgia for the old format at the same time that this new format has worked well in lots of ways. I don't know if the format is the key thing. I think maybe the most important thing is for the group to reevaluate the format and to make changes as they're required.

WILLIAMS: It's nearly seven years now. . . .

DAVIDSON: I don't think we would have survived if we hadn't worked with a new format. And I'm sure the format's going to change again. It's important that we all pitch in and we all say if something's not working correctly.

TOMPKINS: I wish we did more writing exercises, because we always have a good time when we do them. But we're always so eager to get what we're working on read, that we don't do them. We should build it in. We should maybe make ourselves do a writing exercise every week or every other week, for ten minutes or so.

TORGOVNICK: I thought of a really good exercise the other day. I thought wouldn't it be nice to just sit and describe a gift that we had given to one another that had caused our writing to benefit.

WILLIAMS: What gifts have you given? Off the top of your head?

DAVIDSON: I can answer that easily. I took ten years trying to write *Fuji*, and couldn't figure out how I wanted to do it. And then I brought in this section about sleeping in a flophouse when I was sixteen and how this reminded me of sleeping in a Buddhist temple the first time I was in Japan. And the group said, "That's it, you've got it, that's the book." Then I wrote the book in a year. The group showed me that what I needed to do was put myself in the book in a personal and intimate way. I never would have done that without the group, so that was permission. That was a gift.

TORGOVNICK: This particular gift comes from Alice, but there are others that come from Jane and Cathy. When I first wrote on Malinowski, Alice said to me, "You've got this guy, why don't you write about his body," and I went home and did it. I came back, and Jane gave me the gift then. She said, Oh, this seems so much smarter than the original thing that you wrote. The idea that something could be irreverent and unconventional and also smart was a great gift.

WILLIAMS: That was in *Profession,* the piece on "Experimental Critical Writing."

TORGOVNICK: Right, I think that gave away one of our best exercises. That was one of the best gifts the group has given me.

KAPLAN: The biggest gift I've gotten from the group is to stop being so secretive. That's partly from working in a foreign language all the time; I was elliptical in English. But specific things from everybody in the group: Cathy's pacing is incredible, Marianna's forthrightness, just putting her finger on it, and Jane's music. I could go on. We're an amazing collection of different skills.

TORGOVNICK: And the skills travel; they travel from person to person.

DAVIDSON: Yes, we'll say sometimes, "Wow, that was a Marianna revision."

TOMPKINS: When I was working on *West of Everything,* I remember one day that Alice said to me, "Gee, Jane, you can do anything, you've got a license to kill." It was at that moment that I thought, I really can write this book the way that I want to write it. I really don't have to make it look like other books. So that was a gift. But more than anything, I feel I can count on the group. I trust all of you to tell me what I need to know about my work.

TORGOVNICK: When Laurel came to the group, she asked us to decide what was the greatest satisfaction of our meetings. That was what each of us wrote down, the feeling of trust in each other's evaluation. My own feeling is that we're at another stage of critical development, probably because each of us has now completed one or more major projects. But there's always a challenge to accept the new things that people write, because one thing that happens in the profession is that people always want you to be doing the last thing that you did.

KAPLAN: We don't always write in the first person.

DAVIDSON: No, that's a mistake to think we only do personal writing. I'm doing an academic project again, a theoretical study of photography. It's not anything at all like *36 Views of Mount Fuji*.

KAPLAN: And I did a scholarly edition of the letters Céline wrote to his publishers at Little, Brown in the 1930s. The group gave me help in managing vast amounts of information in a readable way.

WILLIAMS: I want to ask two questions about that. I get a real sense of a common project that you have, a common goal and direction. Do you see it that way? And then I want to ask about personal writing, which I think gets a bad rap and is frequently cast as an aspersion. And it's not accurate besides; I think experimental critical writing the better title. Anyway, how do you see your project? To reach a larger audience? Is that the motivating project?

TOMPKINS and KAPLAN: It was. . . .

TORGOVNICK: But I think we have reached larger audiences, so that that's not a motivating project anymore.

DAVIDSON: The project I'm doing is probably going to reach a specialized audience. It's more theoretical and academic again. I'm doing a piece now on Valentino's funeral and photographic movie stills, and I know I'll feel comfortable bringing that to the group.

TORGOVNICK: I'm doing a book called *Primitivism and the Quest for Ecstasy,* which is taking me back into a scholarly mode. I think that the project now has moved from reaching a wider audience to simply being ourselves as writers.

KAPLAN: In order to write *French Lessons,* I had to get beyond the desire to please and learn to say what I thought. That's an awful pressure to put on oneself, to please people—and it makes the writing fraudulent. In that way, simply wanting to reach a wider audience can be a block.

WILLIAMS: Is your project a reaction to the current scene of criticism and theory?

TOMPKINS: I don't think so. We've cemented as a group, so now, at least the way I understand it, we're here to support each other in whatever it is that each person happens to be doing. Another thing that has been really important for me—and, again, it's my interpretation—is that people grow through their writing. Where they're going in their lives and their writing are not two separate things. So it's wonderful to see different kinds of writing evolving.

DAVIDSON: I don't mean to sound fatuous, but I think that we feel secure enough to take risks now, to try things that might not bring glory. That's a privilege, to be able to do writing without the goal of reaching a large audience, or of impressing anyone in your profession. . . .

TOMPKINS: Or any audience . . .

DAVIDSON: . . . but just because that's what you want to do. It's wonderful to have that kind of intellectual freedom.

WILLIAMS: Is it a kind of return to what you got in this business for?

DAVIDSON: Who can remember?

TORGOVNICK: I think one of the things that's been very important is that we each had a career before we joined the writing group. It's not like we were all novices. But I don't think the group is a return to why we had originally gotten into the profession. I think it's a utopian idea of what the profession could be that I wouldn't have dreamed when I started in the profession.

WILLIAMS: How would you distinguish what you do from "personal writing?"

TOMPKINS: We have encouraged each other very much to write from our own voices, because there's been an academic interdict against that. So in the beginning, at any rate, we put a lot of emphasis on that, and it took a lot of effort and courage and faith and our belief in each other. And now Alice's book is out there, and Cathy's book is out there—successful examples of personal writing—so things have changed since then. You don't have to put the effort and concentration on that anymore. I'm doing a personal book right now, largely because of the group. I feel empowered to do it because of what we've done here. But we're not restricted to that.

KAPLAN: But the other thing the label "personal writing" tends to obfuscate is that memoir is a genre, with its habits, its rules and its codes. I taught autobiography and read autobiographies for four or five years before I started *French Lessons*. It was not an unschooled, let-it-all-hang-out undertaking. What we've found again and again in our work in the group is that you have to find a formal solution to the problem of writing about yourself. It's not anti-intellectual. Writing with affect is one big problem that we've been interested in and worked on in this group. But we're also very formally aware of models in literature.

TORGOVNICK: When I was doing the Bensonhurst essay, the first extended piece of autobiographical writing I had done, I remember feeling very strongly that I did not want to feel like I was showing someone a home video of my wedding and saying, "Watch it." Memoir can have that effect; it can be boring. Or it can be chaste and have no emotional impact on the reader, and we've always been going for emotional impact on the reader. If there's going to be exposure, it needs to be exactly the right kind of exposure for you as a writer and to your audience. It's a really disciplined form of writing.

KAPLAN: Several weeks ago, Jane had a formal breakthrough in her work on *A Life in School*. It had to do with her finding a specific kind of dialogue form that really worked in one of the early chapters.

TOMPKINS: But it seems to me that there's no distinction. It's not as if over here there's form and conventions and literariness, and over here there's personal hang-ups. In order for me to say something that was really important for me to say, I had to find the form that allowed me to say what I needed.

TORGOVNICK: I would even go further to say that an essay on some scholarly topic can be personal writing too. I think that the metaphor works both ways. Scholarly material has the inference of impersonality, and the problem with a lot of scholarly writing is that it seems to have been written by a computer and not a human being.

KAPLAN: I'm working on 1945 in France, which is very historical, but my writing problems remain much the same as in memoir: leaving stuff out, being elliptical, putting in too much information, shaping.

TORGOVNICK: I think the other thing that was very helpful to me was finding out I wasn't the only one who didn't produce perfect drafts.

DAVIDSON: We disproved it.

TORGOVNICK: I've done some editing since, but I had not done a lot of editing when the group started. So I was not aware how rare the writer is who produces a perfect draft. When you're in the middle of any project, you have these doubts about whether it's going to work, and it feels like you've never had so much trouble before, but if you look back at all of those drafts, which are records of the difficulties you have had . . .

KAPLAN: The group is very good for seeing how someone else struggles to get a piece right and seeing someone else's process.

DAVIDSON: And we get great suggestions from the group and we rejoice when it hits. . . .

KAPLAN: When someone takes the revision and really runs with it and comes back to the group with something wonderful, I think for me that's one of the most magical things about the group. Someone can be totally off, the group then gives criticism and they feel terrible, and they'll come back with a revision and the group will just say, "You did it," and really be joyful that someone's had a breakthrough. That's the most communal sense operating in the group—the pleasure that someone took our suggestions and got further because of them. And I think we all feel a real sense of pride when it happens.

TORGOVNICK: That's the usefulness of a group. It takes an activity which can be solitary and puts it in touch with other people. It's a long process to achieve a book.

TOMPKINS: Or even an essay.

WILLIAMS: Have you ever counted hours?

KAPLAN: How long it takes to produce something?

DAVIDSON: Oh, I think that would be terrible.

WILLIAMS: Ten hours on a bloody paragraph. . . .

KAPLAN: And then other things write themselves.

DAVIDSON: One chapter in my book I wrote in the morning, just because it was my turn to go before the group and I had to have something. I brought it and thought it was terrible. The group loved it, and I now think it's one of the best chapters. On the other hand, the introduction I wrote about six hundred times. There aren't rules. I don't think you ever fully learn the lessons, and you have to keep relearning them. You learn certain tricks and certain repertoires, but you forget them too, or you have to learn other ones for other situations.

TOMPKINS: Or you have to find them out all over again.

DAVIDSON: And sometimes it's painful. That's the thing with writing.

TOMPKINS: What I love is when—I've been writing this column for a newspaper. . . .

WILLIAMS: Do you write it regularly?

TOMPKINS: Yes, once a month, and sometimes I bring my column, and Cathy walks in and says, "Take this paragraph and put it here, and take this paragraph and put it there, and you don't need to say this anymore, and beef this up a little here, and you've got it, boom, boom, boom, boom." It's sort of like going to a specialist with a broken thing, and they take their tools and it's in shape. Marianna will always find where the fat is, the stuff that doesn't have to be there. She just has an unerring eye.

TORGOVNICK: The flip side of that, though, is that sometimes you expect the group to perform miracles, and it can't.

TOMPKINS: You have to do the evolution yourself.

KAPLAN: That happened to me very much at the end of my book. I got up to a point where the group had read so many drafts, they couldn't help me anymore.

TOMPKINS: Maybe we should tell you about our marathon sessions. There was a time earlier in the life of the group when Marianna, Alice, and I all had completed manuscripts. They were at various stages of being ready. Marianna's was the closest, then mine, then Alice's. I was in California that semester, and at a certain point we mailed each other our manuscripts and I flew back and we had a two-day marathon session.

WILLIAMS: Did you stock in provisions?

TOMPKINS: We went through each manuscript. . . .

TORGOVNICK: Chapter by chapter, it was wonderful. . . .

TOMPKINS: And we recorded the whole thing, so that we would each have a tape to listen to when we wanted to go back and make revisions. We were sort of exhausted and exhilarated at the end, because it was so much work, but it was fantastic.

KAPLAN: And then we did something similar with *Mount Fuji*, we had one [session] that was several hours. . . .

TORGOVNICK: We have an open-door policy to marathons, although they require advance warning. But it's really an invaluable experience to have people read your book, giving you one more chance before it's going out in the world. When the book goes out in the world, you get a different level of feedback.

WILLIAMS: To shift gears a bit, I wanted to ask a question about how you see what you do in relation to other tendencies on the current scene—to, say, confessional criticism, or other kinds of critical writing. Do you have comments on why so many people are doing this at the same time—for instance, Nancy Miller in *Getting Personal* or Lentricchia in *Edge of Night*? Besides those, it seems to me that there are a lot of new kinds of critical writing, like Michael Bérubé's things in the *Village Voice* or Avital Ronell's *Telephone Book*.

TOMPKINS: That's a big question.

TORGOVNICK: I don't feel I can answer that question. I haven't thought about my writing in relationship to those books.

DAVIDSON: I share Marianna's unease about situating my writing in relationship to the field right now. But I certainly remember the first time I read Barthes' *Mythologies*, realizing that I could write a kind of criticism that's different from the kind I'd been taught in graduate school. From Barthes I learned a new world of voice and eloquence and passion and wit. In some way, that became a model for me. I don't know that many people would think that was personal writing, but it just felt connected and passionate. . . .

KAPLAN: Miller has a lot to say about Barthes in *Getting Personal.*

DAVIDSON: He wrote so beautifully. So that was important for me to feel that kind of freedom. I'm not sure I like the personal or not-personal distinction, especially when you're talking about Ronell or Bérubé, who are very different from each other and very different from what we're doing too, but that sense of freedom and that sense you can explore different voices is crucial. It's important to realize you can write intelligently and not use what I'll call the footnote voice. It's part of the poststructural moment, postmodern. . . .

WILLIAMS: The post-poststructural moment. . . .

DAVIDSON: The post-poststructural moment. It's very exciting.

WILLIAMS: What's your read on the scene of criticism right now? It seems to me that we're in a different moment now than we were ten years ago, sort of the last gasp of High Theory.

TOMPKINS: I'm not so sure.

TORGOVNICK: I don't think you can be sure about the end of theory.

KAPLAN: I don't know about the division you're making between personal writing and theory. There's something in me that really resists it.

DAVIDSON: In Barthes, there's both.

TORGOVNICK: Some of the biggest compliments I got about *Gone Primitive* were when people told me I had done theory and personal writing. So I don't buy the distinction.

KAPLAN: I got a lot out of a book that was a general audience book, which was Carolyn Heilbrun's *Writing a Woman's Life.* I read that several times while I was writing *French Lessons.* But also I read technical essays about language acquisition and novels about "métiers," like Richard Ford's *The Sportswriter.*

WILLIAMS: Again, you were saying before that autobiography is very much a form, so the personal is a formal category that's not necessarily opposed to theory. About the current state of criticism and theory, what do you think of the things you see at MLA? If you go to MLA, what are your reactions?

DAVIDSON: I'd say mixed. I go to MLA and some things bore me to death, and other things I find exciting.

TORGOVNICK: There's a lot of interesting stuff going on at MLA. I think that cultural studies has been a significant infusion into what we used to think of as MLA. One of the things which happened really effortlessly was that the subject matter available to literary people has become so much greater.

KAPLAN: One thing that's happening in my own trajectory; when I was a graduate student, I read almost uniquely theory, and now I'd say I read a whole lot more fiction. And it's probably because I got very interested in problems of form, so I wanted to see how writers created form. It's enriched doing the kind of writing that I've been doing, more literary writing. It's also enriched my teaching. I read different kinds of criticism now; I've gone back to some of those French close readers of literary texts and rediscovered rhetorical and genre criticism.

TORGOVNICK: I had a special fixation on fiction when I got out of graduate school. I'm reading more nonfiction now. I still read novels, but I've gotten great pleasure recently from writing about land, for instance, a book called *Dakota* by Kathleen Norris. And I read Norman Maclean's *Young Men and Fire,* and I got a lot of energy from that. The boundary between fiction and nonfiction has broken down to some extent, and a lot of people write nonfiction with the energy that goes into fiction. That's another very important thing that we've all been working on, how to bring that kind of energy to criticism.

WILLIAMS: That brings up another question. Is what you're doing a new belletrism? That's a little bit of a wiseass phrase, but is it a return to literature (which I think is salutary in some ways—god forbid professors write the way they usually do)? On the other hand, is this return to literature or more self-consciously literary writing a return to a humanistic or belletristic ethos? What are the politics implicit in it?

TOMPKINS: Well, I'll speak for myself. Writing in the personal mode has freed me up as a writer and has made me feel that I could do more with the medium. Maybe as a result of that, or because I feel much more in touch with myself in doing this kind of writing, I'm more interested in literature. That is, I'm more interested in the imaginative and creative and magical properties of literature than I was for a long time, doing theory and more politically oriented thinking about it. So that's my trajectory, but it doesn't have any agenda attached to it that I'm aware of. It doesn't mean that I have to read only literature or teach only literature anymore. In fact, the last course that I taught, I taught two classical literary texts, and the only writing that people did in relation to those texts was creative writing or creative living. It's another dimension of literature to which I've returned. I don't even know if I should say returned.

DAVIDSON: *36 Views of Mount Fuji* comes from Hokusai, an early nineteenth-century printmaker, who's taking his inspiration from much earlier Japanese and Chinese sources that resonate with our poststructuralist concepts of relativism and perspectivism. I don't know if I would talk about my interest in writing about Japan in that particular book as humanistic. Zen is very postmodern. I'm just not sure about those kinds of equations of the personal with a certain kind of political agenda. Certainly there is a big political agenda in that book as well the personal agenda. So for me those oppositions don't hold.

TORGOVNICK: You're making me feel as if we need a name for what we're doing, because otherwise somebody else is going to give us a name. I think we've been resistant to giving it a name, but coming off these two comments I would say that to me it's a big mistake to put a divide between criticism and writing. One of the things in which I've found great pleasure is when people ask about the creative process that goes into writing criticism. For me it comes back to feeling that criticism is a form of writing. . . .

KAPLAN: I don't know how I could go back to a time before I studied deconstruction or before I was aware of theory, which woke me up and made me excited about the world and made me see things in terms of signs, and feminism, which made me see myself as constructed. All the things about theory I had learned went into writing a memoir about the construction of my cultural self in the world. So, to call that. . . . You know, when I think of the old humanism and the old belletrism, I think of a kind of dreary literary history, where it's just the theories of guys in salons talking to each other. I mean, I love certain kinds of philology. I think Leo Spitzer's essay on *Phèdre* is one of the greatest pieces of literary criticism ever written, but calling somebody a humanist in the age of theory is an accusation, no?

WILLIAMS: Twenty years from now, couldn't people say that you were in a salon?

DAVIDSON: I don't know, I kind of like the idea.

TORGOVNICK: I don't have any problem with being in a circle. I think we probably do represent a movement, and we are passing up a power-move in not naming it. It's a temptation that women have always succumbed to, not naming the movement, and then some man comes in and names the movement.

DAVIDSON: We'd better come up with a name.

TORGOVNICK: Personal writing is not it. Integrative writing, I think it's a model of integration. . . .

TOMPKINS: But at the same time also permitting fragmentation, permitting lots of different selves, or different aspects of the self. . . .

TORGOVNICK: Creative criticism or writerly criticism?

DAVIDSON: I like creative criticism or writerly criticism better than personal criticism.

TORGOVNICK: Me too.

TOMPKINS: One thing about graduate students these days is that most of them are poets or closet poets. Last year, it seems to me a pretty large proportion of the first-year students were writing poetry. I don't think that's just our students either. There's a tremendous desire on the part of graduate students, and undergraduates too, to do writing that's more creative than the standard critical essay. And they have to lead these split lives or even be ashamed of what they write. I'm sorry, that's really wrong. The profession has shut itself off from a tremendous source of energy, and that just can't go on anymore.

TORGOVNICK: I think that's true, but there's another side. We were the victims but also the beneficiaries of a particular kind of education. We got certain kinds of background that our students don't always get.

TOMPKINS: You mean in writing? In studying?

TORGOVNICK: In studying, in actual content. One of the things that one notices is that there's a tendency to write and construct theory without having some of the background first, and that's not something that I especially want to encourage. There's an imaginative relationship to the material which I think should be encouraged, but I think that certain forms of material demand a particular level of knowledge.

KAPLAN: It's hard to teach today. In my field there's a crisis because of course France is no longer the center of the universe—or even of Europe! The whole corpus has expanded to include all the francophone countries, so the amount of knowledge required has become huge, and the faculty don't always have the expertise to respond to what the students want.

DAVIDSON: One of the reasons I'm excited about teaching and the profession again is that I'm teaching a photography course, and my students know more than I do about the technology of the camera and even about media more generally. They're visually- and media-literate and sensitive. It's exciting to go into the classroom. We spend part of each class not only reading texts about photography, whether it's fictional texts or theoretical texts, but we look at photographs, and my students see differently than I do. It's a different background. Their vocabulary is different. I leave class feeling energized.

TORGOVNICK: On the other hand, there are different kinds of problems. I think it's tough to teach graduate students well; it's tough to read dissertations; it's tough to know exactly what kind of advice to give them. It's hard because today there's a very different landscape from the one that we came up in, not that the one we came up in was all that easy. . . .

DAVIDSON: No, it wasn't easy. . . .

TORGOVNICK: It was a hard one. But this is hard in a different way. Things become familiar and old hat with so much speed.

WILLIAMS: That brings up another point about politics and the profession. It seems to me it's a beleaguered profession. What was the landscape like before, and how do you think it is for students now?

DAVIDSON: Undergraduate or graduate students?

WILLIAMS: Your students in general.

DAVIDSON: I think in English and probably in French too, on the graduate level, it's one of the worst job markets that's ever been, at least since World War II, so there's the blatant problem that some of these brilliant people are writing dissertations and not getting jobs.

KAPLAN: And it was supposed to be different.

WILLIAMS: There were predictions that it would change in the early 1990s.

DAVIDSON: It should be different. The retirements have happened. That's why we're all so overworked. It's happened. People are retiring but not being replaced.

KAPLAN: And the economic crisis.

TORGOVNICK: Universities are about three years behind the general economy, so I think we'll see a reversal. There's a lot of waste going on. There are students who, I think, are much more talented than I was at their age, and who are really struggling.

TOMPKINS: I feel sad that the students have to spend so much time thinking about the profession and how they're going to get a job. From day one, they come in and they're thinking about the job market, and they're twisted out of shape by it. It's awful.

TORGOVNICK: We were touchingly naïve in lots of ways. I remember we compared our professional careers, and it's miraculous that we survived. We took crazy and idiosyncratic routes.

KAPLAN: Now, the pressure to publish while they're still in graduate school, it's terrible. . . .

TOMPKINS: And to be up on everything. They're so afraid not to speak a language of expertise, a technical language. . . .

WILLIAMS: For me, it's a pressing political issue. It seems to me that we're in a devastated profession, that eats its young, although one of my friends says it's a profession that leaves its young out in the desert to starve. . . .

TOMPKINS and KAPLAN: Both are true.

TORGOVNICK: We can change that if we exert constant pressure, but it's going to take a lot of pressure, and faculties often don't have the will for it. When I go around the country, I urge faculties, "Do not accept higher teaching loads, do not accept larger classes, do not allow young people to be squeezed out." That's part of our responsibility if we teach and are in the profession. But the other thing is the relaxing of the retirement age. I guess it will benefit us at a certain age, but what is it going to do to all the kids who are waiting for jobs that aren't going to be opening up. It's really quite appalling.

WILLIAMS: I recently read a statistic that faculties are something like fifty to sixty percent full-time and forty to fifty percent part-time. This fits the general post-Fordist reshuffling of labor: part-timers are very cheap, no benefits, so it's an effective employment practice. But universities used not to do that; it used to be something like ninety percent full-time. How about if we pick up one point from before, relating to the question of politics. You had mentioned, Cathy, that your book is very definitely informed by feminism, so it has the vista of feminist politics. . . .

DAVIDSON: Yes, but not just feminist. It's informed by a constellation of my own personal politics, antiracist politics, multicultural politics, feminist politics, and there's an economic agenda that I put forth. There are a lot of different levels of politics. I'm a political person; politics are a passionate part of my life. One of the projects I'm doing now is with a photojournalist who's photographing the little town of Mebane in North Carolina, which has been hurt by a plant closing. He's doing the photojournalism and I'm doing the text for this book. We're looking at what happened to Mebane, people who were put out of work when the White furniture factory went out of business. So that kind of politics is important to me, too.

KAPLAN: Do you want more testimony?

[Cathy Davidson has to leave for a meeting at this point.]

WILLIAMS: It seems to me that feminism enables the way that you write.

KAPLAN: Well, on a political level, my work has been antifascist, in *Reproductions of Banality*, to the work I did in *French Lessons* about Holocaust revisionism, and on a personal level working through my relationship to my father, who was a prosecutor at Nuremburg. The feminism there is deep; it's not programmatic—it has to do with fathers, mentors, and what it means for an intellectual woman to have an ambition.

TORGOVNICK: My own trajectory has been more concerned with processes of making meaning, although I would not have put it that way early in my career. There certainly was a time when I was upset that the process of making meaning in art did not have to do with politics, but I'm increasingly aware that there is no separation between the two. I have always thought of myself as a feminist but certainly not as a programmatic feminist, and I think a lot of the recent work I've been doing, a lot of the essays in *Crossing Ocean Parkway*, are about various roles that women play in life, both in the family and professionally.

TOMPKINS: My turn. I used to be interested in politics. I don't know how to describe. . . .

TORGOVNICK: You're interested in emotional politics.

TOMPKINS: Well, I was heavily into canon formation when I wrote *Sensational Designs* and believed strongly and still believe that the books that are taught in school send strong messages about who's powerful in the culture and who gets listened to and who can be respected. But my own interests have evolved from institutional polemics to personal development and exploration. I put large portions of my life on hold to become professionally successful, and now I'm making up for that and doing a lot of work on myself. So I'm not involved in critical debates all that much. *West of Everything* does have an agenda, in the sense that it's taking a feminist perspective on fiction and cultural narratives that were written for men and about men. Basically my thesis there was that, in order to think of themselves as persons who could command respect and be successful in our society, men have had to shut down on their emotional lives. The Western hero was a model for how to tough it out in this kind of world. After I wrote the book I discovered that I wasn't just writing about men, I was writing about myself. I'd had to become a man to do what I'd done.

WILLIAMS: Hence why you cook breakfast at Wellspring grocery on weekends, as all the local graduate students tell me?

TOMPKINS: I needed to get out of an academic environment to continue this process of self-recovery. Spiritual life has become important to me. I'm writing about my experiments in the classroom now, where I try to step out of a position of authority and get the students to take over and become responsible for their learning. And I've been trying to understand my own formation as a child in school, how I've been imprinted by authority, where my fears come from. I guess in some sense there could be a systematic or political outcome, at least as far as the way our school systems are organized, but right now I'm not at that level. I'm just trying to find out what happened to me, in order to understand myself.

WILLIAMS: To close, what is everyone working on now?

TORGOVNICK: *Crossing Ocean Parkway* is coming out in the fall. . . .

WILLIAMS: I read "Slasher Stories" [in *Crossing Ocean Parkway*] last night and it almost made me cry, which always is a sign of . . .

TOMPKINS: Well, there you go. . . .

KAPLAN: That's a goal each of us has worked toward, to move people in different ways.

TORGOVNICK: This is a book written from an Italian-American female point of view. Half the essays are autobiographical with some cultural focus, and half of the essays are cultural with some autobiographical perspective. I'm aiming for the warm and the touching, and the integration of personal history and intellectual interests. The project I'm in the middle of is called *Primitivism and the Quest for Ecstasy*. It began as an extension of *Gone Primitive*, but it's much more about primitivism as a displaced form of spiritual expression. I'm dealing with a lot of contemporary phenomena, like body piercing, and then particular case studies, like Georgia O'Keeffe and Dian Fossey. What I'm talking about is a kind of symbolic primitivism, an attraction towards land and animal life, and the desire to obliterate the concept of the self in relationship to the rest of the universe, which is a very deep pattern in religious experience. But it doesn't seem to find fulfillment in our culture, at least within religious institutions. So in our culture it seems to be channeled as a form of primitivism.

TOMPKINS: Didn't you work on Native Americans?

TORGOVNICK: In *Gone Primitive*, Africans were the primary example of the primitive, but in this book Native Americans are the quintessential example of the primitive, in part because I'm talking about a U. S.-based phenomenon.

KAPLAN: I'm just starting some new things. I do have something coming out this summer, an issue of *South Atlantic Quarterly* on Céline's American career, which I've coedited with Philippe Roussin, a colleague at the Centre de recherche sur les arts et le langage in Paris. I'm starting a new book project on the year 1945. That was the year of the liberation and the year a young writer named Robert Brassillach was executed for collaboration. It's very interesting to work on a fascist, closet gay, very sentimental in his fiction but really a very cruel guy who denounced Jews and communists. So I'm interested in that whole culture and how all the intellectuals in Paris positioned themselves in 1945 at the end of the war. Some of them were scrambling to save their asses, they were fighting to see who was going to lead the new generation—a very, very rich moment, and very confusing. So I want to write a book that will be lively. It's not going to be personal, but I want it to have all the energy that a personal book would have. I also think that I might have a novel in me at some point in the future. After writing *French Lessons*, I got interested in writing dialogue and fiction.

WILLIAMS: It doesn't seem as unusual in French intellectual life, one is able to write novels. . . .

TORGOVNICK: Just watch. Lots of people have done them under different names. . . .

KAPLAN: That's true in France, but the French make a really strong division between their persona as critics and their persona as novelists, whereas I don't believe in that. . . .

[This interview with Cathy Davidson, Alice Kaplan, Jane Tompkins, and Marianna Torgovnick took place on January 25, 1994 in Chapel Hill, NC, and was conducted by Jeffrey Williams, editor of *the minnesota review*. Thanks to the writing group for doing it.]

Relevant works:

Davidson, Cathy N. Review of *The Land Before Her: Fantasy and Experience of the American Frontiers, 1630–1860*, by Annette Kolodny. *Ms.* 30 (May 1984).

———. Review of *Sensational Designs: The Cultural Work of American Fiction*, by Jane Tompkins. *Vogue*, June 1985, 152.

———. Review of *The Handmaid's Tale*, by Margaret Atwood. *Ms.* February 1986, 24–26.

———. *The Book of Love: Writers and Their Love Letters*. New York: Pocket, 1992.

———. *Revolution and the Word: The Rise of the Novel in America.* New York: Oxford University Press, 1986.

———. *36 Views of Mount Fuji: On Finding Myself in Japan.* New York: Dutton, 1993.

Kaplan, Alice. *French Lessons: A Memoir.* Chicago: University of Chicago Press, 1993.

———. *Reproductions of Banality: Fascism, Literature, and French Intellectual Life.* Minneapolis: University of Minnesota Press, 1986.

———. "Selling Céline: The Céline–Little, Brown Correspondence (1934–1938)." *Céline, USA,* ed. Alice Kaplan and Philippe Roussin. *South Atlantic Quarterly* 93.2 (1994).

Tompkins, Jane. *A Life in School.* New York: Oxford University Press, 1995.

———. "Me and My Shadow." *The Intimate Critique: Autobiographical Literary Criticism,* ed. Diane P. Freedman, Olivia Frey, and Frances Murphy Zauhar. Durham: Duke University Press, 1993. 23–40. Rpt. from *New Literary History* 19.1 (1988).

———. *Sensational Designs: The Cultural Work of American Fiction 1790–1860.* New York: Oxford University Press, 1985.

———. *West of Everything: The Inner Life of Westerns.* New York: Oxford University Press, 1992.

Torgovnick, Marianna. *Crossing Ocean Parkway: Readings by an Italian American Daughter.* Chicago: University of Chicago Press, 1994.

———. "Experimental Critical Writing." *Profession* 90 (1990): 25–27.

———. *Gone Primitive: Savage Intellects, Modern Lives.* Chicago: University of Chicago Press, 1990.

———, ed. *Eloquent Obsessions: Writing Cultural Criticism.* Durham: Duke University Press, 1994.

16

White-Boy Authenticity

✿

TIM BRENNAN

I

From his parish in Yoro in the coffee regions of Honduras, my uncle used to write me letters. Unfolded in the cramped upstairs library of my parents' home, they were usually short, colored with Spanish words, and filled with anecdotes of travelling by mule. There was only time for a glance at them between football practice and piano lessons, but they were later stamped in my head by a glossy photo of a man in circular-framed glasses, wearing a white cassock, with his hand on a wooden worktable. The letters belonged to the library and existed only there, filled as they were with burros, straw hats, and Carlo Dulce's sculpture of the head of Christ. What I took with me outside the library was the feel and smell of the rice paper coverings, with their faint imprints from a cheap typewriter, and I held them in my hands, not caring very much about Yoro, but wanting to know more about the woven-straw figurines of campesinos and the rough woodcuts of cactuses and vines that accompanied the letters as a reward for writing back.

Of all his nephews, I was the only one who did. The real Catholic. My mom asked me as a matter of charity to give the lonely man in the jungle a needed contact with family—the family he decided never to have for himself. It was a question of self-sacrifice. But not that either, because he was a void to me, a place to cast embellished stories of school triumphs or football victories. When I learned later the effect he'd had, it crept up on me in the form of a memory of grainy black-and-white photos of Mexico I had seen in my school's aging geography textbooks, mixed with the feel of actual, living statues of tightly woven grass. In the moody recovery of those faint words on crisp paper, I had become his anagoge. "Had you lived earlier," my parents would say, "you would have been the family priest."

On a car trip to Irvine, California decades later, I visited him in his exile in Hobbs, Texas, where the Jesuits had banished him as a punishment for working with the Milwaukee poor. Having come back from Honduras in disrepute after a failed coffee cooperative venture, he stopped recruiting for the Church, and gave up his clerical vows of poverty as a hopeless sham to come face to face with the real ugliness of a welfare line. By the early 1980s, as Reagan marched on and Central America rose up, he had thrown his body into peace marches, civil disobedience, indignant editorials—what his Superior angrily called "social justice and other junk issues." On his own (with no money from his Order) he spent his days and nights toiling in a halfway house. He relearned the lesson taught by Gustavo Gutiérrez at a conference of Christian activists in Detroit, where the latter spoke about the fake "romance" of liberation theology once identified with an almost picturesque, and necessarily distant, poverty:

> The universality of the Church in North America has passed through this particularity [of American racial minorities]. . . . Why do we sometimes have this impression that the Latin American theologies are more accepted by some groups than are Black, Indian or Asian theologies of this country? Why? Why? Maybe it's because Latin America is a little farther away.[1]

Visiting in Hobbs, I caught him one day wandering around the mini-oil fields that fill the city's backyard lots. He was having one of those frightening conversations with himself (or God) that marked his later years, those self-dialogues carried long into the night behind the closed doors of his bedroom. By the third day, he had roused himself to talk to me, rather than God, about his unpublished autobiographical play, forty years in the making, entitled "Lavalette of Martinique." It was about a French missionary who had tried to fight imperialism by launching a progressive business venture, but who succeeded only in getting the Jesuits kicked out of France. By the fourth day, I was gone, and we were back to writing letters, quickened by my plan to tell his story in a chapter of an academic book. The letters of my early childhood, then, continued after the lapse of several decades, and we had come to recognize one another again in the issue of Central American war. Interviews in Texas and Milwaukee, a string of letters and phone conversations, armed me with my material checked against local sources. And he still sent me gifts, but modern now, American—Peter Berger's *A Rumor of Angels*, reminding me it was not only liberation but theology on his mind, the supernatural in everyday life.[2]

Fr. William Brennan, S.J. was a Jesuit missionary in Honduras and British Honduras (now Belize) in the 1950s and early 1960s, a personal friend of Fr. Joaquin López y López—one of the five Jesuits assassinated by the Salvadoran military in a celebrated case several years ago in San Salvador. Coming originally from the Midwest, he was a close personal friend in Honduras of the Chicago-based guerrilla priest, Fr. James Carney ("*el padre Guadalupe*"), who was later tortured and then murdered by being thrown from a helicopter at a U.S. military base in 1983. Over ten years, he had been shuffled from one parish to another by his own Order, eager to stop him from speaking about causes ranging from the contras to the war in Iraq. When he returned to the United States, more than a decade after he had left, he assumed the role for which he had been originally trained, taking on the job of English teacher at Marquette High School in Milwaukee, Wisconsin. The Central American training of this Jesuit priest—a political reactionary in the early 1950s, a fan of Wisconsin senator Joe McCarthy—drove him finally to say he admired Trotsky and the Che of the Sierra Maestra. Having personally witnessed the Castillo Armas invasion of Guatemala in 1954 (he was in the Guatemalan airport with my grandparents as loudspeakers announced the coming troops), he found himself identifying with those priests in the field who had made the *formal* declarations of Vatican II and Medellín a formality. "Carney was a rebel from way up the gulch," Bill wrote me once. "He and [the Colombian guerrilla priest, Camilo] Torres cut through all the pious bullshit. They lived it. They are the prophets." Torres had once written: "Revolution is not just permitted; it is the obligation of Christians who see in it the only effective and complete means of realizing the love of all." Bill's position had become, as he put it pointedly to me in one letter, "the radical reform of the capitalistic system."

> Most of my life I've been bothered by people who talked about this threat of atheistic communism; now that I've seen that paper-maché monster crumble, now for the first time people are looking at capitalism with a jaundiced eye; people are beginning to question what [the Protestant theologian] Martin Marty has called "the righteous empire."

He had tried later, unsuccessfully, to return to Central America in the 1980s as a long-term volunteer for Witness for Peace, but his Superior refused him with the words: "we don't need any more dead Jesuits."

II

As a white teacher of black and Latino literatures, I have heard more than once the presumptuous question: "how did *you* get interested in *that*?" It has been enough to make me wonder what a forlorn Jesuit at war with himself had to do with my "unnatural" attachments to the other Americas. After an early bout with college, I found myself dropping out of school and planning a trip to the Lacandon forests of Chiapas and the Yucatán—not as a tourist, but as a roustabout and seeker, using as my informant a local boy who has since died of AIDS. I studied Spanish on the run, without benefit of schooling, and for reasons I do not know—maybe because I had seen Gregory Peck in the Spanish Civil War flick, *Behold a Pale Horse* (one of Hollywood's few), or because I wanted to read Pablo Neruda in his own language after his name came up following a chance viewing of the Cuban feminist film, *Lucía*, in Cambridge, Massachusetts, where I had hitchhiked with my heroin-addict friend, and where I spent an afternoon in a pub with a woman who taught me the words to a José Martí poem. After I had turned down a graduate fellowship to Stanford to work in a Pinto factory in Metuchen, New Jersey, I had memorized long passages of Neruda, and entertained coworkers by reciting them:

> Junto a las catedrales, anudados
> al muro, acarrearon
> sus pies, sus bultos, sus miradas negras
> sus crecimientos lívidos de gárgolas
> sus latas andrajosas de comida
> y desde allí, desde la dura
> santidad de la piedra,
> se hicieron flora de la calle, errantes
> flores de las legales pestilencias. . . .[3]

How does one explain, at any rate, why in college in the mid- to late 1970s—before I had read much history or theory, or before I had done a real lick of organizational work—I wrote long, researched essays on blacks in the Communist Party and on the Fenians? Or why I wrote essays for my English classes on the lyrics of country-and-Western music? Where did those ideas come from? These tastes may have had nothing to do with Fr. Bill, but his stories helped me see them in the subcultural currents of Madison where I went to school, although well after the time of strife for which Madison was known.

But I was also dark—much darker than an Irish-American is supposed to be, so that before I saw how absurd it was, I would play at being foreign in the suburbs when I was young, calling myself a boy from India (my adopted cousin, with whom I grew up playing Civil War games, actually was from India, which gave me the original idea). And there was enough ambiguity in that sallow skin to cause people, even rather late, in the time of graduate school, to peer into my face and ask, "and where are you from?" Even before I had left the suburbs, there was an ethic in the circles I traveled in that one had to be against the "fuds"—the ones who follow their parents' advice because it is good for their careers. And that meant staking out the space where bohemia meets guerrilla—two very different structures that flow together in the mind of a certain middle-class nonconformism. The transformation of the bohemian impulse to a useable politics is surely a neglected process in the issue of white-boy authenticity.

White authenticity has too often seemed to mean planting the flag of ethnicity squarely on the white page: I am Jew (Cynthia Ozick, Paul Rabinow), I am Italian (Marianna Torgovnick, Camille Paglia), I am American Indian (Louise Erdrich), I am Latino (Ariel Dorfman). I repudiate Irish-Americanism as a meaningful belonging for me. American ethnicity was always for me a game of inbreeding, job-trusting, and easy cultural signifiers. We grew up singing "Brennan on the Moor" and had Irish soda bread on St. Patrick's day and drifted dreamlike in clouds of Notre Dame football lore. But the familiar Irish legends, the tiresome family genealogies, always made me feel much more Chicago machine politics than refugees from the famine. I never said I was Irish, and I do not claim it now. Or rather, the Ireland I know is a Third-World country whose interest for me is historical: the Fenians, the memory of Bogside Derry, Bernadette Devlin, and (over here) the Molly Maguires. My formative culture was crisscrossed not by ethnicity but by a web of arbitrary institutional possibilities, which included the Jewish Community Center (I was on their regional swim team in childhood) and the other, more powerful one of the Catholic Church. But I had largely left the Church by my high school years, and so it lived on for me primarily through the influence of my uncle, from a generation for whom the Church still mattered.

But then, why an uncle? Why would that in many ways distant relationship signify more strongly than the suffocating embrace of parents? Because he was close enough to be family, but far enough away to allow a plausible denial of the hereditary necessity of imitative behavior. And *this* uncle meant not Ireland but the immediate, New World identity of a specific and regional people of which I was truly, not romantically, a part; and it meant a class of election joined after a moral rejection of one's own. One had him there at hand to establish precedence for actions one wanted to perform in one's own life, but could always ignore him when the precedence did not suit. Because as a celibate priest and nonconformist, he represented an END to the family line, and, as such, was an antidote to family. The bodily sterility of his vows complemented the great tillage potent in his life-sacrifice. Anyway, he wore black. He was talked about in tones of unmistakeable pity, arriving at Christmas gatherings (to most eyes lamentably) in the company of my old-maid aunt, his sister.

In that, he was set off against a possible, even logical, influence: my uncle Terry (his brother)—a great all-American football player and former coach of Notre Dame, now Chicago stockbroker, who grumbled loudly of his brother's shame. A man of the cloth denouncing the Pope and getting arrested in protests against nuclear waste storage in New Mexico was a disgrace to Terry, the perennial fud. He had had feature articles written about him in *Life*,

Newsweek, and *The Saturday Evening Post* in the mid-1950s and was named (along with Robert F. Kennedy) one of the ten outstanding young men in America in 1955, just as Bill was learning how the military ruled in Honduras during the bloody election campaign of the liberal, Villada Morales. As far as uncles go, Terry was a morose, casually racist, drinking man who understood fame, soothed power, and milked the Irish vote. While not aspiring to Bill's exact combination of burdens, I was drawn to the lessons implicit in the horror of his childlessness. I sought another, more updated version of his isolation, his living afar, and his discipline, for the latter was related (as all religions of the Book are) to fanaticism; and fanaticism, once translated from the language of suspicion, often means this: determination, principle.

III

A specific conjuncture, not racial memory, is what I want to use. Whatever drove me has to do with place and positioning, not lineage. By class, that positioning has been negative and reactive. By geographic location, it was not so much the chance encounter with Bill that inspired as that he and I both, in different ways, grew out of a Midwestern antinomianism. In Bill's case, the influences were at times predictably ascetic—he admired his Jesuit teachers at Marquette for reasons at once "red" and "black": as he put it, they "didn't care what kind of shoes they wore or whether their pants were pressed." But other heroes of this early period for him were much less typical of the son of a lawyer living in a conservative suburb of a major, Northern, industrial city. "In the small print of Catholic social heroes," Fr. Bill explains, "there are very few entries between 1910 and 1930. One of them was Peter E. Dietz—one of the pioneers of Catholic social justice."

Although in the pre–World War II era, the big name in that small circle of clerics doing social justice work was a fellow named Father Johnny Ryan, Dietz was a local hero. After Dietz's vocal support for collective bargaining and unionization, he was expelled from Cincinnati by his bishop, and exiled to what was then the farmlands of Whitefish Bay, just north of Milwaukee— Fr. Bill's boyhood home. The idea of priesthood as an organizational task, mundane and beatific, was imprinted on his mind by Dietz's involvement with Father John Ireland, a famous archbishop from St. Paul, who had begun a school initative called the Fairibeau experiment (after a little town in Minnesota). Those involved wanted to abandon the parochial school, and have the township pay the sisters directly with public funds—not in order to sneak religious instruction into public schooling, but to make school possible for more children by using an available, educated workforce. Dietz was for the plan, while the Jesuits fought it.

The turning point for Bill was his decision to oversee work at Casa Maria, a local refuge and halfway house founded by the Irish lay Catholic social worker, Michael Cullen, who had been deported from the country in the early 1970s for pouring blood on draft records. With roots in the mutiracial activism of Fr. James Groppi, Casa was run mostly on donations, and by joining it, Fr. Bill was cut off financially by his Order, which strongly disapproved of his actions.

At Casa, it was mostly just a matter of "presence" to the poor. "It was a very important time in my life," he said. "I got in touch with poverty, artificially created by a bad system." The work involved going down to help people whose gas had been cut off, feeding them, standing with them in the welfare lines, seeing the welfare system, the ugliness of it. The president of Marquette University at the time was a fellow who really believed that the Church should not be concerned with that sort of thing, since Casa was not what was then technically known as a "religious house." Its residents were about seventy-five to eighty percent black with a few Latinos, and the rest poor whites. Things began to happen. William began sending a regular newsletter on health care issues around the Midwest region to the Jesuit residences. His photo began appearing next to Op-Ed columns in the local newspapers protesting the war in Central America. He applied and was accepted as a long-term guide for Witness for Peace in Nicaragua, but was refused permission to go. "The virtuous and the learned did not want me at Casa because, *tarde o temprano*, I would be picketing Marquette. That's why I was finally removed." He was at this point forced to leave not only Casa Maria, but Milwaukee as well.

The attractive militancy of Torres or Carney is undeniable as a source of emulation and energy in the often grim and usually dull work of social change. And the Midwest did, in fact, offer its own versions of life-drama in the person of Fr. James Groppi of Milwaukee, who was active in precisely the years of Bill's return to the U.S. Groppi had been a man who, in visible solidarity with the black communities in the era of the Black Panthers, filled the position of angry spokesman on the nightly news, and as a leader of loud marches through Milwaukee's usually placid streets, gained national reputation as a civil rights leader. The Irish immigrant, Michael Cullen, had founded Casa Maria in just this period, in alliance with Groppi and a larger Peace and Justice community that Fr. Bill later joined, becoming (like Groppi) an embarrassment to his Order.

In the annals of Midwestern Christian activism, however, such legendary models are scarce. Activists would be more likely to draw for example (as Fr. Bill did) on the more homely example of Fr. Claud Hitehaus, the senior Jesuit overseer of the student newspaper at St. Louis University. In 1945, to protest the refusal of the school to enroll blacks, he wrote an ironic editorial in the mask of a moral theology on Christian cannibalism, citing moral authorities to the effect that Church doctrine did not prevent Christians from eating one another. We are reminded here, negatively, of what the African-American theologian, James Cone, has said about religious practice in this country:

> The sin of American theology is that it has spoken without passion.... When it has tried to speak for the poor, it has been so cool and calm in its analysis of human evil that it implicitly disclosed whose side it was on.[4]

The passion of Hitehaus earned him public censure, and the friendship of Fr. Bill. One takes what one can get.

Conjuncture, not lineage, is what I know and instinctively knew. Victor Berger's "sewer socialism"; the Madison mayoralty of Paul Soglin; James Groppi; the lectures of Madison historian, Harvey Goldberg; and the William Appleman Williams of *The Great Evasion*.[5] I am a white American from the Midwest, and these tastes of mine—although they register today as a peculiar sort of racial betrayal or pretense, as a flight from identity—are situated solidly in my place and time.

Notes

1. Gustavo Gutiérrez, "The Historical Project of the Poor in the Context of the North American Church," *Theology in the Americas: Detroit II Conference Papers*, eds. Cornel West, Caridad Guidote, and Margaret Coakley. (Maryknoll, NY: Orbis, 1982), 84.

2. Peter L. Berger, *A Rumor of Angels: Modern Society and the Rediscovery of the Supernatural* (New York, London, and Toronto: Anchor/Doubleday, 1969).

3. Pablo Neruda, *Selected Poems of Pablo Neruda*, ed. and trans. Ben Belitt, (New York: Grove, 1961), 152. Passage taken from "Los Mendigos" (the Beggars): "Close by the cathedrals, knotted/ to the wall, they hauled/ their feet, their bundles, their black looks/ the pale growth of gargoyles/ their jagged cans of food/ and out from there, away from that hard/ piety of the stone/ they became a street flower/ wandering flowers of legal pestilence" (my translation).

4. James Cone, *A Black Theology of Liberation*, 2nd ed. (Maryknoll, NY: Orbis, 1986), 18.

5. William Appleman Williams, *The Great Evasion* (Chicago: Quadrangle, 1964).

III

Just Do It!

17

Life as We Know It

❀

MICHAEL BÉRUBÉ

In my line of work I don't think very often about carbon or potassium, much less about polypeptide chains or transfer-RNA. I teach American and African-American literature; Janet Lyon, my legal spouse and general partner, teaches modern British literature and women's studies. Nothing about our jobs requires us to be conscious of the biochemical processes that made us—and, more recently, our children—into conscious beings. But in 1985–86, when Janet was pregnant with our first child, Nicholas, I would lie awake for hours, wondering how the baseball-size clump of cells in her uterus was really going to form something living, let alone something capable of thought. I knew that the physical processes that form dogs and *drosophila* are more or less as intricate, on the molecular level, as those that form humans; but puppies and fruit flies don't go around asking how they got here, or how (another version of the same question) DNA base-pair sequences code for various amino acids. And though humans have been amazed and puzzled by human gestation for quite a while now, it wasn't until a few nanoseconds ago (in geological time) that their wonder began to focus on the chemical minutiae that somehow differentiate living matter from "mere" matter. The fact that self-replicating molecules had eventually come up with a life-form that could actually pick apart the workings of self-replicating molecules . . . well, let's just say I found this line of thought something of a distraction. So much so that finally, a friend of ours decided that what I needed was a good dose of demystification. "Michael," he said, stopping me in the middle of one of my frantic-father frenzies, "I know this is all new to you, but look at it this way— it's just DNA making a home for itself."

I recall replying that the spectacle of DNA making its home was plenty worthy of our attention, but I also thought, at the time, that I would never again devote so much attention to it. Not in my line of work—and probably not even with a second or third child, either. I figured that the miracle of human birth, like the miracle of humans landing on the moon, just wouldn't have the same emotional impact the second time around.

When You're Busy Making Other Plans

Five years later, in September 1991, Janet was pregnant again, another fall semester was beginning, and I was up late writing. At 2:00 A.M., Janet asked when I was coming to bed. At 4:00 A.M., she asked again. "Soon," I said. "Well, you should probably stop working now," she replied, "because I think I'm going into labor." At which point she presented me with an early birthday present, a watch with a second hand.

That was the first unexpected thing: James wasn't due for another two weeks. Then came more unexpected things, in rapid succession.

Eight hours later, in the middle of labor, Janet spotted a dangerous arrhythmia on her heart monitor. The only other person in the room was an obstetrics staff nurse; Janet turned to her and barked, "That's V-tach. We need a cardiologist in here. Get a bolus of lidocaine ready, and get the crash cart." (Being an ex-cardiac-intensive-care nurse comes in handy sometimes.) Pounding on her chest and forcing herself to cough, she broke out of what was possibly a lethal heart rhythm. Labor stalled; Janet and I stared at each other for an hour. Suddenly, at a strange moment when she and I were the only people in the room, James's head presented. I hollered down the hall for help. James appeared within minutes, an unmoving baby of a deep, rich, purple hue, tangled in his umbilical cord. "He looks downsy around the eyes," I heard. Downsy? He looks stillborn, I thought. They unwrapped the cord, cut it, gave him oxygen. Quickly, incredibly, he revived. No cry, but who cared? They gave him an Apgar score of 7, on a scale from 1 to 10. I remember feeling an immense relief. My wife was alive, my second child was alive. At the end of a teeth-grating hour during which I'd wondered if either of them would see the end of the day, Down syndrome somehow seemed like a reprieve.

I mention all this because most folks' first reactions to having a child with Down syndrome consist, understandably, of confusion, sorrow, despair, anger. "Relief" isn't usually on the agenda. And it didn't last long, either. Over the next half hour, as the nurses worked on James, and Janet and I tried to collect our thoughts, I realized I didn't know very much about Down's, other than that it meant James had an extra chromosome and would be mentally retarded. I knew I'd have some homework to do.

But what kind of homework were we talking about? Would we ever have normal lives again? We'd struggled for eight years on salaries that left us able to peer at the poverty line only if one of us stood on the other's shoulders. A mere three weeks earlier, the university had hired Janet, thus making us one of the extremely rare dual-career academic couples working in the same department; we knew how lucky we were, and we thought we were finally going to be "comfortable." But now, were we going to spend the rest of our days caring for a severely disabled child? Would we have even an hour to ourselves? Christ, we'd only just finished paying off the bills for *Nick's* birth two months earlier (we had special graduate-student "Swiss cheese" insurance at the time), and now were we going to plunge into the kind of catastrophic medical debt that makes the op-ed pages? These were selfish thoughts, and the understanding that selfish thoughts might be "natural" at such a time didn't make them any less bitter or insistent.

We went over the past few months. The pregnancy had been occasionally odd but not exactly scary. We'd decided against getting an amniocentesis at twelve weeks, on the grounds that a sonogram would pick up nearly any serious problems with the fetus *except* Down syndrome, and the chances of having a child with Down syndrome at Janet's age, thirty-six, were roughly equal to the chances of an amniocentesis-induced miscarriage (1 in 225 and 1 in 200, respectively). Later in the pregnancy there were some hitches: reduced fetal movements, disproportionate fetal measurements on sonograms, low weight gain, and so on. Our worries had been vague but persistent.

Back in the present, over on his table in the birthing room, James wasn't doing very well. He still wasn't moving, he had no sucking reflex, and he was getting bluer. How could his Apgar have been 7? We'd been told everything was all right for a newborn with Down's, but it wasn't, as we found a bit later when James was transferred from the nursery to the intensive-care unit and put on 100 percent oxygen. It turned out that the fetal opening in his heart hadn't closed fully. You and I had the same arrangement until just before we were born, when on our fateful journeys down the birth canal our heart's ventricles sealed themselves off in order to get us ready to start conducting oxygen from our lungs into our bloodstream. But James still had a hole where no hole should be, and wasn't oxygenating properly.

There was more. Alongside his patent ductus arteriosus and his trisomy-21, there was laryngomalacia (floppy larynx), jaundice, polycythemia (an abnormal increase in red blood cells), torticollis, vertebral anomaly, scoliosis, hypotonia (low muscle tone), and (not least of these) feeding problems. That's a lot of text to wade through to get to your kid.

Basically, James was in danger. If he made it through the night, he would still be a candidate, in the morning, for open heart surgery *and* a tracheostomy. Because of the laryngomalacia, which isn't related to Down's, he couldn't coordinate sucking, swallowing, and breathing, and his air supply would close off if he slept on the wrong side. Surgery (the tracheostomy) was therefore a very real option. The vertebral problems, we learned, occur in roughly one of six kids with Down's: his first three vertebrae were malformed, his spinal cord vulnerable. And his neck muscles were abnormally tight (that's the torticollis), leaving him with a 20-degree head tilt to the left. He was being fed intravenously and had tubes not only in his arm but in his stomach, run neatly through his umbilical artery, which was still viable from the delivery. Our first Polaroid of him shows a little fleshy thing under a clear plastic basin, lost in machinery and wires. I remember thinking, it's all right that they do all this to him now because he'll never remember it. But it can't be a pleasant introduction to the world.

Even as I type this, I find that I'm tapping into physical and tactile memories etched somewhere in the contours of my neuromuscular map, evidences of a time when my every sense impression was so vivid as to be unreal. Once last year, at a fast-food restaurant, Janet and I found ourselves mumbling about how we remembered James's time in the ICU, and then mumbling about how strange it was that we'd each remembered the same thing, seemingly unbidden. Only after a puzzling half hour did we realize that the restaurant's bathrooms used the same red, sweet, pungent liquid soap with which we scrubbed ourselves every time we entered the ICU. It may not have been a madeleine, but the smell tapped that structure of feeling with the same primordial, uncanny accuracy to which Proust devoted his prose: all the details of neonatal intensive care came back unbidden, from Jamie's breathing tubes and his oxygen tent to the dim fluorescent lights and disposable scrubbing sponges.

But I'll cut to the chase. Within days, things got better, and one anxiety after another peeled away: Jamie's duct closed, and as I entered the intensive-care unit one morning I found that the staff had erased from his chart the phone number of the emergency helicopter service that would have flown him to Peoria for heart surgery. His blood-oxygen levels got up to the high nineties and stayed there, even as he was weaned from 100 percent oxygen to a level just above the atmospheric norm. A tracheoscopy (that is, a viewing of his throat with an eyepiece at the end of a tube) determined that he didn't need a tracheostomy. He still wasn't feeding, but he was opening an eye now and then and looking out at his brother and parents.

Meanwhile, the Foucauldian social-control apparatus was forming around us with incredible speed: within days we were known to, and put in touch with, a bewildering number of social agencies responsible for different aspects of James's care. We tried to sort out the DSC (Developmental Services Center), DSCC (Department of Specialized Services for Children), and the DSACC (Down Syndrome Association of Champaign County). There would be visits from Diversified Healthcare, speech pathologists, physical therapists, social workers. One too-helpful person started giving us the statistics on the incidence of leukemia in people with Down's, and warned us that little James might display "inappropriate affection," a phrase I've been tumbling around in my head ever since. But for the most part, we were quite happy to be forcibly inscribed into the disciplinary imaginary of the helping professions. They weren't going to institutionalize our baby; they were going to give us all these numbers to call for help.

I got hold of everything I could on genetics, reproduction, and "abnormal" human development, dusting off college textbooks I hadn't touched since before Nick was born. At one point a staff nurse was sent in to check on *our* mental health, and she found us babbling about meiosis and monoploids, wondering anew that Jamie had "gotten" Down syndrome the second he became a zygote. When the nurse inadvertently left behind her notes, Janet sneaked a peek. "Parents seem to be intellectualizing," we read. "Well," Janet shrugged, "that seems accurate enough."

Let's Talk About Sex

Looking over the fossil record, I really don't see any compelling logic behind our existence on the planet. I'm told that intelligence has obvious survival value, since organisms with a talent for information-processing "naturally" beat out their competitors for food, water, and condos, but human history doesn't convince me that *our* brand of intelligence is just what the world was waiting for. Thus, I've never believed that we were supposed to survive the Ice Age, or that some cosmic design mandated the cataclysmic collision in the late Cretaceous period that gave us an iridium layer deep in our soil and may have ended the dinosaurs' 200-million-year reign. Bacteria and horseshoe crabs unmodified for aeons are still with us; but what has become of *Eusthenopteron*, introduced to me by then-five-year-old Nicholas as the fish that could walk on land? If you were fighting for survival 350 million years ago, you'd think you'd have had a leg up on the competition if you developed small bones in your fins, enabling you to shimmy up onto shore. But you'd be wrong: these days, *Eusthenopteron* is nothing more than a card in Nick's "prehistoric animals" collection, alongside the Ankylosaur, the mastodon, and the jessehelms. I figured we were here thanks to dumb luck and blame cussedness, and though we have managed to understand our own biochemical origins and take neat close-up pictures of a crescent Saturn (quite a feat, if you think about it), we also spend much of our time exterminating ourselves and most other species we meet. And nothing in Nick's cards says we too won't wind up as a card in nature's deck of "prehistoric" animals.

A lot of the problem with human neonates, of course, is the dang head. It's too big. As the neck is to the giraffe and the tail is to the peacock, so is the cerebral cortex to the human. Our brains are so outsized and unwieldy that in order to get out of the mother's body, our young have to slide one half of their skulls over the other half, and they come out all distended and asymmetrical (which is one reason why our film renditions of alien intelligent species fixate so obsessively on elongated skulls). Even after we're born, we can't hold our heads up, for though we've got the ecosystem's most elaborate neural net in our trust, its control center is perched atop a weak, skinny, and extremely vulnerable tube called the neck, through which all our food, air, and water have to pass in order to do us any good. As Arthur C. Clarke once pointed out, it's not a very well designed system, especially for one's first few months on the planet.

Still, it wasn't until I got to college and started thinking about sex and drugs in rather immediate ways that I began to realize that the workings of chance on the molecular level are even more terrifying than on the evolutionary plane. Of course, the molecular and the evolutionary have everything to do with each other; it's just that the minutiae of mitosis are more awe-inspiring to me, *because* more quotidian, than the thought of random rocks slamming into my home planet every couple hundred million years. For those who don't feel like cracking open old textbooks, Richard Powers' novel *The Gold Bug Variations* offers some idea of what happens when your DNA gets involved in cell division: "seven feet of aperiodic crystal unzips, finds complements of each of its billion constituents, integrates them perfectly without tearing or entangling, then winds up again into a fraction of a millimeter, all in two minutes" (248). And this is just the ordinary stuff your cells are doing every moment. Sex, as always, is a little more complicated.

So let's talk about sex. But let's leave aside the difficult, political stuff like infant mortality rates and the quality of prenatal and postnatal care for just a second—although smitten folks like me will tell you there's not much that's more indicative of a society's values than these. (Imagine a country in which deeply religious people blockaded streets, harrassed pedestrians, screamed at the top of their lungs, and terrorized their ideological adversaries *all in order to ensure adequate prenatal care for impoverished mothers.* Then remember that the United States has the industrialized world's only *rising* infant mortality rate.) At least fifteen (and at most *fifty*) of every hundred pregnancies end in miscarriage; chromosomal abnormalities account for over half of all miscarriages; and trisomies—the presence of three chromosomes where there should be a pair—account for half of those.[1] Think of it this way: one in every twenty-five human fertilizations goes so severely awry as to produce zygotes with the wrong number of chromosomes. Of the myriad possible genetic mistransmissions in human reproduction, excluding anomalies in the sex chromosomes, it appears that only three kinds of trisomies make it to term: people with three thirteenth chromosomes (Patau's Syndrome), three eighteenth chromosomes (Edwards' Syndrome), and three twenty-first chromosomes (Down's Syndrome, a.k.a. Down syndrome). About one in four or five zygotes with Down's winds up getting born, and since Down's accounts for one of every 600 to 800 live births, it would appear that trisomy-21 happens quite often, maybe on the order of once in every 150 to 250 fertilizations. It turns out, actually, that Down's results from an undivided *twenty-second* chromosome rather than an undivided twenty-first, as had been thought for as long as chromosomes and Down's were known things; but to keep the literature on Down's unconfused, geneticists have renumbered autosomes twenty-two and twenty-one even though the rest of our numbers correspond to the length of the chromosome (starting with 1). The first two of these syndromes, Edwards' and Patau's, were both named in 1960, the year before I was born. Kids with Edwards' or Patau's Syndrome are born severely deformed and profoundly retarded; they normally don't live more than a few months. That's what I would expect of genetic anomaly, whatever the size of the autosome: though the twenty-first chromosome is the smallest we have, little James still has extra genetic material in every single cell. You'd think the effects of such a basic transcription error would make themselves felt pretty clearly.

But what's odd about Down's is how extraordinarily subtle it can be. Mental retardation is one well-known effect, and it can sometimes be severe, but anyone who's watched Chris Burke in *Life Goes On* or "Mike" in McDonald's commercials knows that the extent of such retardation can be next to negligible. The *real* story of Down's lies not in intelligence tests but in developmental delays across the board, and for the first two years of James's life the most important of these were physical rather than mental (though thanks to James I've come to see how interdependent the mental and physical really are). His muscles are weaker than those of most children his age, his nasal passages imperceptibly narrower. His tongue is slightly thicker; one ear is crinkly. His fingers would be shorter and stubbier but for the fact that his mother's are long, thin, and elegant. His face is a few degrees flatter through the middle, his nose delicate.

Down's doesn't cut all children to one mold; the relations between James's genotype and phenotype are lacy and intricate. It's sort of like what happens in Ray Bradbury's short story "A Sound of Thunder," in which a time traveler accidentally steps on a butterfly while hunting T. Rex 65 million years ago and returns home to find that he's changed the conventions of English spelling and the outcome of the previous day's election. As he hit the age of two, James was very pleased to find himself capable of walking; by three, he had learned to say the names of colors, to count to ten, and to claim that he would *really* be turning four. Of all our genetic nondisjunctions (with the possible exception of hermaphroditism), only Down syndrome produces so nuanced, so finely articulated a variation on human reproduction. James is less mobile and more susceptible to colds than his peers (and, accordingly, he's inadvertently cancelled a few of my classes), but—as his grandparents have often attested— you can play with him for hours and never see anything "wrong" with him.

And then there's a variant form of Down's, called mosaicism, which results from the failure of the chromosome to divide not *before* fertilization but immediately *after*, during the early stages of cell division in embryogeny. Only one in a hundred people with Down's are mosaics, but it's possible for such folks to have some normal cells and some with trisomy-21; there's something about our chromosomes, then, that can produce anomalies during either meiosis *or* mitosis. There's also *translocation*, in which the twenty-first chromosome splits off and joins the fourteenth or fifteenth, producing people who can be called "carriers"; they can give birth to more translocation carriers, normal children, or translocation kids with Down's. At this point we get into an area of genetic complexity that's beyond my ability to synopsize, but people with configurations of 21–14 chromosomes can actually have the requisite forty-six (even if they appear to have forty-five). And although everyone knows that incidence of Down's increases with maternal age (or, as the textbooks say, "nondisjunction during oogenesis is thus a function of senescence of the oocytes" [Burns 280]), almost no one knows that three quarters of all such children are born to mothers under thirty-five, or that fathers are genetically "responsible" for about one fifth of them.[2]

So how shall we craft a theory of difference sufficient unto such as James? "For an average human," Richard Powers writes,

> almost every characteristic is homozygous. Only 6.7 percent of human genes are composed of different alleles. From that small fraction, all variability in legacy arises. How small is small? Taking 100,000 genes as a ballpark genome, 6,700 will be heterozygous. That gives 2^{6700} ways of shuffling divergences—a number of more than two thousand digits—to pass on to a child. The growth of genetics has been the growth of realizing how huge the gap between individuals is.
>
> By contrast: the human genome, considered as a whole, represents only the slightest divergence from the closest living trial. More than 98 percent of our DNA is identical to that of both chimp and gorilla. Less than 2 percent of that seven-foot text is proprietarily human. The incredible conclusion is

that two children of the same parents differ more from one another than *Homo sapiens* as a whole differs from the apes. (249–50)

Parents seem to be intellectualizing. And why not? They're watching DNA make a home for itself.

Progress

There has never been a better time to be born with Down syndrome—and that's really saying something, since Down syndrome has recently been reported in chimpanzees and gorillas. Because our branch of the evolutionary tree split off from the apes' around fifteen to twenty million years ago, these reports would seem to suggest that we've produced offspring with Down syndrome with great regularity at every point in our history as hominids—even though it's a genetic anomaly that has no obvious survival value and is not transmitted hereditarily (except in extremely rare instances). The statistical incidence of Down's in the current human population is no less staggering: there may be ten million people with Down's worldwide, or just about one on every other street corner.

But although *Homo sapiens* (as well as our immediate ancestors, all the way back to ramapithecus) have always experienced some difficulty dividing our chromosomes properly, Down syndrome was not fingered and named until 1866, when British physician J. Langdon Down diagnosed it as "mongolism" (because it produced children with almond-shaped eyes reminiscent, to at least one nineteenth-century British mind, of central Asian faces). At the time, the average life expectancy of children with Down's was less than ten. And for a hundred years thereafter—during which the discovery of antibiotics lengthened the lifespan of Down's kids to around twenty—Down syndrome was known as "mongoloid idiocy."

The 1980 edition of my college genetics textbook, *The Science of Genetics: An Introduction to Heredity*, opens its segment on Down's with the words, "An important and tragic instance of trisomy in humans involves Down's Syndrome, or mongoloid idiocy" (277). It includes a picture of a mongoloid idiot along with a karyotype of his chromosomes, and the information that most people with Down's have IQs in the low 40s. The presentation is objective, dispassionate, and strictly "factual," as it should be in a college textbook. But reading it again in 1991, I began to wonder: is there a connection between the official textual representation of Down syndrome in medical discourses (including college textbooks), and the social policies by which people with Down syndrome are understood and misunderstood?

You bet your life there is. Now, anyone who's paid attention to the "political correctness" wars on American campuses knows how stupid the academic left can be: we're always talking about language instead of reality, whining about "lookism" and "differently abled persons" instead of changing the world the way the real he-man left *used* to do. But you know, there really is a difference between calling someone a "mongoloid idiot" and calling him or her "a person with Down syndrome." There's even a difference between calling people "retarded" and calling them "delayed." Though these words may appear to mean the same damn thing when you look them up in Webster's, I remember full well from my days as an American male adolescent that I never taunted my peers by calling them "delayed." Even for those of us who were shocked at the frequency with which "homo" and "nigger" were thrown around in our fancy Catholic high school, "retard" aroused no comment, no protest. In other words, a retarded person is just a retard. But *delayed* persons will get where they're going eventually, if you'll only have some patience with them.

One night I said something like this to Barry Gross of the National Association of Scholars, just to make the point that our terminology *can* matter to our social lives in a nontrivial way. Gross, being a humane fellow, replied that although epithets like "mongoloid idiot" were undoubtedly used in a more benighted time, there have always been persons of good will who have resisted such phraseology. It's a nice thought, the kind you usually hear from traditionalists when you point out the barbarism and brutality of our human past. But it just ain't so. Right through the 1970s, "mongoloid idiot" wasn't an epithet; it was a *diagnosis*. It wasn't uttered by callow, ignorant persons fearful of "difference" and central Asian eyes; it was pronounced by the best-trained medical practitioners in the world, who told families of kids with Down's that their children would never be able to dress themselves, recognize their parents, or live "meaningful" lives. Best to have the child institutionalized and tell one's friends that the baby died at birth. Only the most stubborn, intransigent, or inspired parents resisted such advice from their trusted experts. Who could reasonably expect otherwise?

It's impossible to say how deeply we're indebted to those parents, children, teachers, and medical personnel who insisted on treating people with Down's as if they *could* learn, as if they *could* lead "meaningful" lives. In bygone eras, the parents who didn't take their children home didn't really have the "option" of doing so; you can't talk about "options" (in any substantial sense of the word) in an ideological current so strong. But in the early 1970s, some parents did swim upstream against all they were told, and brought their children home, worked with them, held them, provided them with physical therapy and "special learning" environments. These parents are saints and sages. They have, in the broadest sense of the phrase, uplifted the race. In the fifteen-million-year history of Down syndrome, they've allowed us to believe that we're finally getting somewhere.

Of course, the phrase "mongoloid idiocy" did not cause Down syndrome any more than the word "homo" magically induces same-sex desire. But words and phrases are the devices by which we beings signify what homosexuality, or Down's Syndrome, or anything else, will mean. There surely were, and are, the most intimate possible relations between the language in which we spoke of Down's and the social practices by which we understood it—and refused to understand it. You don't have to be a poststructuralist or a postmodernist or a post-*anything* to get this; all you have to do is meet a parent of a child with Down syndrome. Not long ago, we lived next door to people whose youngest child had Down's. After James was born, they told us of going to the library to find out more about their baby's prospects and wading through horror after textual horror of outdated information, ignorant generalizations, and pictures of people with Down's in mental institutions, face down in their feeding trays. These parents demanded that the library get some better material on Down syndrome and throw out the garbage they had on their shelves. Was this a "politically correct" thing for them to do? Damn straight it was. That garbage has had its effects *for generations.* It may seem to you that it's only words, but perhaps the fragile little neonates whose lives were thwarted and impeded by the policies—and conditions—of institutionalization can testify in some celestial court to the power of mere language, to the intimate links between words and social policies.

Some of my friends tell me this sounds too much like "strict social constructionism"—that is, too much like the proposition that culture is everything and biology is only what we decide to make (of) it. But although James is pretty solid proof that human biology "exists" independent of our understanding of it, every morning when he gets up, smiling and babbling to his family, I can see for myself how much of his life depends on our social practices. On one of those mornings I turned to my mother-in-law and said, "he's always so full of mischief, he's always so glad to see us—the only thought I can't face is the idea of this little guy waking up each day in a state mental hospital." To which my mother-in-law replied, "Well, Michael, if he were waking up every day in a state mental hospital, he wouldn't *be* this little guy."

As it happens, my mother-in-law doesn't subscribe to any strict-social-constructionist newsletters; she was just passing along what she took to be good common sense. But every so often I wonder how common that sense really is. Every ten minutes we hear that the genetic basis of something has been "discovered," and we rush madly to the newsweeklies: Disease is genetic! Homosexuality is genetic! Infidelity, addiction, obsession with mystery novels—all genetic! The discourses of genetics and inheritance, it would seem, bring out the hidden determinist in more of us than will admit it. Sure, there's a baseline sense in which our genes "determine" who we are: we can't play the tune unless the score is written down somewhere in the genome. But one does not need a biochemical explanation for literary taste, or voguing, or faithless lovers. In these as in all things human, including Down's, the genome is but a template for a vaster and more significant range of social and historical variation. That's true even for human attributes that are clearly more "biological" than voguing and reading. Figuring out even the most rudimentary of relations between the genome and the immune system (something of great relevance to us wheezing asthmatics) involves so many trillions of variables that a decent answer will win you an all-expense-paid trip to Stockholm. Nor can you predict allergic reactions from the genes alone: because the body's immune system takes a few years to go on-line, your environmental variables (from dioxin to cat dander) are going to be more important to you than most hereditary "constants" you care to name.

I'm not saying we can eradicate Down's—or its myriad effects—simply by talking about it more nicely. I'm only saying that James's intelligence is doing better than it would be doing in an institution for the "retarded," and people who try to deny this don't strike me as being among the geniuses of the species. And every time I hear some self-styled "realist" telling me that my logic licenses the kind of maniacal social engineering that produced Auschwitz, I do a reality check: the people who brought us Auschwitz weren't "social constructionists." They were eugenicists. They thought they knew the "immutable laws" of genetics and the "fixed purpose" of evolution, and they were less interested in "improving" folks like Jamie than in exterminating them. I'll take my chances with the people who believe in chance.

Indeed, the "science" of eugenics in the early 1900s was not the stuff of fringe crackpots and charlatans: it constituted the conventional wisdom of the time, and dominated damn near every discourse having to do with intelligence quotients, SATs, immigration, race, and the Future of Mankind. And like Rasputin, it's proven extremely hard to kill: even today, anyone with a decent vocabulary, sufficient funding, and a toxic social agenda can make himself rich peddling the claim that human intelligence and achievement are determined at conception, and that democracies need not, therefore (though this proposition follows the last as the haircut follows the appetizer), bother themselves with fostering economic and social justice.

Perhaps there's something very seductive about the thought that Down syndrome wouldn't have become so prevalent in humans for so long without good reason. Indeed, there are days when, despite everything I know and profess, I catch myself believing that people with Down syndrome are here for a specific purpose—perhaps to teach us patience, or humility, or compassion, or mere joy. A great deal can go wrong with us *in utero*, but under the heading of what goes wrong, Down syndrome is among the most basic, the most fundamental, the most common, *and* the most innocuous, leavening the species with children who are somewhat slower, and usually somewhat gentler, than the rest of the human brood. It speaks to us strongly of design— if design govern in a thing so small.

Sweet Baby James

After seventeen days in the ICU, James was scheduled for release. We would be equipped with the materials necessary for his care, including oxygen tanks and an apnea monitor that would beep if his heart slowed, became extremely irregular, or stopped. To compensate for his inability to take food orally, James would have a gastrostomy tube surgically introduced through his abdominal wall into his stomach.

Janet and I balked. If James was going to be sent home into conditions identical to those of the ICU, why wasn't he staying in the ICU? There was no shortage of beds; the only other occupants of the ICU were a few preemies, some born as early as twenty-four weeks. James had recently made progress in his bottle feeding; why do preemptive surgery? We got suspicious. Was the HMO sending James home just to cut costs? Were they recommending a gastrostomy because they consider surgery a quick fix? We recalled one doctor's proposed solution to Jamie's tight neck muscles: cut the muscles and resew them. You don't have to be a post-hippie consulter of crystals and channelers to think that stretching and massage might be a better first option.

We nixed the gastrostomy tube, saying we'd prefer to augment his bottle feedings with a nasal tube and we'd do it ourselves. James stayed three more days in the ICU, during which he was nearly weaned from supplemental oxygen, and came home to a house full of flowers and homemade dinners from our colleagues.

For the most part, I've repressed the details of that autumn. But every once in a while, rummaging through the medicine closet for Ace bandages or heating pads, I come across the Hypafix adhesive tape with which we attached James's feeding tube to the bridge of his nose, or the strap we wrapped around his tiny chest for his apnea monitor. It's like discovering evidence of another life, dim but indelible, and you remember that once upon a time you could cope with practically anything. Running a small tube through your baby's nose to his stomach is the worst kind of counterintuitive practice. You have to do it carefully, measuring your length of tubing accurately and listening with a stethoscope to make sure you haven't entered the lung by mistake. Whenever James pulled out his tubes, by design or by chance, you had to do the whole thing over again, in the other nostril this time, lubricating and marking and holding the tube while you fumbled with the world's stickiest tape. It's a four-handed job, and I don't blame the staff doctors for assuming that we wouldn't undertake such an enterprise alone.

But slowly we got James to bottle-feed. After all, for our purposes, Jamie's nasal tube, like unto a thermonuclear weapon, was there precisely so that we wouldn't use it: each week a visiting nurse would set a minimum daily amount for Jamie's milk intake, and whatever he didn't get by bottle would have to go in by tube. So you can see the incentive at work here. Janet and I would compete each day to see who could get the most fluid into James by bottle, and within a month we were sufficiently adept at it that we began to see glimpses of what James would look like *sans* tube. Then we stopped giving him oxygen during the night, and gradually his tiny nostrils found themselves a lot less encumbered. He still didn't have a voice, but he was clearly interested in his new home, and very trusting of his parents and brother.

Of course, the apnea monitor alarm would still go off in the middle of the night, scaring the bejeezus out of us. Most of the time the electrodes were out of place; sometimes the dang machine's batteries were failing. Come November we got colds, and viewed them as we would have viewed plagues. Visitors wore masks. It was a long winter.

In the midst of that winter James began physical therapy and massages. We stretched his neck every night, and whenever we could afford it we took him to a local masseuse, who played ambient music, relaxed us all, and worked on James for an hour. As one prefers back rubs to calisthenics, so did James like massage better than physical therapy. But his therapist, Ofra Tandoor, was brilliant. Trained in Israel and now working at a nursing home (where James's visits were much remarked upon), Ofra showed us how everything about James was connected to everything else: his neck, if left uncorrected, would reshape the bones of his face. The straighter his neck, the sooner he'd sit up, the sooner he'd walk. If he could handle simple solid foods with equal facility in both sides of his mouth, he could center himself more easily; and the sooner he could move around by himself, the more he'd be able to explore and learn. In other words, his eating would affect his ability to walk, and his thighs and torso would impinge upon his ability to talk. I suppose that's what it means to be an organism.

We not only learned a great deal about the interdependence of our discursive and nondiscursive mechanisms in our very flesh; we also realized (and had to reconfigure) our relations to a vast array of social practices and institutions. *Developmental* turns out to be a buzzword for a sprawling nexus of agencies, state organizations, and human disabilities. Likewise, "special needs" isn't a euphemism; it's a very specific marker. For example, under Illinois law, parents of "special-needs" children are entitled to sixty hours a year of respite care so that they can occasionally go to the movies, get an hour alone, and generally stay sane. Our dear friend and colleague Amanda Anderson went to "special sitters" classes with me, where we learned CPR along with techniques for dealing with children far more endangered and complicated than James. Jamie began speech therapy at Champaign's Developmental Services Center, which gave him more games to play for an hour each week and gave us more feedback on his cognitive and social abilities. We're learning about the differences between "mainstreaming" and "inclusion," and we'll be figuring out the Americans with Disabilities Act for the rest of our lives. We've decided that Foucauldians could stand to be rather less dour about the social services bequeathed us by the disciplinary society of the nineteenth century, and that, on another front, those few remaining Marxists out there who refuse to believe that bodies can be sufficiently "theoretical" have yet to account for James.

The bill for his ICU stay was $30,000, or $10,000 a week—and he was in there short-term compared to the children who were born at 24–26 weeks fetal age, whose stays may run their parents over a quarter of a million dollars. Renting the oxygen wasn't expensive, but the apnea monitor was $300/month. His physical therapy holds steady at $220/hour, or $880/month; speech therapy is a mere $100/hour. The speech therapy costs are absorbed into the state budget by way of some process more complicated than gene splicing. Everything else, with the exception of part of the apnea monitor, was covered by our "high option" insurance, which runs us $175/month (and the University another $400 or so) plus $10 co-pays for our frequent doctor visits and $5 co-pays for each prescription drug. But because Janet, Nicholas, and I all have asthma, we could easily be shelling out over $300 a month for medicines exclusive of James's decongestants and prophylactic antibiotics. It's impossible to tell, of course, whether any of these "costs" are even remotely real, as we learned when we bought an uninsured neck brace for James, a molded piece of foam rubber that ran us $100 but surely cost its manufacturer no more than a quarte. Medical supplies obey a market logic whereby providers bilk insurers and vice versa, with the gentleman's agreement that all costs will be passed on to the "consumer." Yet despite our health-care system's glaring and outrageous shortcomings, we know that James is in many ways extremely lucky to be so well provided for: when every employer is as flexible as ours, when parental leave is the law of the land, when private insurers can't drop families from the rolls because of "high-risk" children, when every child can be fed, clothed, and cared for—*then* we can start talking about what kind of a choice "life" might be.

Because, after all he's been through, James is thriving. He's thrilled to be here, and takes a visible, palpable delight in seeing his reflection in the oven door as he toddles across the kitchen, or hearing his parents address him in the voices of the Sesame Street regulars, or winging a Nerf ball to his brother on the couch. He knows perfectly well when he's doing something we've never seen before, like riding his toddler bicycle down the hall into the laundry room or calling out "Georgia" and "Hawaii" as he flips through Nick's book of the fifty states. He's been a bibliophile from the moment he learned to turn pages—a skill he picked up *before* most children his age. His current favorite is Maurice Sendak's classic *Where the Wild Things Are*, surely a Great Book by any standard; he began by identifying with Max, and then, in one of those "oscillations" described by reader-response criticism and feminist film theory, switched over to identifying with the wild things themselves—roaring his terrible roar and showing his terrible claws.

He has his maternal aunts' large deep eyes, and a beautiful smile that somehow involves his whole body. He's not only an independent cuss, but he has an attention span of up to twenty minutes, or roughly eighteen minutes longer than the average American political pundit. He's blessed with a preternaturally patient, sensitive brother in Nick, who, upon hearing one of his classmates' parents gasp, "Oh, my God" at the news that Jamie had Down's, turned to her and said with a fine mixture of reassurance and annoyance, "He's perfectly all *right*." Like Nick, James has a keen sense of humor; the two of them can be set agiggle by pratfalls, radical incongruities, and mere sidelong looks. He's just now old enough to be curious about what he was like as a baby: as he puts it, all he could do was go "waaah" (holding his fists to his eyes). Barring all the contingencies that can never be barred, Jamie can expect a life of anywhere from thirty-five to fifty-five years. For tomorrow, he can expect to see his friends at day care, to put all his shapes in his shapes box, and to sing along with Raffi as he shakes his sillies out and wiggles his waggles away.

❖

And now Janet and I know what we have in common with Roy Rogers and Dale Evans, and George Will, and Eldridge Cleaver, and Lowell Weicker, and Crimson Tide head coach Gene Stallings: aside from the fact that we're all carbon-based and mortal, we've all been parents of children with Down syndrome. But I've realized a commonality among us humans that goes deeper than this. Before James was born, I frankly didn't think very highly of appeals to our "common humanity." I thought such appeals were well-intentioned, but I didn't think they mattered much to the world. And, in fact, they don't: Muslim and Christian do not bond over their common ancestor in *Australopithecus*. Rwandan Hutu and Rwandan Tutsi do not toast to the distinctive size of their cerebral cortices. The rape of Bosnia, and Bosnian women, does not stop once Serbian soldiers realize that they too will pass from the earth. We share many features in common as a species, but few of these have ever prevented us from drawing and quartering each other; human rights can, in theory, follow either from our belief in God or our belief in chance, but there has never been a time when humans did not deny each other human rights on the basis of race, gender, ethnicity, sexual practice, age, or the ownership of property.

And yet we possess one crucial characteristic: the desire to communicate, to understand, to put ourselves in some mutual, reciprocal form of contact with one another. This desire hasn't proven any better at disarming warheads than any of the weaker commonalities enumerated above, but it stands a better chance nonetheless. For among the most amazing and hopeful things about this species is that its offspring show up, from their day of birth, programmed to receive and transmit even in the most difficult circumstances; the ability to imagine mutual communicative relations is embedded in our material bodies, woven through our double-stranded fibers. Granted, it's only one variable among trillions, and it's not even "fundamentally" human—for all we know, dolphins are much better at communication than we are. Nor is it a "universal" human attribute; the sociohistorical variables of human communication, like the variables in everything else about us, will always be more significant and numerous than any genetic determinism can admit. All the same, it's in our software somewhere, and better still, it's a program that teaches itself how to operate each time we use it.

Whether you want to consider reciprocal communication a constant or a variable, though, the point remains that it's a human attribute that requires other people if it's going to work. Among the talents we have, it's one we could stand to develop more fully. It's only natural: among our deepest, strongest impulses is the impulse to mutual cueing. Nothing will delight James so much as the realization that you have understood him—except the realization that he has understood *you*, and recursively understood his own understanding and yours. Perhaps I could have realized our human stake in mutual realization without James's aid; any number of other humans would have been willing to help me out. But now that I get it, I get it for good. Communication is itself self-replicating. Sign unto others as you'd have them sign unto you. Pass it on.

Notes

1. See Chahira Kozma, "What is Down Syndrome?" in Stray-Gundersen, 1–25. The entire volume is an extremely helpful resource for people who want to learn more about Down Syndrome, regardless of whether they have any immediate relation to a Down's child. See also Burns, 277–87.

2. For the figures on maternal age see Kozma, 10; for the incidence of "paternal error" as a cause of Down's, see "Questions and Answers about Down Syndrome," a small fact sheet available from the National Down Syndrome Society (800-221-4602). As the NDSS sheet notes, "frequency of paternal error is below 10% in other trisomies" (2), which means that paternal error is more than twice as common in Down Syndrome than in any other trisomy. The NDSS adds that "recent research also has revealed that significantly more males than females are born with Down Syndrome in comparison with the general population, with all indications that this ratio holds true in terms of DS conceptions."

Works Cited

Burns, George W. *The Science of Genetics: An Introduction to Heredity.* 4th ed. New York: Macmillan, 1980.

Kozma, Chahira. "What is Down Syndrome?" In Stray-Gundersen, 1–25.

Powers, Richard. *The Gold Bug Variations.* New York: Morrow, 1991.

Stray-Gundersen, Karen, ed. *Babies With Down Syndrome: A New Parents' Guide.* Kensington, Maryland: Woodbine House, 1986.

18

Lives

❖

GAYATRI CHAKRAVORTY SPIVAK

If we are the type that thinks about it, we cannot account for our being here. Many transcendental figurations have been devised to make our lives accountable, in the strongest senses of the pun. It should be possible to think that, as a result of this device or devising—a negotiation represented as that between the "sacred" and the "profane" which we often call "culture"—the temporalizing accounts of a life can come, not as the unique and incontrovertible accounting of a truth, but as factitious responses to what is (or is not) perceived as a challenge precisely for such an account, accounting, accountability.

As feminist students of cultural politics, we questioned the academic pretense of objectivity. Correspondingly, the pressure was strong upon us to use our "lives" ("true" stories of "experience") as unmediated ground of theory steering between these two challenges. I at least found myself constructing Gayatri Spivaks who "represented" various historical and geographic cases. How to distinguish this from a request to speak of the singularity of one's life? I offer three takes.

I

"Asked to Talk About Myself," in 1992, by a Greek-Australian member of a British multicultural collective, who had heard bits of an autobiographical talk I had permitted myself to utter at the University of Cambridge, I first offered a few pages of musings on the thesis that "experience is a staging of experience."[1] Those musings are of course "too theoretical," "not auto-biographical enough," to be included here; although an undoing of that opposition has been at stake in my temporizing of a life.

Yet one word must be added. My account of a middle-class, Hindu childhood which follows is, to quote a caste-Hindu Indian academic woman who heard it at Princeton, "romantic." The point to remember is that it is on the basis of such romantic loyalties that a rather large section of the caste-Hindu Indian middle class has given its support to the Hindu Nationalist Bharatiya Janata Party that may well push the country towards a variety of fascism. So the "cultural difference" that a politically correct U.S. reader may sense here has a hidden agenda. If I write further on this, the piece will be "too political," "not autobiographical enough," although the undoing of this binary makes sense of life now. Read, then:

I was brought up as a middle-class polytheist. (The use of "polytheism" for Hinduism, or strictly speaking, Brahmanism, is a bit dicey—I have written about it here and there—but this is autobiography, so we'll let it pass.) Hinduism was the majority religion, so there was no sense of abnormality in this. Indeed, I felt this to be so normal, and continuous with my growth and development as an enlightened schoolchild and a Left-leaning, English honors student, that I never gave it a second thought, until something peculiar happened in 1981. My sister, who has a Ph.D. in chemistry, and is a highly placed Government servant, is, I believe, bringing up her daughter in the same way. The household was not bigoted. Polytheism was just normal, that's all. The actual ritual details I remember are: getting up at dawn in a certain month from the age of five, gathering a certain kind of grass and leaves of the wood-apple, making sandalwood paste, and putting all of this on the tiny phallus of Shiva in the shrine. My only real feelings associated with this were boredom, that one had to get up so early to do it, and, from the age of seven or eight, pride in the fact that I pronounced the Sanskrit verses correctly—it was a classical language after all—and that I understood them. As for the little phallus, I was not sure what it was and certainly did not find it at all as exciting as the smutty passages in *Forever Amber*, a book that I was surreptitiously reading at nine, or the bits about prostitution in *Charitraheen*, a Bengali novel on every mother's banned list that I managed to lay my hands on at eleven. We sang the hundred-and-eight epithets of Rama on selected ninth nights of the waning moon. There, again, I took good care to pronounce the words correctly. I cannot begin to tell you the officiousness of a Bengali child pronouncing Sanskrit correctly. The fact that it was in the frame of an active, although low-key, bourgeois polytheism was too normal to be noted. Durgapuja was of course a big social occasion, so it doesn't count. The worship of the goddess of learning was another matter altogether. Self-conscious pride in being intelligent as a family was the main thing here. We consecrated the books overnight, and the priest came to perform the service in the morning. I distinctly remember my brother's *Gray's Anatomy* and my *Oxford Companion* reposing in front of the little goddess in her blue-white sari and with her left leg on the swan's head and the musical instrument poised on her knees. Again, one did not contrast this to some monotheist dominant. Polytheism was normal, taken for granted, although it offered an opportunity for staging oneself as monstrant. I remember being transfixed in the crowd in the temple of Jagannath at Puri, identifying madly with the handsome Sri Caitanya who, four hundred years ago, wore away a pillar gazing upon a gigantic icon that would surely strike a Christian as monstrous. Am I equally put off by the bar named *Juggernaut* at the Howard Johnson Motor Inn in Pittsburgh and the sight of cavorting Hare Krishnas in the East Village in New York in memory of that adolescent bliss? The point I'm trying to make here is that one did not have to withdraw from civil space in order to become, specifically, polytheist. It was all the less aggressive because it was middle-class, nonspecial, humdrum. The only other special thing I remember is painting stylized, proleptic footprints with rice paste on thresholds, on the eve of the first full moon in autumn, for the goddess of wealth might step in.

I have no idea if other little girls of my class performed more-or-less polytheist ritual in their everyday. Some of them were Muslim or Christian and seemed a bit unusual but not significantly so. Who knew then that this would be theorized as the ingredients for staging an origin in 1981?

I have to keep you in suspense a bit longer and mention Kali. She was much more pervasive than the other figures I have mentioned but definitely not in a monotheist way. Let me tell you right away that many gods and goddesses are not like many saints. Kali was strongly present in our lives either because my father and then my mother had come under the influence of the wife of Rama Krishna, a nineteenth-century mystic who gained popularity among Calcutta intellectuals, or because my father was from the Kali-based sector of Hinduism by birth. Who was interested in origins? It was (un)felt as (un)staged. One was in place. Polytheism was only normal.

❖

In 1981, a ten-year long close friendship with a man brought up as a believing Roman Catholic in the peripheries of the working class came to an end. Putting myself over against him, we are moving into stagings of cultural inscriptions that come close to stereotypes. At any rate, when the friendship broke up, I was left with a deep sense of loss, and a sense of myself as a violent person. I was in distress, alone in a country which was neither the United States, my place of residence, nor India, my country of origin. Since I doubt I will ever run for elected office anywhere in the world, this is my moment to admit that I went to a psychoanalyst.

I have always been interested in the im-proper functioning of instru-ments. It is interesting to me that a sense of origin was staged for me in this foreign place by this kind analyst precisely because, I think, a "proper" analysis could not take place. I was going to be there only three months. Even initially it was the story of inscriptions. I clung to my "analysis" with all the colloquial fervor of an improper positive transference, until the nature of my inscription suffered one clinamen, and then another, and then got lost in a labyrinth rather far away from my everyday.

The analyst, whom I will call R, knew neither English nor my mother tongue. Gently questioning me in *his* mother tongue, he extracted out of much incidental debris the information that the families of my father and his brother often sang hymns to Kali together all evening, that often driving across Calcutta at night, the children and the parents would sing hymns to Kali together. He made me remember. . . .

I go now to a palimpsestic rememoration, which reminds me of Freud's texts with parentheses within parentheses. I am going to summon up what I said in Cambridge about what R, the European curer of souls, made me remember about my own memories. This is what comes.

R made me remember that Kali was a childlike woman, both mother and daughter. In the representation that I grew up with, Kali was not within the organized familial icon of Goddess. She punished justly, but she punished with the violence that she enjoyed. Kali has been misrepresented as the malev-olent goddess (by Weber for instance). She is irresponsible in her joy in punishing, but she *is* a punisher, not unreasonably malevolent. Now this particular memory began to be put in place by me in response to R's ques-tions. Kali's icon is naked, with the severed head of a miscreant in her hand and a girdle of severed arms around her waist. Her tongue is out in shame because she has put her foot on her husband, the supine and white Shiva. The naked Kali is always celebrated as the childlike, punishing mother-daughter. A site of contradictions easily imagined by the female child.

Finally, the question that R asked before I left the country: How can a man brought up with the Blessed Virgin be able to understand that there can be this model of female violence that is loved and honored? This restoration by R was extremely helpful to me. It helped me rediscover that, although I was not and never would be a believer, ideologically this particular image of female violence as a sort of role model had entered me, so that I was easily shattered by accusations of violence. I was then able to come to terms with it, in a way that was not possible for me before. What I have to talk about now is how I came to realize that this staging of origin, too neat and palliative, was not only medicine but a sort of poison as well, *pharmakon*. It was a gift of a European from within a monotheistic, hagiographic culture. The gift of a

Goddess. As if I too were a monotheist who had organized my self-image by way of a matron saint. As I have argued elsewhere, the monotheist moment is never far away, it does not supervene.

The latter part of my talk at Cambridge, then, was about how I escaped the chair where I sat facing him. How the props of this particular staging of my origin came to be dismantled. In retrospect, I am going to say it stage by stage, in a way that is obviously not quite an accurate account of "what really happened." It will have something like a relationship with the way I narrativized my memories for R.

First, as I began thinking about the ontic—that which is lived so intimately that it is inaccesible to ontology—and restaging it in a very banal, mimetic way as the everyday, I became aware of the fact that in India, in the eighties, the way in which Hindu fundamentalism took hold even of the middle class was precisely through a kind of nostalgia. Through the sort of memory I presented in the beginning of the piece, but also through the monotheistic identification with dominant Gods and Goddesses. This understanding was one of the items that allowed me to dismantle the props. R had been able to organize my life by giving me back a certain calm in the public sphere—the sphere of the state, India not only as the sphere for the staging of the subject's history, but as the staging of the agent's history. This was precisely the kind of restoration that allowed fundamentalism to take hold.

The second item that also worked towards the dismantling of the props was my good fortune in being able to work with Bimal Krishna Matilal on the possibility of looking at Indic performative ethics through the ancient Sanskrit texts. This particular endeavor confronted the fact that India has been diagnosed as lacking a moral philosophical tradition, and that in the European context now, certainly within the Anglo-Saxon context, such philosophers as Bernard Williams, Thomas Nagel, and Jon Elster, were saying that moral philosophy was impossible. And in the continental, post-Hegelian, poststructuralist tradition, the undecidability of ethics was a "position" in Derrida; the last Foucault went toward ethics, because its grounds were "performative" in *The Care of the Self*. If the dominant philosophical critique, then, is that moral philosophy is not coherent or possible, what happens to the old accusation that the Indic context stages the impossibility of moral philosophy? Within that context, as I tried, with Professor Matilal's help, to work through the popular performance of Indic ethics, I began to realize that the question was much bigger than the problems of single, middle-class women, culturally marked by imperialism, and their solution through the single model of the violent Kali. Again I felt that the gift of the European curer of souls, in order that I could confront the accusation of the European companion, was not something that I could cling to as a final resort.

Another thing that also helped, and these things didn't happen in sequence, was the understanding, by way of my work with Mahasweta Devi, that the aboriginal population of India quite often had a kind of counterpantheon. The occasions that were celebrated within Hinduism as triumphs, the most striking being the killing of the buffalo monster by Durga, were sometimes mourned by the aboriginals as defeats. Through my reading of such nonesoteric and available texts as Kosambi's work on history, I knew that Kali straddled the gap between the pre-Brahmanic and the Hindu, but I didn't realize that what I had been given back by R was precisely what I was able to give to him.[2] It was an echo of the Kali that belonged to the Aryanized, middle-class Hindu culture. This was also my first glimpse of the reinscription of the analyst as echo, and my understanding of how little R was able to retrieve of the historical hinterland, simply because I was not in touch with it.

This, then, brought home to me that the friendship which had ended and my traffic with the psychoanalyst honored only one face of Janus: the face of the global feminist that was turned toward the culture of imperialism and toward the postcolonial, emancipated, female bourgeoisie. At that point I was able to break down the walls of the theater where he tried to globalize it in the context not of myself as a suffering *subject*, but of myself as an *agent* of global feminism. I recognized that it was only one face that was being honored and given back to me because it had been disfigured.

As I began to think about the other face, the face that was not accessible to him or, more important, to other global feminists, the face that is turned "backwards" and that is in touch with the "ontic," so to speak, I formulated a simple question, so that I could begin in a space where research is impossible. The question that I asked was not how I was able to cope with my suffering through Kali, but how the women "inside" the Hindu system of belief related to the great Goddesses in their largely male dominated representations and rituals.

Many household Goddesses had emerged in reaction to the Islamicization of the outcastes and the incursion of Buddhism. If I brought them in, it would not, strictly speaking, belong to the staging of my origin, because they were not part of the cultural mulch that I could relate to. They belong more to the disenfranchised rural or urban underclass woman's everyday life. But I kept to the great Goddesses, the ones whom my readership would know, like Kali.

The piece drifts again in directions that would not be conventionally regarded as "autobiographical." I offer now my second fragment, prosaically titled "Narrative Account of My Career," written in 1994, following the directions of a grant-giving authority. I have manipulated a few sentences that would have disclosed the specificity of the project for which I was soliciting released time. It would never have occurred to me that this sort of dry requirement could bring forth a chatty story that would suit a Sunday supplement in a pinch. I asked a colleague who had been successful in winning the grant in question. I was amazed at the coyness of his confection and dashed off a piece in slavish imitation. I feel obliged to include this explanation just in case some gullible reader is taken by its "spontaneity."

II

My ecumenical, secularist, protofeminist, "philosophical Hindu" parents encouraged a grounding in Sanskrit, although my future was clearly in English literature. I elected Sanskrit in High School in Calcutta, and kept it up sufficiently to teach it for four semesters at the graduate level at the University of Iowa in the late sixties. (This was undertaken to persuade the Classics Department that there was sufficient student interest. I stopped when the department hired Sheldon Pollock.)

In 1959, I was graduated first in First Class with Honors in English from Presidency College at the University of Calcutta. In 1961 I borrowed money from a philanthropic financier and came to Cornell University as a graduate student in English. In 1962 I shifted to Comparative Literature for financial reasons and was obliged to learn French and German from graduate courses in French and German literature. (I had three months of private tutoring in German at the age of thirteen, and a semester of French at the Alliance Française in Calcutta in 1960.)

In 1963, with a fellowship from Cornell, I went to Girton College, Cambridge to study under T.R. Henn. In 1964, I taught a seminar on Yeats and Death at the Yeats International Summer School in Sligo, Ireland. In 1965, I became an Assistant Professor at the University of Iowa. I was twenty-three, the only Asian of any kind in the entire faculty, one of two women, the other being the well-known Renaissance scholar Rosalie Colie, then in her forties. At Cornell, I had been the first woman to hold a lodging scholarship at intellectually arrogant Telluride House (I appeared on the cover of and inside *Newsweek* in April, 1963), the only other female resident being Frances Perkins, Franklin Roosevelt's Secretary of Labor, then in her eighties. The faculty Resident was Allan Bloom, who was later to write *The Waning of America*. I mention these details because the times were before academic feminism and multiculturalism. My study of cultural politics was early and practical.

In 1967, I received my Ph.D. from Cornell. My dissertation was on Yeats. In 1970 I received tenure. I published *Myself Must I Remake*, my dissertation simplified in the 1960s mode to be fully accessible to my undergraduates.

It was in 1967 that I bought *De la grammatologie* by Jacques Derrida, a person then unknown to me. It appealed to me greatly because the Algerian author seemed, like me, not-quite-not-Western, as he lovingly critiqued (rather than merely accused) Western metaphysics as an outsider inside. Something of this oblique entry into deconstruction still shows in my relationship to it. I wanted to write something on the book but it seemed a long shot. I proposed a translation to a press. In 1971 I met Derrida. In 1973, with a small grant from the Carver Foundation, I went to France to discuss the Introduction with him. In the meantime, I had to teach myself some philosophy to write it.

In 1975, I became Chair of Comparative Literature. In 1976, Johns Hopkins brought out *Of Grammatology*.[3] I had been promoted to full professorship the year before, on the book's promise. In 1977–78, I was awarded the only important national-level fellowship that I have ever received: to the National Humanities Institute at the University of Chicago. In 1978, I was invited to join the faculty of the University of Texas at Austin.

My institutional experience at Texas was the first example of something many times repeated, most publicly around a collaborative exhibition in London's Whitechapel Gallery in 1992. I am invited as a "deconstructivist" out of touch with "the way things are" but able to add theoretical glamor; it is discovered that I know rather more about the way things are than perhaps my host; the scene changes.

It was with my wonderful students at Texas that I discovered that I was at my best as a classroom teacher—at Iowa I did not know myself as anything else in the public domain. Since then, all my writing has come out of my teaching. I began now to be invited internationally. As a result of a personal crisis, I found myself alone at thirty-nine. To save myself from clinical depression, I decided to accept all invitations; and my mind turned also to the unfinished business of India, a country I had left at nineteen. Two significant invitations will offer a contrast that writes my life still: a rather well-known radical feminist and theoretical department at one of the California campuses, and the Women's Center at the University of Riyadh in Saudi Arabia. In California I was found not to fit a radical mould. In Saudi Arabia my woman students clung to me with a longing that acknowledged the seriousness with which I treated them. (Again, I am speaking of fifteen years ago.) I was sneaked into the men's section of the University for a faculty development seminar. The bold male colleague who had invited me was shifted out of the Education Service after I submitted my report.

In 1987, I finally landed a serious salaried position in India, as Visiting Professor at the Centre for Historical Studies at Jawaharlal Nehru University in New Delhi. New Delhi in the eighties was a far cry from Calcutta in the fifties, my only point of reference in Indian intellectual life. I discovered how riven the elite universities were by Cultural Studies and Third World Feminism stakeouts being fought out in the United States. I taught in the summer at the Centre for the Study of Social Sciences in Calcutta. I discovered how the battle between British empiricism and the French version of "critique" was being fought out there as "Indian scholarship" versus "U.S. theory." I realized that, although I should not give up my renewed connection with Indian academic life, more was needed.

In 1983, I had been appointed Longstreet Professor of English at Emory University, the first female chairholder of color there. Although I enjoyed Emory, I did not enjoy the position. The Indian community that migrated to the U.S. in the mid-sixties is too often mined for affirmative action positions that should go to more "troublesome" constituencies. I left Emory in the fall of 1985–86. I spent a semester at the Society for the Humanities at Cornell and went on to become the first woman of any color to hold a Mellon Professorship at Pittsburgh. It was there that I initiated and directed a Cultural Studies Program that affiliated eleven departments in the Humanities and the Social Sciences, with curricular and budgetary connections. In 1991, I was invited to Columbia. Among many other gifts, the City and the School bring me an awareness that some of us must continue to place the South (no longer only "the Third World") in the history of its own present, instead of treating it as a locus of nostalgia and/or human interest.

In 1987 Routledge published *In Other Worlds*; in 1988, *The Postcolonial Critic. Selected Subaltern Studies* appeared for Oxford in 1989. *Outside in the Teaching Machine*, again for Routledge, appeared in 1994. Donna Landry and Gerald MacLean of Wayne State are editing *A Spivak Reader*. In 1991, the *Compact O.E.D.* cited me for the English word "deconstruction." I remain amazed that people read me.

I met Mahasweta Devi, the Indian fiction writer, interventionist journalist, and activist, in 1979. In 1981, because I thought it was absurd that I was becoming an authority on French feminism, I started translating her. (Absurd not in principle but situationally; I mention this because this difference between principle and situation drives my sense of a life.) This association led to a gradual and profound involvement with indigenous literacy in a small, hilly district in West Bengal. In the late eighties, as I was looking for an extra-academic way to touch the Indian subcontinent, I became gradually involved in what can only be inadequately described as "the training of local literacy teachers" in a rural area in Northwest Bangladesh. Also in the late eighties, beset by the demands of identitarian politics, I asked myself if it was possible to touch other cultural bases. Because of the structural similarities between the histories of India and Algeria, and because I knew French, I turned to Algeria. I started learning Maghrebi Arabic because I was interested in moving out of the international conference circuit, which I have learned to handle with care.

My activities in these three areas relate to my effort to learn to learn from below, to tease out the lineaments of an ethical subject much farther removed from the global dominant than is the migrant underclass. I do not ask for grants to do this because, if I consolidate this work into a proposal, I'll lose the learning. I do not join international organizations because much falls through their net. I do not join indigenous nongovernmental organizations—although in each country I have the confidence of one or two—because, as an intellectual, I must keep my own peculiar learning project "free." I lecture these days only to subsidize this time-consuming addiction. I do not write about these efforts to learn, but I know that they are changing my ways of thinking and teaching. This is evident, I think, at the end of my last book, and in the critical apparatus of my new translations of Devi, collected as *Imaginary Maps* (1994). There are more tangible results that will affect my arguments in more calculable ways: an invitation to the European Parliament from the European Green Party in 1992, to the 1994 ICPD in Cairo from the Asian Women's Human Rights Council.

In 1984, I was asked to theorize the project of the Subaltern Studies group by its leader, Ranajit Guha. This group attempts to rewrite Indian nationalist history from the point of view of peasant insurgency. Some of the conflicts I disovered upon the Indian academic scene were played out in my subsequent collaboration with the group, as an indirect outcome of which the word "subaltern" was picked up and travestied by U.S. radical chic. I believe it is because my writing has changed through my efforts to learn from below that the collective has now asked me to become a full member.

In 1985, I invited Professor Bimal Krishna Matilal, the renowned Oxford Sanskritist, whom I did not then know personally, to the Collège international de philosophie in Paris. We found that we shared certain common concerns: we thought "Indian" philosophy could be an instrument for philosophizing. By 1988, we had decided to work together. Between the decision and starting work came the diagnosis of myeloma. Living Bimal's dying through intellectual work has also changed me. A week before his death, in John Radcliffe Hospital, we read the episode of the extraordinary death of Duryōdhana in the *Mahābhārata* as an ethical instance.

And now, my learning, teaching, dissertation directing, committee work, worldwide recommendation work, activism, writing—all of a piece—leave me no time even for a life.

These two pieces respond, of course, to the current demand that every interesting person show some marginality, some minimally nondominant class or ethnic origin, some otherish gendering. I remain unconvinced of my particularized and differentiated marginality, alas. I have sympathy with the hallucinatory desire that produces Sello in Bessie Head's *A Question of Power*, who, "as an African ... seemed to have made one of the most perfect statements: 'I am just anyone'."[4] I therefore include the following piece— "Excelsior Hotel Coffee Shop, New York, September 13, 1:07 pm"—in its entirety.[5] As the headnote should make clear, it was a staged, momentaneous autobiographical intervention. It is unabashedly "theoretical," yes. At the risk of being universally excoriated, I should reveal that even my mother has complained of my constant ticking over as a theory machine. This is the voice I would like to acknowledge, then, in a rather specifiable time-space, creatively bullshitting; not always in English, not always in accessible spots—but those other babblings would seem heavy-duty if published here. Now the coffee-shop scenario:

III

In response to my letter, Gayatri asks to do an "interview without questions." We agree to meet at an Ethiopian restaurant, but it is not open for lunch, so we start looking for another place. Suddenly, a massive thunderstorm strikes. We run and take shelter under the nearest sign. It turns out to mark the Excelsior Hotel, which, by chance, perhaps, is the space around which Wim Wenders' haunting film "Alice in the Cities" is organized. Sitting at the counter of the coffee shop, with the mist of the rain drifting all the way down towards us through an orange neon sign hanging in the open window promising "Fountain service," we talk.

MARK [WIGLEY]: Look at the rain reaching for us. It's like some kind of Gothic movie.

GAYATRI: Yes, with the wild wind. Shall we order?

MARK: Sure.

GAYATRI: Norwegian lox with cream cheese and a bagel, without the bagel.

WAITER: No bagel?

GAYATRI: No bagel.

MARK: A can of tuna and a toasted bagel with cream cheese.

WAITER: With the bagel?

MARK: With the bagel.

GAYATRI: Let me look at your letter. I deliberately made myself not think of a rap for this. Why organize a rap before and do it "like" an interview? It should be totally time-bound in a certain way. I always prepare for interviews because

I don't like to be surprised. I don't like to do something without being prepared, but I was attracted by the notion of violence and space. Time becomes violent in the space of an interview. The time frame here is a kind of violence. Time becomes violent in displacements. I have thought of this before when considering the displacement of liberation theologies of individual transcendence by an animist liberation theology. I don't particularly think liberation should need theology. You're better off if theologies are not there. But theology is an extremely powerful instrument. I have thought of a theography, as it were, which would be an animist liberation theology in which the human being is written in space rather than transcending itself in time, which is the situation in theology as we know it now, Judeo-Christian or Islamic. One does violence to the other because the battleground between old animisms and relatively new religions like Christianity and Islam is really a battleground, the site of so much ongoing violence, violence that is very much on my mind right now.

One can see this in everything, everything. I'm with people who are into allegories, like old Baudelaire, because I am a modernist, not a postmodernist, and Baudelaire is the best example of modernism that you can think of in terms of displacing the Enlightenment. You know, the Baudelaire who walks through, right? In one of the great walks through Paris, as he says, everything becomes an allegory. If you tow that line, as you know Benjamin argues, then allegory is the spacing of our time frames which gives violence to meaning. So, since everything becomes allegory for me, allowing a violent interview to take place, unprepared, improvised, like the rush of examinations and evaluations, is appropriate. Even though, especially, if it does not transcribe well.

Anyway, back to your letter: "Each writer will be given the same space in the journal." So you're being allegorical also. The page becomes the allegory of space and violence. But the funny thing about space is that it is layered, and you can't layer a page except by giving it a time. That's another of my little thought bites, as it were. You know, we could even do this whole thing through the tiny area of thought bites and not explain. The violent trouble then becomes the academic's trouble, someone else's thesis, and you don't really feel it any more. Less violence.

Here's another bite then: Jacques Derrida is not a postmodernist. Do you know that?

MARK: mmm hmm

GAYATRI: What do you mean "mmm hmm"?

MARK: I said "mmm hmm."

GAYATRI: Yes, but . . .

MARK: What did you think I said?

GAYATRI: That you agree.

MARK: I agree.

GAYATRI: But do you also disagree?

MARK: No. I think I agree, but I was immediately wondering what you were going to say that postmodernism was, because I would also say that Derrida was not postmodern, though maybe from a different angle.

GAYATRI: Well, I see Derrida constantly rereading and constantly emphasizing the old rules. The old that rules our lives and is actually the only way of life. Old fragments always renewed, everything always second hand, every second everything renewed again, and so on. This seems to me not at all like post-modern performance. You know what I mean?

MARK: Yes.

GAYATRI: It's just everyday life, so its not a heavy-duty thing. I don't see it as a performance. It may look like a unique kind of performance in a collo-quial sense because it doesn't look like traditional writing. But it's not really. At the same time, it effects a critique of the limits of the individual deliberative consciousness identified with the self. The subject is generally transcenden-talized, in our case it's made into predestination, but not in Derrida. And that's where the sacred stands. In some sense, Derrida is like going back to the eternal verities and talking, while the postmodern tries to talk back at the word eternal.

So, following that (and I'm deeply, deeply influenced by that part of Derrida, as you well know), I cannot separate out the time-movement in spac-ing. In fact what I'm interested in, like Freud in some ways, is delaminating the time line. I would not call it the primary form of intuition. I would call it a limit that we cannot in fact perceive in real space. Time is constantly dilating because we are flashes in the time-violation of space. It would mean that architects today produce flashes of the violation of space because they are building time machines, each producing their machines, right? I'm talking a kind of low-cut Deleuze and Guattari. We are producing machines and, in another way, we are excrements of these machines. We are ourselves reproduc-tion producing machines, as we are made we are cut, we are made as space is cut, just as we cut menstruation in order to get better organized. Space has to be violated in order to reproduce itself.

MARK: You are talking of an unavoidable, if not human, violence of the machine.

GAYATRI: Absolutely. That is the human in space. The human being, in an integral sense, is a machine of violence, and talk of pure space is already compromised by that founding violence. When I talk about animist liberation theology, I have to think about this violence that we are. Long before the thought that we are culture and not nature and all that nonsense, we are violating machines in space because the way in which we are in space, we are not, by definition, in the real. In that sense, talk of pure space is for me just talk, time-talk in space about space. That's why I'm trying to think of this as an allegory of space, which is not one given thing, even if, as your letter says, each of the writers will be given the "same space."

Space is always layered beyond the boundaries of the machine that we are. What we have to do is to make accommodations for that by calling for that other thing which seems to be beyond the human machine: space. This would be theography then. I'm not talking about museumizing animist cultures, that's nonsense. I'm talking about longing to enter, learning to enter, in the most time-bound way, with compromised, embattled, politically mobilized ways of thinking, making an incursion into the possibility of animism in the broadest sense. I'm not talking postcolonial blah blah blah, but it relates to my thinking about subaltern mind-sets. Learning to enter is the hardest possible thing. But animism is the only way in which we can get at all close to notions of meaning, alterity, and space. It would be interesting really to give it that name, animism, because we have to name ourselves with something of the other, right? Is this enough?

MARK: I have no idea what "enough" would mean here. Actually, I don't even know what "this" is. What are its limits? How much is this? Can we exclude the bagels from this allegorical riff around space, for example? And what would it mean to do so? If the space of the riff itself was in some way produced by ordering then withdrawing a bagel, shouldn't we publish the menu?

GAYATRI: It would be a compromise not to.

MARK: A violent one?

GAYATRI: Absolutely, but it would be equally violent to include it. After all, no normal eye could read the extremely small print.

MARK: We could provide some kind of prosthetic attachment for the reader's eye.

GAYATRI: No, don't provide a lens. The issue is about the violence of space after all. You know, that reminds me of something else. I went to Roosevelt Island the other day with a journalist and saw the project by Kawamata. I liked this Kawamata. The curator and my friend were talking with him and were both into the whole issue of public space, but this guy was more like Derrida than the pure-space brothers, so I asked him a few questions. He was saying that what he was doing was treating the space as a private space which was a public space before and will have to be public space again, since it was an installation, after all. Now, he was using an older terminology, but what he was really talking about when he spoke of private space was the human violating machine or, rather, the human interferer as a variation of the human violator, interference being as little as you can do to the self-consciousness of violation. If we long to call absolute alterity "space," we must acknowledge that we are, by being human, violators of the purity of space. Therefore we must try to reduce violation into interference. And I'm giving the word "interference" its fullest value here. In a sense, you could say that he was allegorizing the moment of interference as one of the private spacing of a movement from space being public in one way before and in another way now. What he does is to get wood from demolition sites and literally cover the space over. Borrowing the materials and then giving them back again, but now to different people, the homeless. In the meantime, he uses it to displace the space. He borrows in the way one borrows the mother tongue, that which has a history before us, a history after us, into which we are inserted in the mother's name, but then think is our own, the material with which we create and recognize reality and express ourselves, the material which we then pass on to others and leave when we die, but which has been altered, just slightly, by our own occupation and use of it. This is another allegory of the way we turn ourselves from violating machines into humble interferers. Because a mother's debt is never paid, and space is the mother in which we are placed. Kawamata's notion of private space is a way of coming to terms with what I'm talking about. When a government violates space by displacing people who have lived in a place for thousands of years for a big project, like a big dam, built under policies of sustainable development orchestrated by the World Bank, one of the only ways of mobilizing people against this monolith is through a sense of the sacredness of space, one that can be culturally patronized by people like us. That's all.

MARK: What you're saying about space seems to add something very crucial to to the argument which I think is written into most of your work, usually tacitly but sometimes very explicitly, about the inevitable violence written into the construction of identity.

GAYATRI: Yes, and also, in a way, ontologically. I'm interested that in the history of thinking, the ethics of ethics is prior to ontology. If being is defined as the violation of space, it's already an ethical question. But since it's not just a question of moralism, it's really a preethical question. Architecture is also the violence of space. But I'm not morally against architecture. I'm not even against the great individual expressions in art and intellectual systems, except I would like it to be acknowledged that they are violent. It's an aporia. You cannot put space and cultural production together in the same position, you have to choose one or the other. It's a genuine aporia because we have no basis on which to choose. And yet all aporias are also always broken. We always choose, and in general we are obliged to take it in the other direction and privilege cultural production, even in the pages of *Assemblage*, while we talk here about the purity of space. So that's it. No more explanations.

MARK: Coffee?

GAYATRI: Coffee.

Notes

1. Spivak, "Asked to Speak About Myself," *Third Text* 19 (Summer 1992), 9.

2. Damodar Dharmanand Kosambi, *Ancient India: A History of Its Culture and Civilization* (New York: Pantheon, 1965).

3. Jacques Derrida *Of Grammatology* (Baltimore: Johns Hopkins University Press, 1976).

4. Bessie Head, *A Question of Power* (Oxford: Heinemann, 1974), 11.

5. *Assemblage* 20 (April 1993), 74–75.

19

Laos Is Open

❧

STEPHEN GREENBLATT

For your next vacation I do not recommend the River View Hotel in Vientiane, the capital of Laos. A large, dreary concrete block, converted with Soviet help from a warehouse, it is utterly without charm. At the entrance, to be sure, there is a welcoming gesture: two life-size cardboard figures of smiling Laotians in the prayerlike, palms-together posture of greeting, called a *wai*. But the colors are faded and the cardboard disintegrating, as if to signal what lies within. Whoever designed the bathrooms evidently had had little previous experience of indoor plumbing; how else to explain the quaint decision to place the toilet inside the shower? And I had no idea that electric bulbs of such low wattage could be produced—though the gloom had the advantage of keeping us from looking too carefully at the sheets or deciphering the ominous smudges on the walls. My wife Ellen and I took the liberty of grumbling a bit to Amkha, the Lao Tourism guide who had been assigned to our family of four, but he shamed us by finding our complaints incomprehensible. The hotel is excellent, he declared with manifest conviction, though he regretted that it was enormously expensive—about twenty dollars a night, or half the monthly salary of an office worker or a teacher.

Why the warehouse was converted to a hotel is something of a mystery, though perhaps no greater mystery than why the warehouse was built in the first place—commerce being not much more evident than tourism. There are some small shops now in Vientiane and, in the modest covered market, an unprecedented if still very tentative display of big-ticket items: a few washing machines, stereos, and televisions. But it is difficult to see where Laotians will get the money for such purchases. One of Laos's principal sources of foreign currency is the sale of air rights for overflights; another is the export of used U.S. bomb casings dug up by peasants who frequently get blown up by the ones that failed to explode the first time round. There are, to be sure, unofficial sources of income: major opium production, stolen antiquities from the largely unguarded temples, the illegal cutting of timber, and—or so I was told by a Thai environmentalist— the illegal capture and export of exotic animals eaten as aphrodisiacs by wealthy Japanese. But there is almost no industry, no infrastructure, no sign of domestic manufactured goods. This is an unimaginably poor country.

On our first night in the River View Hotel, we dined entirely alone—not in the melancholy dining room which was darkened and empty, but on the rooftop, a huge, empty expanse of tar paper, lighted like a basketball court by a long row of glaring flourescent streetlamps. It was atrociously hot. Our meal was carried up four flights of stairs and served by a delicate young woman in a long wraparound skirt and embroidered blouse and an even more delicate young man with rings on his fingers, startlingly long fingernails, and a coy smile. Neither of them seemed to break a sweat.

Somewhere in the darkness flowed the Mekong, but there were no signs of life on the river, only a few lights on the Thai side, no cars or bicycles on the street below, and apparently no one else in the hotel. At breakfast the next morning, however, there were two other guests. The first was an American, paunchy, balding, and loud, in a sweat-stained polyester suit. He was a lawyer, he said, a "consultant" to the Lao government. What did he consult on?

"Anything they ask me to. Socialism is dead, they know that. But they don't know how to do anything different. The fault is the United Nations. Their bureaucrats are everywhere, and they give the Laotians endless money, so they have no incentive to develop their economy. It makes me sick. You see the bureaucrats—Indians mainly, who spend their lives shuffling forms—having dinner at the best restaurant in town, where they charge three times the price anywhere else. Their cars and drivers are sitting outside waiting for them. A little money gets through, of course, but ninety percent goes to pay their salaries. It makes me sick."

He had lived in Asia, he said, for more than twenty years—he arrived then, like so many of our other exports, with the Vietnam War—and "everyone knew him." But a few minutes later he said that he had lived for a year recently in Yugoslavia. And a few minutes later still he said he had been living in Florida where his daughter was in college. Had she grown up in Asia, we wondered. "No, on my yacht in Coral Gables."

The other guest at breakfast was a genial Indian who had listened with a smile to our compatriot's ramblings and who worked, he said, for Unilever. "What is Unilever doing in Laos?" we asked. He chuckled, "Having breakfast."

As we got up to leave, another foreigner hurried into the hotel, a lean American in his mid-thirties, with grease-slicked wiry hair and a loud Hawaiian shirt. He was carrying an attaché case and asked to see the manager. He was going to stay for a month, he said, and wanted a fifty percent reduction in the price of the room. He would have many visitors, he added, "my wife, my girlfriend, my father, my friends," and would have them all stay at the hotel. He spotted the "consultant"— "Am I glad to see you!" —and the two of them rushed off to a corner and began to talk earnestly in low tones. My younger son, Aaron, who used to be a great lover of Tintin comic books, looked at them with excitement: "Opium!" he whispered.

We didn't stay around to spy on the sinister pair, for it was time to see the sights of Vientiane, which is a capital largely without sights. A long history of defeat and domination—by the Thais, the Burmese, the Vietnamese, the Khmers, and the French—has taken a heavy toll on the dusty old city. There are a few Buddhist temple compounds, several quite lovely, but all of them on a modest and subdued scale compared to the glittering opulence of the *wats* of Bangkok. We resisted the temptation to pocket some fine old Buddha images in Wat Si Saket—there were thousands of them in dovecot-like niches along the cloister walls—but it was clear from the empty niches that others had not resisted. Everywhere there was an air of desolation, destruction, pillage: buildings razed in war, temples falling into ruin, melancholy reminders of famous treasures taken to Siam, murals flaking apart, headless and armless statues thrown in heaps. And the fact that we were alone at all of these sites intensified the poignancy and the sense of loss.

Thailand, just across the river, is overrun with tourists, but the Laotian government, though hard-pressed for foreign capital, is showing few signs of welcoming tourists. In fact it was remarkably difficult for our family of four, hard currency in hand, to get visas. We tried first in the United States, after we had heard from a friend of an anthropologist friend that Laos was "open" after so many years of being tightly "closed." For Americans who came of age during the Vietnam War, Laos has an extraordinary resonance: it conjures up a special outrage, for it was there, in the Annamite Mountains, along the Mekong Delta, and on the Plain of Jars, that the fatal combination of American arrogance, violence, and futility reached its zenith. The outrage, intensified by my generation's quaintly idealistic belief that the United States was supposed to behave justly, was oddly mingled with what Victorians must have felt at contemplating the implausible names of those whose faraway lands their empire was ravaging. For a few years our newspapers were filled with exotic characters— Prince Souphanouvong, the sinister General Phoumi

Novasan, the Pathet Lao leader Kaysone Phomvihane, gallant, courageous Prince Souvanna Phouma, King Sisavang Vong and his son King Savang Vattana— who seemed to inhabit a Gilbert and Sullivan opera, even while our B-52s bombed and bombed and bombed. At first the bombing was "secret"— the planes flew under different markings, and our government systemically lied about what it was doing—but even when we finally admitted what we were up to, there was not much of an explanation or excuse. Without a declaration of war, and hence without either congressional debate or legal authorization, the United States dropped more bombs per capita on remote, weak Laos than we did on Germany in World War II.

My family and I had been planning a trip to neighboring Thailand anyway, and something about this resonance, along with those words, "open" and "closed"— as if a country were a strongbox or a long-buried tomb—made us want to go to Laos. Memories of the devastation we visited on one of the poorest countries on earth were paradoxically intertwined with the tourist's dream of the unspoiled: if only you can get there, the *Lonely Planet Guide* declares, Laos offers you "an unparalleled glimpse of old South-East Asia." The world is full of places about which everyone says maddeningly, "You should have been here twenty years ago, before it was ruined": Chiang Mai, Rio, Berkeley. At last we would get to a place before it was ruined. We would be in on the ground floor of touristic spoliation. Years from now we could say to friends, "If only you had visited Laos when it was first opened to foreigners."

There is a Lao-American Tourist Association, in Elgin, Illinois. I imagine that it is located in Elgin because a bureaucrat in Vientiane looked at a map of the United States and put his finger down more or less in the middle. We had an elaborate and, in its odd way, warm exchange of letters with this office—I explaining to Ms. Marla that we did not want a package tour, Ms. Marla assuring me that we would be welcome on our own, that we would certainly receive visas, that we had only to fill out the applications in triplicate and tell them a bit more about ourselves and our reasons for wanting to visit. Applications duly sent; then long delays, more letters, more assurances, more delays, futile phone calls to Elgin and then to Washington, mumbled but evidently heartfelt apologies, still no visas—and then it was time to leave for Thailand.

In Bangkok we made our way to the Laotian embassy for another try. It took us almost two hours to get to the embassy through some of the worst traffic in the history of the world, the air insufferably heavy and full of exhaust fumes. We stood in line while two young Italians threw a prolonged histrionic tantrum at the demure young clerk behind the desk who was not giving them a visa. Finally, she relented, instructing them to leave their passports and return the next day. We had been told by the friend of the friend that the Laotians despised displays of anger, and valued gentleness and good humor:

even after all we did, she said, they prefer Americans to the Russians, because we smile so much more. We approached the desk wreathed in forced smiles, a family of Malvolios. The clerk smiled in return and instructed us to fill out new applications. But when we presented these applications—duly filled out in triplicate, with grinning photographs—she quietly said that we would not receive visas. "Why not?" She only shrugged. "But why did the Italians get visas?" "They not get visas. I only tell them come back tomorrow. But no visas." So, in a way, our smiles had been rewarded.

Still we had wasted the better part of the day and had no visas to show for it, and we wandered around Bangkok's Chinatown disconsolately. It was amazingly hot and humid, and the traffic was hideous. We ducked into a warren of alleys to get out of the sun, but it was almost as hot back there in the dark, and it was difficult to walk, because the ground was thick with refuse and the space almost completely filled with cooling ducts, pipes, electric wires—the stuff of unregulated, uncontrolled construction. Out on the snarling street again, we looked for a taxi. My older son Josh cooled his hands in the melting ice of a fish stall; we pointed out to him that the water was of dubious cleanliness. He has the regrettable habit of biting his fingernails from time to time.

The next morning Josh fainted on the airport bus taking us to a flight to Chiang Mai. Admittedly, that bus was crowded and hot—I felt faint too—but we took his temperature and knew that when we landed we had to get him to a doctor. The same anthropologist friend who put Laos into our heads had given us the name of another friend of his, an American-born lawyer who had married a Thai woman, become a Buddhist, practiced law in Bangkok, and—crucial for our purposes—commuted to Chiang Mai where he and his family lived. His wife was at home when we phoned and said she would come immediately to the hotel: "I was just going to drive to that part of town anyway." In her mid-40s, Ti Garden was cheerful, soft-spoken, immensely kind, and—in a way immediately apparent though difficult to define—not completely of this world. Where does one get such an impression after ten minutes' conversation, preoccupied by a feverish child and constrained by the formality of a first meeting? From very obscure signals: a certain timbre in the voice, the way sentences take form and trail off, a posture that somehow conveys the indwelling of the spirit. This will sound absurd—doubly so when I add that Ti Garden had gone from high school in Chiang Mai to Radcliffe, drove a big Range Rover, and had two teenage children. Less sylphlike than sturdy, quick to laugh, and utterly unpretentious, she nonetheless immediately struck all of us as the native of a different planet.

We talked about what to do with the suffering Josh. Ti knew a Western-trained doctor in town, but she urged us to do first what she would do with her own children: go to a Buddhist healer in a forest monastery on the outskirts of town. "I happen to be going there this morning anyway, so it's not out of my way. I'll take you." Josh is sixteen and is developing a sense of irony as well as a capacity for despair. He groaned audibly.

We piled in the Range Rover, and Ti drove us to the monastery, our son swearing quietly in the backseat. The saffron-clad monk, sitting in front of a hut in the forest, wore wire-rimmed glasses, which was vaguely reassuring. He did not look at Josh—that was less reassuring—but listened attentively to a description of his symptoms, then brought out a glass of water and a paper packet of herbal pills and told him to take ten of them immediately. He noticed that we looked askance at the water and explained that it was rainwater. We evidently looked unconvinced, because he went inside the hut and brought out a glass of what he said was boiled rainwater. Fifteen minutes after Josh took the pills his fever was completely gone. There was no charge.

It was cool in the forest, and we walked around the monastery, listening to the crickets and the howling of a gibbon, hidden somewhere in the trees. Ti said she wanted us to meet someone. In a cell by a small pond she introduced us to a middle-aged German who had become a Buddhist monk, a coarse-featured, hairy-chested man, his shaved head nicked by his razor, with a big paunch under his saffron robe. He was from Hamburg, he said, and was raised as a Lutheran. He had run away from his mother and stepfather when he was sixteen; then lived a wild life in Sweden; then followed Rudolf Steiner; then found Buddhism. Even during his years sharing "the material affluence and sensuous gratification of Swedish youths" (which he pronounced unsettlingly like "Jews"), he had been seeking something. He had lived in the cell by the pond for seventeen years. Did he think that he would ever leave? Perhaps not, he answered, though he would like to go to Laos.

Ti also longed to go to Laos—"it's deeply Buddhist, very unspoiled." Back in the hotel, we saw an ad for a tourist agency in Chiang Mai—the aptly named Exotissimo Travel—that claimed it could book trips to Laos; a week later (for an extravagant sum that more than made up for the no-cost medical treatment) we had our visas.

❧

At the River View Hotel we wondered whether we were missing the Buddhist epiphany that Ti and the German monk both associated with Laos. The capital certainly did not seem a notably mystical place. The temples, or *wats*, were empty; the only place where we saw worshipers was at the ugly, modern site of the city pillar—an ancient stone column set into the ground—where a handful of women knelt on the linoleum and made offerings to an image said to bring luck. We went to a forest temple just outside of town—a place with the imposing name of Wat Mahaphutthawongsa Pa Luang Pa Yai—where toothless nuns in white robes gave us herbal saunas and pleasant massages, but it all seemed more like Calistoga than Nirvana.

The most striking thing about Vientiane is not the aura of religious life but the sense of being in the provinces' provinces. In one direction along the river from our hotel, there were lots of young people sitting on small wooden decks built out on the banks. They were chatting and smoking and quietly laughing. They probably lived in the horribly squalid concrete apartment blocks behind us, with their glimpses through curtainless windows of bare rooms, lit by a single naked bulb or a long fluorescent light, cracking paint and plaster, with blotches of water stains, scraps of corroding metal. In the midst of these, there survived a few dilapidated French-style houses, with long shuttered windows, as if lifted from a town in Normandy. A small food shop or two were the only signs of commercial life, and even these seemed shut, so that a young couple could sit by their bicycle (a passenger seat cleverly fitted on to the frame) and hold hands and feel quite alone (until, that is, the girl noticed the unfamiliar sight of the American tourist strolling towards them). In the other direction from our hotel, the pavement gave out after a block or two, and the dirt lane was lined with bamboo houses on stilts, with pigs and chickens in the space below. There were woodcutters lopping off branches with machetes, fishermen casting graceful nets into the flooded rice fields to catch minnows, and farmers, plodding behind their water buffalos, turning the heavy mud. Here a few shops were open, selling tiny selections of fish and meat, and two or three vendors were making small rice cakes. But all was quiet, except for the crackling voice on the loudspeakers attached to concrete poles, broadcasting the news, I suppose, or the latest production figures from Savannakhet, or the Party's latest manifesto.

The loudspeakers were one of the very few signs of ideological life, though the Pathet Lao remains very much in power. We seemed to be the only visitors at the Lao Museum of the Revolution, in an old, faded mansion. The Museum is an odd place. Its account of World War II completely suppresses the fact that the Americans fought the Japanese, who surrendered to "the Anti-Fascist Alliance." (But then the East German Museum at Buchenwald concentration camp, near Weimar, scarcely mentioned that Jews died there; and the Musée de l'Armée at the Invalides in Paris does an impressive job of minimizing the American role in the liberation of Europe, celebrating instead what it shamelessly pretends was a widespread French resistance to the Nazis.) There are news photographs of Johnson and MacNamara ordering the bombing of Laos and painful photographs of children burned by "U.S. imperialist napalm" and a few old rifles and charred pieces of American planes. Above all, there is much celebration, in the old Maoist manner, of Comrade Kaysone: his heroic exhortations to the people, his life hidden in caves (one display case shows the exercise cables—just like I had as a kid!—with which he kept fit while in hiding), his surprise attacks, and his plans, as one caption rather nakedly put it, "to seize power." But outside the museum there were few signs of indoctrination—no elaborate posters, no flags and photographs, no parades. At the same time, there were virtually no books or magazines and very few televisions, and though there must have been newspapers somewhere, we never saw one. Perhaps indoctrination seemed beside the point.

There were some of the familiar signals of the police state at the airport, where we went to catch a plane to Luang Phabang: photography forbidden, papers stamped and counterstamped by sour-looking bureacrats and customs officials, a distinct sense of disapproval though no very clear indication of what any of us had done wrong. We would have preferred to go by bus or still better by boat. But the river in the summer months was too low, and the road, we were told, was impossible. "Why impossible?" "I don't know," said our guide, "Maybe mines, maybe Hmong guerillas." The Air Laos flight didn't seem much safer. The small twin-engine Chinese plane couldn't get much altitude, and we bumped along perilously close to the rugged mountaintops, skimming (within automatic weapons range, I thought) over the isolated Hmong villages where the CIA recruited its army and where much of Laos's opium is grown. The plane grew tremendously hot, the cabin filled with smoke—just normal condensation, we were told—and several passengers became violently ill. Then the mountains came still closer—they seemed about to scrape the bottom of the plane—and we were landing at Luang Phabang.

❖

In the mid-nineteenth century a French naturalist, M. Henri Mouhot, travelled through Southeast Asia on behalf of the Geographical and Zoological Societies of London, collecting specimens, making scientific drawings, and writing reports. In July, 1861, after a nightmarish voyage on elephant, beset by mosquitoes, ox-flies, and leeches, he reached Luang Phabang. "It was a charming picture," he wrote in his journal, "reminding one of the beautiful lakes of Como and Geneva. Were it not for the constant blaze of a tropical sun, or if the mid-day heat were tempered by a gentle breeze, the place would be a little paradise"[1] I can corroborate both the torrid heat—two of the passengers collapsed on the short walk from the plane to the little shed that serves as the terminal— and the intense beauty, though the steep jungle cliffs and magnificent temples seem very far from the Alps.

Poor fever-ridden Mouhot! By the time he reached Luang Phabang, with his precious cases of beetles and butterflies, he must have been dreaming of lively Italians and yodelling Swiss peasants. The Laotians seemed to him disagreeably passive and withdrawn—not hostile, exactly, but indifferent, unhelpful, and lacking all normal curiosity. Before he set out, a Chinese merchant had warned him to carry a good stick, the longer the better: "Put all delicacy aside," the merchant advised, "Laos is not like a country of the whites." The somber words continue to echo weeks later in his journal entries. "I am getting tired of these people," he writes, "a race of children, heartless and unenergetic. I sigh and look everywhere for a man, and cannot find one; here all tremble at the stick, and the enervating climate makes them incredibly apathetic."

Though the king of Luang Phabang received him with great pomp, Mouhot's mood did not improve, even when he had the pleasure of watching the natives kill a rhinoceros. Despite his long stick, he could not seem to compel service; and even gifts, the kindler, gentler alternative to beatings, were not properly recompensed. The Laotians seemed to him ungrateful and egotistical: "they not only will give you nothing—one has no right to expect it—but after taking presents from you, they will make you no return whatever." From morning to night the priests continually made their "frightful noise," but everyone else seemed "indolent," cultivating only enough rice to survive and then—as Mouhot puts it with fine Victorian exasperation—"lounging about the woods." They weren't even picturesque: "I saw some pretty young girls with intelligent faces; but before the females attain the age of eighteen or twenty their features become coarse and they grow fat. At five-and-thirty they look like old witches." Only the elephants seemed to him entirely admirable in their patience, goodness, and intelligence.

Mouhot labored on to collect his specimens, but his wanderings in the mountains near Luang Phabang—his own purposeful version of lounging about the woods—broke his health. By September his journal entries have become little more than lists of place names, interrupted by complaints about the tormenting mosquitoes and leeches; by October they have become for the most part unreadable:.IP5,4/

15th October. 58 degress Fahr.—Set off for Louang Prabang.

16th. - . . . . . .

17th. - . . . . . .

18th. - Halted at H. . . .

19th. - Attacked by fever.

29th. - Have pity on me, oh my God. . . !

Mouhot died in delirium on November 10, 1861. A large beetle was named in his honor, *Mouhotia gloriosa.*

✿

There was a *Mouhotia gloriosa*, or one of its close relations, in our hotel room in Luang Phabang. It was too big to squash—it would have been like smashing a squirrel—so I picked it up in my son's baseball hat and escorted it outside. This was our principal experience of the area's wildlife—the tigers and rhinoceroses are all gone—if you except the drowsy civet cat in a very small cage and a monkey on a very long chain in the hotel's garden. We did not try to find any leeches, and we wore enough repellant to ward off every mosquito in Southeast Asia. The incidence of malaria in the region is astonishingly high, as is the general level of disease that so dismayed (and finally killed) Mouhot.

Good as its word, Lao Tourism had sent a guide to the airport to meet us—a sweet, quiet, sad-eyed young man named Tongchan who spoke some French and a few words of English and had one exceptionally long, indeed finger-length fingernail on his pinky. I asked him why. "Useful," he said, and mimed cleaning his ears with it. He took us sightseeing—for the most part, *wat*-hopping. We were, as far as we could tell, the only tourists in Luang Phabang and were the sole visitors in all of the splendid temples and in the former royal palace at the center of town. On the second day we did, however, meet another American while we waited on the steps that led down to the Mekong for a long-tail boat that would take us about thirty kilometers upriver to caves with famous Buddhist carvings. Our compatriot was a somewhat brassy Laotian woman, originally from Luang Phabang. She had been in a refugee camp in Thailand, she said, then in the Philippines, and now in Oakland where she had become a U.S. citizen and lived near 35th Avenue. She had the Laotian's ready smile, but all of the diffidence was gone: she was expansive, irrepressible, and above all loud. It was impossible for us to tell, of course, if she had left Laos because she was so loud, or if she had become loud in America: some are born loud, some have loudness thrust upon them. "You should take pictures where they tell you not to," she boomed at us. Tongchan looked away, as if lost in thought.

Along the river, in the event, we were not asked to refrain from photography. The long-tail boat swooped in close to a half-sunk U.S. patrol boat, Vietnam War vintage, and stopped at a riverside village where rice wine—here called "Lao-Lao"—is brewed. This was, quite obviously, the standard tour. But in the village I was forcibly struck by something I had already noticed in Luang Phabang: no one was interested in selling us anything. Indeed there was virtually nothing for sale. I had wandered around the town for several hours looking for something to buy, even a postcard, and the best I could come up with was a small bamboo stick crudely decorated with an odd checkerboard design. I asked what the design was meant to signify, but I couldn't make out the answer. At the riverside distillery, similarly, there were no souvenirs for sale. Two large, rusted barrels were sitting over a wood fire on the bank; a woman was pouring river water into the barrels through a homemade strainer; a bamboo pipe dripped the wine into dark earthenware pots. I was invited not to buy but simply to taste: the cup was a Sprite can, with the top removed and the edges smoothed. Tongchan ladled some Lao-Lao into this cup by dipping what appeared to be the top of an old antifreeze container into the pot. Preferring death to dishonor, I gingerly drank some, but even then there was no hint that I might want to buy a bottle to take with me.

Laos was, I realized, the culture least oriented to selling anything that I have ever encountered. This restraint or, to use Mouhot's term, indifference extends to places where you would most expect a sales pitch: market stalls, shops, hotels, restaurants (where you are never urged to have any drink but water). There was, to be sure, the rapacity represented by the absurd sum that the government charged for a tourist visa, but that sum seemed largely to function as a device to discourage visitors and inhibit commerce. Indeed I never saw anyone in the country actively trying to make money. No one tried to interest us in commodities or sell us services; no one seemed eager to initiate exchange of any kind. Even in the handicraft village to which we were taken (and where again we were quite alone), the weavers did not display goods by their looms or urge them upon us; instead all of the women sat chatting with one another around the perimeter of an open-sided wooden shed and, if we happened to glance in their direction, held up their goods. Prices were rather high, and there seemed to be no interest in bargaining, just as there seemed to be no frustration, anxiety, or disappointment at not making a sale. So too in the appallingly poor little villages along the river at which we asked the boatman to stop, there was virtually no grasping after us, even among the children. It is not that the children or, for that matter, the adults were, to use Mead's and Bateson's famous term for the Balinese, "away." No, the kids giggled and dared each other to approach us and say "Sa-bai-dii" (hello); the adults smiled, and responded to our greetings; a few went further and expressed some quiet amusement or interest in our presence. But the villagers seemed to lack any of the familiar signs of social *desire*—to sell, to acquire, to impress, to touch, to improve their lot, to signal their presence in the world.

This was what it meant then to reach a place untouched by tourism, the place that our acquaintance Ti and her friend the German Buddhist monk dreamed of visiting: we had reached the Land of No Desire. Now and then there were signs of activity: two young men cutting planks with a long saw, a few dugout canoes, some villagers coming down to the river to fetch water. But the villages, though full of people squatting by their bamboo huts, seemed oddly still, and the wide, muddy river, flanked by jagged limestone cliffs and lush mountains, was empty and silent. Was it beautiful? Yes, of course. But I found it strangely unsettling that no one seemed to want anything from us. It is the intense mutual exploitation of tourism—the sense of consuming and being consumed, the search for a "bargain" and the fear of being ripped off— that conditions the dream of an escape from tourism; without the exploitation, without a feverish climate of exchange, the actual escape seemed unnerving. Moreover, I am more of a Victorian than I had realized: it was impossible for me not to feel some half-repressed version of Mouhot's horror, a version focused on the big-bellied children caked with mud and mucus. We had read that Laos has one of the highest infant mortality rates in the world: that was, in the villages along the Mekong, not an invisible statistic but a graphic reality.

Tongchan took us to his village, one of the poorest we had seen on the river and one of the most disheartening. But in the midst of the disorder, with huts falling into ruin, pigs rooting about the midden, children wandering about naked and coughing, there was a central meeting hall of sorts—a row of plank benches under a thatch roof—and a small *wat* with simple, touching paintings of the life of the Buddha. Tongchan led us to the hut where he was born and introduced us to his parents. His mother was a thin, toothless woman with an elegant face. She held her grandchild, the daughter of Tongchan's sister whose husband had been killed while serving as a soldier. Tongchan's father, an emaciated seventy-year-old, was a blacksmith; a fire grate, a small vat of water, and a few simple tools were the signs of his trade. We drank tea. The old man cleared his throat and remarked that the river was low. We agreed—as if we had some idea of its usual height. He said it would rise later in the season. We agreed again. The conversation gave me the chance to look at the tattoos on his chest and arms. I realized that they were the same odd checkerboard design that was on my stick, and I asked what they signified. They keep the poisonous snakes in the river from biting, he said. Mystery solved.

I was safe from snake bites, then, but not from the sadness that welled up from the great brown empty river and the ragged children and the sight, as we returned, of the sunken U.S. patrol boat. Back in Luang Phabang the feeling was only intensified by a visit to the National Museum. This large, rather graceless building on the riverbank had served as the royal palace until the 1975 revolution. Then the king, who had made the mistake of backing the United States and counting on its support, was sent with his wife and five children to a "reeducation camp" in northern Laos. They have not been heard from since.

The museum's great treasure is the "Pha Bang" from which the town (Luang means "big") gets its name: this is a deeply venerated first-century standing Buddha, supposedly made of solid gold. Displayed in a cluttered room and seen through a locked grate, it looked rather unimpressive and, more to the point perhaps, fake. But who can tell? Perhaps it was simply cheapened by the surrounding elephant tusks and Chinese porcelein vats and small bronzes—second-rate loot in a well-traveled Edwardian gentleman's country house. No doubt it was more impressive when it was washed ritually every year by the king in a solemn temple ceremony; judging from the dust, it had not been washed since 1975. I looked dutifully for the requisite minutes, daydreaming that I was in Nabokov's Zembla, and then moved on to the rest of the palace.

The whole house—a succession of reception rooms, bedrooms, a modest bathroom, and a small library that contained only a single immensely large history of the Ming and Ching dynasties—had an air of desolation. King Savang Vattana may be officially the enemy of the people, but the guards in the museum gave the distinct sense of being in deep mourning. Why didn't the king try to escape? we asked, thinking of our South Vietnamese allies. "The king did not leave Laos because he decided to die with his people," came the answer. Perhaps. Or perhaps he was naïvely confident in the power of his allies. Among the array of official gifts to the royal family was a medal with Lyndon Johnson's picture on it, a piece of the moon given by Richard Nixon, and, in the place of honor, the key to the city of Los Angeles, presented by the mayor, Sam Yorty.

❖

On our last morning in Luang Phabang, I awoke at 4:30 A.M., couldn't get back to sleep, and tiptoed out to have a last walk around the town. A line of monks was going on their alms round, each carrying a covered bowl and receiving offerings—a bit of meat, fish, or rice—from passersby. They turned into Wat Mai, the temple where the king used to wash the Pha Bang. I decided to climb to the top of Phu Si, the steep hill that dominates the town, so I scrambled over the locked gate and, in the very great solitude of a city filled with solitude, hiked up the path to the top, past the frangipani trees, the *bodhi* tree sent from India, the tangle of vines and palms and flowers. There was a strange birdcall and the cry of a gibbon.

From the foot of the *stupa* on the summit, I looked out at the mist-shrouded river and the temple roofs, but I couldn't bring myself to sit in solitary contemplation for very long, so I hiked down again and continued my walk through the largely deserted streets. Several small shops and tiny repair sheds were opening, a few parents were out with their children, and a solitary *samlor* pedaled by. Mostly there was emptiness and silence.

I reached Wat Xieng Thong, a marvelous seventeenth-century temple complex at the northern end of town. I hadn't realized that I had walked so far, and I suddenly felt tired. There was no one in sight, but the side door of the main *sim*, or chapel, was open a crack, and I took off my sandals and entered. There are no windows in the *sim*— the roof in the Luang Phabang style sweeps almost down to the ground—and very little light came through the door. Wats have neither the massive solidity of Romanesque nor the soaring, dazzling light of Gothic. Rather, and especially in Laos, they seem to be entirely about darkness, enclosure, withdrawal. Here it was almost pitch-dark, though I could just make out a glint of gold from the enormous Buddha at the end of the hall. At first all that was visible was part of the arm; then very gradually, as my eyes adjusted to the darkness, I deciphered more of the huge figure, along with the smaller figures standing in the strange, stiff "Calling for Rain" posture—arms held rigidly to the side, fingers down—characteristic of Laotian Buddhism. I tried, in a half-comic, half-serious way, to pray, or rather to clear my mind. If it was going to happen for me, whatever it was that Ti and the German monk longed for, it would happen here and now. But I was too preoccupied, worrying about whether Josh had been completely cured, about whether Ellen was enjoying herself, about my work, about the sick children in the villages, about the possibility of getting locked in the *sim*, about the flight back to Vientiane. As a Buddhist I was a complete failure. All that had happened was that my eyes had involuntarily adjusted to the darkness. And then I realized, with a flash that even my relentless irony couldn't entirely undermine, that adjusting to the darkness was the best I could hope for.

Note

1. M. Henri Mouhot, *Travels in the Central Parts of Indo-China, Cambodia, and Laos*, 2 vols. (London: John Murray, 1864).

20

Damaged Goods

❀

BRUCE ROBBINS

Not long before he died, my grandfather took me with him to the track, I was
visiting him in Miami, where he had moved after my grandmother died and
an experiment living with another woman in the Bronx hadn't worked out.
(My mother said, obscurely, that the woman in the Bronx was "too demanding.") He had quit his job as a shipping clerk at the Pennsylvania Railroad
when my grandmother got sick. Then he found a job supervising a team of
young messengers at Lehman Brothers on Wall Street. Before leaving for
Florida, he used to drop hints that working for Lehman Brothers gave him
access to inside information about the stock market.

If inside information was a perk of the job, we never saw the benefits of it.
My father continued to pay his father's rent in Miami as he had in Brooklyn.
But I'm not sure I was aware of that then. I *was* aware that my grandfather had
a lot of inside information on subjects I hadn't learned about in school, and
wasn't likely to.

We went to the track in a van with a crowd of noisy regulars. I was shown
off. I was at Harvard. But it was my grandfather's knowledge that everybody
seemed to want, not mine. He was having trouble with his eyes by then, so we
didn't fight for a place by the rail. I can't remember him, or anyone else, actually watching the horses go by. I don't remember even *seeing* horses. What I
remember is my grandfather's friends—he called them his "cronies"—crowd-
ing around him, trying to find out his opinions on the day's horses and jock-
eys and odds. The moment that sticks in my mind is the moment he looked

up and noticed I was watching the men around him, how they wheedled and joked to find out his picks and his reasons for them, how the old, lined faces strained toward his face as if he were a TV monitor or a racing paper. That was when he broke away from the group, took me by the arm, and led me a few steps away. He said, "You're a writer. Someday you should write about all this."

He swept his arm over the whole scene, including the distant and invisible horses. I must have said something, trying to joke, about how much I didn't know about the ponies. But he was serious, and of course the impossible thing I was immediately nodding and promising to do was not to become a chronicler of the racing scene. It was to preserve the right memory of him, which was the memory of the recognition he was receiving and had received from the cronies, who *did* know about the ponies—to preserve if I could the results of a lifetime of scrupulously attentive devotion to the object of their shared passion.

My grandfather never got further in school than second grade, so he didn't know that I wasn't a "writer," or how poorly graduate studies in English had been preparing me to describe the world he belonged to. Some would have called it the underworld. Not us, though. As far as my family was concerned, that world of gamblers and small-time crooks had taken its definitive, for-general-audiences form in Damon Runyon and in the famous musical made from his stories, *Guys and Dolls*. "I Got the Horse Right Here" and "Luck Be a Lady" were like family anthems. When I was small, my grandfather took me on the subway from Avenue J to Lindy's in midtown. *Guys and Dolls* had only called it Lundy's to avoid legal trouble, he said. He ordered cheesecake for me and told me names of gangsters who used to hang out there. Maybe he even knew where they used to sit.

My grandfather's more flamboyant younger brother, Uncle Willie, who for many years ran the numbers operation where my grandfather worked, made it into Damon Runyon under his nickname, Willie the Fish. (Their father had sold fish at one time on Fulton Street.) We always spoke of him as if he were an honorary cast member of *Guys and Dolls*. I never met him. He died on the run from the mob, in California, having borrowed all but a hundred dollars of my father's savings account. His Irish widow always called me by my full name: Bruce William.

Morris the Fish (more often Moishe, even to his Irish sister-in-law) had his claims to glory, too. He had met Dutch Schultz and Lepke. (One of them, I forget which, had distinguished himself by his politeness: "How *are* you, Mr. Rabinowitz? And how is *Mrs.* Rabinowitz?). And together with my grandmother, Mrs. Rabinowitz, he had gone on some double dates with Mae West and her boxer boyfriends during Prohibition, thanks to my grandfather's knowledge of where good booze was available. He spoke with respect of Mae West: "She always paid her own way." I respected her, too, but what I thought of lines like "Is that a pistol in your pocket . . . ?" was not the sort of thing I thought I could share with my grandfather. Lord knows how much he felt he could not share with me. I know he was a collector of gambling debts and that he carried a blackjack in his pocket. He never told me about any violence he committed, or even saw.

At college in 1970 or so, I read Robert Lowell's "Memories of West Street and Lepke." In the poem Lowell, serving time as a conscientious objector, meets Lepke, serving time for altogether more serious infractions. It was a rare instant for me. Lepke? The guy who had been so polite to Pa? My grandfather's halting, heavily censored stories about his life had suddenly intruded into my new college life, with its ironic, ambivalent poetry and its straightforward demonstrations against the war in Vietnam. But now that I think of it, there must have also been other intrusions.

Why was I so interested, for example, in the story of strong, upwardly mobile sons and weak, downwardly mobile fathers that I found over and over in nineteenth-century novels and that I followed, in my undergraduate thesis, into twentieth-century writers like Joyce and Céline? I wasn't the strong son of a weak father. But my father was. It was my grandfather who had talked big and gambled and never won enough, who hadn't been able to keep his family from being put out on the street or even to keep the family together. (My father was sent off to live with Uncle Willie nearby and then later with Aunt Gussie in New Jersey.) And what I was replaying in my head it was my father's story of upward mobility, the story of how he rescued his father and his family and carried them out of poverty. I replayed it over and over, making it mine by reading it into the books I read, making it what I studied and why. The traumas of the Depression became the novels of Dickens. My father's personal progress became a collective political progressiveness—a progress that made room for me, too.

It's not an unfamiliar pattern among people of my generation, mainly men. As friend and colleague Michael Sprinker pointed out one day, children of working-class and lower-middle-class immigrants, or of the children of immigrants, can find in cultural Marxism or other styles of cultural critique a comforting sense of synthesis between one generation's deprivation and the next generation's struggles toward upward mobility. Identify both with your educated teachers and with your uneducated family, and the result may be a politicized attitude toward culture that combines, more or less successfully, loyalty to where you're trying to get to (the culture) and loyalty to where you've been (the politics).

But this wasn't the whole story, even for my undergraduate thesis. No, my grandfather wasn't just the unhappy starting point required by his son's and grandson's push toward a happy ending. In fact, he was where my story went *after* my father, and where my thesis went after it left the nineteenth century. The definitive scene for me—where the rising curve of the Young Man from the Provinces was finally checked and flattened, according to my thesis, and therefore what I put on the first page—was the opening scene of Samuel Beckett's *Malone Dies*: an old man alone in bed, getting more and more decrepit, waiting to die, telling stories. It never occurred to me at the time that for me, Malone was my grandfather, helplessly but somehow virtuously left behind by the inexorable progress of my father. Nor did it occur to me that in letting him take center stage from the son who had risen so far and supported him for so long, I was also doing a little upstaging myself. Beckett's modernism, where the thesis began and ended, was a moment of blockage when progress abruptly went out of style. Not coincidentally, it was also the moment when professional literary criticism came into being. Helpless but somehow virtuous, literary critics acquired a heroic identity from the fact, if it was a fact, that progress had turned out to be a lie. It was because they, or rather we, agreed to see our time as one of ever-increasing commercialism and decay that we could claim credit for reverentially salvaging the great cultural artifacts of the past. It was a convenient story for critics engaged in trying to make a place for themselves as opposed to the scientists and businessmen, and it was a convenient story for me as I tried to make a place for myself separate from and maybe even equal to that of my businessman father.

Years later this same narrative turned into the vocational allegory I proudly discovered and criticized, though without referring to my family, in a book on the professional identity of literary critics. Repeating myself like a broken record. That book could only have been written, I suppose, once I stopped recognizing myself and criticism generally in the worldly paralysis my grandfather compensated for by gambling hopefully or ironically with words. Logically, I would have to have moved on to some other story, it would seem, in order to be critical of that one. But someone else will have to say what the new story might be. In the meantime, progress remains an unfashionable idea for critics, and the status quo is always rich in targets. It's easier to think of criticism as my daughter did when she was asked, in second or third grade, what her father did for a living. She replied: "Daddy is a criticizer."

My grandfather can't have liked being supported by his fourteen-year-old son's after-school job as a delivery boy, or getting his first legitimate employment when the same son, now seventeen, gave up his job in an aircraft parts factory near Yankee Stadium to join the Army Air Corps in 1941 and managed to pass the job on to him. It isn't hard to understand his impulse to criticize. He ran into Woody Allen's father once in Miami. They had lived on the same street in Brooklyn. My grandfather said to Mr. Konigsberg, "My son's in the curtain-and-drapery business. Doing very well. And your boy—still writing jokes?" My grandfather was very funny about the way the other Florida retirees compared the size of their children's cars. But when I mentioned this to my father, he looked surprised. His father had complained, he told me, that the rented car my father drove up in was too small. On the evidence of my family, criticism seemed to be a matter of unpredictable investments rather than regular rules or laws. Sitting in front of the TV during a gunshot-filled preview of *The Magnificent Seven*, I remember hearing my father count, slowly and with emphasis: "Magnificent six.... Magnificent five.... Magnificent four...." *That* was criticism.

My grandfather found it easier to invest in my future than in my father's. His hopes for me did not focus on literary criticism, or even on education. An assimilationist ("My name was Kelly," he used to say; "I changed it because Kelly is too common") and a patriot, he wanted my success to be success at the all-American game of baseball. There is an old black-and-white photo of him teaching me to swing a bat on the back porch of our old house. I couldn't have been more than two. My hands were too small, so he used the handle of one of my father's golf clubs. We're not looking at each other, but we're both ecstatic. Later, whenever he came from Brooklyn to visit he would bring me a pink rubber ball he called a spaldeen. (It was years before I realized this meant Spalding, the company that made them.) I was supposed to walk around squeezing the ball all the time so as to build up my right forearm and throw a better curve. For a while it seemed to work. When he could, he came all the way out from Brooklyn to see the Little League games I pitched. But I did not become a right-handed Sandy Koufax. My control wasn't bad, and I would gladly have played in the World Series on the High Holy Days—the World Series *was* my High Holy Days. But I was never going to have Sandy Koufax's back muscles or his fastball. Luckily I was not told how much of a disappointment this was.

When my father knew he was dying, in 1990, he told me that his father had been a socialist. In fact, he said, all my grandparents had been socialists. This was not a surprise about my mother's father, a housepainter who was active in his union, and who died in an industrial accident when my mother was sixteen. It was a surprise about both grandmothers, one of whom had been blind since her thirties and neither of whom had ever said a word to me about politics, though they knew it mattered to me. And it was a surprise about my father's father, whose only political opinion that I could recall was that Robert Kennedy was "arrogant." My father did add, with a laugh, that his father hadn't been a very observant socialist.

Among my father's many gifts to me, this was the one he withheld the longest, and it may have been the one he chose for me most carefully. It was a sort of guarantee, like so much else he did and said, that my politics, my way of looking at the world would not begin and end in Oedipal revolt. My grandfather had less to give, but what he gave, like the Lindy's cheesecake and all the spaldeens, had a fitness about it that went straight to the heart. On Sunday mornings he would drive up to our house in his black Chevy, and when we ran out to greet him he was already opening up the trunk. In the trunk were always two wooden crates, always one full of grapefruit and one full of oranges. Damaged goods, I heard someone say. They came from my grandfather's respectable job in the freight yards. I remember thinking it funny that you couldn't *see* any damage. All my life I have found it almost impossible to see oranges and grapefruits without tossing one of them up in the air, hefting its weight as it falls, and spinning it upward again. I squeeze it like a spaldeen, knowing there may be damage to the fruit, and I feel the familiar tautness in my pitching arm. I catch it lightly as if it were part of my hand. I can't help myself, even though there's a risk I'll break something or that people will think I'm bored. It's not boredom. It's something about the rising arc and the soft fall.

21

Junctions on the Color Line[1]

❖

WILLIAM L. ANDREWS

"Why the colored, Bill?" my mother inquired in the summer of 1972 during a conversation we had after I told her I had decided to write a doctoral dissertation on an African American writer named Charles W. Chesnutt. "Why are you so interested in colored authors?" My mother's tone was more nonplussed than disapproving. I don't recall how I responded to her, but it was probably vague, deliberately so. A product of the post–World War II suburban South, I had learned almost nothing in my education about how to talk about race in my own family, let alone communicate my growing sense of intellectual commitment to investigating the color line in turn-of-the-century American literature.

For two years I had been pursuing, largely on my own, an inquiry into race via American literature, my avowed major field in graduate school at the University of North Carolina at Chapel Hill. I had managed to keep my official and unofficial literary studies in tandem, steering my way through comprehensive exams in Medieval, Renaissance, and Nineteenth-Century British literature while imagining projects I might undertake in black American literature; volleying oral examiners' questions about eighteenth-century women writers, Philip Freneau, and Henry James while wondering whether anyone would ask me about Phillis Wheatley or Charles Chesnutt; planning a dissertation on American naturalism while researching an article on Chesnutt's novel, *The House behind the Cedars* (1900). But as my enthusiasm for Stephen Crane, Jack London, and Theodore Dreiser began to wane, I would recall my three-day visit to the Fisk University Library in 1971, where

I'd delved as deeply as I could into Chesnutt's scrapbooks, journals, manuscripts, and correspondence. One of my professors had used some of his travel money to help me buy a round-trip Trailways ticket to Nashville. The only black professor I'd ever studied with had telephoned his friend, the special collections librarian at Fisk, to announce to her that he had "a chap in my office who wants to go out there and read some of the Chesnutt papers." "He's white," my professor added, smiling at me as he leaned expansively back in his chair. "But we won't hold that against him," he chuckled into the phone.

The trip to Nashville was no intellectual road to Damascus for me. Despite the beckoning gesture I received from Du Bois's statue on the Fisk campus, I did not know exactly what I was doing in that environment, and neither did the staff at the library, despite their impeccable politeness. By the end of my visit, all I was sure of was that Chesnutt had proved even more interesting than his books made him appear. I had obtained a glimpse into the mind of a writer who seemed more tangibly and feelingly connected to the world I had grown up in, the world I was still trying to come to terms with, than virtually any other eighteenth- or nineteenth-century American author I had read. Gradually, as naturalism seemed increasingly alien to me, and Chesnutt's life, writing, and socioliterary concerns felt more and more natural and understandable, I came to the conclusion that I *could* write a dissertation on Chesnutt with a lot more intellectual satisfaction and professional efficiency than one on Crane, Dreiser, London, and the rest.

"But why the colored, Bill?" my mother had asked. Not *this* colored man—*any* colored. Although I dodged her question and its implications, the subject kept on confronting me as I pursued my studies of African American literature in my postgraduate career. "I know who you *are*, William Andrews," a fellow editor told me when we met at the organizing meeting of the *Norton Anthology of African American Literature* in Ithaca in the fall of 1987. "What I want to know is, how did you get *here*?" Her smile of genuine invitation, not skeptical challenge, should have helped me explain more coherently than I did what had brought me to the work I'd been doing in African American literature for the past fifteen years. As I recall, however, "I'm a Southerner," was about all I mustered up in reply to my colleague's question. As far as it went, my answer bore witness to my conviction that the single most important personal factor that has influenced the direction in which I've gone as a scholar has been the fact that I was born and raised a white Southerner. But as a Southerner, I was raised to say the least about what I feel the most strongly about. Thus I've never sought an opportunity to write or speak autobiographically about my work in African American literature. Now it seems I have the chance, and maybe even the obligation, to talk about the impetus behind this work.

❧

I suspect that many whites who grew up as I did had little if any understanding of who it was we had been segregated from throughout our lives in the South. My family (and everyone else I knew) lived in such complete racial isolation that virtually the only blacks we were acquainted with were the "colored girls" who rode the bus from Richmond, Virginia's inner city to our modest subdivision to do domestic chores. The elderly, bow-legged, impassive black woman whom I knew only as Florence the maid was the only African American I ever had any interaction with during my growing-up years.

We didn't exactly get to know each other. At least, I never found out much about Florence. Florence spoke only when spoken to, and I had no idea what a boy like me would talk about with a woman like Florence anyway. Other than remarking with approval (when invited) on how tall I was getting or how much I looked like my father, Florence had nothing to say to me that I can recall. Nor do I recall her and my mother having a conversation about much of anything other than the weather or the high price of food in the grocery store. Mostly they worked in silence at their separate duties: Florence dusting as my mother vacuumed, Florence washing the bathrooms while my mother did the laundry. Florence was as quiet and unobtrusive as the pieces of my grandmother's china that she cleaned and polished in the forbidden curio shop that was our living room.

At first the silence that seemed to envelope Florence in our house pricked my curiosity. It wasn't that I wanted to talk to her—it was hard enough talking to old white people. Florence's starched institutional-green cleaning dresses warded me off like armor. I had neither the experience nor the boldness to approach her. But I did wonder what she was thinking as she worked. Why didn't she ever talk? And why, when she did talk, did it always sound like a recording of what she had said the week before, and the week before that? I soon learned that, by eavesdropping on Florence when she was ironing in the utility room or drying bathroom mirrors with newspapers, I could sometimes detect her humming to herself. It sounded like hymns, but not the ones I knew. The tunes did not take memorable shape, but once in awhile a phrase would escape her lips—"take my hand" or "light of the world." But if she knew anyone was around she kept it all muffled. I could never figure out why Florence seemed so secretive. You couldn't even tell when she went to the bathroom, I marveled to one of my friends down the street.

Florence always ate by herself at our house. She waited until after my mother had served me and my brothers the tomato sandwiches that were as predictable as the heat at lunchtime in the summer. After we had all left the room, Florence made herself a sandwich and drank a glass of milk. She partook of nothing else from our world. She didn't watch our TV, although it sat within arm's reach across from her in a corner of the kitchen. She didn't read our newspaper, although it usually lay next to her on the end of the table. She just sat, chewing her food deliberately and gazing out the window at the clothesline. When her workday came to an end, she retrieved her pocketbook from the front hall closet, put on her hat, and took a seat in a straightback chair in the living room. There she remained mutely ensconced until my mother got her car keys to transport her to the bus stop. They drove away in silence, with Florence in the backseat.

Once when I was a child I asked where colored ladies like Florence lived. "Colored women," my mother corrected me. White ladies, colored women—it wasn't clear to me what the difference was, but as usual in these matters the older I got the less I asked, even though I couldn't figure out exactly what it was that I was supposed to understand. I began to feel that understanding race was like understanding sex. To be accepted as one who understood hinged on how well you acted the part of one who already knew. Asking questions about race was likely to evoke the same patronizing reaction you got when you asked about sex: if you've got to ask, you're not old enough to understand. Thus the unspoken message: don't ask, just accept; just accept, then you'll *know*. Eventually accepting and knowing became the same, and there wasn't anything left to ask questions about.

❖

Negotiating the disparities between accepting and knowing incurred a debt to self-doubt as I pondered the struggles over racial justice in the South during my teenage years in the late 1950s and early 1960s. Unsure of the world and my place in it, my mind cluttered with questions I could not answer, I had little of the impervious confidence in my own personal resources and moral vision that was to become stereotypical of my 1960s generation. When the Southern college to which I had been accepted in 1964 informed me that it was admitting for the first time American Negro applicants to our incoming freshman class, I thought seriously about volunteering to be a roommate for one of these new students. The idea appealed to my sense of college life as a new beginning for me in a freer environment. But in less expansive moods I wondered, what did I know about living with a Negro, even one who came from a background like mine? I consulted my father about the matter. He counseled me against volunteering. "You don't know what the situation is like down there," he pointed out. "It would be better to wait and see how the land lies." Partly disappointed, partly relieved, I did what I knew my father wanted me to do.

I emerged from Davidson College in 1968 aiming to get a Ph.D. in English and become a professor of British literature in a school pretty much like the one I had come from. When I informed my mother of these plans she replied, with incredulity, "Teach? Is that all you want to do?" Eventually she became reconciled to the idea that I was not going to become a lawyer or a newspaper editor, as she had hoped. Meanwhile my graduate school interests shifted from British to American literature to African American literature, turning me into an oddity to some even as I felt myself coming more and more into my own, in a curious sense coming home. Unlike most of my white graduate school colleagues, the route I had followed into African American literature had not started in the big northern cities of Baldwin and Baraka, Cleaver and Malcolm X. My journey had begun in a down-home jook joint known as the Golden Day in the company of the Alabama-born narrator of *Invisible Man*. Spurred by the mocking laughter of the Invisible Man's once-enslaved grandfather, I had gone searching back into the nineteenth century, where I met Charles W. Chesnutt, quite by accident, in the spring of 1970 after purchasing a copy of *The Wife of His Youth and Other Stories of the Color Line* (1899).

Chesnutt became for me a conductor, a manager of literary passage, on the color line, especially in the South, where we had both grown up. With him in charge, the color line tracked something more than a racial divide. It provided a vantage point from which a reader could see over social and racial barriers. Intended to separate, the color line often marked the margins of encounter between whites and blacks in Chesnutt's fiction. But Chesnutt's literary world was studded with junctions along the color line, where the fates of whites and people of color intersected in spite of the supposedly discrete course that segregation had charted for each race. Conducting me, his white reader, to these junctions, and then beckoning me to look, Chesnutt gave me more of a shock of recognition than almost any American writer I had ever encountered. It was not myself that I recognized at these junctions; it was the world I had grown up in, the half-world of segregation, which like the moon had presented only one face to me when I observed it, though I could not help but know that another was also there, shadowed in vague outline.

During that same spring of 1970, when the racial, political, and social polarization of the United States seemed to be reaching its breaking point, I enrolled in a graduate seminar on black American autobiography. Encouraged by my professor, a black Southerner who took an avuncular interest in my progress, I learned of the contributions of Southern black people such as Frederick Douglass, William Wells Brown, James Weldon Johnson, and Maya Angelou to a literary tradition that had been virtually invisible to me throughout my undergraduate and graduate training in English. Later in the semester, in the wake of the U.S. invasion of Cambodia and the killings at Kent State and Jackson State, many of my graduate school colleagues went on strike from their classes in an effort to register their protest against these atrocities. I continued to attend my seminar, however. The more radically committed of my fellow students may have judged my business-as-usual behavior an insult to the gravity of the crisis we were in. But although I too supported anti–Vietnam War efforts, I could not see the use of opting out of the only systematic study of African American literature I would ever have a chance to take. If social "relevance" was the key to the value of one's education, what I was reading by black writers gave me plenty to ponder about my relationship to the war as well as to race. During a rally one Saturday afternoon during that turbulent spring I got a lesson in "double-consciousness" that I probably would never have had if I hadn't been reading W.E.B. Du Bois's *The Souls of Black Folk.*

After marching in a demonstration through downtown Chapel Hill, waving particularly at the dark-suited men who filmed and photographed us and then drove away in what most assumed were state cars, I joined two hundred others at a massing spot on campus to hear speeches. Some of the speakers I knew from the English department; they were now planning demonstrations instead of classes and converting their teaching talents to this vastly more stimulating platform. Accompanying them on the makeshift stage were two men in uniform, their uncovered heads buzzed in a fashion reserved usually for relatively new army recruits. They glanced around over the heads of the crowd, unsure of what to do with their hands, clearly unused to this kind of rally, plainly uncomfortable in front of this audience. Yet here they were, two enlisted men from Fort Bragg in Fayetteville, on hand to take part in this demonstration against a war they were almost certainly being trained to fight.

Introduced by the rally organizers, each soldier made a brief statement of his opposition to the war. As the crowd cheered and I joined in the applause, my mind shuttled back and forth between two perspectives. I could not forget that in two more years I too would become a member of the U.S. Infantry and possibly a unit commander for such men as these, just as disaffected by the war as I was, just as confused about what to do when faced with the ultimate decision. My recent reading of the narratives of Douglass and William Wells Brown added another layer of significance to the event, through which I could see the soldiers as contemporary versions of fugitive slaves who had been put on exhibit by well-meaning antislavery activists thinking little about what it felt like to be an object lesson in someone else's lecture. As the main speakers of the rally took up the brave examples of the two soldiers, my mind followed them to the rear of the stage, wondering: How did those guys get here? Did their CO know where they were? What would be the repercussions if they were found out? Did the rally's organizers know or care? My solicitude for the men mounted until suddenly it hit me: who was I—the slavemaster/officer they were running away from, or the antislavery/antiwar comrade they were hoping, if only temporarily, to find?

Perhaps I thought that somehow they could answer that question for me. At the least I wanted them to know that their presence at that rally had touched me more deeply than the speeches that were made of them. After the rally, I sought them out as they stood under a tree nervously smoking and accepting the congratulations of a student or two. I asked them what they were going to do for supper. Were they going back to Bragg that night? Did they have a ride back? Yes, they answered, they were going back, but it turned out they weren't leaving until later that night. So I asked them to come over to my basement apartment for beer and burgers. They could bring anybody they wanted. I'd invite a few friends over. They accepted.

During the impromptu party I put on in their honor the two soldiers seemed for the most part just as ill at ease as they had been on the platform at the rally, just as reserved in what they said, polite but unwilling to jump into any sort of one-on-one discussion of the war and our places in it that I vaguely hoped might develop between us sometime during the course of the evening. Their ride came fairly early in the evening, leaving me with a sense of a missed chance. Yet as I cleaned up afterwards, I began to see how unlikely it was that we really could have talked even if it had been just the three of us alone that evening. I remembered the scene in Mr. Emerson's office in *Invisible Man* when Emerson's son, the conflicted liberal whose double messages evoke such perplexed suspicion from the Invisible Man, announces, "With us it's still Jim and Huck Finn." The soldiers from Fort Bragg, I realized, were like Ellison's black narrator on the run but not sure where to go. I had played the part of Emerson's son, a figure of privilege in their eyes, whose attempted identification with them must have seemed strange and, though perhaps well-meaning, unexpected and potentially exploitative enough to warrant guardedness. Just because I had made a gesture of solidarity didn't mean that the differences, whether of class or of color, that estrange us even from those with whom we feel a bond would simply relax and disappear. Those tensions had to be acknowledged. They could not be put aside in order to have a talk. They were, willy-nilly, what the talk was already about.

Whether as an army officer dreading to assume the responsibilities of his commission, or as a Southerner trying to understand his role in the changing racial scheme, I could not think about the antiwar soldiers any more than I could read black American writers without feeling my own unreconciled twoness. Was the respect and allegiance I felt for the soldiers' opposition to the war invalidated by the fact that I was an officer, at the bottom of the chain of command but still implicated in its power? They were enlisted men; they *had* to wear the uniform. I, on a four-year deferment granted by the Army for graduate school, didn't even own a uniform. How much easier for me to be opposed to the war in Vietnam. By the same token, was the seriousness of my interest in black American writing, especially the autobiographies I was read-ing, not challenged by my privileged situation as a white Southern male, who could read black writers all he wanted without materially affecting his place and prospects in the social and economic status quo?

I had no answers for these questions. Fortunately, or perhaps not so for-tunately, my professor in the autobiography seminar didn't ask any of me. Reading African American autobiography that semester became a way for me to reconsider the accumulated memories, the unresolved confusion, the still-unexamined lessons of a lifetime of segregation. The course exerted a crucial influence on me as a reader, a professional scholar, and a Southerner. In *I Know Why the Caged Bird Sings* (1970), Maya Angelou revealed something it seemed I had always sensed but had never articulated to myself about how segregation creates (rather than merely enforces) a sense of racial difference that leads to a dehumanizing otherness. In her home town of Stamps, Arkansas, Angelou wrote:

> the segregation was so complete that most Black children didn't really, absolutely know what whites looked like. Other than that they were differ-ent, to be dreaded. . . . I remember never believing that whites were really real. (20)

To Angelou as a child, everything about whites—their clothes, their man-ners (or lack of manners), their color, right down to the way they walked and the size of their feet—made them creepy and threatening:

> I couldn't force myself to think of them as people. . . . People were those who lived on my side of town. I didn't like them all, or, in fact, any of them very much, but they were people. These others, the strange pale crea-tures that lived in their alien un-life, weren't considered folks. They were whitefolks. (21)

The similarities between what the young Angelou learned to feel about whitefolks and what I grew up thinking about the colored gave me, ironically enough, a sense of commonality with Angelou that overrode in my mind the obvious differences between her childhood in Arkansas in the 1930s and mine in Virginia in the 1950s. What Angelou's account of her childhood in Stamps, Arkansas, showed me was how omnipotent and pervasive segregation was in her South. Even Annie Henderson, Angelou's proud and capable grand-mother, despite her unparalleled position of respect among whites (she was the only black woman in town ever to have been referred to as Mrs.), so feared and despised whites that "she didn't cotten to the idea that whitefolks could be talked to at all without risking one's life" (39).

Given such total estrangement of the races, to the point where there was neither talking nor listening across the barrier of segregation, Angelou's portrait of the South in the 1930s and early 1940s offered little of the hope for racial dialogue that I found glimmering, albeit faintly, in the fiction Charles Chesnutt had written decades earlier. Reading Angelou, I could find no points of junction along the color line in Stamps, Arkansas. By whatever means stammering Marguerite Johnson had been transformed into eloquent Maya Angelou, it hadn't happened in the segregated South. In the South of *I Know Why the Caged Bird Sings*, even the most talented of its black children learned that there was nothing to say to whitefolks since they were literally too far beyond the pale to hear or care, anyway. The only way to break *through* the color line was to break *out* of the world it so tightly enclosed. And yet, as I realized after finishing her autobiography, Angelou had revealed the South she had broken away from in such a way as to break through to me, a white Southerner of another generation. Her delineation of her growing up in a separate black Southern community had helped me begin to recognize what my own growing up in segregation had taught me to ignore: not simply the injustice of segregation to black people, but the disquieting sense of white disjunction, of self-complicitous denial of my own lingering awareness of the lapses and contradictions and silences that had structured my coming of age in the South.

My fascination with the external signs and internal effects of segregation led me to pursue the implications of W.E.B. Du Bois's classic description of segregation in *Dusk of Dawn* (1940), another African American autobiography I was introduced to in the spring of 1970. Recounting his own initiation into "the American concept of race," Du Bois admitted the difficulty of conveying to "others" (that is, whites like me) the "full psychological meaning of caste segregation":

> It is as though one, looking out from a dark cave in a side of an impending mountain, sees the world passing and speaks to it; speaks courteously and persuasively, showing them how these entombed souls are hindered in their natural movement, expression, and development; and how their loosening from prison would be a matter not simply of courtesy, sympathy, and help to them, but aid to all the world. One talks on evenly and logically in this way, but notices that the passing throng does not even turn its head, or if it does, glances curiously and walks on. It gradually penetrates the minds of the prisoners that the people passing do not hear; that some thick sheet of invisible but horribly tangible plate glass is between them and the world. They get excited; they talk louder; they gesticulate. Some of the passing world stop in curiosity; these gesticulations seem so pointless; they laugh and pass on. They still either do not hear at all, or hear but dimly, and even what they

hear, they do not understand. Then the people within may become hysteri-
cal. They may scream and hurl themselves against the barriers, hardly realizing in their bewilderment that they are screaming in a vacuum unheard and
that their antics may actually seem funny to those outside looking in. They
may even, here and there, break through in blood and disfigurement, and
find themselves faced by a horrified, implacable, and quite overwhelming
mob of people frightened for their own existence (130–131).

Initially what arrested me in this passage was its complex, graphic metaphor of segregation as a state of simultaneous visual connection and aural isolation. Segregation, Du Bois stressed, was designed to ensure that a race could
be seen but not heard. The more I thought about this bleak racial parable of
twentieth-century America, however, the more disconcerting it became. Du
Bois was arguing an appalling irony: the attempt to be heard, to establish a
bond of humanity with whites on the other side of the segregation barrier, the
motive I most admired in black writers like Chesnutt and Angelou, could easily backfire into the most counterproductive, self-defeating thing a black person could do.

According to Du Bois's parable, blacks who tried to communicate with
whites via the norm of calm and logical discourse would soon find that, in the
soundproofed social vacuum of segregation, they could not be heard. They
would have to resort to extreme measures to be noticed at all. The more exaggerated the effort to get whites' attention, the less likely whites were to
respond positively. The more bewildered and frustrated blacks felt by the failure of their efforts, the more alienated they would become from the courteous
and reasonable persons who started out trying to communicate in the first
place. Screaming and hurling themselves against the invisible barrier, the pris-
oners of segregation might "break through," but only at the cost of their "disfigurement," which would underscore their otherness to the whites who,
finally, could see and hear them. Having broken through, the bleeding and
exhausted blacks would discover too late that they had divested themselves of
the protection that the wall of segregation had provided. They would have to
face the implacable fear and horror of white racism alone.

The ending of Du Bois's parable, in which an attempt to break through
the barrier of segregation arouses a lynch-mob reaction from whites, provided
strong justification for the contention later in *Dusk of Dawn* that planned,
cooperative "self-segregation" from whites could promote African American
advancement on a number of fronts, from economics to art and literature,
better than the protest and integration efforts that Du Bois himself had helped
to spearhead ever since the turn of the century. As for white reaction to this
revision in his racial philosophy and political strategy, Du Bois in 1940
professed little solicitude:

Whether self-segregation for his [the African American's] protection, for inner development and growth in intelligence and social efficiency, will increase his acceptability to white Americans or not, that growth must go on. (306)

What troubled me most about *Dusk of Dawn* was Du Bois's dismal assessment of the capacity of whites in general to realize the folly and harm of the color line and rid themselves of it. Refusing to give up on the idea of ultimate equality and harmony between the races, Du Bois nevertheless emphasized that, insofar as segregation was concerned, "What was true in 1910 was still true in 1940 and will be true in 1970" (310). As I read this statement in *Dusk of Dawn* in the spring of 1970, I could not help thinking ruefully of George Wallace's still-current cry of white defiance: "Segregation now! Segregation tomorrow! Segregation forever!" Had Du Bois's prophecy for 1970 been borne out by the likes of Wallace? Was the best hope for an end to the color line a rededication, on the part of black people, to "the segregated Negro institutions" that, Du Bois maintained, had always been "the best and most compelling argument for the ultimate abolition of the color line" (310)? If so, what role did whites have in "the ultimate abolition of the color line"?

I could not find in *Dusk of Dawn* any advice to whites about what they should do in the event that African Americans decided to practice segregation instead of agitating against it. In light of the trends in the early 1970s away from integration and towards Black Nationalism, a Black Aesthetic, and separatist Black Power in general, I wondered if what was becoming important to me in my encounters with black writers would have any particular use or value in a future in which segregation would be accepted as both a social fact and a tactical political necessity. In such a future, what would become of the classics of black American literature that were just now, finally, escaping the segregation of American literary history and making their mark on the consciousness of whites like me? Would white students from the South read Douglass, Chesnutt, Du Bois, Angelou, and other black writers with a Southern heritage? Would these students have a chance to discover as I had how effectively the color line had inscribed our sense of identity and circumscribed our capacity to envision an alternative for our future individually and as a society? Was it not possible that intellectual encounters, literary junctions between white readers and black writers, could yet play a part in breaking down barriers, opening up minds, and providing a ground for dialogue and mutual understanding?

The imperativeness of preserving some sort of dialogue between white readers and black writers became clearer to me after my first encounter with *Black Boy* during that same spring of 1970. Uncovering the raw wounds of segregation in the Deep South, Richard Wright showed me how little I had really fathomed of the meaning or effect of the color line. I remember asking myself as Wright's narrative piled up successive indictments of Southern racism, could it have really been *that* bad? Like Abraham prevailing on the Lord to spare Sodom if just fifty, just thirty, just ten godly people could be found there, I refused to believe that there had been no decent whites in Wright's entire growing-up experience in the Deep South. Because the whites he recalled from his childhood seemed so cruelly alien to my idyllic middle-class Southern childhood, I found myself resisting, complaining that the whites in *Black Boy* were unbelievable, that they were caricatures, grotesques, gargoyles. Not until I read Angelou did I understand that in the eyes of black Southern children the ultimate terror of whitefolks was that they *didn't* seem real or human. White hostility to black people exceeded the limits of what seemed rational or credible; it was the stuff of nightmare. How, then, was a black boy to survive in a world in which segregation had turned reality into a nightmare that tested the capacity of the imagination to represent what had to seem, to an outsider, surreal and incredible?

At the end of *Black Boy* Richard Wright addressed that question of survival. "What was it that made me conscious of possibilities? From where in this southern darkness had I caught a sense of freedom?" (282). This was, for me in 1970, the crux of *Black Boy*. How had a black youth not only survived the ravages of the worst segregation I had ever been shown but preserved within his own consciousness the conviction that he, on his own, against all the odds, could still find a liberating alternative to his pathological circumstances? Wright's answer to this conundrum moved me deeply:

> It had been only through books—at best, no more than vicarious cultural transfusions—that I had managed to keep myself alive in a negatively vital way. (282)

No student who still hoped to become a professor of relevant literature could have clung more tenaciously than I to this endorsement of what books could mean and be. As I read him, Wright was crediting his encounter with literature, in particular the works of classic American and European novelists, with sustaining him and showing him a way out of his "southern darkness." If, as Wright claimed, the work of Theodore Dreiser, Edgar Lee Masters, H.L. Mencken, Sherwood Anderson, and Sinclair Lewis could inspire Wright's black boy to imagine something better than segregation, to believe "that America could be shaped nearer to the hearts of those who lived in it" (283), surely, I concluded, the same lesson would hold true for young white readers when introduced to black American writers. I had found such inspiration in the books of Chesnutt and Du Bois, Angelou and Wright. These writers were certainly no less motivated than a Mencken or a Masters to shape their America "nearer to the hearts of those"—black as well as white—"who lived in it." If white American literature, some of it unmistakably racist, could play a major part in the redemption of a black youth from Mississippi, black American literature had at least equal potential to inspire not only young black readers but white ones, especially whites like me from the South, as well.

In 1970 I paid little mind to Wright's caveats about the limits of what books could give to someone seeking in at least a "negatively vital way" to keep his mind and spirit alive. It never occurred to me to question whether I might not be seeking "vicarious cultural transfusions" from reading Wright and Angelou and the other African American writers from the South who made such an impact on me in 1970. Whatever qualms I might feel now about my motives then do not counterbalance my conviction that African American writers, especially those from the South, gave me in some ways for the first time in my life as a reader a sense of what literature could do to open up one's vision of community and give purpose to intellectual work. For the first time I felt that I was beginning to understand my place, my part, my reason for being a student and, I hoped, a teacher. While many of my colleagues abandoned graduate school in disgust and cynicism, I persevered more out of a sense of faith than with a clear plan of how I was going to share the insights I had gained from my dialogues with Angelou, Du Bois, Wright, and the other writers in their tradition. All I was sure of was that, somehow, I was going to find ways as a scholar and a teacher to help other readers, especially white readers, discover what Ralph Ellison's Invisible Man meant when he insisted on reclaiming his heritage and his future as "a world of possibility."

Informed by the many questions that arose from thinking about the color line in and through that seminar, my reading elicited a more personal response from me to literature than I had ever felt before. The *Autobiography of Malcolm X* spoke to me, the Southern white legatee of segregation, in tones more demanding and evocative than any I heard emanating from the work of Emerson, Henry James, or even William Faulkner. The words that arrested me had to do with what "sincere" whites could do to address the injustices of racism and segregation. Instead of trying to prove to black people how sincere we were, we needed to be confronting ourselves, our own people, with the heritage and consequences of white racism. If the South in particular needed to unlearn its racist myths and confront its racial history, white Southerners had to feel a special mission in this regard.

Many white Southerners with "a mind to stay here" in the South held on through the reversals, betrayals, and tragedies of the 1960s to maintain a biracial movement for racial justice and social change.[2] When I finished graduate school, my job opportunities took me out of the South, first to west

Texas, and later to Wisconsin and Kansas. Although some of my colleagues seemed as puzzled by my interests in black writers as my mother had been, I continued as a scholar-critic to do my part to build bridges of awareness between readers of today and the efforts of African American writers of the past. Feeling a special sense of obligation to the writers and the tradition I met in the spring of 1970, I set for myself ten years later a long-term goal: to help reconstruct the history, key texts, and critical assessments of the African American autobiographical tradition. Working in this vein has made it possible for me to form collaborations with a number of black scholars who have interests similar to my own, which have led to some of the most valuable and memorable junctions that my study of the color line has brought me to.[3]

The one question I am most often asked after I give a talk or a lecture is how I, a white man and a Southerner, got into the work that I do. What I have written in this brief space may not provide an adequate answer. But more important than whether my confession as a critic is satisfying or even convincing is the question of the usefulness or applicability of the story I have tried to outline here. The story is one of self-discovery and vocation, two standard themes in the tradition of autobiographical confession that goes back to St. Augustine and forward to Malcolm X. My sense of vocation is hardly comparable with theirs, of course. But as a white critic in a world of black texts I hope my work helps to keep open a channel, if only on the lower frequencies, so that others, especially whites who have ears to hear, can learn a way to listen and find new ways to speak.

Notes

1. This essay is composed of excerpts from the Epilogue to my book, *Junctions on the Color Line: Black-White Dialogue in Southern Literature*, forthcoming from Oxford University Press.

2. For a compelling gallery of portraits of black and white Southerners committed to interracial dialogue and understanding in the South after the Civil Rights Movement era, see Egerton.

3. These junctions include two ongoing editorial projects, the *Norton Anthology of African American Literature* and the *Oxford Companion to African American Literature*.

Works Cited

Angelou, Maya. *I Know Why the Caged Bird Sings*. New York: Random House, 1970.

Chesnutt, Charles Waddell. *The Wife of His Youth, and Other Stories of the Color Line*. Ridgewood, N.J.: Gregg Press, 1967.

Du Bois, W.E.B. *Dusk of Dawn: An Essay toward an Autobiography of a Race Concept*. New York: Schocken Books, 1968.

Egerton, John. *A Mind to Stay Here*. New York: Macmillan, 1970.

Ellison, Ralph. *Invisible Man*. New York: Random House, 1952.

Wright, Richard. *Black Boy*. New York: Harper & Row, 1966.

Malcolm X. *The Autobiography of Malcolm X*. New York: Ballantine Books, 1965.

22

"Why Am I Always the Bad Guy?"

A Reverie on the Virtues of Confession

❁

Judith Newton

Why Am I Always the Bad Guy?

This question from my lover came to haunt me during a period of reflection on my current work. Although answers to questions such as this are inevitably complex—and one response surely is that *my* perception of our personal dynamics is somewhat different from his—my lover's challenge reverberated in an unsettling way with uncertainties I had already been sorting through before we met. These prior uncertainties, which arose in the course of my participation in a collaborative oral history project on the intellectual and political trajectories of radical, academic males, had to do with the relation between feminism and progressive men. More specifically, they had to do with the relation between what seemed at first to be male intransigence and feminist rectitude and what appeared at last to be something more—something involving difference, the different materialities of our male subjects' lives, and what appeared to be not feminist rectitude so much as feminist narcissism and egocentricity. My difficulties, that is, had to do with sorting out a relation between the political and the personal, the social "public" and the social "private." They had to do with facing up to the realization that after several months of reading my transcripts of male-authored, oral history texts I felt less confident than before, to put it bluntly, about who the "bad guys" always were.

How the Critics Came to Confess

Confession: 1. an admission of fault, etc. 2. acknowledgement of a sin, especially to a priest to obtain absolution 3. something that is confessed 4. a
church group having a particular creed.

In the fall of 1991 my collaborator, Judith Stacey, and I began to collect
oral histories about the intellectual and political trajectories of largely white,
heterosexually identified, radical, academic men. These were men, who like
ourselves, had been active as graduate students in sixties politics and who had
made some translation of those politics into their academic work.[1] As leftist
and antiracist feminists, we were particularly interested in the ways that our
male peers would narrate their relation to feminist and antiracist politics and
scholarship over the last thirty years and in the degree to which they would see
themselves as having taken on feminist and antiracist analyses and priorities
in their work and lives.

Our interest in this project stemmed in part from our having arrived at an
age when narratives of a life or of a career are common, when telling one's
own story in one's own words becomes a defensive measure against the
inevitable telling of that story from less sympathetic quarters. We were curious, frankly, about what our participation in thirty years of feminist and
antiracist struggle had "meant," and we were aware that an important part of
its meaning lay in its various effects upon the minds and hearts of those
whom the movements we had been a part of had tried critically to engage.

We came to this project, as well, out of an interest in and commitment to
broader political alliances. The conservative political climate of the last twenty
years, economic restructuring, the growing inequalities between rich and
poor, mounting racism and homophobia, the anti-PC backlash and its succes-
sor discourse, centrist and conservative articulations of "family values" (now,
surely, the dominant form of political rhetoric in the U.S.) had convinced us
anew that feminism could not be "for women only." Our positive experience,
moreover, with cross-racial and cross-gender coalitions in building a multicultural women's studies program on our campus also fueled our burgeoning
investment in diverse political alignments. If we tended, therefore, on the one
hand to regard the anticipated stories of our male peers as part and parcel of
our own, we conceived these stories, on the other, as something more. For
textual and face-to-face experiences with feminists of color over the last
twenty-some years had taught us valuable lessons about the role of "learning
to listen" in the forging of alliances with different "others."

These, at least, were the priorities and motives which we were initially
willing to acknowledge. What we were later prompted to reveal, and to reveal

in print, was that the project had been also conceived with a good deal of potential pleasure in our minds. We thought it would be fun to work together, to avoid nineteenth-century archives or lonely, ethnographic drives into Silicon Valley. It seemed refreshing to think of talking with progressive men for a change rather than just to feminist women. Since one of us was in the process of separating from her husband, a scholarly project licensing her to meet and talk at length with politically sympathetic men seemed far from a social liability. Anticipated pleasure, a certain weariness of twenty years in mainly female communities, a liking for progressive men, the heterosocial erotic, these constituted the feminist unspeakable which we were later to "confess."

Many feminists our age, of course, once belonged to a "confession," a church or group whose particular creed, in this case, had embraced the virtues of public revelation of the "private." Indeed, the act of describing one's personal, familial, and sexual life, while it might involve divulging "un"- or prefeminist feelings and behaviors, was seen, in the seventies, as an act of political defiance, as insistence that the individual and the structural were linked, that the familial was political, and that academic norms forbidding the use of "I" and references to the domestic everyday were politically repressive.

From at least the mid-eighties on, feminist and nonfeminist critique of the unitary "I's" around which such narratives were often organized and of the latters' humanist, linear, and teleological logics were to throw the project of writing the personal under an intellectual and even moral cloud. (I can remember being so stymied by the difficulties of avoiding these particular theoretical embarrassments that I refused an invitation to contribute to an anthology of autobiographical narratives by first-wave feminist critics, a project I really longed to be part of. The personal, for the moment, felt ruled out of bounds and had become, practically speaking, for me, inaccessible.)

It is hardly necessary, however, as many have subsequently observed, to employ a unitary I or linear logics in writing the personal (although these conventions may be difficult to avoid, given the weight that traditional storytelling norms continue to exert upon narratives of a life and a career.) There are pressing reasons, moreover, for keeping the activity of writing the "personal" alive, and specifically the personal in its relation to the political. Indeed, to employ and validate this particular discursive norm need not represent a turn away from theory and politics but may, as I wish to suggest, represent potentially significant components of "doing" both.

What the Critics Learned from Their Confession

Our confession, to a largely female, feminist readership from whom we desired, if not priestly absolution, then sisterly empathy and mutual revelation, had to do with an area of life that has long dominated the confession of fault or sin. It had to do, that is, with pleasure and, in this case, with hetero-social pleasure, with the presence of it in feminists and in their scholarship in 1994. Had our work been informed by *homo*social pleasure, of course (as our alliances with feminists certainly have been) we could have spoken of it without seeming to "confess." For within academic, feminist circles homo-social pleasure and homosexual desire continue to have a privileged place, while heterosexuality is regarded these days as an embarrassment of sorts, as boring and predictable, if no longer politically retrograde. (The irony of this reversal in an obscenely homophobic culture like our own, beset by conserva-tive paeans to the never-divorced, heterosexual couple is something, of course, to also savor.)

Our confession might also have remained unspoken were it not that self-reflexivity had presented itself to us as a current, although far from universal, discursive norm. Having engaged in a quasi-ethnographic project, understanding and embracing the theoretical position that self-reflexiveness is an ethnographic, feminist, and postmodernist *desideratum*, we felt compelled to write a reflection piece on our ethnographic selves, on our relation to our native "subjects," and on the politics of initially writing about white, hetero-sexually identified, radical, academic men. As good girls, and as smart girls too—since if we denied it our critics would be sure to call us to account—we forced ourselves to examine our heretofore secret pleasures in our work, our liking for, our collegiality with, our male peers and the varying degrees of heterosocial pleasure which the intimate interview situation evoked. We enjoyed our work, we were prompted to confess, a bit too much.

Following some dictates of the "new" and of feminist ethnography, our initial response to the prospect of having to confront the secret pleasures of our work in public was to process them rigorously in terms of their shaping influence on our power and the power of our subjects. Were we recentering white (albeit progressive white) academic men? we asked ourselves and were asked repeatedly by feminist respondents to our first collaborative essay on academic males. Did the heterosexual dating codes that informed the inter-view situation empower them, or did these codes empower us? Whose plea-sure entrapped them most? Who were the bad guys here? But the analysis we produced in our initial draft left us queasy. In "speaking with" and feeling collegial toward "the enemy" (in early, white feminist terms) we were obvi-ously guilty as we assumed we would be charged. But adding to our uneasi-ness was the fact that there was still more to confess. It was only in "public," in discourse slated for publication and for a readership of female feminist peers, that we felt bad about ourselves. In private, between the two of us, we felt justified as well.

It was the process of having to confront these tensions between our secret satisfactions in our work (and our even more secret sense of feeling justified in having them) and the anxiety induced by feeling required to bring these satisfactions and this justification to some public feminist account that forced us, once again, to contemplate the limits and exclusions of various white, feminist positions about men, heterosexuality, and power. It was our act of "confession," moreover, which brought us up against the surprise of our own lingering immersion in these discursive slots. In the abstract, that is, we had assumed our distance from the way that even some postmodern feminisms can posit men as a unified cast of "bad guys" and heterosexuality as undeviating and a political dead end. Both seemed retrograde in an age of multiple and fluid sexualities and selves, not to mention coalitions across them. Our long years of work with female feminists, moreover, had taught us that alliance involved not only power but also collegiality, friendship, shared discourses, pleasures, and desire. Yet in our public, feminist accounting of our work with men, these were the very qualities of relationship that we felt prompted to disown.

Our initial, unreflecting reduction of our political and collegial relationships with our subjects to a matter of unequal power, moreover, began to seem part and parcel of other feminist practices in which we had occasionally engaged with men—our tendency to assume our own rectitude, for example, and a partial sympathy with the "damned if you do, damned if you don't" conundrum that has informed many feminist critical relationships with profeminist males. The more we contemplated the contradictions of our "private"/"public" split, the more it appeared to us, indeed, that female feminists could sometimes be the "bad guys" too.

The Slope Is Too Steep

My lover, in a reflective moment, used this phrase to explain his resistance to being asked how his childhood and specifically his relation to his mother might be entering into our life together. To ask this question too early on in our efforts to "talk out" one of those murky instances of human misunderstanding was to sweep him too quickly out of his own accustomed discourse into my own. He did not object, in principle, to the occasional translation out of his own accustomed mode into the unfamiliar one of the psychoanalytical, but "the slope was too steep." He couldn't get there at the pace that suited me. I have been trying since to alter my discursive habits, to become more patient and to break somewhat with the habit of asserting the validity of my own approach. I have been trying to let him get to his mother, if he will, at his own speed. That he consents occasionally to arrive (at this topic so crucial to my understanding of human relationship) is part of our ongoing and reciprocal negotiation.

That I myself arrived at this point in my romantic history—first choosing to be with someone who speaks different languages from my own, then acknowledging that, despite everything, he will continue to speak differently from me, and, finally, seeing that this initially discouraging piece of news might not be all that bad, bears some dialectical relation to my work on men. For the initial shock of my and my collaborator's interviews with progressive, academic males was that our own apocalyptic language of feminist first encounters ("the scales fell from my eyes"), and even our assessments of what men's languages would be, were not reflected in our subjects' narratives. Having invited our male peers to confess to the "impact" of feminism on their lives, to reveal their previously concealed shock, anxiety, outrage, and possible liberatory excitement over feminism at first encounter, we were daunted to find that their acknowledged responses were not at all what we had assumed we would find.

Most of the men we interviewed, indeed, appeared to be suffering from a mild form of fem-amnesia: "Could we have talked about (feminism) and I not remembered?" "It's a blank, an interesting blank." From the moment of our entry into the "field," the narratives we elicited directly challenged and ultimately rewrote our initial egocentric assumptions about feminist "impact." We were not as central to their lives as we had assumed. Or, at least, we were not as central in the ways we myopically imagined we must have been. (Hadn't we learned this already in our private histories with men? Did we really think that feminism must have changed all that?)

What we read in our oral histories, then, was not the kind of "confession" we had thought we would find. Early encounters with feminism, by and large, had had little overt "impact" on our subjects' consciousness as constructed in their stories of their works and lives. Feminism, indeed, seemed linked to the personal and domestic elements of our subjects' lives, which also had less "impact" on their narratives than we assumed we would find. Most of the men we interviewed, that is, did not spontaneously introduce the subjects of feminism, the personal, or the domestic in the early segments of their oral histories—this despite our previously announced interest in the role of feminism on their political, intellectual, and personal histories. Indeed our subjects' voluble and polished narratives appeared at first to be organized along the lines of traditional masculine life histories, in which the so-called public realms of published scholarship and, in this case, anti-imperialist or antiracist political struggle were center stage. The personal and domestic, along with feminist politics, which has often focused, of course, on just these areas, did not seem, for the most part, to have been previously integrated into their official stories of themselves as politically minded intellectuals. Our interviews, indeed, often initiated a halting integration of these realms into our subjects' narratives of their work and lives.

Most of our mens' life stories, then, in contrast to most female, feminist narratives by women of our age, initially maintained a separation of "public" and "private," a separation expressed in the way that the domestic and the feminist, which was often linked with sexual and personal politics, failed spontaneously to appear in their narratives of political and intellectual development. The initial submergence of feminism in our men's narratives, moreover, was mirrored in what they reported, and what we sometimes witnessed, about the role of feminism in their teaching and their scholarship. Most of our subjects, that is, had reportedly confined critical gender analysis to the relatively private space of the classroom until at least the late 1980s. It was not until critical gender analysis became established as a legitimate and well-published branch of theory, thereby "masterfully" entering our subjects' most "public" sphere, that it made its entry into their published work.

Since feminism and critical gender critique had entered academic conversations, among some of us at least, almost twenty years before, it might seem difficult to claim that, for our subjects, "the slope had been too steep," that the translation from one accustomed language into a new one had been required too quickly. And yet the late entry of critical gender analysis into our subjects' scholarship did, it seemed to us, have much to do with the temporal persistence of certain languages and discursive norms. Feminisms in the seventies, for example, offered a set of narratives which were very different, in some respects, from those offered by the political movements which had gone before. The narratives of the Civil Rights and the antiwar movement, in which most of our subjects had been engaged, had focused on issues associated with the public sphere—imperialism, legal rights, economics—had privileged public and large-scale forms of protest, and had assumed male leadership. Feminisms, in contrast, focused on the private sphere as well. Indeed sexual politics, the politics of the personal, was a major emphasis of white mainstream feminism in the early seventies. Feminist protests, moreover, were usually smaller in scale than in the earlier movements while small consciousness-raising groups, rather than open meetings, were the primary form of organizing. Finally, of course, the narratives of mainstream feminism cast white men, in particular, not as political leaders or even allies, for the most part, but as the problem. For many of the men we interviewed, the narratives of feminism seemed to offer men no place "to put your body on the line" and in some instances were difficult to see as properly "political."

Many of the men we interviewed, finally, entered into their first jobs just as the political movements in which they had been most involved—an integrated Civil Rights Movement, the students' and antiwar movements— were ending or winding down, and as second-wave feminism was developing. For many of these men, entering into the establishment functioned as a moment of shifting gears. If they did not exactly leave their politics behind, they organized their energies differently, focusing less on challenging "the establishment" and more on securing some position within it. The dominant discourses of academe were hardly conducive to their taking on gender betrayal and feminist politics.[2] In the seventies and early eighties, as one of our subjects pointed out, there were established discursive slots in academia for antiracist and anti-imperialist white Westerners, but there were no compelling slots for antisexist men. Since feminist politics are centrally grounded upon an analysis of the structural links between the "the personal" and the larger social, moreover, it is also significant that until recently there have been few discursive norms, for male academics in particular, which have not constituted a division between the personal and the public as a given of serious scholarly production and which have not constituted writing the personal as "confession," as itself an act of fault or sin. Finally, it is also significant in this context that the few men in our study who did do critical gender analysis before this time—in the seventies for some, and early eighties for others—and who developed this analysis most fully in their work often reported they had done so because feminism had touched their personal or domestic lives. It was critical reflection upon the personal or domestic, that is, that precipitated an opening to critical gender analysis in their work and a fuller incorporation of feminist politics in their day-to-day behavior.

Our subjects' initial reflections on the personal, of course, were rarely carried on in published discourse, and so my reference to the potentially progressive role of personal reflection might constitute the grounds for nothing more than a modest argument that private reflection on the personal is potentially a good thing for the soul and for feminist politics as well and should be engaged in frequently. I might stop there, too, if it weren't the case that the critical reflections in which academics seem most willing to engage are those most likely to wind up in published texts and to swell a vitae. Musings which seem doomed, by our discursive norms, to remain confined to the closet of the unread text are not, in our publication-driven world, liable to be much valued or rigorously pursued. It is in these contexts, at once material, discursive, and political, that arguments positing a necessary cleavage between the personal and the political or casting public writing about the personal as itself the fault or sin (which is what the equation of writing the personal with "confession" tends to do) seem themselves politically problematic.

Not on Your Terms Alone: The Return of the Father

It was the interview I conducted with an African-American scholar and friend that impressed upon me, perhaps more than any of the others, the one-sidedness of many feminist conversations with progressive men:

I've had fairly intense arguments with black feminists, black lesbians, about this, where they sort of say, "You men can't get it right." And I say, "But if the terms of getting it right—whatever 'it' is, whether it's emotional relationships, or political responses—if getting it right is simply only determined by your construction of the feminist, then no we can't. But if getting it right means that we can come together and talk about the ways in which possibilities might unfold from those two points then maybe we could do something."

These words made their way to the surface over the last few years, as I began to revise my romantic life and to study masculinities with less automatic suspicion than before (although a healthy suspicion remains a valuable quality in this world). I have been thinking of late, for example, about the current phenomenon, across a wide range of political and mass media discourses, of the return to the father, surely the biggest revisionist discourse on masculinity that we have encountered since second-wave feminisms hit the scene. The skeptical feminist in me tends cynically to observe that patriarchally inclined men now have a seemingly respectable but actually deeply regressive image of masculinity around which to coalesce, for fathers and specifically "the father" are now at the heart of many conservative discourses, from the political to the popular. Fathers, for example, are key to conservative and centrist discourse on "family values," as fatherless families are routinely claimed to be the cause of every social and economic disaster from which we currently suffer. It is in conservative family-values discourse that the return to the father most clearly signals a form of gender nostalgia, an effort to recoup traditional masculine authority ("Fathers who make the family effort," according to William Safire, "need recognition as 'head' of a household") and a form of racist and gender scapegoating as well. (Fatherless families most often translate as lower-class, black, female-headed households run by overbreeding teenage mothers.) It is here that the return to the father appears most blatantly as an effort to further delegitimize state responsibility for poverty and injustice, and as an effort to erase "the economy, stupid" as a point of reference. It is here that the return to the father offers a renegotiated economic individualism, through which middle-class, father-headed, two-income families will participate in a NAFTA- and GATT-deregulated struggle for survival.

But a second, also feminist, voice in me suggests that the return to the father cannot be so simply dismissed. Perhaps this phenomenon, like other efforts to reconstruct masculinity, must be read from several unfolding perspectives rather than just one. The mainly white, middle-class, so-called "men's movement," which focuses almost solely on failing fathers and the relations between male peers, for example, might be read both as an evasion of feminist challenges to rethink the power relations of gender *and* as an effort to recast hegemonic masculinity in a more feminist direction, as more empathetic, at least, and less armored. Perhaps the evasion of feminist challenge in itself is rooted in the desire to elude the rigidities of feminist discourses that continue to hold men's self-abasement as a prerequisite for solidarity.[3] If black nationalist idealizations of the committed husband, the responsible, loving father, and hard-working community leader, who is also "king in (his) personal kingdom" at home may be read, to some degree, as an effort in the direction of middle-class respectability, gender nostalgia, homophobia, a return to masculine political authority, and an evasion of black feminist calls for equality, they might be read more complexly as well.[4] They might also be read as efforts to curb the racist scapegoating of conservative and centrist family-values rhetoric, to offer some alternative life narrative to lower-class, black males, and as a response to black feminist demands for more male responsibility, more respectful (although hardly progressive) discourse on women, and a less bounded set of masculine behaviors.

What the current rage for fathers might require in its articulation across a wide spectrum of political discourses and forms of popular culture—I think here about the spate of PG-13 movies that my nine-year-old daughter and I have recently sat through: "Mrs. Doubtfire," "Junior," "The Lion King," and "Santa Clause"—is something more from female feminists than the cry that this is not what we had in mind. That the return to fathers in mass media often avoids issues of personal relation between adult women and men within the home (in father-centered sitcoms, moms are largely absent or displaced by nonauthoritative female figures such as the mother-in-law, Mary, for example, in the black show "Me and the Boys") should not lead us automatically to assume that the return to the father is, on every level and across every site, just another detour around feminism and the female, or even that its meanings are a matter of sexual politics alone.

Economic restructuring—for example, the decline of male wages, and the inadequacy of a single family paycheck—has dislodged middle-class, white men, in particular, from a primary-breadwinner role while stripping many lower-class black men of the ability to win bread at all. It may not be surprising that some men turn inward to the family—with encouragement, of course, from conservatives and from centrists both—as a site on which to rearticulate a social significance that, in the arena of the market, seems increasingly insecure. (Since fathering has been defined, for white middle-class men in particular, in terms of this chief provider function, the traditional significance of fathering has also been emptied out.) Since many feminisms, finally, have tended to offer men the role of undeveloped bad guys who "always get it wrong," it may not be surprising that male efforts to reinvent themselves have focused on working out their relationships to children rather than to the far more critical adult women in their lives.

Coda

As I end this piece, I am conscious of not wanting to deny or to underestimate the role of progressive men's intransigence, their fear of and rage at women, or their varying investments in unequal power, but I am conscious of feeling, too, that feminism cannot be a political movement for women only, and that it is not male intransigence alone that must account for the fact that female feminists have had to write the founding narratives of critical gender analysis, sexual politics, and familial and social revolution in language and in terms almost entirely of their own.

I am aware, as well, of an element of guessing and speculation in much of what is written here. I am aware that when I work on men I lack the authority I feel when I write on women. I am conscious both of the great familiarity of "men" in feminist discourses and of what I construct of their mysteries and the multiple differences among them. I think about the great clarity with which I have analyzed my lover and of my utter failure at times to comprehend his point of view. I begin to wonder how much about themselves the many men in my life have ever told me and how attentively I have ever listened, listened, at least, to what was different. When I work on men, I am conscious of my anger at the cruel resurgence of conservative patriarchy on the national, state, and local levels—I live in California, where cuts of welfare to children and their mothers are a common budget strategy and where anti–affirmative-action sentiment runs high. I am conscious of my own continuing frustrations with the intransigence of many white, progressive men, of my desire not to let them off the hook or to offer premature absolution, of a desire to insist on accountability and struggle. These sit in an uneasy mix with my, now-daily experiences of positive alliance with men, white men and men of color, as some of us begin to forge a cultural studies program on our campus. I am conscious, as well, of what feels like a greater openness and humility about myself born of many things—age, critiques of mainstream feminism by women of color, and now this scholarly engagement in "learning to listen."

It is in female feminists' interests at the moment, I have come to feel, to invite male allies or potential allies to tell their stories, and to attend to what we hear. It is in our interests, for this reason, to further deconstruct the traditions of academic masculine life histories and of current theory that relegates the private to the untheoretical realm of confession, fault, or sin. Rather than pitting the personal against the political and theoretical, it would seem more fruitful to work toward the legitimation of writing the personal as the political, to work toward the legitimation of this as a form of theory and as a respectable discursive slot—not just for female feminists nostalgic for the early seventies but for all of us. For without more labor, critical self-reflecting labor, on the part of men who are or would be allies, gender analysis, sexual politics, and feminist social change will continue to be defined on female feminist terms alone. Those terms, I am convinced, have never been, are not now, and will never be enough.

Notes

1. Our larger project incorporates white men and men of color, gay and heterosexually identified men, men of forty-five to fifty-five and men who are younger as well. Our initial published work, however, has focused on white, heterosexually identified, leftist men, identified or in some way related to cultural studies. For more detailed accounts of our project see the following: Judith Newton and Judith Stacey, "Learning Not to Curse, or Feminist Predicaments in Cultural Criticism by Men: Our Movie Date with James Clifford and Stephen Greenblatt." *Cultural Critique*, 23 (Winter 1993); "Ms. Representations: Reflections on Studying Academic Men," in Ruth Behar and Deborah Gordon, eds., *Women Writing Culture* (Berkeley: University of California Press, forthcoming); and "The Men We Left Behind Us, or Reading Our Br/others: Narratives Around and About Feminism in the Lives and Works of White, Radical, Academic Men." In Elizabeth Long, ed. *Sociology and Cultural Studies* (New York: Blackwell, forthcoming). My account here of our project draws from these earlier papers.

2. For feminist women, entering into a male-dominated academy seemed itself a revolutionary act, a mode of changing and radicalizing a mainstream institution. Taking one's first job was less likely to signify leaving politics behind than to offer the mixed blessing of making a career of political struggle.

3. I owe much of my thinking here to Fred Pfeil's work on the mythopoetic men's movement. See his forthcoming *White Guys: Studies in Postmodern Domination and Difference* (London and New York: Verso, 1995). I am paraphrasing his citation of Aaron R. Kipnis, *Knight Without Armour: A Practical Guide for Men in Quest of Masculine Soul* (Los Angeles: Jeremy P. Tarcher, Inc. 1991), 59.

4. Nai'im Akbar, *Visions for Black Men* (Nashville: Winston-Derek Publishers, 1991), 15. See also Haki Madhubuti, "Black Man: Obsolete, Single and Dangerous?" in Nathan Hare and Julia Hare, eds. *Crisis in Black Sexual Politics* (San Francisco: Black Think Tank, 1988), 35–44.

23

Let's Get Lost

❊

JANE TOMPKINS

Sixteen men on a dead man's chest,
Yo ho ho! and a bottle of rum.

It was the best course I ever taught. I even got the course description right. So the students who signed up—twelve graduate, three undergrad.—had self-selected for it. Things began slowly, as always, but even on the first day, when they were in small groups, there was an excited hum in the room.

When I reach back in my mind for what happened next, there's nothing. I kept no journal of the course because I was happy. For me course journals are a way to keep fear under control and to rationalize impending failure. When things are going well, I don't keep them.

But records or no, it's hard to tell a straight story, hard to get at the reality of what happened in a class, either on a given day or over time. Anxiety and desire for success distort the record. Wanting to succeed, I gloss over difficulties, forget things. At the same time, being prone to a victim mentality, I frequently rush in to admit failure. Embracing defeat, mentally, before anyone else can criticize me, I end up obscuring the truth in the other direction. When I embarked on my experiments in teaching, I thought I was putting the performance mentality behind me by putting students at the center of things. But now I see that the experiment itself has become my performance. Only now my success or failure depends on the performance of the students. The ego's need to be reflected *one way or the other* intrudes everywhere.

The other problem in telling the story is, I can't do it in anything like an objective, reportorial manner. Or rather, I could, but it wouldn't mean anything. I've realized that the story of this course is about issues that have long lain dormant in my teaching life, at the bottom of a pool inside me, like monsters in a fairy tale. They control the agenda here. And the story will come out or not according to their desires. The good news is, that having discovered these backstage artistes, having had to acknowledge the dimensions and depths of classroom experience, I know that not only this course but all our teaching, what we do in class day after day, is a text—beautiful, strange, many-layered, frightening—woven out of the memory and desire of every person in the room. We never look at this tapestry, almost. It hangs there on our collective mental wall, oscillating gently, sinister, inviting. Its brilliant, darkly textured world is worth the risk of entering, despite the danger. Let's get lost.

What I have are images—of the students' faces, of their voices, of memorable moments; they come in spurts—peaks and valleys of emotional intensity. Even now, tears well up inside me as I write. I loved the course so, and the students—well, they felt all different ways about it. I wanted them to love it as much as I did.

At the end of Sylvia Ashton-Warner's *Teacher* (New York: Simon & Schuster, 1963) there's a chapter that begins with this anecdote:

> What is it, Little One?
> I kneel to his level and tip his chin. Tears break from the big brown eyes and set off down his face.
> That's why somebodies they broked my castle for notheen. Somebodies.
> I sit on my low chair in the raftered prefab, take him on my knee and tuck the black Maori head beneath my chin.
> "There . . . there . . . look at my pretty boy . . .
> But that's only a memory now. A year old. (216)

The anecdote is cryptic at first. The words of the child, awkward and painful. By the end of the chapter, when she quotes them again, we know what they mean. Ashton-Warner's ideas for teaching children, the methods she's built up with so much love and work and imagination over the years, have been rejected by the authorities. Her little school has been torn down. In its place a grand one, where children who used to dance and cry and laugh and sing and paint and argue and shout now sit quietly in rows. At the end of my course last fall I felt like that: "they broked my castle." They, the students, the ones I'd been so proud of, so happy for, after all we'd done—the singing, playing, shouting, painting—on the last two days they tore the course apart. Four mornings in a row I cried over what happened, so I could get through the rest of the day. Now, the whole thing sits in the back of my throat, waiting to be resolved.

So let me begin again.

First, Ocracoke.

The name of the course was American Literature Unbound, and the idea was, we would use the texts we read, *Moby-Dick* and *Beloved* (only those, for the course was to be uncluttered, unrushed, a pure opportunity for absorption in great works of literature—time to wallow in and be drenched by their beauty and profundity, nothing in the way), the books were to be used as avenues *into* the world, rather than as a retreat from it. The books would lead us into all kinds of experience, especially sensory, imaginative, and emotional experience—the kinds that usually get left out in school. So Ocracoke (one of the barrier islands on the North Carolina coast) was to introduce us to the sea, or rather, since everyone had seen the ocean before, be a way of realizing, physically, something important about Melville's novel. A chance for Ishmaelian reverie, a combination of water and adventure.

The other purpose of the trip was to provide a bonding experience. I'd learned the previous fall that there's nothing like an overnight trip to make students and teacher feel more at home. It puts relationships on a different basis. You can't be intimidated in the same way by people you've slept in the same room and shared a bathroom with, who you know that they use dental floss compulsively, or maybe that they fart.

The deep text was my own need to feel accepted by the students. To be part of something they were part of. Not to be alone.

We meet on campus at 4:30 A.M. in front of the chapel. I get there a little late. Almost everyone's there. Three female students who have banded together act as combination mothers and teenage gigglers—they've brought coffee in thermoses. Someone's brought donuts. Someone's brought bagels and cream cheese. Thank God! They're coming through. Everyone shows up. Four cars. Fours designated drivers—me, Mark, Ryan, and Bernard. Excited, uncertain, half asleep, we nervously check directions and bundle into the cars. We're late. All in a row, we barrel off into the morning darkness. We have exactly four hours to make the ferry.

Charlie S., a young man from the law school and James M., another law student, both smart, alive, with-it kind of guys, are in the back seat. In front, Sonya, an exchange student from Germany. At first it's awkward, but Sonya and I discover we can talk, so we do. Charlie and Jim converse sporadically in the back. After worry about following road signs has worn off, the road unfolds steadily before me. We're doing it. We're on the way. Fifteen people going to an island on their own recognizance. No one said we could. No one said it was okay. We're just doing it because I thought it would be fun to try and the students were willing.

They planned the whole trip. Ferry reservations, cars, drivers, estimated costs—food, gas, lodging—estimated travel time, itinerary, directions. Feng

Liu, from the People's Republic of China, has booked the motel at a remarkably low rate. Paula, from Iowa, has organized most of the rest. New York Sarah has stepped in at crucial junctures to take responsibility. I'm in good hands.

We make it to Kinston, our halfway stop, on schedule. I turn into Bojangles. They don't want to sit—just pee, get biscuits, and go. Off again. Now it's light, the driving's easier, Charlie takes the wheel. I sit in front with him. It's fun. But time is short. Around Beaufort we lose sight of the other cars. We're late. We're barreling down beautiful roads now—the bay waters sparkle, marshlands spread right and left, tiny towns whiz by. If they're still behind us we'll never make it. On the long bridges and empty straightaways there's no sign of them. We're fucked. But Charlie drives like a demon and when we get there—there they are! They took a shortcut. Paula's negotiating with the ferry people. She's got us on. We're the last cars on the ferry. It's heaven.

On the ferry, water stretching everywhere, high sun, sea gulls, wind. We explore the boat, cluster in little groups, nap. I doze in the back of the Oldsmobile, Zarena sleeps in front. The trip is long—two, two and a half hours—yet it doesn't seem that way.

I've never been to Ocracoke before but had heard about it for years. A barrier island, I read in the book I've brought, is something solid that's always changing. The way to preserve it is to let it be destroyed. "In my end is my beginning."

The harbor is bright, the buildings sharply etched and clean. On the lawn of the Visitors' Information Center stands the vertebra of a whale, humongous—Moby-Dick! We've come to the right place. Inside we read about pirates. A kind, elderly man gives us directions to the beach and to the motel. We're on our way.

Blackbeard's is attractively funky and down-at-heels. Roomy and warm and friendly. All the men in one big room on the first floor. The women split between two. I'm in with the students. Off to lunch.

The beach at Ocracoke is clean and empty, a long straight stretch of greyish-white sand backed by a long dune topped with pale green grass. The ocean is gleaming blue-grey-green, and playful, not rough. Early on I worry about students drowning—there are no lifeguards—but they all seem okay in the waves. We swim and sun, drink sodas, take walks. I've asked them each to spend some time alone. My alone time takes place on the dunetop, hunkered down near some bushes in a hollow of sand. This place seems miraculous to me. Round shiny leaves of bushes, thin spears of faded grass, the smooth surface of untouched sand. The precision and exactitude of outline, the contrast of textures, the delicate palette—life here seems intense, perfect, and abundant. A mini-paradise.

Back on the beach I start to worry. We're doing nothing. I ask myself "Is this education?" But what can you do on a beach so beautiful but enjoy it? Isn't that the point?

At night we get down to work. No. At night we carry out something that looks like a classroom activity. First we make a fire on the beach. (I'm proud of this. I brought the wood from home; Paula called the park ranger and found out if fires were allowed). I've brought my guitar. We pass around a bottle of rum someone's bought (what sailors drank in the nineteenth century). I sing the whaling song I know and try to teach it to them. Pass the guitar around. Sing some more. Then, the assignment: to read or tell about an experience we've had with water. This is the best part—I think—although the stories alone are not what works the magic. The almost-full moon rides at the center of a huge night sky, the breezes are soft, the fire glows, I savor the cigarettes I've been bumming from Sonya, and the rum is warm. The sharing of stories is somewhat formal, more or less embarrassed, always revealing. It draws a line around each person, sets them off, even as the night sky and moon, breeze, fire, sand pull us together. And, just as the night divides us body from body, the stories knit us up, soul to soul.

The experiences are intense and different one from another. Bernard out with a friend in a rowboat in waves they can't handle, laughing uncontrollably. Charlie running away from home. Sarah W. carrying water from Lourdes. Michael having a mystical vision of the moon over the Aegean while his parents eat and drink in a restaurant. Jim lying all day on the beach in Los Angeles after his sister's suicide. New York Sarah on the dock at night, sensing the presence of a huge fish. Erin ocean-drunk from sailing.

Three things stand out after that. Reading aloud from *Moby-Dick*, while we eat brunch in an airy upstairs room with a view of the marsh. Feng Liu reads the same passage as Michael (does he know it?), the conclusion to "The Whiteness of the Whale"—the German accent and the Chinese rendering the philosophical vocabulary with equal strain and equal force of conviction. On the tongues of the students among the clatter of knives and forks Melville's language sounds different from itself. Their reading brings out tones and feelings I've never heard before. Breakfast is abundant and delicious. It's noisy in the restaurant, but the language spills over everything, a rich, complex sauce.

Near where the cars line up for the ferry, Ryan discovers a volleyball net on a field of grass between the dock and the ocean. He's brought a volleyball, and the students split into teams. I sit leaning against a stump and watch them. The day is bright and blue. In the background, ocean water. The students stumble and cavort on either side of the net in a mood between mellowness and hilarity. For me, this is the moment of greatest joy. A gift from nowhere. Sheer, unexpected. After a timeless time, the motors of the cars in the line start up; we pile back into ours. The trip is over.

On the way home, I commit an error. We get to Kinston—our halfway stop—and the lead car (Ryan's) pulls into McDonald's. Maybe it's because I'm tired, but suddenly I fling out of my car and over to the hamburger lovers' and burst out with a diatribe on the evils of meat-eating, cattle-raising, and rain forest destruction. I don't normally impose my vegetarian beliefs but in this situation, out of its hiding place comes the desire to rule, comes the need to be right about something. The students are cowed. As soon as I've done it I know I've blundered, but it's too late. On the way to *my* choice (Taco Bell, of all things), we lose one of the cars. Serves me right.

The fit of pique coming out of nowhere should have warned me, I guess. It signaled a bridge troll somewhere in the vicinity, but I looked in the wrong place. I said to myself: "I'm glad that *I'm* the only one who goofed." But it wasn't true. There were some things the students did that I didn't like. The three who stayed late on the beach after everyone had gone back to the motel. Drinking, maybe smoking dope. And two of them snuggling in the back of the car on the way home. Did they sleep together, somehow? One of them was married. None of my business I said to myself, but I was pissed.

❖

What the trip was for the students I can only guess. What it was for me, I know, at least in part. Seeing Feng Liu's head against the sky and dune, chin raised, squinting at the sun through his glasses. Hearing Michael's trained Germanic baritone on the American strand. Rum and cigarettes. Swimming before breakfast. The delicious mixture of omelettes and literary language. Tumbling in and out of cars, restaurants, the group feeling. Beach beauty.

On our return the students' energy is high: they carry the classes on their shoulders like athletes. They are unstoppable. Usually, in my experimental classes, things are still up for grabs and I am still terrified even in the sixth week. But this class was different. I had no fears. It seemed a miracle.

A week or so after we got back, there was vigorous debate over grades. I'd originally offered the course Credit-No Credit—with this kind of experiential agenda, how could I give grades?—but the graduate school had ruled against it. I turned the problem over to the students. One aim of the course, I'd said, would be to reflect on the mode of teaching that the course represented. Issues of power, authority, fear of performing, learning for yourself versus learning for the teacher came tumbling out. Finally, a three-person committee proposed that the class get a group grade: that way, they reasoned, the pressure of competition, of individual against individual, would be lifted. It was a joint venture we were engaged in, and the class should stand or fall as a group. Credit would be given for every kind of contribution—for cutting up vegetables for dinner at Erin's, calling motels, pricing rental vans, managing the class calendar—the nuts-and-bolts stuff that courses depend on but that have no cachet academically. In the final week, they would decide together what grade they deserved. I agreed to all this. Besides, by this time people were tired of the subject of evaluation, they had ideas they wanted to carry out.

I'm a little fuzzy on what we did next. Some of it I missed. I'll tell you why in a minute. We had a small group discussion on Melville's rhetoric; there was a videotape on issues of political power and authority composed of clips from contemporary films (*Grand Canyon, Malcolm X*); there was a series of skits on gender, papers on epistemology and homosocial desire.

If you'd asked me at the time, I'd have said that the Ocracoke trip had had no clear influence on our understanding of *Moby-Dick*; the impact was all on the group dynamics. But looking back now, I think the trip affected our relation to Melville profoundly. Because all our attention at Ocracoke had been on physical things—getting from here to there, sleeping, swimming, eating— and on psychological-social things—who was getting close to whom, what people were like, whether the class would work—and because when we got back the discussions of *Moby-Dick* were planned by a different group of students every time, there was no official line to follow in interpreting the novel. It was mine, it was theirs, it was anybody's. The vague iconoclasm of the atmosphere, the sense that no one was checking up on us, being nontraditional and emphasizing sensory experience and physical activity—all this gave *Moby-Dick* to us permissively. It was come as you are.

To me it gave permission to enjoy what I'd always loved most about the novel—its language. Until now, I hadn't realized to what extent I'd hidden my love of Melville's language because I was afraid I'd be ridiculed for it. It hasn't been the fashion to care about style for a long time, and it's never been fashionable to say passionately that you *loved* a novel's language, and to go overboard about it in class. But this time round I began the course by reading an entire chapter aloud to the students, the one where Melville describes his "mysterious divine Pacific" and how he beheld it for the first time rolling before him "a thousand leagues of blue." It was this language that made me an Americanist. I loved it, but I don't think I ever explained why.

As a graduate student in the mid-sixties I'd been grading for Richard Sewall's tragedy course at Yale, and one day when he read aloud from the stage in Woolsey Hall passages from the chapter where Melville explains what the white whale was to Ahab, I decided to write my dissertation on Melville's style.

> All truth with malice in it, all that stirs up the lees of things, all that cracks the sinews and cakes the brain, all evil, to crazy Ahab, was visibly personified and made practically assailable in Moby-Dick.

I'm quoting from memory now. The sentence that did it, that put me over the top was:

> He piled upon the white whale's hump the sum of all the general rage and hate felt by his whole race from Adam down and then, as if his chest had been a mortar, he burst his hot heart's shell upon it.

I didn't identify in the least with Ahab, not consciously anyway, but it was Ahab's hate so eloquently expressed that determined what I would spend the next year—and most of the rest of my life—doing. I didn't know it then, but what you wrote your dissertation on determined your professional field. I wonder, now, after all these years, why it was the passages on rage that drew me. The description of Ahab's immitigable hate, so abundantly *thorough* and satisfying, could it have called to an anger buried in me, so deep I had no idea it was there? I know the prose of *Moby-Dick* backwards and forwards now. It's in my bones. I can quote patches and snatches of it, and one long lyrical sentence from a chapter called "The Dying Whale." But I'm still not too well acquainted with the sources of my rage.

Of my long intimate relation to Melville my students knew nothing. I spoke once to the class, formally, about *Moby-Dick*. A fifteen-minute talk on the characteristic form of sentences and chapters in the novel, and how these are related to the mentalities represented by Ahab and Ishmael. I rather liked what I said but don't think it made a great impression. But I didn't care. If the students weren't particularly interested in talking about the language, neither was I. I just wanted to glory in it, to revel again, as in the old days, in the genius with which Melville put sentences together. His perfect ear, his sense of rhythm, his feel for imaginative texture, his knowledge of when to keep something in the air and when to close. A friend from graduate school, A.N. Kaul, once quoted to me a line from R.P. Blackmur that has always seemed to me to sum up the truth about Melville's style. "Melville habitually used words greatly." It was so. And this time around, it was enough for me. I didn't need to prove to anybody that I could discourse about epistemology or make dutiful observations about structure and point of view, or justify the chapters on cetology. This time, I would just let myself savor and marvel at the unbelievable feats of verbal artistry that novel contains.

Some of this, I think, rubbed off on the class. People started writing poetry and creative prose. Language was in the air; people read things aloud as if they cared how the words sounded. We were *doing* language, not just talking about it.

So what do you think? Should I have told the students more? Held forth? Given them more to hold on to? I seem to remember a remark or two from the students about being overwhelmed. But I didn't want my Melville to stand in the way of theirs. I conceived my job as allowing them to get lost, and maybe to find themselves, in *Moby-Dick*'s unnavigable maze. I gave them a lot of time to do it in.

❖

What happened next was, my father died.

My father, who'd been in chemotherapy all summer with apparent success, was suddenly given four to six weeks to live, and then next to no time. One week, two weeks. Anytime.

My father loved literature for most of his life. He read aloud to me when I was little, and later on recited poetry from memory as we did the dishes together. When I was in grade school, he made up stories to tell me and my friends, and after he retired from the telephone company, wrote mysteries that got published in *Ellery Queen* and *Alfred Hitchcock* magazines. Though my mother was a reader and read aloud to me too, my love of literature I've always attributed to him. It was his emotional relation to it that stuck. He loved the sounds of words, and the romance of them, and passed this on to me as surely as the shape of his brow. I can hear his voice reciting, with great conviction and emphasis on the beat, "Gunga Din" and "Danny Deaver"— long poems by Rudyard Kipling that nobody reads anymore. I can hear him read the opening line of Dickens's *A Christmas Carol*—"Marley was dead"— with an intonation that promised such pleasure to come.

As he lay in the medical unit of the retirement community, I read to him from collections of poetry he had around the apartment, Victorian and Edwardian poems, mainly, some Renaissance. I discovered, as I did this, that nearly every poem worth its salt, if it's not entirely about death, has something about death in it. And I discovered another thing, too. There are some books you can read while sitting at a deathbed, and some you cannot. It wasn't a test I would have wished to make, but there it was. Sitting at my father's bedside while he rested or slept, I read to myself from *A Week on the Concord and Merrimac Rivers*, the book we were doing next in my undergraduate class. As Thoreau paddles up the Concord, nattering on about whip-poor-wills and such, he is never not conscious of some other river and shore to which this one refers. It was in that realm, as I sat and sang with my father, and read to him, and we talked that I felt we were, though our bodies were here in a hospitallike room with faintly pinkish walls, and a Greek-looking design that ran around the walls just under the ceiling. Though I had with me a copy of *Moby-Dick* I was never once tempted to open it. My much-beloved and labored-over Melville, struggling magnificently to stem the tides of this world, was too tumultuous and effortful to read in the presence of extremity.

❖

It's not exaggerating to say that the intensity of feeling I experienced in this course was surpassed only by the joy and pain of being at my father's bed-side. I had to tear myself away from my teaching to go to him and my mother in Philadelphia, and it took three days to realize I couldn't return home for a while. The strength of my reluctance to leave the students took me by surprise. It was as if I were abandoning my own children, choosing between them and my parents. If this depth of involvement in my courses is a good thing or a bad, I don't know. All I know is that it was so.

❖

I'm not going to tell about the second half of the course. Its structure was the same as the first. Dominated by a fantastic trip, student-conceived and organized, to Somerset Place plantation near Edenton, North Carolina, where we spent time doing work that slaves had done and wrote about it afterwards. (I won't forget the gritty-salty taste of the corn bread we fried in fatback or how Erin looked, her blond hair wrapped in a cotton turban). Later in the motel we had a discussion about our own experiences of oppression that was as good a discussion as I've ever been in. One student found it so uncomfortably intense, she had to leave the room twice; another burst out at the end: "It's a privilege to be in the same room with you guys!" and then he dove out the door. Talking it over later, the first student, the one who'd had to leave, said: "There were sixteen rooms in that room"—meaning, there were sixteen different experiences of what that discussion had been. At the time, though, the only one I wanted to acknowledge was mine.

And that, as Melville would have said, is the key to it all—my refusal to admit that there were sixteen different stories going on simultaneously. I was happy, so that was the only story I wanted to hear. Can you blame me? The course fulfilled old longings that were bound up with my love of Melville, and of *Moby-Dick*. The novel is a protest against cosmic injustice, a defiance of all constituted authority; it played into my ancient sense of victimization at the hands of power. *Beloved* did too, for that matter. So I loved our rebellion against grades and rules and conventional procedures, and I loved the group ethos. For both novels are also celebrations of communion and spoke to my longing to be rid of loneliness.

❖

The student presentations on *Beloved* were antic, inventive. I saw no signs of disaffection, though they must have been there. We watched Alvin Ailey dance videos, listened to recordings of call-and-response songs like those the slaves had sung; some of us joined in. Michael sang "Every time I feel the spirit" *a capella*, sitting with his back against the wall and it was as if his voice were coming straight out of his chest. We read aloud passages from a flail made of paper strips that was passed around the room, each strip with a quote from the novel or a related text. We drew pictures of the box in Georgia where Paul D. had been incarcerated, no two pictures the same. And squeezed ourselves under the table and talked about what it was like to feel trapped, closed in. (Do you see what I mean? Do you see how great it was?) On another day, the students pulled down all the shades, pushed the table over to one side of the room, turned off the lights, lit candles, and we sat around in a circle, reading aloud quotes from *Beloved* that had been passed out to us in advance.

I would like to stop writing right here. For now my throat clenches and I have trouble focusing my attention. On the last two days of the course, the students read aloud their evaluations. I had no idea. I'd expected celebration, mutual congratulation, fond reminiscence. What they did was criticize. Lack of structure, said New York Sarah; unfocused discussions, said Hilary; too much time spent planning and arranging things, said Bernard; too much time spent talking about evaluation, said two or three others; not enough disagreement, said someone else; it was utopian to think we could become a real community, said Sonya. There was tension between the norms of the institution and what we'd been trying to do, deliberated Erin. A few students said only positive things but I hardly heard them. I was devastated. For me the course had been a wondrous series of events; I began to wonder if I'd been living in a dreamworld. When it came my turn—last—with tears in my eyes and a quavery voice, I read my evaluation, full of pride and joy in the accomplishments of the class, and of my own happiness at what we'd been able to do together. And called for a vote. There was no time to talk about what happened. It was time for the grade. The students from the class after ours had been standing in the hall for ten minutes. The class split between an E (in our system, the equivalent of an A), and an E–. For an awful moment I thought I'd have to break the tie, but then Zarena switched her vote to an E and it was over.

Another person might have taken it better, not been so sensitive. But the students had unknowingly found me out. Criticism was what I'd been trying to avoid all along, criticism of any kind—literary criticism, and criticism of myself as a teacher, my having to criticize them. Why else go to beaches, work as slaves, light candles, and put on little plays if not to escape the steel trap of judgment? With creativity and imagination you could sidestep the need to measure and find fault, either with the students or with yourself or with the texts we read. I wanted to be safe, "safe from the wolf's black jaw and the dull ass's hoof," as Ben Jonson had said. I'd been criticized too early in my life and for too long. Now, I wanted to be free from judgments and from judging, and was offering that freedom to the students. But they were still learning to criticize, and I had been trying to take that opportunity from them.

They got me, all right, maybe in the deepest place. Taking criticism too much to heart; wanting to be free from it entirely. All along I'd known in the abstract that I taught from places inside me that needed healing. Well, here was my chance. To forgive myself for fearing judgment so much, to forgive myself for wanting to escape. For wanting to be in school and out of school at the same time. No wonder I thought Ocracoke was heaven.

❀

Later, someone asked me if this way of teaching gave students deeper insights into the texts, or even stronger feelings about them, than the usual way of teaching would. The question assumes that "we," the readers, will somehow be better off if we have "insight" into "them," the texts. For us it was topsy-turvy. The texts became the scaffolding for the building we were constructing. They were the road we walked on to wherever we were going—the road that allowed us to see those houses, that sky, these trees. They were the occasion for the show we put on for each other in our father's barn. Our carnival.

The texts fell to pieces under the onslaught of the students' energy. They gave, graciously, like old pieces of fabric, in several different places. We tore them apart, like animals, consumed their energy and fire to make ourselves live. Sported their great lines like trophies—"How loose the silk. How fine and loose and free"—this one, from *Beloved* was worn by both Jim and me. By the end of the course, *Moby-Dick* and *Beloved* were in tatters, strewn about our collective mental room like something children leave behind after they've played with it.

❀

Was it a success? What would that be? Everybody feeling good at the end? Why not? That was what I wanted. But in this case, that would have meant not to have been broken open, like the clam the seagull drops on the rocks from a great height so he can eat it. Not to have felt the pain of failure and so not to have dived into the pool where rage, the need for ego gratification, self-absorption, loneliness, and fear of criticism lurked, waiting.

I said to myself, after it was over: if only we had had those last two days in the middle of the course. If only I'd had the sense to stop around the seventh week and say—how're we doing? How's it going for you? Is there anything you'd like to change? But you see, I'd learned the year before to take the trip in the third week so the students could bond early. And they had, we had, and our energy was released. In the seventh week people were dying to *do* things, not to criticize and reflect. The course was riding high then, and then I went to Philadelphia. . . .

Each course has its own trajectory, its own momentum. You can talk about scheduling the moment of breakdown and self-criticism so it lands where it's supposed to, but things aren't like that. Next time, if I get that one right, some other part of the vessel will burst at the seams and we'll be awash.

❖

How does it end? It doesn't, really. The course ended. We'll never be in the same room together again. But Jim came in to my office shortly after that awful last day and took back everything he'd said. Feng Liu came to talk about his Ph.D. prelims, and Maurice about his dissertation plans. Sonya—the one who said we'd failed at community—came to my office and told me not to be dismayed—it was good that the students felt free to criticize the course, a healthy thing. Erin called me up and asked if I'd like to go for coffee at the Columbia Street Bakery. Ryan suggested lunch—we went to Hazel's Home Cooking,—we're planning to have lunch again. Sarah W. asked me if I knew a good dentist, and if I'd like to have coffee some day; we had a two-hour conversation at Ninth Street. Bernard gave me a chapter from his novel and I criticized it for him—at his request. Michael mentioned dinner with some other students when he passed me in the hall and later he came in to thank me for the course. Today I met Paula and she said she'd been thinking about me, and maybe we could organize a get-together.

This is the way my courses continue now. The visible part. When I see students I've had on one of these Odyssean ventures, often we embrace. It's like running into someone you went to camp with in New York City over Christmas vacation. Your eyes light up with the memory of experiences shared that set the two of you apart for that moment from the rest of humankind.

One day, after Christmas break, I got this card in the mail. Salvador Dali's *Metamorphosis of Narcissus* on one side, and on the other it read:

> The more time I have to think about American Lit Unbound the more I like it. I have been considering how to communicate my gratitude for last semester's experience, however my prose pales in comparison to the attachment I felt towards our class. I came to Duke hoping to find teachers like you and classes like ours. I was challenged, stretched, stumped, excited—but more importantly, I was responsible. I was responsible for our course. It was this onus of responsibility that added an entirely fresh dimension to the course and required all of us to engage in some self-examination. This is not always a pleasant experience and looking into that pool of water can be startling. Thank you for taking the risk to teach that class. Thank you for extending yourself far beyond the role of traditional teacher. And thank you for teaching me about literature, academia, and myself. Sincerely, Mark G.

That was Mark's story, a month later.

I, of course, am still wondering what happened. I still want to know why the students couldn't see how great they'd been. What kept them from appreciating all the fun they'd had, their spontaneity, and wit, and gumption. Why couldn't they see that this *was* the earthly paradise? It *was* what all the theory and criticism of literature was pointing toward, had hoped some day could be achieved? Why couldn't they understand that we're just like the barrier island, the ribbon of sand, that's always being created and destroyed, always changing, never the same? That we were perfect, and that our imperfections were all that we would ever have?

I'll never know the answer to these questions. But I feel it's okay not to know. To just go on and let the experience be. I cling to the metaphor of the barrier island, which tells us not to cling. When you teach like this you don't know what failure is anyway, or success. What looks like victory could turn out to be defeat, as well as the other way around. You just do it, as the Nike ads say, and hope for the best.

Contributors

❖

CHARLES FRANCIS ALTIERI is Professor of English at the University of California, Berkeley.

WILLIAM L. ANDREWS is Joyce and Elizabeth Hall Professor of American Literature at the University of Kansas.

MICHAEL BÉRUBÉ is Associate Professor of English at the University of Illinois, Urbana-Champaign.

TIMOTHY ANDRES BRENNAN is Associate Professor of English at the State University of New York, Stony Brook.

GILLIAN BROWN is Associate Professor of English at the University of Utah.

RACHEL M. BROWNSTEIN is Professor of English at Brooklyn College and the Graduate Center of the City University of New York.

CATHY N. DAVIDSON is Professor of English at Duke University.

ELIZABETH FOX-GENOVESE is Professor of History at Emory University.

DIANE P. FREEDMAN is Assistant Professor of English at the University of New Hampshire.

MARJORIE GARBER is William R. Kenan, Jr., Professor of English and Director of the Center for Literary and Cultural Studies, Harvard University.

GERALD GRAFF is George M. Pullman Professor of English and Humanities at the University of Chicago.

STEPHEN GREENBLATT is Class of 1932 Professor of English at the University of California, Berkeley.

MARIANNE HIRSCH is Distinguished Research Professor in the Humanities at Dartmouth College.

ALICE YAEGER KAPLAN is Professor of Romance Studies and Literature at Duke University.

AMITAVA KUMAR is Assistant Professor of English at the University of Florida.

CANDACE DuBIGNON LANG is Professor of French and Italian at Emory University.

JUDITH LOWDER NEWTON is Professor and Director of Women's Studies at the University of California, Davis.

LINDA ORR is Professor of Romance Studies at Duke University.

VINCENT P. PECORA is Associate Professor of English at the University of California, Los Angeles.

BRUCE ROBBINS is Professor of English at Rutgers University.

DAVID SIMPSON is Professor and Chair of the Department of English at the University of Colorado, Boulder.

GAYATRI CHAKRAVORTY SPIVAK is Avalon Foundation Professor in the Humanities at Columbia University.

MADELON SPRENGNETHER is Professor of English at the University of Minnesota.

JANE TOMPKINS is Professor of English at Duke University.

MARIANNA TORGOVNICK is Professor of English at Duke University.

H. ARAM VEESER is Associate Professor of English at Wichita State University and was Visiting Scholar at the Center for Literary and Cultural Studies, Harvard University, in 1995.

JEFFREY WILLIAMS is Assistant Professor of English at East Carolina University and Editor of *the minnesota review*.